IMPORTANT! Be sure to read the installation instructions in the introduction to this book before installing this disk.

Sound Blaster: The Official B

*Valuable information for game enthusiasts, bus...
multimedia, and developers who wish to program the...*

Software Included with This Book

Disk Contents:

☐ **Blaster Master** A dynamite digital sound editor. With it you'll be able to record sound samples and add special effects like fades, echoes, and stereo pans. You can even eliminate vocals from a sound track and slow playback without changing pitch!

☐ **Sputter Monitor (SPUTMON)** This utility will add sound to your DOS environment, making your computer come alive with sound. This is certain to put a smile on your face whether you are 6 or 106.

☐ **SoundSculptor** Explore the wonders of creating music with your FM synthesizer. SoundSculptor allows you to create and edit FM instruments and sounds.

☐ **Sound Samples** You're going to like the unique sound samples we've included, which you can use with Sputter Monitor or edit with Blaster Master. Surprise everyone when your computer suddenly screams from the other world or crackles with the breaking of glass. Turn to Chapter 9, "Making Your System Come Alive with SPUTMON," to learn how to use SPUTMON to play the sound samples.

☐ **Music Files** We've given you music files for jazz, pop, and classics in the three most popular music file formats. Play these with SPUTMON and with the Creative Labs programs that were included with your Sound Blaster card. Watch that computer boogie! Turn to Chapter 9, "Making Your System Come Alive with SPUTMON," to learn how to use SPUTMON to play the music files.

☐ **SBSIM** Learn how to program the Sound Blaster with the sample C program we've provided for the Sound Blaster Simplified Interface Module (SBSIM). Incorporate this into your own game software to play .CMF music files, .MID midi music files, or digital audio voices from disk or memory. The example C program and supporting files are discussed in Appendix C, "Programming the Sound Blaster Family."

System Requirements: IBM PC or compatible Intel 8086 machine or higher, MS-DOS 3.3 or higher, and 640K of memory with at least 1.2MB of disk space, Sound Blaster card. A mouse is necessary for running some of the programs.

Installation Instructions: For brief installation instructions, see the Introduction of this book. For more detailed information on Blaster Master, SPUTMON, and SoundSculptor, consult the appropriate chapters of this book.

WARNING: BEFORE OPENING THE DISK PACKAGE OPPOSITE, CAREFULLY READ THE TERMS AND CONDITIONS OF THE DISK WARRANTY FOUND ON THE BACK OF THIS PAGE.

DISK WARRANTY

This software is protected by both United States copyright law and international copyright treaty provision. You must treat this software just like a book, except that you may copy it into a computer to be used and you may make archival copies of the software for the sole purpose of backing up your software and protecting your investment from loss.

By saying, "just like a book," Osborne/McGraw-Hill means, for example, that this software may be used by any number of people and may be freely moved from one computer location to another, so long as there is no possibility of its being used at one location or on one computer while it is being used at another. Just as a book cannot be read by two different people in two different places at the same time, neither can the software be used by two different people in two different places at the same time (unless, of course, Osborne's copyright is being violated).

LIMITED WARRANTY

Osborne/McGraw-Hill warrants the physical diskette(s) enclosed herein to be free of defects in materials and workmanship for a period of sixty days from the purchase date. If Osborne/McGraw-Hill receives written notification within the warranty period of defects in materials or workmanship, and such notification is determined by Osborne/McGraw-Hill to be correct, Osborne/McGraw-Hill will replace the defective diskette(s).

The entire and exclusive liability and remedy for breach of this Limited Warranty shall be limited to replacement of defective diskettes(s) and shall not include or extend to any claim for or right to cover any other damages, including but not limited to, loss of profit, data, or use of the software, or special, incidental, or consequential damages or other similar claims, even if Osborne/McGraw-Hill has been specifically advised of the possibility of such damages. In no event will Osborne/McGraw-Hill's liability for any damages to you or any other person ever exceed the lower of the suggested list price or actual price paid for the license to use the software, regardless of any form of the claim.

OSBORNE, A DIVISION OF McGRAW-HILL, INC., SPECIFICALLY DISCLAIMS ALL OTHER WARRANTIES, EXPRESS OR IMPLIED, INCLUDING BUT NOT LIMITED TO, ANY IMPLIED WARRANTY OF MERCHANTABILITY OR FITNESS FOR A PARTICULAR PURPOSE. Specifically, Osborne/McGraw-Hill makes no representation or warranty that the software is fit for any particular purpose and any implied warranty of merchantability is limited to the sixty-day duration of the Limited Warranty covering the physical diskette(s) only (and not the software) and is otherwise expressly and specifically disclaimed.

This limited warranty gives you specific legal rights; you may have others which may vary from state to state. Some states do not allow the exclusion of incidental or consequential damages, or the limitation on how long an implied warranty lasts, so some of the above may not apply to you.

Rich Heimlich, David M. Golden,
Ivan Luk, and Peter M. Ridge

Sound Blaster:
The Official Book

Osborne **McGraw-Hill**

Berkeley New York St. Louis San Francisco
Auckland Bogotà Hamburg London Madrid
Mexico City Milan Montreal New Delhi Panama City
Paris São Paulo Singapore Sydney
Tokyo Toronto

Osborne **McGraw-Hill**
2600 Tenth Street
Berkeley, California 94710 U.S.A.

For information on translations and book distributors outside of the U.S.A., please write to Osborne **McGraw-Hill** at the above address.

Sound Blaster: The Official Book

7890 DOC 99876543

ISBN 0-07-881907-5

Publisher	**Copy Editor**	**Illustrator**
Kenna S. Wood	Carol Henry	Susie C. Kim
Acquisitions Editor	**Proofreader**	**Cover Designer**
William Pollock	Carol Burbo	Mason Fong
Associate Editor	**Indexer**	**Book Development and Technical Advisor**
Vicki Van Ausdall	Matthew Spence	David M. Golden
Project Editor	**Computer Designer**	
Janis Paris	J. E. Christgau	

To our parents: Richard and Phyllis Heimlich,
Wayne and Victoria Ridge, Tony and Jenny Luk,
Jacqueline Golden and the memory of Robert Golden

Contents

Part I • Creative Labs and the Sound Blaster Family

1 Anatomy of the Sound Blaster Family 3

Part II • Software Bundled with the Sound Blaster Family

2 Basics of Sound and the Sound Blaster 31

3 Sound Blaster Software Toys 59

Part III • Using the Software Included with This Book

Part IV • *Hardware and Software Enhancements*

11 *Third-Party Software* 235

12 *Getting the Most Out of Your Speakers* 279

Part V • *Appendixes*

Acknowledgments

It is impossible to thank everyone who has made a contribution to this book, but we'd like to start out with a special thanks to Adrienne Cousins, the author of SPUTMON, Gary Maddox, the author of Blaster Master, and Cindy Kear of Ibis Software for SoundSculptor. Thanks to Adrienne, Gary, and Cindy for letting us include such high-quality software on the disk that comes free with this book. We are confident that you, the reader of this book, will find SPUTMON so much fun it will become part of your everyday computer activities. Sound Blaster owners (who have been wanting to customize their digital audio recordings but have been working with only VOXKIT) are in for a very pleasant surprise—possibly like the shock accompanying a jet streaking overhead. Anyone interested in music and FM synthesis must check out SoundSculptor, a program for creating custom instrument sounds.

Thanks to the software and speaker companies who contributed products and documentation for us to review. In almost every case, they bent over backwards to help us by shipping their product overnight—or by making their top engineering and marketing staff available to us.

Naturally we are indebted to the folks at Creative Labs, both in the San Francisco Bay area and in Singapore. Special thanks to W.H. Sim, H.Y. Chong, Scott Sindorf, Benita Kenn, and Larry Samuels for reviewing this book and keeping its technical content accurate and honest. Creative Labs' contribution of technical information and insight was invaluable.

Special thanks also to: Jonathan Pynchon, Craig A. Lemas, T.L. Goh, Jacqueline Chia, Shelley Williams, Kelly Pittman, Kim Federico, and Arnold Waldstein.

Thanks to John Beekman of Voyetra.

The unsung heroes of this project are the people at Osborne/McGraw-Hill. Thanks to Bill Pollock, Jeff Pepper, Cindy Brown, Janis Paris, Carol Henry, Vicki Van Ausdall, Carol Burbo, Susie Kim, Eric Christgau, and many others who worked their magic in record time. They never wavered from demanding the best from themselves and from the authors.

Introduction

This is the most up-to-date and comprehensive book available on the Sound Blaster family of sound cards. It is also the only official Creative Labs guide. *Sound Blaster: The Official Book* is loaded with valuable information for the game enthusiast, the business person interested in multimedia, and software developers who wish to program their Sound Blaster.

About This Book

This book is very different from the all-too-typical computer book that rewrites the manufacturer's manual, providing little more than extra pictures, fancy formatting, and a few tips. We've plugged the gaps in your *Sound Blaster User Reference Manual* by delivering a wealth of information not found in your manual. Due to our unique relationship with Creative Labs, this book includes lots of previously unavailable information about the Sound Blaster and its software—information that you won't find anywhere else.

How this Book is Organized

This book is divided into five parts so that you can easily dive into the material you are most interested in.

Part I provides an overview of the Sound Blaster family of cards, including both a history and a description of the newest member of the family: the Sound Blaster 16 ASP.

☐ Chapter 1 takes you inside the Sound Blaster for a little anatomy lesson so you will understand what's going on in your fancy piece of hardware. We explain and compare every member of the Sound Blaster family, down to a description of the jumpers, connectors, and most significant electronic circuitry.

Part II, "Software Bundled with the Sound Blaster Family," is everything you need to know to fully exploit the software programs provided with your sound card.

☐ Chapter 2 (the first chapter in Part II) gives you a good leg up on the basics of sound with explanations of MIDI, General MIDI, FM synthesis, digital audio sampling, analog-to-digital and digital-to-analog conversion, and a host of other technical topics.

☐ Chapter 3 gives you tips and tricks for using the sofware toys that come with your Sound Blaster, such as Dr. Sbaitso and the Talking Parrot.

☐ Chapter 4 focuses on the command line utility programs for recording and playing back sound files, as well as for converting from one type of sound file to another.

☐ Chapter 5 fills in the gaps about VOXKIT, the sound editor that comes with Sound Blaster, and VEDIT2, the one that comes with Sound Blaster Pro.

☐ Chapter 6 is aimed at Sound Blaster Pro owners. It provides a comprehensive description of the programs for controlling the mixer, which is new to the Sound Blaster Pro.

☐ Chapter 7 is your reference guide for creating multimedia presentations with the software that comes with your sound card.

☐ Chapter 8 dives into facets of Sequencer Plus Pro, the MIDI sequencer software package that comes with the Creative Labs MIDI Kit. We have tried to cover the most common stumbling blocks for users of this MIDI music composition package.

Part III, "Using the Software Included with This Book," shows you how to get the most out of the utility programs bundled with this book: namely SPUTMON and Blaster Master. (SoundSculptor is briefly documented in Appendix E of this book.)

☐ Chapter 9 shows you how to use SPUTMON (short for Sputter Monitor) to attach sound effects or music to hundreds of events in your system. SPUTMON will let you do things like play a "scream" whenever you delete a file.

☐ Chapter 10 tells you how to use Blaster Master, a digital audio sound recorder and editor. Blaster Master lets you record speech or music, edit pieces, and even add special effects like fades and slowing your playback speed without changing the pitch.

Blaster Master is more flexible and powerful than the VEDIT2 editor that comes with the Sound Blaster Pro. Sound Blaster owners, who are still working with the rudimentary VOXKIT editor bundled with their sound card, are in for a very pleasant surprise.

Part IV, "Hardware and Software Enhancements," presents a concise summary of many leading software and hardware products that can be used with your Sound Blaster. This section should give you the background to ensure that you are satisfied with any speakers or additional software you have purchased for your sound card.

☐   Chapter 11 provides short descriptions of well-known third-party software programs that work with the Sound Blaster family. Both commercial products and less expensive shareware programs are described, along with addresses and phone numbers so you can contact these companies. Don't forget to check out the coupons provided with *Sound Blaster: The Official Book* to see if you can buy one of these products at a reduced price.

☐   Chapter 12 provides information on how to select a speaker for your Sound Blaster and lists many of the companies who have a presence in this marketplace.

Part V, "Appendixes," contains a wealth of reference information, including the very latest information about the newest member of the Sound Blaster family, the Sound Blaster 16 ASP.

☐   Appendix A supplements the installation chapter of the Sound Blaster User Reference Manual, providing a complete step-by-step guide for installing the sound card. If you have any problems with the card installation—or problems later on, when using your card—either Appendix A or Appendix B, the troubleshooting section, will come to your rescue.

☐   Appendix B covers the most common problems encountered with Sound Blaster...and provides solutions, direct from the technical support staff at Creative Labs.

☐   Appendix C is a reference section for programmers. It contains detailed, register-level information for controlling the sound card hardware, as well as documentation for the SBSIM interface that provides a unified and simplified interface to the Sound Blaster.

☐   Appendix D describes the Sound Blaster 16 ASP. You'll get a glimpse into the next generation of sound card hardware and software—and you'll find out whether its time to upgrade!

□   Appendix E contains a concise introduction to SoundSculptor, a fun utility for programming custom instrument sounds into the FM synthesizer. SoundSculptor is included with this book.

Note   Because Blaster Master and SoundSculptor are graphically oriented programs, they will not run without a mouse.

Installing the Disk for Sound Blaster: The Official Book

The accompanying 3.5" 720K disk contains valuable software programs, as listed on the first page of this book. If your machine doesn't accept this size disk, call Osborne/McGraw-Hill, in Berkeley, California, at 1-800-227-0900 or 1-510-549-6600 (8:30 A.M. to 4:30 P.M., Pacific Time) for a replacement 5.25" 1.2M disk.

Before beginning the install process, read the README file on the *Sound Blaster: The Official Book* diskette. To do so, change to the drive that contains the disk and type **README** at the DOS prompt. Use the UP ARROW and DOWN ARROW keys to scroll through the information. When you're done reading, press the ESC key to return to the command prompt.

Note   At various times during your installation of the *Sound Blaster: The Official Book* disk, you may be called upon to edit your AUTOEXEC.BAT or CONFIG.SYS files. See "Editing ASCII Files" in Chapter 2, "Basics of Sound and the Sound Blaster," of this book for information on editing these files or consult your favorite DOS manual.

Installation Requirements

The installation program and related batch (.BAT) files require DOS version 3.3 or higher and slightly more than 1.2 Meg (megabytes) of space on your hard disk. Before beginning your installation, note the following:

□   INSTALL may be canceled at any time by pressing the ESC key. If you press the ESC key to exit the INSTALL program before it has finished, you will receive instructions to run SETUP as if you had completed the installation. Running SETUP at this point will produce unexpected results because only some, if any, of the disk will be on your hard disk. If this describes your situation, make sure that you have run the

INSTALL program to completion before searching for another solution to your problem. See the beginning of the troubleshooting section that follows for a cautionary note on rerunning INSTALL.

☐ SETUP.BAT must be run from the directory on which you installed your disk. For example, if you installed to the C drive, that directory will be C:\SBDISK. If you encounter a problem running SETUP, make sure that you are in the appropriate subdirectory.

☐ Should you have problems running SPUTMON, you may need to add a SHELL statement to your CONFIG.SYS file. If you can't run SPUTMON or the other programs provided on the disk, you may need to modify the PATH statement in your AUTOEXEC.BAT file. This is discussed in the troubleshooting section that follows.

How to Install the Disk

1. Place the disk into your floppy disk drive and close the drive door.

2. Type the letter of the disk drive that contains the *Sound Blaster: The Official Book* disk, followed by a colon, and then the word INSTALL. For example, if your disk is in drive B you would type **B:INSTALL**. Press ENTER and the first screen in the Install program will pop up.

3. The installation screen will ask you for the source of your disk, where you wish to install the disk from (default is the current floppy drive, the drive you specified in step 2). The installation program will also ask you for the target for your installation, the hard drive you'd like to install to (default is the C drive).

 Note   If you want to install to another drive, such as the D drive, press the TAB key to highlight the drive letter to the right of "to Hard Drive." Then type the desired drive letter.

Now press the F10 key to start the installation process. Follow the directions on the next screen, pressing ENTER to continue the installation or ESC to cancel.

4. When the INSTALL program finishes it will ask you to press the ESC key. Press ESC.

You will be asked whether C:\SBDISK should be added to the PATH statement in your AUTOEXEC.BAT file. You should answer yes. Answering yes will modify AUTOEXEC.BAT and save the original file as AUTOEXEC.SB. You may also be notified that the FILES statement in your CONFIG.SYS file needs to be updated. You should answer yes. Answering yes will modify CONFIG.SYS and save the original version as CONFIG.SB. The INSTALL program will then state that installation is complete—but you're not quite done yet.

5. You should now see a screen titled "**IMPORTANT **" that asks you to run SETUP.BAT. Type **SETUP** at the \SBDISK> prompt (step 4 should have left you in the \SBDISK directory on your target drive) and press ENTER to run the setup program. This action will bring up the SB Environment Configuration Screen.

6. You will be prompted by SETUP for the target drive (the drive you'd like to install to); the default is C. Press ENTER to use the default selection.

 Note   If you're installing to a disk other than the C drive, you should see that drive letter here. Press ENTER to install to that drive.

7. SETUP now prompts you for the appropriate I/O Base Address. The default address is 220. Press ENTER to accept this, or type the correct number if you didn't use the default settings when you originally installed your Sound Blaster card. SETUP then asks for the appropriate IRQ interrupt (IRQ). The default is 7. Press ENTER to accept this, or type the correct number. SETUP now displays the settings you just entered, and asks you if this is correct. Press Y to go onto the next step, or press N to revise these settings.

 Note   If you don't know your Sound Blaster's I/O address and/or the IRQ interrupt (IRQ), check Appendix A for a description of Sound Blaster's test programs to determine the settings. Most sound cards are installed with the default settings of 220 for address and 7 for IRQ. To quit step 7, press Q when prompted by the "Is this correct (Y or N):?" question.

8. SETUP will then ask you whether you want SPUTMON loaded automatically when you start your computer. Press Y to add instructions for SPUTMON to your AUTOEXEC.BAT file so SPUTMON will always be loaded when you turn on your computer. If you press N you can still run SPUTMON, but you must enter the commands by hand, as explained in the section that follows on SPUTMON.

 Note   If you are connected to a network or have a lot of TSR (Terminate and Stay Resident) programs or drivers loaded in your machine, you should answer no, N, when asked if you want SPUTMON loaded automatically. This will help to eliminate potential TSR conflicts that you may encounter when running SPUTMON.

9. You've now finished the disk installation. Remove the disk from your floppy drive and reboot your machine by pressing the following keys at the same time: CTRL, ALT, and DEL.

How to Install and Run the Programs

Batch files in the \SBDISK directory make it easy to access the programs provided with your book.

 Note   The installation program modifies the AUTOEXEC.BAT file, adding \SBDISK to the PATH statement for locating files. If you've already rebooted your computer, you can skip step 1 in the instructions below.

Blaster Master

1. Switch to the SBDISK directory by typing **CD\SBDISK** and then press ENTER.

2. Type **BMASTER** and then press ENTER.

Blaster Master may refuse to run for various reasons. Potential problems and their remedies are as follows:

☐ Blaster Master requires a mouse to function. If it can't find one, it refuses to start.

☐ Blaster Master checks to see that a Sound Blaster card is installed. Its automatic scanning feature should detect your sound card automatically. If it doesn't, and you know that your card works correctly, check that you have a SET BLASTER= environment variable in your AUTOEXEC.BAT file. See the section "Setting the Blaster Environment" in Chapter 10, "The Blaster Master Sample Editor," for more information on this topic.

☐ If you get the message "Not Enough 640K Memory Free" when you try to start Blaster Master, see the section by that name in the troubleshooting section of Appendix B of this book.

☐ If you're having problems with Blaster Master that cause your machine to crash, you probably need to make more memory available by removing TSRs and unnecessary drivers. This is also discussed in the troubleshooting section in Appendix B of this book.

SPUTMON

1. Switch to the SBDISK directory by typing **CD\SBDISK** and then press ENTER.

2. To turn on SPUTMON, if it isn't currently active, type **SPUTON** and press the ENTER key. To turn off SPUTMON, type **SPUTOFF** and press the ENTER key.

Note   Don't be surprised if you see the DOS command prompt twice when SPUTMON is running. It is executing a command that you cannot see at the first prompt.

If SPUTMON doesn't work for you, please see the section "Troubleshooting Your *Sound Blaster: The Official Book* Disk Installation," later in this introduction.

Loading SPUTMON Manually

The instructions above assume you've told the installation program to install SPUTMON automatically. If you answered no, N, preventing the install program from adding the SPUTMON instructions to your AUTOEXEC.BAT file, you can still load and run SPUTMON. When you're ready to install SPUTMON, type the following commands at the command prompt. Press the ENTER key after you type each line:

```
\SBDISK\SBENV /q
\SBDISK\SPUTON
```

SPUTMON will now be loaded and turned on until you reboot, turn the machine off, or give the SPUTOFF command to temporarily disable SPUTMON. The two command lines above are the same commands that the install program attaches to the end of your AUTOEXEC.BAT file.

SoundSculptor

1. Switch to the SBDISK directory by typing **CD\SBDISK** and then press ENTER.

2. Type **SS** and press ENTER.

Note   SoundSculptor will refuse to run if it can't locate your mouse.

Troubleshooting Your Sound Blaster: The Official Book Disk Installation

Due to the nature of the programs contained on the *Sound Blaster: The Official Book* disk, you may encounter problems with your installation. Do not despair. The following is a list of helpful techniques and common problems and their solutions.

If your particular problem is not covered in the list below, reread the installation directions above to make sure that you did not miss any steps. It would also be a good idea to test that your Sound Blaster card works with other software, such as that received from Creative Labs, to ensure that your Sound Blaster card is installed correctly.

 Caution   Be aware that if you run INSTALL more than one time, it will modify your AUTOEXEC.BAT file more than once. If you have run INSTALL more than once, make sure that duplicate lines do not exist in your AUTOEXEC.BAT file. The following techniques will help in this situation.

Technique: How to Examine Your AUTOEXEC.BAT File

With the following command you can examine your AUTOEXEC.BAT file to see what changes were made to your PATH statement. Type the following command, followed by the ENTER key, to display your AUTOEXEC.BAT file on the screen:

```
TYPE C:\AUTOEXEC.BAT
```

If the AUTOEXEC.BAT is so long that it scrolls off the top of the screen before you can read it, try the following variation of the type command. Press ENTER to see the next screen:

```
TYPE C:\AUTOEXEC.BAT | MORE
```

Technique: How to Examine Your CONFIG.SYS File

With the following command you can examine your CONFIG.SYS file to see whether you have a SHELL= statement and to examine the FILES= and BUFFERS= statements. Type the following command, followed by the ENTER key, to display your CONFIG.SYS file on the screen:

TYPE C:\CONFIG.SYS

If the CONFIG.SYS is so long that it scrolls off the top of the screen before you can read it, try the following variation of the type command. Press ENTER to see the next screen:

TYPE C:\CONFIG.SYS | MORE

Technique: How to Restore Your Original CONFIG.SYS and AUTOEXEC.BAT Files

You can restore your original AUTOEXEC.BAT file by typing the following commands, in the order shown, at the DOS command prompt. The original version was saved as either AUTOEXEC.SAV (prior to changes by SETUP.BAT) or AUTOEXEC.DB (prior to changes made by INSTALL.EXE). Don't be concerned if you get the message "file not found" when you type the second command line—it means that the installation process didn't have to make a backup copy of your AUTOEXEC.BAT file at that stage. Press the ENTER key after you type each of these command lines:

COPY C:\AUTOEXEC.SAV C:\AUTOEXEC.BAT
COPY C:\AUTOEXEC.DB C:\AUTOEXEC.BAT

The installation procedure also saves your CONFIG.SYS file. You can restore the original version by typing the following two command lines:

COPY C:\CONFIG.SAV C:\CONFIG.SYS
COPY C:\CONFIG.DB C:\CONFIG.SYS

Common Problems and Solutions

Following is a list of common problems you may encounter. If you're having difficulty with installation or use of the software on the disk, this is the first place to look. Most likely you will find the solution to your problem here.

Problem: When I type SPUTOFF to unload SPUTMON I have no problem. But, when I type SPUTON to turn on SPUTMON, my system locks up.

Solution: You are probably encountering a dreaded TSR conflict. Try one of the following remedies:

1. SPUTMON is a TSR (Terminate and Stay Resident) program. When loaded, it runs unseen, in the background. Like all TSRs, SPUTMON may interfere with other programs, such as network drivers. If you are connected to a network and are encountering problems running SPUTMON, create a boot disk for connecting to the network without SPUTMON. On the boot disk, use the original AUTOEXEC.BAT and CONFIG.SYS files, the ones you had before installing the disk that accompanies this book. Make certain to check that command lines in the AUTOEXEC.BAT and CONFIG.SYS files that reference files on the hard disk are preceded by the drive letter for the hard disk. For example, the command line C:\WINDOWS\HIMEM.SYS will always work correctly but \WINDOWS\HIMEM.SYS won't locate the windows directory if you boot from a floppy.

2. If, when running SETUP, you answered yes to the question "Do you want SPUTMON to load automatically....," your AUTOEXEC.BAT will contain the following lines, which load SPUTMON automatically when you power up:

```
CALL C:\SBDISK\SBENV.BAT /q
CALL C:\SBDISK\SPUTON.BAT
```

Try "remarking" these lines out of your AUTOEXEC.BAT to see if your problems disappear. Do this by typing the abbreviation REM before each line, followed by a space, as follows:

```
REM C:\SBDISK\SBENV.BAT /q
REM C:\SBDISK\SPUTON.BAT
```

Remarking these lines out of your AUTOEXEC.BAT will make them inactive. SPUTMON will not be loaded automatically when you boot up. Reboot to have these changes take effect.

Problem: When you try to run SBSTATUS, BMASTER, SPUTON, SPUTOFF, or SS from any directory other than \SBDISK, you encounter one of the following:

☐   You see a "bad command or file name" message

☐   Odd things happen to your machine

☐   Your machine crashes.

Solution: If your AUTOEXEC.BAT has a PATH statement, make sure that the path listed below was added to your PATH statement:

```
C:\SBDISK
```

For example:

PATH=C:\;C:\DOS;C:\UTIL;C:\SBDISK

Note   If the floppy disk contents were installed to a drive other than C:, that drive letter must appear in the PATH statement. For example, if, when running INSTALL, you selected your D: drive, your PATH should contain D:\SBDISK rather than C:\SBDISK.

Note   If you do not have a PATH statement in your AUTOEXEC.BAT file, you must add one. Using an editor or word processing program designed for revising ASCII text files, add the line below to the beginning of your AU-TOEXEC.BAT file:

PATH=C:\SBDISK

Problem: You receive one of the following error messages or a similar message:

☐   "Out of environment space"

☐   "Memory allocation error. Cannot load COMMAND, system halted"

☐   "Cannot load Command"

☐   An error from your memory manager, such as an exception error from QEMM.

Solution: Increase the size of your DOS environment. If your CONFIG.SYS file doesn't contain a SHELL statement, add one as follows. Using an editor or word processing program designed for revising ASCII text files, add the following line to your CONFIG.SYS file. You must have at least one space after "COM" and after "1024," and no other spaces within the command line:

SHELL=C:\COMMAND.COM /E:1024 /P

Note   If COMMAND.COM exists on a different drive or directory, adjust the SHELL statement accordingly. It's often found in the \DOS directory.

If your CONFIG.SYS has a value of less than 1024, change it to 1024 as shown above. If your CONFIG.SYS already has a /E: value of 1024 or greater, increase the value by another 200 to 300 if the problem persists.

Problem: You want to return your computer to how it was before you ran INSTALL, so you can redo the installation, but you're not comfortable with the idea of editing CONFIG.SYS and AUTOEXEC.BAT files. Is there an easier way to do this?

Solution: Follow the instructions for the technique described above under the heading: "Technique: How to Restore Your Original CONFIG.SYS and AUTOEXEC.BAT Files." The installation process has probably created the directory \SBDISK on your hard drive even if you prematurely terminated the installation. As a result, when you rerun the INSTALL program, it will report that the installation disk files are already found on the hard disk. You will then be prompted for a Yes/No response on whether to overwrite these files. Answer Y to every question. This is less work than deleting all the files and subdirectories within \SBDISK prior to rerunning INSTALL.

Problem: Now that you've installed the disk, you have problems running your other programs. For example, SBTALKER only talks once and then goes silent, and the VEDIT2 screen has junk displayed. Some of your other programs don't seem to work right either.

Solution: Sputter Monitor can conflict with other programs. If you suspect this is the case, temporarily disable SPUTMON with the SPUTOFF command before running these other programs to prove whether SPUTMON is the source of the conflict. If necessary, you can permanently disable SPUTMON by editing the AUTOEXEC.BAT file. You can also add the PS (program suspend) command to SPUTMON.DEF (Sputter Monitor's configuration file) to cause SPUTMON to automatically disable itself when certain programs are run. This works, for example, for VEDIT2 but not for SBTALKER. See the section "Suspending SPUTMON's Operation" in Chapter 9, "Making Your System Come Alive with SPUTMON," for further information.

PART I

Creative Labs and the
Sound Blaster Family

CHAPTER

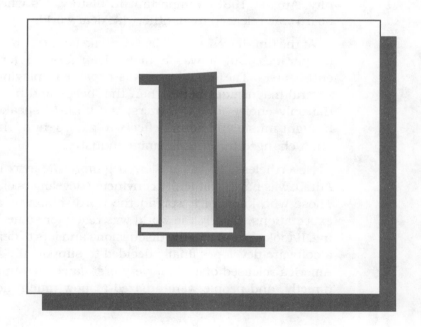

Anatomy of the Sound Blaster Family

*I*n this chapter you'll learn about some history about sound card development, and basic information about the hardware in the Sound Blaster family of cards.

The Beginning: AdLib

In the grand scheme of things, the month of August 1987 will be as forgotten as any other month in history, but in the sound board community, August 1987 is important in history. It's when the AdLib sound board was released to an otherwise deaf world.

At the time it was a small feat, with no fanfare, no confetti and certainly no parades, but it was a major leap forward for PC entertainment enthusiasts. The AdLib card was capable of playing sounds that were several magnitudes better than the "beeps and boops" that came from the only choice for PC owners: the built-in speaker. The AdLib card brought music and sound effects to games, and when it finally caught on, it changed the entire gaming industry.

Nevertheless, it was a slow beginning. Martin Prevel, president of AdLib, was having difficulty convincing developers of his card's potential. Those who knew of it spread the word, however, and sales exceeded expectations. Clearly the world was ready for something new and exciting. It took several lengthy discussions and lots of demonstrations before a software developer finally decided to support the AdLib card. Taito of America released one of the very first games to support the AdLib card directly, and people were amazed at how much more fun a computer game could be.

Competition

Over the course of the next few years AdLib sold tens of thousands of boards, and game company support grew. It's not difficult to understand why the AdLib card caught on: Good sound wasn't impossible to come by; you could find it on computer systems like the Amiga, Apple, or an Atari ST. But the PC had nothing but that abominable and nearly useless built-in speaker. The AdLib card was the first of its kind for those of us with a "real" computer, and at the right price to boot. Anyone who took their gaming seriously rushed out and bought an AdLib card as soon as one of their favorite games supported it. When they heard the difference, they convinced their computing friends to buy one, too.

AdLib had a virtual monopoly on the market from 1987 until 1989. Not that competition was foreign to AdLib—competitors hoping to cash in on this new market showed up from all over. Oddly, no one wanted to "share" this burgeoning market with AdLib. Rather, everyone had their own idea of how a sound board should work. In addition, no one wanted to give AdLib credit for making the right choices at the right time. The companies producing sound boards wanted the entire market for themselves, so they created new, incompatible products that each required direct support from game developers.

The problem with this approach became obvious almost immediately. Why should a game developer support a new sound card when almost no one owned one, and while the AdLib card was reaching more and more people every month? From the beginning, none of the new sound boards could gain a foothold, and through it all, support for AdLib continued to grow. Then, in November 1989, Creative Labs released the Sound Blaster. Not just another competitor, Sound Blaster was different in one major way: It was fully AdLib-compatible.

Enter Creative Labs

Creative Labs didn't just happen along onto the sound board scene. In fact, the company had been involved with sound long before anyone heard AdLib play its first note.

Creative Labs was brought to life as Creative Technology, by 26-year-old Sim Wong Hoo in Singapore. This early version of the company had begun by producing high-speed cassette systems for the venerable TRS-80s and memory cards for Apple computers. In 1983 they produced the Hanyu card, a milestone speech-synthesis card and the first one capable of speaking Chinese. The groundwork for the Sound Blaster can be traced to August 1987, when Creative Technology released the Creative Music System (CMS) 12-channel AM synthesizer card. Ironically, this was the same date AdLib first appeared.

After much success in Singapore and other parts of the world, Creative renamed their Creative Music System as Game Blaster and headed for the United States. Unfortunately, Game Blaster showed up about a year too late; by the time it arrived in the U.S., the AdLib card was already well on its way to the top. On the surface, Game Blaster seemed as though it could compete: It could play 12 stereo instruments simultaneously, compared to AdLib's 11 monaural instruments. The deciding factor came down to competing technologies. Game Blaster used AM (amplitude modulation) synthesis, a method for simulating sounds that was older than the AdLib's FM (frequency modulation) synthesis. As a result, Game Blaster, even in stereo, didn't sound as good as the AdLib in mono, and Game Blaster quickly became a footnote in sound board history.

The Birth of Sound Blaster

Determined not to be vanquished by the failure of Game Blaster, Creative Labs went to work on a new project, code-named the Killer Card. Sim developed a plan based not only on his own ideas, but also on feedback gathered from the industry at large. Ken Williams of Sierra On-Line, as well as many others, made major contributions to the early design of the new card.

One thing was fairly obvious. The AdLib card was doing so well at this point that if the Killer Card was to have any chance at all, it would have to be fully AdLib-compatible. And this aspect alone wouldn't be enough to take on AdLib, so the new card was expanded. Creative added a joystick port, speech synthesis capability, a MIDI interface, and most importantly, an ADC and DAC. The ADC (analog-to-digital converter) allows the board to record music, speech, and sound effects. The DAC (digital-to-analog converter, pronounced "dack") allowed playback of actual speech and sound effects. With the AdLib card, you needed a separate joystick card to play games, and the sound effects were no better that what could be simulated by the FM synthesizer. But having all these features on one board made the Killer Card the only game card anyone would need, and a selection of software was finally created to let users work with all the included features.

Welcome, Sound Blaster

In November 1989, the Killer Card was formally named the Sound Blaster and was released to the public. In only one year it surpassed the AdLib card as the best-selling sound board in the world.

Looking back, it's possible to see how the Sound Blaster was able to accomplish this feat. An AdLib card added an "emotional edge" to games, in much the same way that an orchestra adds texture to silent movies. But the AdLib did no more than that, as it was limited to playing music alone. Sound Blaster, on the other hand, was able to do much more: It could play recorded speech and sound effects, which really made people's computers come alive. It is fair to say that Sound Blaster revolutionized the gaming world just as the "talkies" changed the motion picture industry forever.

Simply put, Sound Blaster does for the PC what color does for television—it brings new life to an artificial environment. No longer do you have to listen to the all-too-common beeps from your IBM PC and its countless compatibles. With Sound Blaster, a myriad of software—from games to business applications—take on new meaning as they play music and even talk back to you.

The Role of FM Synthesis in the Sound Blaster Story

People often ask why AdLib "allowed" Creative Labs to move in and take over the sound card marketplace; how could Creative Labs legally create an AdLib-compatible card? The answer is simple: Sound Blaster isn't really AdLib-compatible at all; it's Yamaha FM synthesis-compatible. The fact is, both the AdLib and Sound Blaster cards are based on an established technology that has been around for years—it's called *FM synthesis*. With FM synthesis, you can synthesize, or imitate, musical instruments using the sine waves generated by FM signals.

The Japanese megacompany Yamaha produces computer chips that generate FM music, and the AdLib card is designed around these FM-synthesis chips, which can be purchased by anyone. Creative Labs simply purchased the same components AdLib was using, and put the products into a card of another design.

The Sound Blaster Pro and Multimedia

Multimedia accomplishes the blending of sound and video into the text-based world of computers. Multimedia has gone beyond just pictures in a document, though; you now see applications that span from talking reference books to databases that store digital video images of local real estate. And to run these applications, you need a Multimedia PC (MPC).

The MPC standard was set by the Multimedia PC Marketing Council to eliminate a lack of consistency in hardware requirements for multimedia applications. The current minimum MPC requirements are an 80386SX processor, a CD-ROM drive fast enough to run multimedia titles, support for MIDI and digital sound, and Microsoft's Windows 3.1.

The Sound Blaster Pro version fulfills the sound requirements of the MPC specifications (you'll learn more about Sound Blaster versions later in this chapter). By combining Sound Blaster Pro (SB Pro) with the Creative Labs CD-ROM drive, you have an easy solution for multimedia. In fact, Creative Labs makes a Multimedia Upgrade Kit that has everything you need in one package: the SB Pro card, a MIDI Kit, the CD-ROM drive, Windows 3.1, and over $3,000 worth of software on CD-ROMs. If you already have an SB Pro card, you can buy just the CD-ROM Upgrade Kit to bring your computer up to MPC specifications.

Anatomy of the Sound Blaster Family of Cards

The manual that came with your Sound Blaster card goes into some detail about where jumpers are located and what the card can do. Unfortunately, it doesn't say much about how it all gets done. The purpose of these next few sections is not to make you a hardware engineer, but rather to show you what all those chips and other components do. We'll talk you through each card in the Sound Blaster family, pointing out their similarities, differences, and even some features that aren't commonly known.

The Sound Blaster 1.0/1.5/2.0

Creative Labs has released three versions of the original Sound Blaster, model numbers 1.0, 1.5, and 2.0. These three Sound Blaster cards can be used on an IBM PC/XT, AT, 386, 486, PS/2 (models 25/30), Tandy (except 1000 EX/HX), and compatible computers.

The original Sound Blaster is an 8-bit card that incorporates 11-channel FM synthesis, 8-bit digital sound recording and playback, and a joystick/MIDI port. What this means to you is that you can play up to 11 musical instruments simultaneously, bringing new depth to games and presentations. On top of that, the 8-bit digital recording and playback capabilities allow you to add special sound effects and speech. For occasional gamers as well as serious game enthusiasts, a built-in joystick port means you don't have to buy another card to use joysticks; you just plug in the Sound Blaster. And for those who want to explore music, a MIDI (Musical Instrument Digital Interface) port is included, as well, so that MIDI-compatible keyboards and synthesizers can be easily connected to your computer without the expense of additional MIDI cards.

Sound Blaster 1.0 and 1.5, shown in Figure 1-1, are essentially the same card, except that the 1.5 card does not include the Creative Music System upgrade (CMS chips). This upgrade was originally offered by Creative Labs to provide backward compatibility with the older Game Blaster (discussed above). The CMS chips use AM technology to synthesize musical instruments, though they are not as good as the newer FM technology that has subsequently been incorporated into Sound Blaster.

Support for the Game Blaster, and thus the CMS chips, has gradually fallen off and is almost nonexistent today, although you can still obtain the CMS chips and add them to your Sound Blaster. However, given the lack of support for them, there would be very little you could gain by adding them.

Sound Blaster 2.0, shown in Figure 1-2, is quite different from the 1.0/1.5. It makes use of *surface mount* technology, the state-of-the-art in circuit board technology; as a result, Sound Blaster 2.0 is smaller and more reliable than its predecessors. It can play back digital files at sampling rates as high as 44.1 kHz, as opposed to the 1.0/1.5 limit of 23 kHz; and it can record at sampling rates as high as 15 kHz, as opposed to the 1.0/1.5 limit of 12 kHz. Thus the sound quality of digital recordings

Sound Blaster 1.0/1.5

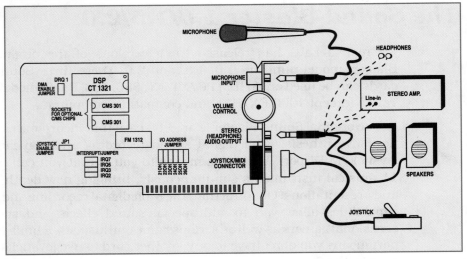

on the 2.0 is quite a bit better than the 1.0/1.5. (See Chapter 2 for more information on sampling.)

Beginning with version 2.0, the Sound Blaster has a line-level input connector in addition to the microphone input. The line-in connector is right above the microphone connector; see Figure 1-2 for its location.

Note   The best way to distinguish between the different Sound Blaster models is to use the test program TEST-SBC.EXE. See Appendix A, which covers installation, for more detailed information on running TEST-SBC and determining the version of your sound card.

The Chips for Sound Blaster 1.0/1.5/2.0

The chips used on the Sound Blaster are what bring all of its extraordinary features to life. These chips include the FM synthesizer, the Digital Sound Processor (DSP), and the bus interface.

Digital Sound Processor (DSP) Chip

The most versatile chip on the Sound Blaster is the DSP (Digital Sound Processor) chip; it processes all the commands that come from an

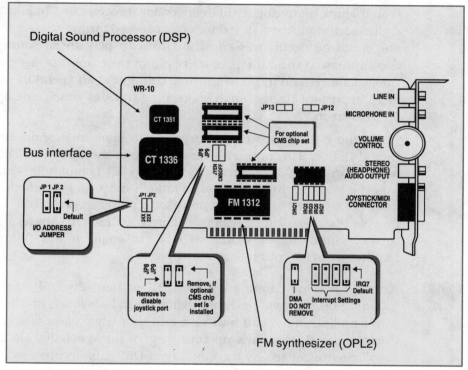

FIGURE 1-2 Sound Blaster 2.0

FM synthesizer (OPL2)

application. The DSP chip must also instruct all the other sound chips on your Sound Blaster in order to produce the sounds you hear.

As shown in Figure 1-1, the DSP chip is numbered CT1321 on the 1.0/1.5 card and is the largest chip on the card. On the 2.0 card it's labeled CT1351, as shown in Figure 1-2.

When a presentation program wants to play notes through the FM synthesizer, the DSP must accept the data from the computer and instruct the FM chip how to play the music. When a game wants to surprise you with a digitally recorded explosion, the DSP accepts the sound data from the computer and converts it from digital to analog form so that you can hear the sound.

The DSP is responsible for sending and receiving the MIDI data used by electronic keyboards and synthesizers. The DSP also performs the analog-to-digital and digital-to-analog functions that allow you to do digital recording and playback of music, sound effects, and speech. (You'll learn more about this conversion process in Chapter 2.) Some digital sound files are stored in a compressed format to save disk space and must be decompressed. The DSP can play these sound files by decompressing the data as it arrives from the computer. By performing the decompression in the chip, your computer can spend its time doing more important things, such as keeping track of your game opponents on the screen.

You may be interested or surprised to know that some versions of Sound Blaster 1.5 come with version 2.00 of the DSP chip. DSP 2.00 is faster than the 1.05 version and is Windows 3.1-compatible. Version 1.05 was the latest technology when Windows 3.1 was published, but Windows 3.1 requires more sound processing power than the DSP 1.05 could provide. As a result, a DSP 2.00 is offered by Creative Labs as an upgrade to the Sound Blaster's original DSP, to conform with Windows 3.1 requirements for sound processing power.

Note If you are running Windows 3.1 without the DSP upgrade from 1.05 to 2.00, you will find that digital sound playback in Windows can waver and stumble. You may also find that some games, such as Wing Commander II, may lock up your system unexpectedly. Both of these problems are caused by the inability of DSP 1.05 to process sound fast enough. If you currently have a Sound Blaster 1.0 or 1.5 with the 1.05 DSP, you can upgrade to a 2.00 DSP by calling Creative Labs, Inc. At this writing, the cost of the DSP 2.00 is $30, plus shipping and handling and any applicable sales tax. You may instead want to simply upgrade from Sound Blaster 1.x to the faster DSP and extra features of Sound Blaster 2.0, or even to Sound Blaster Pro; these newer cards are better suited to the requirements of today's software.

The FM Synthesizer Chip

The FM synthesizer chip is the same on all three versions of the Sound Blaster card, as shown in Figures 1-1 and 1-2. The FM chip is responsible for synthesizing the sounds of musical instruments. This chip, numbered FM1312 (and also known as the Yamaha 3812 OPL2), can play up to 11 instruments simultaneously. It does this by manipulating sine waves to approximate the waveforms created by real instruments. Chapter 2 goes into more detail on FM synthesis and how it works.

Other Chips on Your Sound Blaster

The rest of the chips on the Sound Blaster card are support chips, including gates, buffers, and amplifiers that help the main chips communicate with your speakers, microphone, joystick, and computer. On Sound Blaster 2.0, the many chips used to communicate with the computer have been replaced by the CT1336 bus interface chip, as shown in Figure 1-2. This integration not only reduces the cost and size of the card, but greatly increases its reliability.

The Connectors for Sound Blaster 1.0/1.5/2.0

Figures 1-1 and 1-2 point out the various connectors on the Sound Blaster 1.0/1.5 and 2.0 cards. These connectors provide a means for passing sound from the card to speakers, stereos, and headphones, and for receiving sound from a microphone, tape player, or stereo. There are three connectors on the 1.x cards, and four on the 2.0 card.

☐ The microphone jack is the first connector on the 1.x cards (look at the very top of the card in Figure 1-1), and it is the second connector on the 2.0 (as shown in Figure 1-2). It is a 1/8-inch monaural minijack.

☐ The topmost connector on the 2.0 card is a line-in connector for hooking up to the line-out from a tape deck, stereo, or CD player, as shown in Figure 1-2. It is a 1/8-inch stereo minijack.

☐ The connector just below the volume knob, as shown in Figures 1-1 and 1-2, is the speaker output. It, too, is a 1/8-inch stereo minijack. The speaker-out connector has a built-in amplifier that can output up to four watts of power per channel, so be sure to turn down the volume before connecting anything to it. Also, do not connect a mono 1/8-inch miniplug to the speaker output, as this can short-circuit and damage the amplifier.

☐ The last connector is a 15-pin, D-sub connector used for joystick input and MIDI input/output. This connector is shown in both Figures 1-1 and 1-2 and is the same on both cards. The joystick/MIDI port can support one or two joysticks. Using two requires a Y-adapter available from Creative Labs; generic Y-adapters from other vendors may not work properly. Two pins on the joystick/MIDI connector (pins 12 and 15) are used for MIDI Out and MIDI In, respectively. This allows you to connect MIDI keyboards and synthesizers to the Sound Blaster with the optional MIDI cable.

The Jumpers for Sound Blaster 1.0/1.5/2.0

The jumpers are used to configure the card so that it doesn't conflict with other cards in your computer. These jumpers set the card's configuration when you install your sound card. Their labels and locations can be seen in Figures 1-1 and 1-2.

☐ Jumper JP1 on the Sound Blaster 1.x (Figure 1-1) or JP8 on the Sound Blaster 2.0 (Figure 1-2) allows you to turn the built-in joystick on or off. The only time you will need to remove the jumper is if you have another joystick port in your computer. Many combination I/O cards have a joystick port that is turned on by default. If you have such a card, check the documentation for the card to see if the joystick is enabled. If it is, disable the port on either the I/O card or the Sound Blaster, but not on both.

☐ The DRQ1 jumper, as shown in Figures 1-1 and 1-2, enables the DMA (direct memory access) channel on the sound card for digital sound recording and playback. Do not remove this jumper, as the sound card cannot perform digital sound functions correctly without it.

☐ The IRQ jumpers select the hardware interrupt number of the card, which is also known as its IRQ. These interrupts are compatible with XTs, ATs, and later machines. The interrupts are used for digital sound recording and playback, as well as MIDI input.

☐ Jumpers 210 through 260, as shown in Figure 1-1, select the base I/O address of the 1.0/1.5 cards. The I/O address is the location of the communications channel that the computer uses to send and receive data from the Sound Blaster. Notice that Sound Blaster 2.0 only allows selection of ports 220H or 240H, as shown in Figure 1-2.

Sound Blaster Pro (CT1330), Pro 2 (CT1600), and Pro Basic

The Sound Blaster's FM-synthesized music, 8-bit digitized sound recording and playback, and built-in joystick and MIDI ports are fine for some people. But these features represent only the most basic level of the Creative Labs Sound Blaster family. Sound Blaster's successor, the Sound Blaster Pro, brings stereo to all the sound output capabilities of its little brother.

There have been two models of the Pro: CT1330 and CT1600 (also known as the Pro 2). The Sound Blaster Pro (CT1330) is shown in Figure 1-3. The Sound Blaster Pro 2 (CT1600) is shown in Figure 1-4. The Pro Basic is exactly the same as the Pro 2 except that it is packaged without a MIDI adapter and sequencing software.

FIGURE 1-3   Sound Blaster Pro (CT1330)

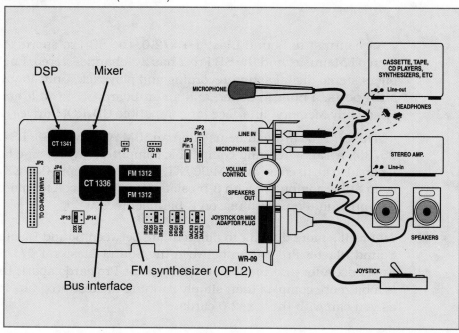

FIGURE
1-4

Sound Blaster Pro 2 (CT1600)

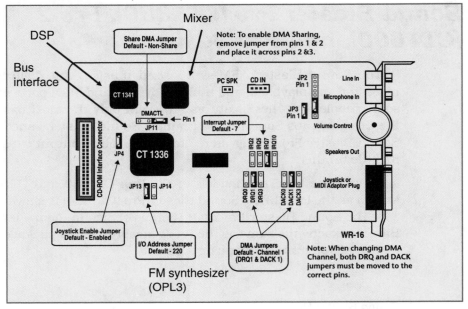

In contrast to Sound Blaster 1.x/2.0, the SB Pro sports 22-channel stereo FM music, and the SB Pro 2 has 20-channel stereo. Each Pro also offers stereo digital sound recording and playback, built-in joystick and MIDI ports, a built-in mixer, and an on-board CD-ROM (Compact Disk Read Only Memory) interface for compatible CD-ROM drives.

The SB Pro card can be used on an IBM AT, 386, 486, PS/2 (models 25/30), a Tandy AT, and compatible computers. With some limitations, it can also be used on an IBM PC/XT, a Tandy (except 1000 EX/HX), and compatible computers with 8-bit slots. See Appendix A for more information on limitations with use on 8-bit machines.

Note   It's more difficult to differentiate between Sound Blaster Pro and Sound Blaster Pro 2 than between the Sound Blaster 1.0/1.5/2.0. See Appendix A for information on telling these Pro cards apart; the process is a bit more complex than simply running the test program TEST-SBC, as you can with the 1.x/2.0 cards.

The Chips for Sound Blaster Pro/Pro 2/Pro Basic

The chips used on the Pro, Pro 2, and Pro Basic bring to life all its extraordinary features. These chips include the Digital Sound Processor (DSP), FM synthesizer, the mixer, and the bus interface.

The Digital Sound Processor (DSP) Chip

Both Sound Blaster Pros use a newer DSP chip, labeled CT1341 in both Figures 1-3 and 1-4. This chip can digitally record and play back in mono or stereo. It also has a high-speed mode that allows it to record and play back at sampling rates up to 44.1 kHz (44,100 cycles per second) in mono, or 22.05 kHz in stereo. The CT1341 can decompress digital sound files as they are played back; thus no processor time is needed from the computer when playing compressed files. The DSP also handles all the MIDI input and output functions, and controls all the other sound chips on the card.

The FM Synthesizer Chip

The Sound Blaster Pro model CT1330 has two FM chips. On the board in Figure 1-3 you will see two chips labeled FM1312; these are also known as OPL2 FM chips. Each one produces 11 FM instruments, and since the Pro card has two of them, it is capable of 22 FM instruments.

The Sound Blaster Pro 2 model CT1600, on the other hand, does not have dual OPL2 chips. Instead, it has the newer stereo OPL3 FM chip, labeled YMF-262-M in Figure 1-4. This chip is backward compatible with the older chips that use two-operator FM synthesis, but also has a new four-operator mode that produces better-sounding instruments.

Note   While in four-operator mode, the Pro 2 card is limited to a maximum of six simultaneous instruments.

The Mixer

Another new chip introduced on the Pro cards is the CT1345 mixer. This chip allows you to adjust and mix the sounds from the microphone, line-in, CD input, and the digital sound output. This way you can hear a blend of sounds, such as your voice from the microphone while FM music, digital sound, and CD audio play in the background. On the Sound Blaster 1.x/2.0, you can only hear FM and digital sound at the same time. You cannot, however, digitally record from multiple sources simultaneously. Only one recording source can be selected by the mixer. If you want to record from the microphone and a tape player, for example, you will need an external mixer.

With this built-in mixer to control volumes, you may be wondering what the manual volume control is for on the Sound Blaster Pro. The manual volume control sets the final volume of the output. With this manual volume control, you know that when you turn down the volume, there's no way that the computer can override your setting.

The Bus Interface

The CT1336 bus interface chip, shown in both Figures 1-3 and 1-4, passes messages between Sound Blaster Pro and the computer. It is the same chip used on Sound Blaster 2.0, shown in Figure 1-2.

The Connectors for Sound Blaster Pro /Pro 2/Pro Basic

Figures 1-3 and 1-4 point out the various connectors on the Pro cards. Connectors are used for passing sound from the card to speakers, stereos, and headphones, and for receiving sound from a microphone, tape player, or stereo.

Four connectors are accessible from the outside of the computer.

☐   The line-in jack is shown at the very top of the card in Figures 1-3 and 1-4. It is a 1/8-inch stereo minijack, and is used to hook in the line-out from a tape deck, stereo, or CD player.

☐   The next connector on the card is the microphone connector; it is a 1/8-inch mono minijack.

☐   The connector just below the volume knob is the speaker output. It is a 1/8-inch stereo minijack. The speaker-out connector has a built-in amplifier that can output up to four watts of power per channel, so be sure to turn down the volume before connecting anything to it. Also, do not connect a mono 1/8-inch miniplug to the speaker output, as this can short-circuit and damage the amplifier.

☐   The 15-pin D-sub connector is used for joystick input and MIDI input/output. The joystick/MIDI port can support one or two joysticks. Using two requires a Y-adapter available from Creative Labs; generic Y-adapters from other vendors may not work properly. Two pins on the joystick/MIDI connector (pins 12 and 15) are used for MIDI Out and MIDI In, respectively. This allows you to connect MIDI keyboards and synthesizers to the Sound Blaster with the included MIDI cable.

Note   The Sound Blaster Pro Basic does not include the MIDI cable.

There are also three connectors on the card that are accessible only from the inside of the computer: JP1, J1, and J2, all shown in Figures 1-3 and 1-4.

☐   The JP1 connector allows you to connect the motherboard speaker output to the Sound Blaster Pro. The pin configuration for this connector is given in Table 1-1.

Caution   If you connect JP1 to your motherboard, be prepared for the resulting loud volume level of the computer's beeps. The input on JP1 is not connected to the Sound Blaster Pro's mixer and can only be adjusted with the manual volume control.

PC Speaker Connector (JP1)

Pin	Signal	I/O
1	+5V	IN
2	SPK	IN

☐ The J1 connector is a Molex-type connector for the CD-ROM drive. It passes stereo audio from the CD-ROM drive to the Pro card. The pin configuration for this connector is shown in Table 1-2 for both the Pro and Pro 2.

☐ The J2 connector is the CD-ROM data cable connector. The data cable that runs between J2 and the CD-ROM drive allows the Sound Blaster Pro to directly control the CD-ROM drive. It is a proprietary interface connection for Creative Labs CD-ROM drives and some Panasonic/Matsushita drives. Contact Creative Labs, Inc., for exact model information. J2 cannot be used by just any CD-ROM drive, and it is not an SCSI (Small Computer Standard Interface) or a subset of an SCSI-type interface.

The Jumpers for Sound Blaster Pro/Pro 2/Pro Basic

The jumpers are used to configure card so that it doesn't conflict with other cards in your computer. These jumpers are set in the card's configuration when you install your card. Their labels and locations can be seen in Figures 1-3 and 1-4.

☐ Jumper JP4 lets you turn the built-in joystick on or off. The only time you will need to remove the jumper is when you have another joystick port in your computer. Many combination I/O cards have a joystick port that is turned on by default. If you have such a card, check the documentation for the card to see if the joystick is enabled.

TABLE 1-2   CD IN Connector (J1)

Pin	Signal	I/O
1	Ground	IN
2	CD left channel	IN
3	Ground	IN
4	CD right channel	IN

If it is, disable the port either on the I/O card or the Sound Blaster Pro, but not on both.

☐ Jumpers JP5 through JP7 and JP15 through JP17 select the DMA channel of the sound card. The DMA channel is used when playing and recording digital sound. Choose from channels 0, 1, or 3. Channel 0 will only work on ATs and higher.

☐ Jumper JP11 is available on the CT1600 to allow the Pro 2 to share its DMA channel with another device that is using the same DMA channel. The only time you will need to use this function is when all the DMA channel selections are being used in your computer. This jumper will work only if the other device is also designed to share its DMA, so leave it disabled unless you are absolutely certain that the other card in your system can share its DMA. Otherwise, data could be lost, or one or both cards could be damaged.

☐ Jumpers JP13 and JP14 select the base I/O address of the card. The I/O address is the location of the communications channel that the computer uses to send and receive data from the Sound Blaster Pro. You can choose between addresses 220H and 240H.

☐ Jumpers JP18 through JP21 select the hardware interrupt number (IRQ) of the card. The interrupts are used for digital sound recording and playback, as well as MIDI input. Choose from 2, 5, 7, and 10. IRQ 2, 5, and 7 are compatible with XTs, ATs, and higher machines. IRQ 10 only works on ATs and higher class machines.

☐ Jumpers JP2 and JP3 are different from all the other jumpers on the board. They do not change the configuration of the board. Instead, JP2 and JP3 are an extension to the audio connectors on the board. Their pin configurations are shown in Tables 1-3 and 1-4.

In Figures 1-3 and 1-4, notice that there is a jumper on pins 6 and 7 of JP2 and pins 1 and 2 of JP3. Removing these jumpers will prevent sound from coming out of the Speaker Out connector on the board.

Warning Do not experiment with the Audio Extension jumpers unless you are experienced with audio electronics. A mistake in making connections here can damage the sound card.

Connector JP2 Pin Configuration

Pin	Description
1	MICR (microphone input, right channel). Input range 0.004 to 0.7 V rms.
2	MICGEN (microphone input ground).
3	MICL (microphone input, left channel). Input range 0.004 to 0.7 V rms.
4	SPKGND (speaker output ground).
5	SPKR (speaker output, right channel). Maximum output voltage 3 V rms at 4 ohms.
6	SPKL (speaker output, left channel). Maximum output voltage 3 V rms at 4 ohms.
7	SPKRL (speaker output return signal, left channel).
8	SPKRR (speaker output return signal, right channel).

Connector JP3 Pin Configuration

Pin	Description
1	SPKR (speaker output, right channel). Maximum output voltage 3 V rms at 4 ohms.
2	SPKRR (speaker output return signal, right channel).

Sound Blaster MCV

The Sound Blaster MCV (Microchannel Version), shown in Figure 1-5, incorporates 11-channel FM synthesis, 8-bit digital sound recording and playback, and joystick/MIDI port. The Microchannel is simply the connector on the motherboard used to interface with peripheral cards. A regular AT card will not plug into a Microchannel machine because the connectors are different.

The phrase Microchannel Version refers to proprietary architecture developed by IBM to eliminate competition from clone manufacturers. The Sound Blaster Microchannel Version was developed to support this Microchannel architecture.

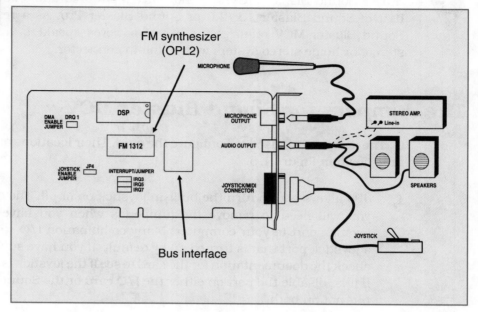

FIGURE
1-5

Sound Blaster MCV

The Sound Blaster MCV card can be used only on the IBM PS/2 model 50 and higher, or computers that are 100-percent compatible with IBM PS/2 with Microchannel bus architecture. The Sound Blaster MCV cannot be used on PS/2 models below 50 because they do not use the Microchannel architecture.

The Chips for Sound Blaster MCV

The Sound Blaster MCV's chips are identical to those in Sound Blaster 2.0. Figure 1-5 shows where each chip is located.

The Connectors for Sound Blaster MCV

The Sound Blaster MCV connectors are exactly the same as those on the Sound Blaster 1.0/1.5, except that Sound Blaster MCV does not have a line-in connector. Refer to Figure 1-5 for the location of the connectors.

Note   Sound Blaster MCV does not have a powered audio output like that of Sound Blaster 1.x/2.0 or Sound Blaster Pro. As a result, the Sound Blaster MCV requires the use of powered speakers, a portable stereo, or home stereo system with a line-in connector.

The Jumpers for Sound Blaster MCV

The jumpers are used to configure the card. Their locations and labels are shown in Figure 1-5.

☐   JP4 allows you to turn the built-in joystick on or off. The only time you will need to remove the jumper is when you have another joystick port in your computer. Many combination I/O cards have a joystick port that is turned on by default. If you have such a card, check the documentation for the card to see if the joystick is enabled. If it is, disable the port on either the I/O card or the Sound Blaster, but not on both.

☐   Jumper DRQ1 enables the DMA channel on the sound card. Do not remove this jumper, as the sound card cannot perform digital sound functions correctly without it.

☐   The IRQ jumpers select the hardware interrupt numbers for the card. The interrupts are used for digital sound recording and playback, as well as MIDI input.

Sound Blaster Pro MCV

The Sound Blaster Pro MCV (Microchannel Version), shown in Figure 1-6, has 20-channel stereo FM music, stereo digital sound recording and playback, a built-in joystick/MIDI port, and a digitally controlled mixer.

The Sound Blaster Pro MCV card can be used only on the IBM PS/2 model 50 and higher, or computers that are 100-percent compatible with IBM PS/2 computers with Microchannel bus architecture. The Sound Blaster MCV cannot be used on PS/2 models earlier than model 50 because they do not use the Microchannel architecture.

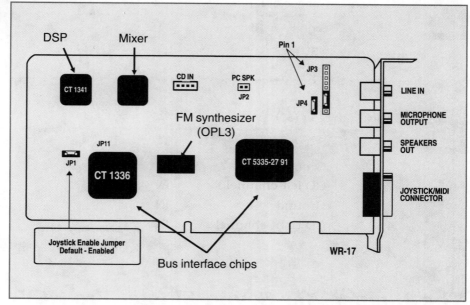

FIGURE
1-6
Sound Blaster Pro MCV

The Chips for Sound Blaster Pro MCV

The Sound Blaster Pro MCV uses the same chips as the Sound Blaster Pro 2, including the OPL3 FM synthesizer. The major difference is the addition of the CT5335 bus interface chip in the Pro MCV, to communicate with the Microchannel bus. See Figure 1-6 for the location of the CT5335 bus interface and other chips on this card. Also, refer to the previous discussions about Sound Blaster Pro 2 for more information on the functions of each chip.

The Connectors for Sound Blaster Pro MCV

The Sound Blaster Pro MCV has the same connectors as the Sound Blaster Pro 2, except the Pro MCV does not have a connector for the CD-ROM data cable. See Figure 1-6 for the specific location of the connectors. Tables 1-5 and 1-6 show the pin configurations for JP2 and J1. (Note that these are labeled differently on the Pro 2 card.)

TABLE 1-5

PC Speaker Connector (JP2)

Pin	Signal
1	+5V
2	SPK

TABLE 1-6

CD IN Connector (J1)

Pin	Signal	I/O
1	Ground	IN
2	CD left channel	IN
3	Ground	IN
4	CD right channel	IN

The Jumpers for Sound Blaster Pro MCV

The jumpers are used to configure the hardware on the board. Their locations and labels can be seen in Figure 1-6.

☐ Jumper JP1 allows you to turn the built-in joystick on or off. The only time you will need to remove the jumper is when you have another joystick port in your computer. Check the manuals that came with your system to see if you already have a joystick port in your machine. If you're still not sure, run the test program to check for conflicts with the MCV Pro card, as outlined in Appendix A.

☐ Jumpers JP3 and JP4 are different from all the other jumpers on the board; they don't change the configuration of the board. Instead, JP3 and JP4 are extensions to the audio connectors on the board. Their pin configurations are shown in Tables 1-7 and 1-8.

The tables below point out the functions of each pin. Notice that there is a jumper on pins 6 and 7 of JP3 and on pins 1 and 2 of JP4. Removing these jumpers will prevent sound from coming out of the Speaker Out connector on the board.

Connector JP3 Pin Configuration

Pin	Description
1	MICR (microphone input, right channel). Input range 0.004 to 0.7 V rms.
2	MICGEN (microphone input ground).
3	MICL (microphone input, left channel). Input range 0.004 to 0.7 V rms.
4	SPKGND (speaker output ground).
5	SPKR (speaker output, right channel). Maximum output voltage 3 V rms at 4 ohms.
6	SPKL (speaker output, left channel). Maximum output voltage 3 V rms at 4 ohms.
7	SPKRL (speaker output return signal, left channel).
8	SPKRR (speaker output return signal, right channel).

Connector JP4 Pin Configuration

Pin	Description
1	SPKR (speaker output, right channel). Maximum output voltage 3 V rms at 4 ohms.
2	SPKRR (speaker output return signal, right channel).

Warning   Do not experiment with the Audio Extension jumpers unless you are experienced with audio electronics. A mistake in making connections here can render the sound card useless.

Sound Blaster's Future

Today there are over one million Sound Blasters in use, in addition to thousands of Sound Blaster Pros. The Sound Blaster legacy has reached computer users worldwide, and is still growing strong. Just take a walk into your local computer software store and look at the section on recommended hardware for any game. Sound Blaster is supported on virtually every piece of PC entertainment software shipped today. Also, Microsoft Windows 3.1 is shipped with drivers for Sound Blaster, so that the entire Windows environment and all Windows-compatible software can take advantage of the card's capabilities.

The development of the Sound Blaster family continues to push forward, with enhancements and technical improvements being added all the time. By the time you read this, Sound Blaster 16 ASP (SB16) will be out. It can record and play back digital audio with 16-bit resolution at sampling rates up to 44.1 kHz in full stereo. That's the same high-quality digital audio used in CD and DAT (Digital Audio Tape) players. SB16 also has a new mixer that will allow you to digitally record from all of its sound sources (FM, line-in, microphone, and CD-Audio) simultaneously. You also get bass and treble controls, in addition to gain control of the input and output amplifiers for recording even the tiniest signals.

The SB16's MIDI port is now compatible with the popular Roland MPU-401 hardware, so you won't have to have Sound Blaster-specific drivers to use the MIDI port. There is also a special connector on the card for the Wave Blaster sound module which, when plugged into the SB16, will produce the realistic instrument sounds used by professional musicians. To top it all off, a new processor chip has been added. It's called the ASP (Advanced Signal Processor) and can be programmed by software applications for operations such as real-time compression and decompression, without the need for hardware upgrades.

With its worldwide support and continuing technological breakthroughs, the Creative Labs Sound Blaster family can be expected to remain the sound card standard for the foreseeable future. The following chapters in this book will show you how to get the most out of your Sound Blaster and how to make it even more of a staple in your computer diet.

PART

II

Software Bundled with the Sound Blaster Family

CHAPTER

Basics of Sound
and the Sound Blaster

*I*n this chapter you will find important basic information about working with sound on your computer. Other chapters of this book contain references to this chapter. These discussions of topics such as software drivers, digital audio files, sampling rates, packing, and so forth will not only explain the concepts to you, but also will prove helpful in getting the best performance from your Creative Labs Sound Blaster hardware and software.

Note   In this chapter, the term Sound Blaster refers to all versions of the Sound Blaster card except when explained otherwise.

The sections about MIDI and the FM Synthesizer are the most technical of this chapter. The MIDI section introduces MIDI concepts, and then launches into interesting, although somewhat more difficult material. The FM Synthesizer section is compact and straightforward. It will give you an excellent introduction into FM synthesis theory, and you'll find out what's involved in programming at the level of the FM synthesizer chip.

At the end of the chapter is a brief but very important glimpse into the future, when 16-bit digital audio will replace 8-bit digital audio, and wave table technology will supplant FM synthesis technology.

Note   You don't need to read this section now if you're in a hurry to start enjoying your Creative Labs sound card. But you should at least scan the section headings, so you will know what information is available here.

Using Your Sound Blaster Software

This section provides general information on how to find the programs that came with and are related to your sound card, and also explains some of the conventions used by the software and throughout this book. You'll find information about fixing or avoiding common problems in the use of your software, such as how to eliminate popping and pauses when you play back your sound files.

Locating the Programs

If you follow the installation procedures found in your Creative Labs Sound Blaster reference manual and in Appendix A of this book, your programs will be in a directory named either \SB or \SBPRO. (Appendix A tells you what directory the various Sound Blaster versions are stored in.) The instructions in this chapter assume you are using these directory names. Occasionally you'll read instructions for switching to another directory.

Command Syntax

To use your sound card and software effectively, you will enter commands instructing the software to take action. Usually these commands are entered on the DOS command line. There are syntax rules for commands and their parameters, but you needn't be concerned with capitalization within the commands—Sound Blaster software is not case-sensitive. For example, all of the following commands will work:

```
VPLAY CONGA.VOC
vplay conga.voc
VPlAy CoNGA.voc
vplay conga.voc /T:5 /Q
vplay conga.voc  /q /T:5
```

Notice that in the last two commands listed just above, the two command switches following the command (/q and /T:5) are reversed, yet they work the same way. Though command options may be typed in any order, you do need to be careful to type the complete filename correctly, such as CONGA.VOC, using the appropriate filename extension (such as .VOC) when you know it. You should always use the extension, although most programs will correctly guess the appropriate file extension. Avoid typing spaces between the filename and its extension. Also avoid typing spaces between a command switch and its parameter, as in /T:5.

Editing ASCII Files

In order to use a particular Sound Blaster program, you may need to create or modify a plain-text (ASCII) file. For example, the Sound Blaster Pro has a software program called MMPLAY, which is used to create audio/visual presentations. When using MMPLAY, you create a plain-text script file that includes instructions for playing specific music and animation files.

Plain-text files are called ASCII files because they use only the printable ASCII characters. ASCII files are different from the files that most word processing programs work with. Most word processors, such as Microsoft Word or WordPerfect, embed special characters in their document files to specify formatting information. These formatting codes are likely to interfere with the ability of other programs to read these files.

Recognizing the need to create or edit ASCII text files, most word processing applications offer command options that allow you to work with files without embedding the special formatting characters. For example, in WordPerfect 5.x these commands are the Text-in and Text-out commands. In Microsoft Word you can use the Save As Text option. And in Windows 3.1, the Write application allows you to save work as an ASCII file by selecting the File Save As Word for DOS/Txt Only menu option.

In addition to using your word processor to work with ASCII files, you can use a simple text editor such as the one that comes with DOS. In your DOS directory you may have EDLIN, a programmer's tool, or EDIT (MS-DOS 5) or EDITOR (DR DOS). You can use these tools to directly create or edit an ASCII file. You can also use these editors to verify that your word processor or text editor is really creating an ASCII file, by typing the resulting file to the screen using the DOS TYPE command. For example, suppose you have a file called TESTFILE.TXT. Type **C:>TYPE TESTFILE.TXT** and press ENTER. If your file is truly in ASCII format, you will see the entire file on the screen. If it is non-ASCII, and has embedded control characters, you will see unrecognizable symbols on the screen.

Managing Your Driver Software

Drivers are small software programs that allow an application program, such as Dr. Sbaitso the talking analyst, to be customized to work with any PC hardware, and specifically with Sound Blaster sound cards. Although there is only one Dr. Sbaitso application, each version of the Sound Blaster sound card has its own driver program. Drivers shield application programs from having to know the specifics of the hardware they run on, such as the differences between Sound Blaster 1.5 and Sound Blaster Pro 2. A software driver is like a limousine driver—just tell it where to go, and it handles all the details. Your Sound Blaster driver handles all the details of communicating with the sound card.

Drivers are typically loaded as needed by an application. For example, when you first install a word processing program, it asks you to pick from a list of printers. Later, when you print a file, the driver for the printer you've selected will be loaded automatically by the word processing program. The word processing program doesn't need to know much about the printer because the printer driver, as the intermediary, figures out how to print italic, underlining, strikeover, and other similar tasks.

Having the correct driver—one that works well for the hardware—is just as important as having a smoothly running transmission. Small problems with either one can completely disable your machine.

How the Sound Blaster Programs Use Drivers

The software that comes bundled with your Creative Labs hardware, as well as the programs included with this book, rely on drivers to communicate with the sound card. You will sometimes need to load a driver explicity (that is, by typing its name at the DOS prompt); at other times drivers will be loaded automatically. For example, when you use the program PLAYCMF, you must first load the driver called SBFMDRV that controls the FM synthesizer part of the sound card. On the other hand, the FM Intelligent Organ automatically loads a driver called ORGAN.DRV.

Creative Labs does not recommend loading drivers into high memory, using a memory manager such as the MS-DOS 5 EMM386 driver. You may discover that some drivers, such as SBFMDRV, do work correctly in high memory, but there is little to gain in loading such a small driver into that part of your system.

 Note   Drivers can be shared by many programs. For example, once the SBFMDRV driver is loaded, you can use PLAYCMF without having to load another copy of the driver.

Unloading Drivers

If you load a driver explicitly, by typing its name at the DOS prompt, you are also responsible for unloading it and removing it from memory. Software drivers consume from 30K to 110K of conventional memory. If you forget to unload the driver, it will occupy conventional memory that may be needed by your other programs, affecting their performance or even preventing them from running at all.

The drivers described in this chapter are typically unloaded by typing the driver name followed by the /U command option. For example, typing **SBFMDRV /U** will unload the SBFMDRV driver. If a software program loads a driver automatically, it will typically unload it automatically when you quit the program.

 Tip   Should a program crash, a driver may be left in memory. You will have to reboot your computer to remove it from memory.

Running Sound Blaster Programs under Windows 3.1

The following discussion alerts you to some of the issues and difficulties of running Sound Blaster in the Windows environment. Check with Creative Labs, Inc., to get the latest information about running their programs within the DOS compatibility box of Windows 3.1. (The DOS compatibility box is provided in the Windows 3.1 environment so that you can continue using your favorite DOS applications for which you don't have a Windows counterpart.)

Sound card-related utility programs such as VOC-HDR and JOINTVOC that don't talk to the sound card should work fine in the DOS compatibility box. On the other hand, programs that are real-time (meaning they probably can't tolerate any delays), such as game and music software, may not work reliably in DOS within Windows. Examples of such real-time aplications include Sound Blaster's PARROT, SBTAL-KER, Dr. Sbaitso, VOXKIT, and VEDIT2 programs. At a minimum, Windows 3.1 must be run in 386 Enhanced mode, and these real-time applications must be given exclusive use of resources. See your Windows user's guide for more information on how set up a PIF (program information file) to accomplish this.

The reason real-time programs do not operate reliably in the Windows 3.1 DOS compatibility box is because Windows 3.1 is a *time-slice multitasking operating environment*. This means Windows 3.1 permits each application that is running concurrently (multitasking) to take control (a time slice) of the PC intermittently. This interrupted access poses a problem for real-time applications, and an audio or video application is usually a real-time application that will not behave properly unless it has exclusive control of your PC. Windows cannot grant some real-time applications enough time for them to run correctly.

Note With most applications you can't detect this rapid switching from program to program that happens with time-slice multitasking, but you will notice timing problems with real-time audio and video.

Windows-Compatible Sound Blaster Applications

You cannot run one of the Creative Labs DOS programs in the DOS compatibility box if you've already installed the Windows 3.1 drivers for the Sound Blaster. When Windows loads, its drivers take total control of the Sound Blaster. Windows will reject your attempt to run a DOS program that tries to access the same hardware.

Though it's not recommended that you run Sound Blaster real–time DOS applications in the Windows 3.1 DOS compatibility box, you needn't be too concerned. Creative Labs and Microsoft have provided you with several excellent Windows-based programs that take full advantage of the Windows graphical environment. In fact, you'll probably have more fun using the Microsoft Media Player and Sound Recorder and the

Creative Labs Jukebox under Windows than you will with their DOS equivalents.

Sound File Principles and Concepts

This section provides some essential basic technical concepts. Understanding them will let you push your Sound Blaster setup to its full potential.

About Digital Audio Files

Digital audio files are files that contain sound converted to digital form so it can be stored in your computer's memory or on disk. Once sound has been converted to digital form it can be easily modified with an editor, such as VOXKIT (Sound Blaster) or VEDIT2 (Sound Blaster Pro). With an editor such as VEDIT2 you can amplify a selection of sound, fade it in or out, insert and delete words from speeches, and make endless other changes.

Digital audio files are stored in either the Creative Labs *voice file* format, indicated by a filename extension of .VOC, or in the Microsoft *wave file* format, indicated by a filename extension of .WAV. Nearly all of these files are "raw" data—that is, bytes that represent the sound. The .VOC and .WAV file formats both have identical raw data. The main difference between these file formats is the header, which is an introduction at the very beginning of the file that identifies the file's type. For digital audio files, this header characterizes the file as wave or voice; designates whether the raw data should be played as stereo (all the odd-numbered bytes go to one channel and the even-numbered bytes to the other) or monaural (all bytes go to the same channel); and so forth.

 Note   In the DOS environment you are likely to work with .VOC files; in the Windows environment you will work with .WAV files. The Sound Blaster Pro provides utilities to convert your digitized audio files from .VOC to .WAV and vice versa.

Controlling Popping and Pausing

If you hear pops or have pauses when you play digital audio files, you can solve the problem with additional *buffering*. Buffering uses part of memory as a temporary staging area to smooth the flow of digitized audio data between your computer's central processing unit (CPU) and the hard or floppy drive.

Many of the programs that come with the Sound Blaster cards feature the optional /B*kk* setting for disk buffer size. The default setting (the one you get when you don't include this command option) should be fine for most computers. However, if you have a slow computer such as an XT-class (8088) machine, or you're saving to floppy disk, you may need additional buffering.

Sampling: Analog-to-Digital Conversion

Before your computer can record and manipulate sound, these sounds must be transformed from audible sound to digital form by a process called analog-to-digital conversion (ADC). In this process, sound is converted to an analog (continuously changing) electrical signal by the microphone. It is then converted from a continous signal to a series of discrete values by measurements taken at a constant rate. This process is known as *sampling*. If the measurements (samples) are done at a sufficiently high frequency (sampling rate), they can do a good job of approximating the analog sound wave.

Figure 2-1 below depicts how analog-to-digital conversion is performed. Notice how the continuous wave is approximated by a series of point values.

When the digitized audio file is played back, the digital data is converted from a stream of byte values to an analog electrical wave by hardware called a DAC, a digital-to-analog convertor. The analog signal is then fed to the speakers or headphone from which you hear sound. The illustration below depicts this conversion. Digital audio stored on disk is represented at the top of Figure 2-2 by a tape reel with data.

FIGURE
2-1
Analog-to-Digital Conversion (ADC)

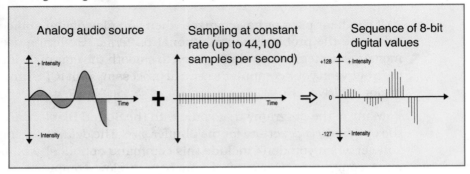

Sampling Rates and Sampling Sizes

The quality of digital audio sound is dependent on two key factors: the number of samples taken per second (sample rate) and the sample size.

The sampling must be so frequent that high-frequency sounds, such as the ringing of a crystal wine glass or the bowing of a violin, are captured accurately. To faithfully replicate a sound, the sample rate must be at least twice the highest frequency component. Since the highest frequency that can be perceived by normal human ears is a little over 20 KHz (20,000 vibrations per second), the maximum sampling rate of the Sound Blaster cards (44,100 kHz) is usually adequate. This is the sample rate used by today's CD players. According to many audiophile enthusiasts, CD audio lacks a certain richness in sound. This may well be due to the sample rate being just a little too low to accurately reconstruct the highest-frequency components.

FIGURE
2-2
Digital-to-Analog Conversion (DAC)

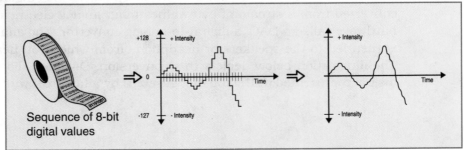

The other factor in the quality of digital audio is the sample size. The current generation of consumer sound cards, including the Sound Blaster family, are mostly 8-bit sound cards. This means the dynamic range (variation in signal strength) is only 8 bits, a maximum of 256 steps. CD players, in contrast, have a 16-bit sample size. Their dynamic range is 256 x 256, or 65,535 steps. The human ear perceives a world of difference between these two sample sizes. Your ears are most sensitive at detecting pitch (frequency), but are also quite sensitive to sound intensity. Human ears are capable of detecting sounds that vary in intensity by orders of magnitude, and 8-bit sound is perceived as lethargic and noisy in comparison to 16-bit sound.

Digital audio files can be recorded with your choice of sampling rate. The higher the sampling rate, the better the sound quality. For example, 6,000 Hz (6,000 samples per second) is fine for a typical man's voice, but not good enough for the typical woman's voice, which has higher frequency components. A sampling rate of 8,000 Hz would provide a higher-quality recording of a woman's voice. The highest sampling rate available to you depends on which sound card you have, as shown below:

Card	Max Record Rate	Max Playback Rate
Sound Blaster 1.0, 1.5	13,000	13,000
Sound Blaster 2.0	15,000	44,100
Sound Blaster Pro	44,100	44,100

The Sound Blaster Pro cards are capable of recording and playing in stereo. Since both a left and right channel measurement must be taken, the top sampling rate is 22,050. Both the Sound Blaster and Sound Blaster Pro take 8-bit (1-byte) sound samples; each measurement consumes one byte of storage in your computer's memory or disk. The typical CD player stores music in 16-bit (2-byte) samples. The future generation of sound cards, in order to record speech and music with fidelity equivalent to today's CD players, will process 16-bit samples. As a consequence, these cards will consume memory and disk space at twice the rate.

You may not be able to use the highest sampling rates for several reasons. First, high sample rates require a lot of storage capacity. Each sample consumes 1 byte of memory or disk space. At a sample rate of 6,000 Hz, one minute of recording will fill a 360K disk. At the peak Sound

Blaster Pro sample rate of 44,100 Hz (for monaural sound) or 22,050 Hz (for stereo), an empty 10MB hard disk will be filled in just four minutes! You will be even more constrained if you record to memory rather than to disk. For example, when you use VEDIT2 (the Sound Blaster Pro's sound editor) on a typical PC with 640K, you can only record about six seconds of stereo at 22,050 Hz before filling up conventional memory.

There are other sample rate restrictions. These will be discussed in detail for each utility program. The key restriction is that you cannot use too high a sample rate if you plan to pack (compress) your files.

File Packing and Compression

Digital audio files are very large, and can easily consume many megabytes of hard disk storage. Your Creative Labs software and hardware provides tools for reducing the storage requirements of digital audio. Two techniques for *packing* (which is file compression specific to Creative Labs .VOC digital audio files) are available: replacement of silence periods with silence blocks, and compression of data blocks. With these packing techniques, files can be reduced to just one-quarter of their original, unpacked size. There are trade-offs involved, however:

☐   There is some degradation in audio quality.

 Tip It's easy to find out how data packing changes your recording's audio quality. Using Blaster Master, or Sound Blaster's VOXKIT or Sound Blaster Pro's VEDIT2, you should repeatedly load a sample digital audio file, pack it, and then listen to the results.

☐   Packed files cannot be converted to another format, such as Microsoft wave (.WAV).

☐   Sophisticated voice editors such as Blaster Master and Sound Blaster Pro's VEDIT2 cannot be used to further modify your voice file.

☐   Packing cannot be done on voice files recorded at a high sampling rate. For these files you can use a tool like VEDIT2 to reduce the sample rate before packing is done.

Silence Block Packing

Silence packing is a technique for replacing stretches of silence or near silence with a special marker that represents a period of silence. This marker, called a *.VOC file silence block*, tells your sound card how long to "speak" silence. This can make voice files containing speech much more compact by eliminating the silent data that is heard as pauses between words and sentences. Note the stretch of silence in an actual waveform shown in Figure 2-3; this can be replaced by a silence block. The shaded region illustrates the Silence Window, which is superimposed upon the wavefront.

Silence packing is effective because a silence block is very small relative to the stretches of silent audio it replaces. When a silence block is encountered during playback, the sound card's DSP (digital signal processor) is smart enough to be silent for the time duration encoded in the silence block.

Note   Silence blocks are part of the Creative Labs .VOC file format but are not supported by the Microsoft .WAV file format.

 FIGURE 2-3   Audio data that can be replaced by silence block

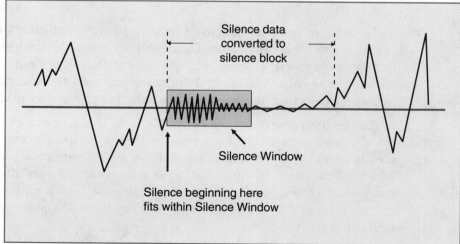

Data Block Packing

The Sound Blaster cards are capable of playing .VOC digital audio files in which the data blocks (the part of the file that contains audio data) are compressed. There are various techniques for data compression. Some techniques compress files without the loss of information, so that when the file is decompressed, the original file is restored.

Data block packing in audio files is somewhat similar to the type of compression done by file compression tools such as PKZIP and LHarc. In essence, their trick is to look for repeating patterns of characters and then substitute markers for every occurrence of the pattern after the first one. Since word processing files, for example, contain many blank spaces and frequently repeated words, you can easily get compression of 80 percent or more, which reduces the file size to 20 percent of the original.

Tip   LHarc was used to squeeze the Sound Blaster Pro software onto the installation disks. In fact, the complete LHarc compression program, written by Haruyasu Yoshizaki, is in your SBPRO directory. As this program is shareware, you are free to use this software as long as you adhere to the guidelines presented in the documentation file. The documentation file is named LHARC.MAN, and the program files are LHARC.EXE and LHARC.LZH.

The type of compression used by your sound card differs from general-purpose file compression. The beginning of the file (the header) must not be compressed, since it contains information that identifies the file as a Creative Labs .VOC digital audio file and tells the sound card how to play it (including the sampling rate, whether it is stereo, and so forth).

Rather than compress the entire file, only the data blocks within the file are compressed. The compression technique used is fast and simple—a necessity if speech and music are to be compressed on the fly. When playing back a sound file, your Sound Blaster card doesn't have the luxury of scanning through the entire file before starting to play music. It must play the file quickly, byte by byte, so there won't be any unnatural pauses.

While the compression technique used for quick decompression is simple and fast, it results in some information loss. In particular, the 8-bit sample size is reduced to as few as 2 bits. This provides considerable economy in storage, but considerably reduces the dynamic range (the range of sound intensity heard), degrading the sound quality in the process.

Data packing is a two-step process. First, the .VOC digital audio file is compressed. Second, the file is decompressed when played. The compression is done by software, after the sound file has been recorded; both the VOXKIT and VEDIT2 editors perform this compression for you. Decompression is done by the Sound Blaster cards' hardware during playback, by means of the digital signal processor (DSP), which is like a small computer in its own right.

Although you can do data packing with as much as 4:1 compression, you must take several factors into consideration before selecting the amount of compression. Extreme compression, such as 4:1, will cause too much distortion to be practical for music and even speech. This amount of compression is suitable for sound effects only. The 2.6-bit compression is appropriate for speech. Compression is not recommended at all for recorded music.

You will also want to select your sample rate with an eye toward your intended compression type. Decompressing a file places an additional burden on your sound card's DSP. As a result, the sound card cannot play back packed voice files as quickly as unpacked ones. The recommended maximum sample rate varies according to the compression selected (see the following table). If the sample rate exceeds the maximum shown below, your sound card will be unable to play the file fast enough, and the audio output will sound "slow."

Compression Type	Maximum Sampling Rate
8-bit uncompressed	44.1 kHz (Sound Blaster Pro and Pro MCV)
	15 kHz (Sound Blaster 2.0)
	13 kHz (Sound Blaster 1.5 and MCV)
2:1 compression	12 kHz
3:1 compression	13 kHz
4:1 compression	11 kHz

Note   The minimum sample rate is 4 kHz.

Sound Recording and the Role of Filters

Your Sound Blaster has one or more input sources, depending on which card you have. With older Sound Blasters (1.5 and earlier), there is only one input: microphone. With version 2.0 there is both microphone and line-in. Beginning with the Sound Blaster Pro, there are three inputs: microphone, line-in, and CD-ROM. In addition, line-in and CD-ROM can now handle stereo.

An artifact of recording in 8 bits is that a high-frequency ringing noise is always added to the source sound. This noise is due to a process called *aliasing*, a phenomena inherent to the analog-to-digital (ADC) conversion process. This noise component can be reduced by *filtering*, that is, by an input filter that is also known as a *recording filter*. Aliasing is less pronounced or even nonexistent when recording in 16 bits at a high sampling rate.

When you play back a sound file, your sound card performs digital-to-analog conversion (DAC). It reads a byte of sound data and creates an electrical signal whose strength is equivalent to the numeric value of the byte. This signal, which actually consists of many discrete steps, will look similar to a staircase that follows the form of the original signal. A *reconstruction filter* is then used to smooth out the signaling—a process called *convolution*. This resulting signal is then fed to your headphone or speaker to create sound.

Sound Blaster and Sound Blaster Pro cards have a recording filter that reduces high-frequency noise. A "low-pass" filter attenuates (reduces the strength of) sound components above a given frequency. Sound Blaster versions have a single, fixed-setting input filter, and Sound Blaster Pro cards have two settings: high and low. The high setting begins attenuation at a higher frequency than does the low setting. Though filter selection is really a matter of personal taste, there are some general guidelines. The low filter setting is intended for microphone input. The high filter setting is suitable for high-sample-rate speech or music. The default settings are On and Low.

Sound Blaster and Sound Blaster Pro cards also have an output filter. Like the input filter, this is a low-pass filter. It behaves similarly to the input filter that is set to high. The output filter also has a similar purpose: to reduce the high-frequency noise often encountered in real-world recordings. You should enable (turn on) the output filter whenever playing .VOC or .WAV digital audio files. When playing your CD player or line-in source, on the other hand, you will get superior sound by disabling (turning off) this filter, because these sources are very high-fidelity and very low in noise. The default setting for the output filter is On.

Understanding MIDI

The Musical Instrument Digital Interface (MIDI, pronounced "middy") has completely reshaped the music world, by delivering sophisticated music recording and performing capability to amateur musicians. Since MIDI was introduced 10 years ago, it has become a worldwide standard for electronic music. It is the standard by which synthesizers, keyboards, sound modules (electronic instruments), and computers talk to each other.

The MIDI topics that follow describe a MIDI network, explain what MIDI music data is, and describe how to connect MIDI instruments. Finally, there is a discussion of how the FM synthesizer on your sound card relates to MIDI music. (The section that follows, "Understanding FM Synthesis," provides a more expanded discussion of the FM synthesizer, including an introduction to how FM audio synthesis works.)

What Is a MIDI Network?

Anything you play on your computer's keyboard, or on an external MIDI keyboard, can be recorded by the computer. Likewise, any MIDI data in your computer can be played back on the keyboard's synthesizer or on a MIDI sound module. Of course, you need a sequencer software package to accomplish the recording and playback. Creative Lab's MIDI Kit includes a sequencer program created by Voyetra Technologies, and an interface cable to attach your sound card to a MIDI keyboard or other MIDI device.

MIDI consists of a digital protocol for representing musical notes and actions, and a network protocol for transmitting music data between MIDI-compatible devices. The digital protocol allows MIDI to describe music in a digital fashion, that is, as a sequence of byte values with musical meaning. These byte values can be recorded on disk by a digital computer such as your personal computer. The network protocol refers to the network software protocol used to pass music data between MIDI devices, including your computer.

When you hear the word *network* you probably think of Novell's NetWare or Artisoft's Lantastic or a similar local area network (LAN) used to connect personal computers. A MIDI network is really a very similar beast. Consider a typical business LAN that connects PCs containing network adapter cards. Once connected, the PCs can share documents and resources, such as printers, fax machines, and hard disks. Similarly, a MIDI network is a music network that connects PCs and musical instruments that have a MIDI interface. Once connected, the MIDI devices can exchange music data and share resources in the form of electronic instruments.

Many keyboards and electronic pianos today have a MIDI interface built in. You can easily add a MIDI interface to your computer by inserting one of the Sound Blaster or Sound Blaster Pro cards. The smallest MIDI network consists of just your PC, containing a Sound Blaster card, and an external MIDI device such as a MIDI keyboard. The sequencer program running on your PC performs two functions: It can record music created by playing keyboards and other instruments on the network, and it can control the MIDI network when it plays back previously recorded MIDI data. The FM synthesizer on your sound card can be addressed as a MIDI device. Together with an external MIDI keyboard, you have a small, yet complete MIDI network.

MIDI Music Data

Rather than musical sounds, MIDI consists of instructions on how to play music. When a sequencer program, such as Sequencer Plus Pro (Sp Pro) stores music as a MIDI file on your disk drive, it records MIDI instructions that specify what instrument to play, what key to press, with how much strength and when to press it.

MIDI files are signficantly different from digital audio files such as .VOC and .WAV files. Digital audio files contain actual sound, recorded in digital form by taking thousands of samples each second. MIDI music, on the other hand, contains only instructions on how to play an instrument. Digital audio files may require millions of bytes of data to play just a few minutes of music, but you can play hours of music with a MIDI file of just a few thousand bytes of data.

A MIDI file is not only more compact than a digitized audio file; it is also completely editable. An appropriate comparison of these two types of files might be with a fax document and a word processing file: The fax document can be read, and the digitized audio file can be played, but you can't modify either one much except for cutting and pasting to move the pieces around. A MIDI file, on the other hand, is like a word processing file; you can modify it endlessly.

The MIDI file is the computer equivalent of sheet music that is read by a conductor or musician. A MIDI sequencer program displays the music composition on the screen, showing the notes for each instrument on its own track. With the sequencer, you can not only effortlessly edit a composition, but also have your "orchestra" play the music back, immediately and flawlessly.

MIDI Messages, Channels, and Instruments

MIDI data consists of a variety of messages. The most commonly used are Note Number (what note to play), Note On (when to play a note), Velocity (how hard to hit the note), Note Off (when to release a note) and Channel Number (what instrument should play the note).

Sixteen *channels* are available on a MIDI network, which means you can play up to sixteen instruments simultaneously. A channel is actually more like a numbered seat in an orchestra pit than an instrument itself. Just as only one person at a time sits in a specific chair in the orchestra, only one instrument at a time is assigned to a channel.

Your sound card's FM synthesizer can simultaneously play many voices. The term *voice*, when used to describe electronic music, means an instrument sound. For example, your FM synthesizer can simulate drum, violin, and electronic piano sounds simultaneously. As an aside, if your PC were serving as conductor of a MIDI network with a drum-sound module, you would create drum sounds with the drum module rather than your sound card's FM synthesizer. A dedicated sound module is almost certain to have a finer sound than the equivalent voice from your sound card's general-purpose FM synthesizer.

Each instrument is assigned a number, called a *patch* or *program number*. Microsoft Windows and the Sound Blaster conform to the General MIDI (GM) standard, which designates specific program numbers for each instrument. Thus, a MIDI file using program number zero for a piano will produce a piano sound when played back through all GM-compliant synthesizers, regardless of the manufacturer. Prior to the General MIDI standard there was no guarantee what instrument would be heard if you played someone else's composition.

Note If you need to play MIDI files that do not adhere to the GM standard, you'll need to match up a program number with the correct instrument, using a MIDI mapper. Microsoft Windows 3.1 provides such a program, called MIDI Mapper.

The MIDI Interface

Most sound cards today, including the Sound Blaster and Sound Blaster Pro, provide a joystick connector on the sound card. This connector has been assigned a dual purpose, by utilizing two pins that are unneeded by the joystick. One pin receives MIDI data (MIDI In) and the other sends MIDI data (MIDI Out). By connecting a MIDI interface cable to the joystick connector, you can connect your PC to a MIDI device. If you own a Sound Blaster Pro, the interface cable necessary for MIDI connection is included. If you own a Sound Blaster 1.x/2.0 or a Sound Blaster Pro Basic, you can purchase the MIDI interface kit from Creative Labs.

The MIDI interface cable has a 15-pin male connector on one end that plugs into the MIDI/joystick port of your sound card. On the other end of the cable are three connectors: one female 15-pin connector and two 5-pin DIN-type connectors (the round ones). The female 15-pin connector is physically identical to the female 15-pin MIDI/joystick connector on your sound card, and you can continue to use a joystick by plugging it into this connector. The two 5-pin DIN connectors are the MIDI In and MIDI Out connectors, which are attached to any keyboard or sound module that adheres to the MIDI standard. The MIDI In and Out connectors are labeled accordingly.

When connecting a MIDI instrument such as a keyboard, the Out cable from the Sound Blaster MIDI interface connects to the In port on the back of the keyboard. In a similar fashion, the In cable of the Sound Blaster MIDI interface connects to the Out port of the keyboard. This may sound backwards at first. Just remember that data that comes *out* of the Sound Blaster goes *into* the keyboard, and the data that comes *out* of the keyboard goes *into* the Sound Blaster.

Some keyboards and synthesizer modules also have a MIDI Thru connector. This connection simply passes any MIDI data that comes in the In port. The Thru connector provides the means to "daisy chain"—to connect several MIDI devices along a single cable. This is the same technique used to connect SCSI devices on a Macintosh or PC. This subject can get complicated very quickly, and entire books have been written about MIDI devices, so we won't explore it much further here. It is sufficient to know that your PC, running a sequencer program like Sp Pro, can be attached to an external MIDI keyboard that will then play your sound card's FM synthesizer. You can even attach a small orchestra of MIDI instruments, all of which can be computer controlled.

MIDI and the FM Synthesizer

When you use a sequencer program to play or record MIDI music, it can control either external MIDI devices connected to the dual joystick/MIDI port, or it can control the FM synthesizer on your sound card. The Sound Blaster program disks include a device driver for the FM synthesizer. (See "Managing Your Driver Software" early in this chapter.) When you use a sequencer such as Sp Pro to record or play a MIDI file, the sequencer uses this driver to communicate with the FM synthesizer.

For the sequencer to drive an external MIDI device through the joystick/MIDI port, you must change the port assignment of the sequencer program so that it sends its music data out of the joystick/MIDI port instead of routing the music data internally to the driver for your sound card's FM synthesizer. For the Sound Blaster and Sound Blaster

Pro, the sequencer can talk to the sound card's FM synthesizer by addressing port 2, or to the MIDI output port by addressing port 1. The Sp Pro manual discusses this further in the chapter on FM synthesis.

The Sound Blaster Pro's FM synthesizer is capable of playing up to 16 FM-sythesized voices; Sound Blaster 1.x/2.0 can play up to 11. The Sound Blaster Pro cards, when running in the Windows environment, are limited to 6 voices, because the Windows driver uses four operators per voice, rather than the two used by the DOS driver. The Windows four-operator sound has much better quality than the two-operator sound you hear when running DOS programs.

Understanding FM Synthesis

Both the Sound Blaster and Sound Blaster Pros can produce music using their FM synthesizer. The FM synthesizer (called just "the synth" by most musicians) is a modern invention for producing a wide range of sounds, both music and special effects, using a simple approach invented by John Chowning of Stanford University in 1971. Prior to the discovery of FM audio synthesis, electronic music was created by complicated, expensive equipment. Chowning discovered that a wealth of musical sounds could be created by the mixing of two sine-wave (simple) sound sources, using the FM (frequency modulation) technique to create a third, frequency-modulated output sound. This process can be done with very inexpensive equipment and, in recent years, has been reduced to a single integrated circuit smaller than a fingernail.

This section provides an introduction to the theory behind FM synthesis, with a specific explanation of two-operator versus four-operator sound synthesis, and information about your sound card's FM synthesizer.

The Theory of FM Synthesis

The terms *FM* and *AM* will be familiar to anyone who listens to the radio. The technique underlying FM-synthesized music is exactly the same method used to produce FM radio broadcast signals: mixing low-frequency (audible to the human ear) speech and music with a pure, very high frequency electrical wave to create an FM-modulated electrical wave. This electrical wave, due to its very high frequency, can travel through the air. After your FM radio receives and amplifies the FM electrical wave, it is mixed with a signal produced within the radio that has the same high frequency used by the radio station—for example, 99.7 MHz (megahertz). When the broadcast signal and the local signal are combined, one of the results is a wave that is the exact difference between the signals. If your radio is precisely tuned, you will hear the speech and music that was sent piggy-back on the very high frequency radio wave.

 Note In case you are not familiar with the technical meaning of *frequency*, it is used here to describe an electrical signal in terms of the number of vibrations per second. For example, when you hear "99.7 FM on your dial," the announcer is telling you that the radio frequency is 99.7 MHz. A hertz is the technical term for a vibration, so MHz means megahertz, or one million vibrations per second. As a reference point, the extent of human hearing is roughly 20 Hz to 20 KHz (one thousand hertz).

FM audio synthesis, on the other hand, is done by mixing together two pure, low-frequency waves of similar frequency, resulting in the creation of additional waves. The resulting sound is very complex, as it contains components of both the two original frequencies and many *harmonics* (sums and differences of the two waves). Research into electronic music over the last 20-25 years has provided a key insight: *Timbre*, the musical term for richness of sound, is determined to a large extent by the variety and relative strenth of these harmonics. Since FM audio synthesis provides a technique for mixing signals in a very controlled fashion that also produces rich harmonics, it is capable of creating a wide range of musical sounds.

Chowning's discovery for synthesizing music sounds is both simple and versatile. The FM technique is so simple that a single integrated circuit by Yamaha, which is the industrywide standard for FM sound creation, can simulate over 100 different instruments. There is a drawback to the technique, however. Since the basis of FM synthesis bears little direct relationship to the physics of the musical instrument sound being synthesized, the creation of sounds that resemble familiar instruments is done by trial and error. In less polite and more scientific terminology, FM synthesis is a "black art."

Two-Operator FM Synthesis

The Sound Blaster and Sound Blaster Pro cards prior to Pro 2 use the Yamaha 3812 OPL2 integrated circuit (chip) that produces FM-synthesized sound by two-operator synthesis. The 3812 chip has 12 *operator cells* that can be combined into 6 pairs for creating 6 FM-synthesized sounds. In addition, the chip has special programming for simulating 5 percussion instruments: snare drum, bass drum, tom tom, top cymbals, and high hat. In total, the 3812 can create 11 simultaneous voices (instrument sounds). Figure 2-4 illustrates two-operator FM synthesis.

The timbre of a sound is only partly a function of the frequency of the two operator cells. A wide range of parameters for these operators can be controlled, creating sound of very rich texture. Each of the following operator cell parameters can be controlled in the Yamaha chip to create a unique sound:

- ☐ Frequency
- ☐ Envelope type (percussive or nonpercussive)
- ☐ Envelope amplitude
- ☐ Attack/decay/sustain/release (ADSR) rates
- ☐ Key scaling rate
- ☐ Waveform selection (sine or nonsine)
- ☐ Vibrato depth
- ☐ Tremolo depth

FIGURE 2-4   Two-operator FM synthesis

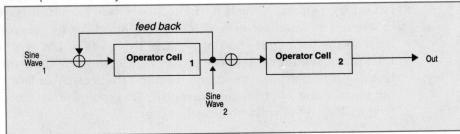

Two of the operator cell parameters, envelope type and ADSR rates, have a major influence on the timbre. These two parameters can be easily understood through pictures, and this will give you a good idea of what's involved in programming an FM chip (not recommended for anyone but the most hard-core music programmers!).

The Yamaha chip supports two envelope types. The envelope with diminishing sound simulates a percussion instrument; the one with continuing sound better simulates a nonpercussion instrument (see Figure 2-5).

The attach/decay/sustain/release (ADSR) parameters control the relative extent of these four phases in the lifetime of a note. Note that "Key on" in Figure 2-6 indicates the interval of time during which a note is held down.

Stereo Sound

The Sound Blaster Pro card (prior to Pro 2) has two 3812 chips. As a result, it can produce as many as 11 stereo voices or 22 monaural voices. Of the 11 stereo voices, 6 are instruments and 5 are percussion. The Sound Blaster Pro 2 was built with the latest Yamaha chip, the YMF262 OPL3, which is capable of four-operator synthesis. The YMF262 is "almost" downward-compatible with the earlier 3812. As anyone who has worked with computers knows, "almost" compatible is never compatible enough. Though the 3812 has 11 voices, and the early stereo Sound Blaster Pro has two 3812 chips for 22 voices, the newer Sound Blaster Pro 2 with the YMF262 chip has only 20 voices, 15 are instruments and

FIGURE
2-5

Envelope type

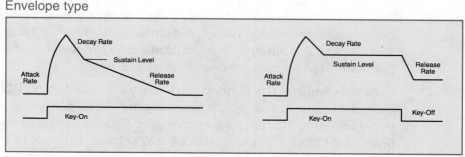

FIGURE
2-6

Envelope ADSR

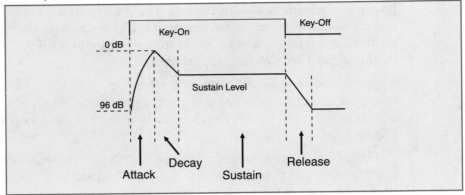

5 are percussion. The 20-voice limitation doesn't have much practical impact, as 20 monaural voices or 10 stereo voices are usually quite sufficient—few people need to compose music for more than 10 instruments at once!

Note Another limitation, applicable when playing the FM synthesizer with MIDI data, is that you can play no more than 16 monaural voices at once because MIDI only supports 16 channels.

Four-Operator FM Synthesis

The Sound Blaster Pro 2, with the newer Yamaha chip, can do either two-operator FM synthesis or four-operator FM synthesis. The advantage of two-operator synthesis is that it ensures compatibility with existing drivers and supports up to 12 synthesized voices. The advantage of four-operator FM synthesis is that the FM synthesizer can create very rich sounds by utilizing twice the number of operators. The drawback is that the Pro 2 is limited to 6 synthesized voices, because two operator pairs are used for each voice instead of one pair.

At this writing, the Windows 3.1 drivers for the Sound Blaster Pro 2 support four-operator FM synthesis only; DOS drivers only support two-operator synthesis. As a result, your Windows programs will probably sound better. You can obtain from Voyetra an upgrade to your Sp Pro

Sequencer program that includes a DOS four-operator driver for the FM synthesizer.

Creative Labs Developer's Kit

If you're interested in experimenting with the FM synthesizer, you can obtain a third-party utility for programming it. If you are a software developer, or interested in prospecting the depths of your Creative Labs sound card, you should purchase the Creative Labs software developer's toolkit package. This provides extensive documentation on how to program the Yamaha FM integrated circuit, as well as a description of the .VOC file format and related topics.

Future Technologies

This section provides a quick snapshot of future technology in sound cards. These technologies exist today, but only on truly professional-caliber equipment. Soon, however, the cost of these technologies will be driven down so much that they will appear on home computers. The two most significant technologies are 16-bit digital audio sampling, and wave table sampling.

For more information on digital audio files, refer to the earlier sections in this chapter, "About Digital Audio Files" and "Sampling: Audio to Digital Conversion."

16-Bit Sampling

Digital audio recording, which converts sound to digital values that are then recorded in memory or on disk, has made rapid advances in recent years. The current standard for inexpensive sound cards is 8-bit (1-byte) samples, with up to 44,100 samples per second. The sampling rate of 44,100 kHz, is sufficient to cover the breadth of human hearing (approximately 20 Hz 20,000 Hz), but the sample size of 8 bits provides inadequate dynamic range. Today's CD players play back 16-bit sound, at 44,100 samples per second. With the price of disk storage dropping rapidly, it will soon be practical to store 16-bit sampled data, and 16-bit digital audio will become the standard. In fact, tomorrow's technology is here today. An example of this future generation of sound cards is the new Creative Labs Sound Blaster 16 ASP card, discussed in Appendix D.

Wave Table Sampling: The Future for Music Generation

FM synthesis has been the key to advanced electronic music, and which has made sound cards possible. Another technology, however, is about to ascend: Sound Blaster 16 with the Wave Blaster daughter board employs *wave table* technology. Wave table technology stores digitized audio samples of actual instruments. When you play your sound card or electronic instrument, you will hear sounds recorded from instruments regarded as the finest examples of those instruments. (The electronic instrument cannot sound exactly like the real one, since only representative notes are recorded, and variations in sound due to the softness or tempo of play are digitally produced.)

You may already be familiar with this technology. Perhaps you have listened to or played one of the full-size electronic pianos that sound similar to a real piano. Many of these pianos can switch their sound output from that of a regular piano to a grand piano, or to an organ or other instrument. With prices for computer memory (needed to hold the wave tables) and dedicated microprocessors (like the one in your computer but dedicated to music production) dropping rapidly, the coming generation of sound cards will use wave table technology rather than FM synthesis.

CHAPTER

Sound Blaster
Software Toys

The delightful programs described in this chapter provide a fun introduction to your Creative Labs Sound Blaster. (The Sound Blaster Pro version adds stereo sound.)

☐ The Talking Parrot plays back digitized audio messages, demonstrating the power of even simple multimedia: the integration of sound and animation. It's a guaranteed crowd pleaser that sometimes "parrots back" what you say and often speaks its own mind.

☐ SBTALKER illustrates how a computer can read and speak. It pronounces words you type from the keyboard or that it reads from a file.

☐ Dr. Sbaitso, another text-to-speech conversion program, is your personal, no-hourly-fee therapist, who can converse intelligently on a wide range of topics. Be open with the Doctor; he forgets everything when you reboot!

☐ FM Intelligent Organ lets you create music with the FM Synthesizer. It's so easy and fun to use that even people who hate music will begin to dream of their Carnegie Hall debut.

 Note   Throughout this chapter you will encounter these abbreviations: SB (Sound Blaster and Sound Blaster MCV) and SB Pro (Sound Blaster Pro and Sound Blaster Pro MCV).

The Talking Parrot (SB and SB Pro)

The naughty Talking Parrot, shown in Figure 3-1, demonstrates speech synthesis and the excitement generated by sound and animation. The Parrot reacts to both speech input and keystrokes. Talk into a microphone, and the Parrot will usually "parrot" you, but it often comes up with its own zany comments. If you don't have a microphone, don't worry. The Parrot isn't shy about speaking to strangers. Just press a few keys and you'll really excite it.

FIGURE 3-1   The Talking Parrot

Loading and Setting Up the Parrot

Here are the steps to load the Parrot program in Sound Blaster and Sound Blaster Pro. In addition to loading the program, you need to adjust the microphone input.

Note   The Parrot program assumes you have a microphone. Even if you don't have one, you must still do steps 3 and 4 to adjust the microphone input before you can use the Parrot program.

1. Switch to the Sound Blaster directory.
    SB users: Type **CD \SB** and press ENTER.
    SB Pro users: Type **CD \SBPRO** and press ENTER.

2. Load the Parrot program by typing **parrot** and then press ENTER.

Note   If you have a CGA monitor, you will see the "big" parrot. If you have an EGA or VGA monitor, you will see the "little" parrot. Sound Blaster owners can force display of the "big" parrot on EGA/VGA monitors by adding the /T switch to the command in step 2 (type **parrot /T**).

3. Now you need to estimate the background noise level. You will see a graph indicating the noise level picked up by your microphone. Press ENTER. Notice the peak height of the noise; it's measured by a number along the vertical axis. In reading this number, don't worry about precision; rounding to the next 10 (to 130 or 140, for instance) is good enough.

4. Enter a number on your screen 10 counts above the measured noise level (the number you estimated in step 3), and press ENTER.

Running the Parrot

There are two ways to communicate with the Parrot—with a microphone or via your keyboard.

If you have a microphone connected to your system, speak into the microphone and listen to the Parrot's response. The Parrot will usually echo what you say, but sometimes it gives a random reply, such as "Don't talk nonsense." If the Parrot doesn't hear anything from you, it will get impatient and say things such as "I'm a talking parrot."

If you haven't got a microphone hooked up, try pressing various keys on your keyboard and listen to the Parrot's response. For example, when you press any of the letter or number keys, the Parrot will respond with a message such as "Ouch."

You will find most of the Parrot's responses listed in the Creative Labs Sound Blaster manual, but there are a number of additional, undocumented replies. Also, some of the "random" messages are actually tied to specific keys. For example, if you press the 3 key (the one at the top of your keyboard, not the function key), you will hear the undocumented reply "Hey buddy."

Mastering the Parrot

You can customize both the look and sound of your Parrot.

Giving the Parrot a New Look

To change how your Parrot looks on screen, and even substitute entirely new pictures for the four-cell (four-picture) animation, all you need is a paint program that saves pictures as .PCX files, such as the Paintbrush program that comes with Microsoft Windows.

To change the Parrot image, you need to replace or edit the Parrot files that have the filename extensions E0/E1/E2/E3 (for EGA or VGA monitors) or C0/C1/C2/C3 (for a CGA monitor). The following instructions will guide you in modifying the existing image.

Before you edit the image files, it's a good idea to make a copy of them. At the command-line prompt, switch to the Parrot subdirectory (\SB\PARROT or \SBPRO\PARROT), and type the following:

```
COPY parrot.C* parrotC.C*
COPY parrot.E* parrotE.E*
```

Later, if you want to restore your original Parrot images, delete the revised ones and rename the backups, by entering

```
DEL parrot.C*
REN parrotC.C* parrot.C*
DEL parrot.E*
REN parrotE.E* parrot.E*
```

Now here are the steps to modify your Parrot image files:

1. Run your paint program.

2. Load an image file into the paint program. Locate the image files in the Parrot subdirectory (\SB\PARROT or \SBPRO\PARROT).

3. Load the PARROT.E0 file if you use an EGA or VGA monitor, or PARROT.C0 if you use a CGA monitor. These files contain images of the Parrot at rest, before it tries to speak. The files with extensions E1/E2/E3 and C1/C2/C3 contain the other three animation cells.

 Note Since the Parrot program has its own color palette, the Parrot's colors in the paint program will be different from what you see when Parrot program runs.

4. Modify the image file as desired. Then save it, replacing the original file. When you next run the Parrot program, you will see the new Parrot.

Giving the Parrot New Messages

The Parrot's messages are stored as voice (.VOC) files that have been combined into a single file called PARROTV.VCB in the Parrot subdirectory. You can record your own set of messages by using the voice-record programs VREC/VOXKIT for Sound Blaster and VREC/VEDIT2 for Sound Blaster Pro. Bear in mind that you must create all 21 voice files, from PVOC-A.VOC through PVOC-U.VOC. You cannot replace selected voices only.

Voice files PVOC-A.VOC through PVOC-U.VOC must have a sample rate of about 10,000 Hz and must be unpacked, as explained in Chapter 2. Each voice file must average no more than 10,000 bytes, or, on average, no more than one second each.

Once you have created the voice files, place them into the Parrot subdirectory. Then run the MAKEPV program to create a new PARROTV.VCB file, as follows:

1. Change to the Parrot subdirectory and press ENTER.

2. Rename your original Parrot voice library file to protect it. Type **REN PARROTV.VCB PARROTV.ORG** at the prompt and press ENTER.

3. Now type **MAKEPV** and press ENTER. If the MAKEPV utility finds all the voice files it needs, it will respond with a message that you have been successful. If not, it will respond with error messages.

Replacing Selected Messages

You can really surprise someone by replacing several of the standard Parrot messages with "custom" ones, though the process to do this is somewhat tedious. Here are the general steps:

Note   SB Pro users must use VEDIT2 or Blaster Master to replace the standard Parrot messages. SB owners must use Blaster Master only. Chapter 10 contains a discussion of Blaster Master, which is included free on the disk attached to this book. See Chapter 5 for information on working with VEDIT2.

1. Add a header to PARROTV.VCB by using VOC-HDR utility. This is necessary so VEDIT2 and Blaster Master will recognize PARROTV.VCB as a .VOC file and let you load it.

 Note VOC-HDR is discussed in Chapter 5 of this book. Blaster Master is discussed in Chapter 10.

2. Use VEDIT2 (for SB Pro) or Blaster Master (SB) to extract the messages you want to change from PARROTV.VCB. Save each message as its own voice file, named PVOC-A.VOC through PVOC-U.VOC.

3. Use VEDIT2 or Blaster Master to record your custom messages.

4. Use the MAKEPV utility to incorporate all the new message voice files into the PARROTV.VCB Parrot voice library.

SBTALKER (SB and SB Pro)

The Sound Blaster talk program, SBTALKER, is an interesting example of a basic program for text-to-speech conversion. You type in text, and it is converted by the program into speech.

Although SBTALKER is on the surface a very simple program, text-to-speech conversion is not a simple matter at all. All languages consist of many *phonemes*, basic units of speech such as /ba/, /bee/, /boo/, and so forth, and a text-to-speech conversion program must have digital audio recordings of these phonemes. (The real challenge is to figure out from the spelling of a word what phonemes must be spoken.)

SBTALKER speaks in American English (actually, with an American computer accent) when you type in text or have the program read text from a file. The English language presents a relatively difficult task for text-to-speech conversion. Because English is such a blend, it has many phonemes, a very rich vocabulary, and (an even bigger obstacle) many exceptions to standard spelling. Text-to-speech conversion is much easier in Spanish, for example. Since the written language is very regular, it can be pronounced well by a person (or a machine) with an elementary knowledge of the language.

Some languages contain fewer phonemes, making text-to-speech conversion easier. For example, Japanese has a very limited set of phonemes. Japanese text written in its two phonetic alphabets is easy to pronounce. The drawback to a language with few phonemes, however, is that it has many *cognates* (words that sound the same but have different meaning, such as *their* and *there*). As a result, speech-to-text conversion is made more difficult because many words can be identified only from context.

Once you experiment with SBTALKER for a while, you will have a good understanding of the problems involved in text-to-speech conversion—as well as why speech-to-text conversion machines are only just now coming out of the laboratory.

Loading and Running SBTALKER

 Warning   Before running SBTALKER, you must temporarily disable your computer's memory managers. SBTALKER will conflict with QEMM, 386MAX, and EMM386, as well as with HIMEM.SYS, the Windows memory manager. Memory conflicts with SBTALKER, when they arise, can result in catastrophic loss of data on your hard drive!

To disable your memory managers you will have to edit your AUTOEXEC.BAT or CONFIG.SYS files with an ASCII text editor (see Chapter 2). Enter an **REM** at the beginning of the line referencing the memory manager, and then reboot your machine. Alternatively, you can create a DOS boot disk to be used prior to running these programs.

 Warning   SPUTMON can interfere with SBTALKER. If you're using SPUTMON, disable it temporarily by typing **SPUTOFF** and press ENTER.

Here are the steps for loading and running SBTALKER:

1. Change to the SBTALKER directory (C:\SB\SBTALKER in Sound Blaster, or C:\SBPRO\SBTALKER in Sound Blaster Pro) and press ENTER.

2. Type **SBTALK** and press ENTER.

The talk program and its driver will be loaded into memory.

Note   Since SBTALKER is a memory-resident program, remember to type **REMOVE** at the DOS prompt when you are done with it. If you don't, there may be insufficient memory for your other programs to load or run properly.

Using SBTALKER

You can tell SBTALKER to respond to one line only of text that you enter, before returning to the command-line prompt. However, it's easier to use SBTALKER if you tell it to respond to every line of text that you type. You can also tell SBTALKER to read an entire file. Here are the procedures for all three modes.

To Hear Only One Line of Typed Text

Type **READ** at the command-line prompt, press SPACEBAR, type the text that you want SBTALKER to read, and press ENTER. Here is an example of this command:

READ your wish is my command

Tip   If you want to hear the same text with shorter, more natural pauses between words, surround the text with double quotes like this: **READ "your wish is my command"**.

To Hear Line After Line of Typed Text

At the command-line prompt, type **READ** and then press ENTER. Your cursor will appear on the left edge of the screen, without the command-line prompt. SBTALKER is now ready to read every line you type. To quit and return to the command-line prompt, press CTRL-C (hold down the CTRL key and press C).

To Hear an Entire File of Text

At the command-line prompt, type **READ**, followed by the less than sign (<) sign, followed by a filename. Press ENTER to issue the command.

For example, to have SBTALKER read the ASCII text file named SBTEST.TXT in the SBTALKER subdirectory, type

READ < SBTEST.TXT

and press ENTER.

To have SBTALKER read a file in a directory other than the current directory, you'll need to specify a full path after the <, such as C:\SB\SBTALKER\SBTEST.TXT to read file SBTEST.TXT in the \SB\SBTALKER subdirectory.

To quit before reaching the end of the file, press the ESC key.

Tip   Normally, when SBTALKER reads a file, it will pronounce the text without showing it. To have SBTALKER display on the screen the lines of text as they are spoken, use the /W switch with the READ command. For an example, type **READ /W < SBTEST.TXT**.

Mastering SBTALKER

Although SBTALKER has an unlimited vocabulary, it doesn't always guess the correct pronunciation. It can be easily fooled.

For example, feed SBTALKER the word *Chicago*. Notice how it pronounces /ch/ as /sh/. Then try words with a harder /ch/ sound, such as *chunk* or *hitch*. Notice that SBTALKER is either not smart enough to recognize that /ch/ at the end of a word is pronounced with a harsher sound, or it lacks this phoneme in its speech vocabulary. This example illustrates the challenges of creating natural-sounding speech output, not to mention learning English as a second language.

Also notice that because SBTALKER is programmed with American English phonemes, it butchers words in other languages. For example, type in the Spanish for *good night*, **buenas noches**, and hear what happens.

Note   If you wish to experiment further with text-to-speech conversion, you can do so from within Dr. Sbaitso, discussed just below. Dr. Sbaitso uses SBTALKER to communicate with you, and will optionally read from an ASCII file. The advantage of using Dr. Sbaitso is that you can control the volume, pitch, overall tone, and, most importantly, the speech speed.

Dr. Sbaitso (SB and SB Pro)

Dr. Sbaitso is your personal consultant on matters of the heart (see Figure 3-2). He reads what you type, ignoring words such as *and* and *the*, while looking for provocative words like *envy*. (To save you the embarrassment of having to ask Dr. Sbaitso such an obvious question, we'll tell you that Sbaitso is an acronym for Sound Blaster Artificial Intelligence Text to Speech Output.)

Caution   You must temporarily disable your computer's memory managers before running Dr. Sbaitso! Dr. Sbaitso will conflict with popular memory managers including QEMM, 386MAX, and EMM386, as well as HIMEM.SYS, the Windows memory manager. Memory conflicts with these programs, when they arise, can result in catastrophic loss of data on your hard drive.

To disable the memory managers you will have to edit your AUTOEXEC.BAT or CONFIG.SYS files with an ASCII text editor, inserting an **REM** at the beginning of the line referencing the memory manager, and then reboot your machine. Alternatively, you can create a DOS boot disk

FIGURE
3-2

Dr. Sbaitso's opening screen

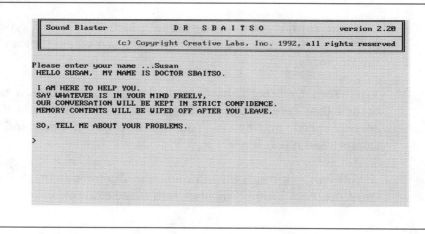

to be used prior to running these programs. See Chapter 2 for information on editing ASCII files and how to edit your AUTOEXEC.BAT or CONFIG.SYS.

Loading Dr. SBAITSO

To load Dr. Sbaitso, switch to your Sound Blaster subdirectory (\SB for Sound Blaster or \SBPRO for Sound Blaster Pro). Then type **SBAITSO2** and press ENTER.

To leave Dr. SBAITSO, type **Quit**, **Bye**, or **Goodbye**.

Note   If you own a Sound Blaster Pro you can hear Dr. Sbaitso in stereo, with an echo, by adding the /S switch to the startup command, like this: *SBAITSO2 /S*.

Using the Doctor

Once Dr. Sbaitso has been loaded, he will prompt you to enter your name. After that he will introduce himself, and you can ask any question on your mind. The Doctor will display a > prompt when he is ready for your next question. Follow each question by pressing the ENTER key.

Dr. Sbaitso emits a lot of initial chatter after you enter your name. To skip over this, enter your name and press ENTER as usual, and then press ESC.

If you are not communicating well with the Doctor, type **help** to get instructions, and then type **m** twice to learn which topics most interest the Doctor.

Tip   Your Creative Labs Sound Blaster manual lists a table of commands that control the Dr. Sbaitso program, including tone, volume, speech speed, and colors. You can also give a command to have the Doctor read a text file.

You can ask math questions of the Doctor by entering the keyword **CALC** at the > prompt, as shown in these examples:

CALC 2/3
CALC 1+2

The first command divides 2 by 3, and the second adds 1 and 2.

 Caution   Watch your language: Should your side of the conversation be off-color, expect a temperamental reprimand. If you upset the Doctor you will need to type **.WIDTH 80** to wrest control of your screen away from the Doctor. This command restores your screen to the normal 80-character display.

FM Intelligent Organ (SB and SB Pro)

The Intelligent Organ, an electronic organ, is a wonderful instrument. The opening screen for the Organ, with function keys for the main menu on the bottom of the screen, is shown in Figure 3-3.

Loading the Intelligent Organ

Here are the procedures to load the Intelligent Organ:

1. Switch to the Intelligent Organ subdirectory.
   SB users: Type **CD \SB\FMORGAN** and press ENTER.
   SB Pro users: Type **CD \SBPRO\PRO-ORG** and press ENTER.
   (Be careful to type the hyphen key in the command, not the underscore.)

2. Start the Organ.
   SB users: Type **FMORGAN** and press ENTER.
   SB Pro users: Type **PRO-ORG** and press ENTER.

Using the Intelligent Organ

Suppose that you want to do three things with the Intelligent Organ: play a song (automatically stored to memory when you play); replay your

FIGURE 3-3 Intelligent Organ opening screen

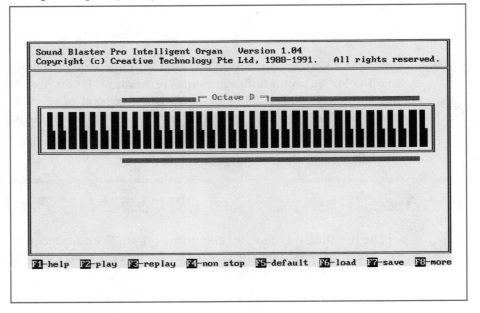

song to check your composition; and then save your song to disk. Here are the general steps to do this, beginning from the main menu represented by the function keys shown along the bottom of the screen in Figure 3-3. You'll learn more details about some of the Organ's settings and features throughout this section.

Setting Up the Organ

Your first step is to set up the Organ in the key you want it to play in, and make other settings to control the Organ's sounds.

1. At the main menu, press F5 (default) to display the Default Settings screen (Figure 3-4).

2. Type **O** to restore default values, and then change these as you wish.

3. When you're done with the settings, type **T** (for Title) and enter your song title.

4. Press ENTER until the main menu reappears.

FIGURE
3-4

Intelligent Organ Default Settings screen

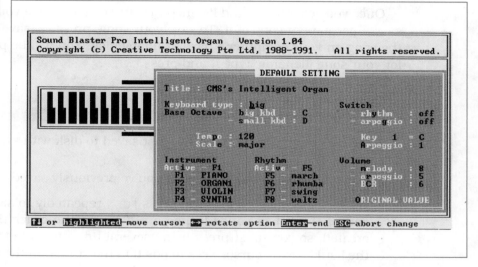

Recording Your Song

1. On the main menu, press F2 (play) to begin recording your song.
    Don't pause too long before beginning your masterpiece—the Organ
    assumes your hesitation is an intentional silence at the beginning
    of the composition and records it as such.

2. Press ESC as soon as you are done to avoid recording silence at the
    end of the composition.

Replaying Your Song

When you have finished recording, replay your song by pressing F3
(replay). Your song is stored temporarily in your computer's memory.

Caution   Don't press F2 (play) to replay your song, or it will be be erased
from memory because you haven't yet saved it to disk. Pressing F2 tells
the Organ you want to record a new song.

Saving Your Song

Once you've recorded and listened to your song, decide if you want to save a permanent copy of it. To save your song, press F7 (save) to store the song on your computer's hard or floppy disk. You will be prompted for your song filename; type it and press ENTER.

Retrieving (Playing) Your Song from Disk

To retrieve and play the song you just saved to disk with F7:

1. Press F6 (load) to retrieve a song you've previously saved.

2. When the Song Box appears, press PGDN repeatedly to skip to the end of the list of songs (songs are listed in the order they were created, so you must press PGDN several times to go to the end of the list.) Use the cursor keys to position the cursor on the song you just recorded.

3. Press ENTER to select and then F3 (replay) to play that song.

Quitting the Intelligent Organ

1. If you haven't already saved your song, do so now by pressing F7.

2. Press F8 (more) to bring up the auxiliary menu, which is a menu with more command options.

3. Press F4 (quit) and then type Y to confirm your command.

Deleting Intelligent Organ Files

To delete songs you saved to disk with F7 (save), you must first go to the command-line prompt. Follow these steps:

1. From the Intelligent Organ main menu, select F8 (more) to display the auxiliary menu.

2. Press F3 (shell) to go temporarily ("shell out") to DOS.

3. Delete the song files using the DOS DEL command. Song files have an .ORG filename extension. For example, to delete the file named MYFIRST.ORG, type **DEL MYFIRST.ORG** and press ENTER.

4. When you're finished deleting files, type **Exit** and press ENTER to leave DOS and return to the Intelligent Organ.

Mastering the Intelligent Organ

The following sections introduce you to some Intelligent Organ features musicians will really appreciate. In addition to playing notes and changing instruments, you can adjust volume and tempo, and even have the Organ add harmonious and rhythmic accompaniments to complement what you play.

The Melody: Selecting Notes, Instruments, and Volume

Once you press F2 F3 or F4 from the main menu, the Play menu will be displayed. To begin playing the Intelligent Organ, you can press a key on your computer keyboard to play a note. You will now be in PLAY mode and you'll see the Play menu. By pressing keys such as A, S, D, or F, you play the notes that make up the melody. When you play a note, the Organ on the screen will show you which piano key you played by making that key grey in color. Your Creative Labs Sound Blaster manual contains two illustrations that show you which piano keys are played by the various keys on the computer keyboard.

From the Play menu, you can switch to any of 20 instruments by pressing function keys F1 through F4 on the Play screen. The name of the currently selected instrument is displayed in contrasting color to the right of the function key on the Play screen. Press F1 to rotate through five different instrument selections, F2 to rotate through another five instruments, and so forth.

Press the HOME key to increase the melody volume, and the END key to decrease the volume.

Adding Auto-Bass-Chord Accompaniment

To enliven your music, the Intelligent Organ can add accompaniment that complements your melody, in the form of a bass line, harmonizing chords, or a rhythm section sound. Choose the type of accompaniment you want by pressing function keys F5 through F8 on the Play screen. Each function key lets you rotate through a choice of four accompaniments. The sounds are recorded along with your song and can be saved to disk with the song.

Press the spacebar to toggle the accompaniment on and off. Press the ENTER key to end the accompaniment. To increase the Auto-Bass-Chord volume, press PGUP, or PGDN to decrease the volume.

Using Auto Arpeggio

In addition to the Auto-Bass-Chord accompaniments, you can use Auto Arpeggio to add a harmonious melody to the main melody that you play by pressing either of the bracket ([or]) keys on your computer keyboard. As you press the bracket keys repeatedly, you rotate through the various arpeggios available; the number for each arpeggio is displayed, and you can hear the arpeggio as well.

To turn off the arpeggio, press the quotes key (the one that has both an apostrophe and double quotation marks). Press the UP ARROW key to increase the Auto Arpeggio volume, or DOWN ARROW to decrease the volume.

Adding Artificial Melodies

Instead of using the Auto Arpeggio, you can add four fill-in musical patterns, such as a trill. To do this, press the following keys on the top row of your keyboard: 9, 0, - or +. The 9 key—the trill—is the most fun. These keys will add character to long notes in a song.

The volume control for these fill-in patterns is the same as for the Auto Arpeggio. Press UP ARROW to increase the artificial melody volume, or press the DOWN ARROW to decrease the volume.

Controlling Tempo

Two other important keys on the Play menu are the ones that control tempo (the speed of play):

☐   The INS key increases tempo

☐   The DEL key decreases tempo

Features for Advanced Players

Now that you've mastered the fundamentals of the Intelligent Organ, you're ready for the more powerful features. This section tells you how to add polish to your performance, using techniques such as transposing to other keys.

Scale Selection

While playing a song, you can select either a major-scale or minor-scale accompaniment from the Play menu by using either of the following:

☐   F9 produces a major-scale accompaniment

☐   F10 produces a minor-scale accompaniment

Transposing

You can transpose your music into a higher or lower key from the Play menu by pressing these keys as you play:

± key	One semitone up
− key	One semitone down
SHIFT and + or =	A perfect fourth
SHIFT and _ or –	A perfect fifth

You can then save your transposed song.

Changing Octaves

You can directly address four octaves with the large keyboard, the one that appears by default on your screen. You can switch to another four octaves within the seven octaves accessible to the FM organ by pressing the cursor keys. Press the RIGHT ARROW key to move to a higher octave. Press the LEFT ARROW key to move to a lower one.

Switching to the Small Keyboard

When you begin playing the Intelligent Organ, you get a large keyboard that spans four octaves and plays with the white keys only. If you want to use the black keys, you can switch to a smaller keyboard that allows you this access (but it only has two octaves). Press the TAB key to toggle between the keyboards. You can tell which keyboard you are playing by looking at the width of the Octave bar above the piano keyboard.

Tip   While playing the large keyboard, you can play accidentals—occasional notes foreign to the key you're playing in—by holding the SHIFT key down while playing.

Playing with a MIDI Keyboard

You can play the Intelligent Organ with a MIDI keyboard by adding a MIDI adapter cable. These are available from Creative Labs. Refer to your documentation for more information on hooking up a MIDI keyboard and for using MIDI with the Intelligent Organ.

Intelligent Organ Files

The Intelligent Organ files (.ORG) are unique to the program. They cannot be played or edited by Sequencer Plus Pro (discussed in Chapter 8), Blaster Master (discussed in Chapter 10), or the Creative Labs utility programs. The .ORG files are actually MIDI files, but with a special Creative Labs header that defines the instrument patches (instrument assignments) for you.

CHAPTER

Play and Record Utilities

This chapter introduces the following utility programs that play or record digital audio and music files. You will encounter at least some of these utilities in your work with Sound Blaster.

- ☐ VPLAY
- ☐ VREC
- ☐ PLAYCMF
- ☐ PLAYMIDI
- ☐ CDPLYR
- ☐ Microsoft Media Player
- ☐ Multimedia Jukebox
- ☐ Microsoft Sound Recorder

The first five of these programs are DOS programs, and the last three run under Windows 3.1. Multimedia Jukebox is produced by Creative Labs. Media Player and Sound Recorder are provided by Microsoft as part of the Windows 3.1 environment, and are well documented in the Windows 3.1 user's guide.

VPLAY and VREC are easy-to-use DOS programs that play and record digital audio files in the Creative Labs .VOC format. The files are created by recording your voice through a microphone (with VREC) or from another source, such as CD or line-in (using a more sophisticated software utility such as VOXKIT or VEDIT2). The sound is converted to digital data stored either in memory or on floppy or hard disk. The primary use for a digital audio recording is to add a voice-over or special effects to a multimedia presentation. The VREC and VPLAY utilities can be great fun—like playing back your friends' laughter.

Note Any *serious* recording should be done with VEDIT2 or Blaster Master . VPLAY and VREC are for quick-and-dirty handling of voice files.

PLAYCMF and PLAYMIDI are your avenues for converting that boring computer into an exciting Multimedia PC, adding great background music to your presentation. PLAYCMF plays Creative Music Files (.CMF);

PLAYMIDI plays MIDI music files. If you have a compatible MIDI keyboard, you can use the Creative Labs MIDI kit to attach the keyboard to your Sound Blaster card. The MIDI kit comes bundled with the Sound Blaster Pro card, and is also available separately for Sound Blaster, Sound Blaster Pro Basic, Sound Blaster MCV and Pro MCV. With the MIDI kit you will be well on your way to becoming the world's next musical prodigy.

Sound Blaster Pro ISA (not MCV) owners who have a CD-ROM drive shouldn't waste a minute before checking out CDPLYR, the DOS CD player program, and Microsoft Media Player, a Windows applet (an *applet* is a little application) that controls your CD-ROM drive as well as other devices. These two utilities have easy-to-use graphical interfaces.

The Multimedia Jukebox utility is like a real jukebox, letting you stack enough MIDI songs to keep the music blaring until your boss or friends turn your computer off for your own good.

The Microsoft Sound Recorder, as well as Media Player, are provided by Microsoft as Windows 3.1 applets. Both Sound Blaster (version 2.0, and 1.5 with updated DSP) and Sound Blaster Pro owners can use these applets. The Media Player plays MIDI music files and .WAV digitized audio files. The Sound Recorder records and plays .WAV files and can do limited editing. It has record-and-play functions that are similar to VREC and VPLAY, but with an easy-to-use interface. Sound Recorder's editing capabilities, such as the ability to insert and mix (overlay) sound files, complement VEDIT2.

 Note   Throughout this chapter you will encounter these abbreviations: SB and SB Pro. SB refers to Sound Blaster 1.0/1.5/2.0 and the Micro-channel version. SB Pro refers to the Sound Blaster Pro, Pro 2, Pro Basic, and Pro MCV, unless otherwise specified.

VPLAY (all cards)

VPLAY is a voice utility that plays .VOC (Creative Voice File) format digital audio files such as those created by VREC, VOXKIT, and VEDIT2. VPLAY makes it a snap to listen to your audio files.

 Note   More recent versions of VPLAY can play audio files too large to fit into available memory. The Creative Voice Disk driver (CTVDSK.DRV)

makes this possible. Look for this file in your \SB\DRV or \SBPRO\DRV directory. If you don't have it, check the Creative Labs bulletin board (BBS) for an update to your VPLAY, or call the Creative Labs support line.

Running VPLAY

As usual, the commands to run VPLAY vary based on which Sound Blaster card you own.

1. Switch to the appropriate subdirectory.

   SB users: Go to the VOXKIT subdirectory by typing
   CD \SB\VOXKIT and then press ENTER.

   SB Pro users: Go to the VEDIT2 subdirectory by typing
   CD \SBPRO\VEDIT2 and then press ENTER.

2. Type **VPLAY** followed by a voice filename. For example, for SB users to play TV4.VOC, type

   VPLAY TV4.VOC

   and press ENTER. For SB Pro users to play BBCNEWS.VOC, type

   VPLAY BBCNEWS.VOC

   and press ENTER.

 Note   To get help with VPLAY, type **VPLAY** and press ENTER.

Mastering VPLAY

VPLAY is easy to use. All its command switches are optional. The /T switch (for timer) is the most useful option for most people.

VPLAY Command Switches

VPLAY has a number of optional command switches that allow you to control its actions. These switches include

- [ ]   /T:*n* specifies the maximum duration for play, in seconds. For example, /T:5 limits playback to a maximum of five seconds.

- [ ]   /Q, the Quiet option, suppresses the on-screen appearance of messages from VPLAY.

- [ ]   /B:*n* specifies the buffer size. This is described in more depth in your Sound Blaster manual.

- [ ]   /X= is used to activate DOS program execution. After recording is started, the DOS command line you enter following the = will be executed. If you have the proper equipment, this switch can be used to send a command to a serial or parallel port to cause an external device like a CD laser disc player to advance to another image.

 Note   You cannot use both the /X= and /T: switches in the same VPLAY command.

Here is an example of two of these switches used to play the FROGS.VOC sound file for a maximum of two seconds:

VPLAY FROGS.VOC /T:2 /Q

 Tip   The Sound Blaster Pro toolkit, SBSIM, includes a program called VOICE that also plays .VOC files. VOICE has many more features than VPLAY, including the ability to pause and resume audio output. See Chapter 7 for more information on SBSIM.

VREC (all cards)

VREC is a voice recording utility that records audio input directly to disk. VREC creates a file in Creative Voice File format (.VOC), which you can play with VPLAY.

Running VREC

The commands to run VREC vary according to which Sound Blaster card you have.

1. Switch to the appropriate subdirectory.

    SB users: Go to the VOXKIT subdirectory by typing
    CD \SB\VOXKIT and then press ENTER.

    SB Pro users: Go to the VEDIT2 subdirectory by typing
    CD \SBPRO\VEDIT2 and then press ENTER.

2. Specify the voice file you want to create by typing **VREC** followed by the filename. For example, to record your voice from the microphone and save it in file MYVOICE.VOC, type

    VREC myvoice.voc

    and begin talking when you press ENTER.

3. When you're done, terminate recording by pressing the ESC key. *Don't forget to do this*—if you forget to terminate recording, VREC will fill your floppy or hard disk with one very long voice file!

Note   To get help with VREC, type **VREC** alone and press the ENTER key.

Mastering VREC

Both the Sound Blaster and Sound Blaster Pro versions of VREC have the following optional switches:

☐   /B:*kk* controls the buffer size. Omitting this switch results in a default value that usually works well. Don't worry about this switch unless you hear popping sounds when you play your digital audio file. (Popping and hissing are discussed in Chapter 2.) See your manual for more information on possible values for *kk*.

☐   /S:*n* is the recording sample rate. The *n* range is from 4,000 Hz to 13,000 Hz (Sound Blaster 1.5); 15,000 Hz (Sound Blaster 2.0); or 44,100 Hz (Sound Blaster Pro). Sound Blaster Pro owners should note that selecting stereo recording automatically sets the sample rate to 22,050 Hz, and this rate cannot be overridden by the /S switch. The default, if you don't use this switch, is 8,000 Hz. This rate is fine for both male and female voices, but you may want to set it lower for male voices. See the section on sampling rates in Chapter 2 for more information.

☐ /T:*n* sets the timer period, where *n* is from 1 to 65,535 seconds. When the timer expires, recording stops.

☐ /Q enables the Quiet mode. This suppresses on-screen message display by VREC.

☐ /X= is used to activate DOS program execution. After recording is started, the DOS command line you enter following the = will be executed. This could be used to send a command to a serial or parallel port, causing an external device to begin playing.

Note You cannot use the /T: switch and the /X= switch in the same VREC command.

The following example combines some of the optional switches listed above. This command records to the file PARROT.VOC at a sample rate of 10,000 Hz and for only one second, in Quiet mode to suppress all messages other than error messages:

VREC parrot.voc /S:10000 /T:1 /Q

Note Regardless of the filename extension you suggest, VREC will create a file with the .VOC extension.

Sound Blaster Pro Enhancements

The Sound Blaster Pro version of VREC has been significantly improved. It has the following additional command options:

☐ /A:*recording source*. Although Sound Blaster's VREC records only from the microphone, Sound Blaster Pro can choose between microphone, line-in, and CD input (MIC or line-in for Sound Blaster 2.0). Use switches /A:MIC for microphone, /A:LINE for line-in, and /A:CD for CD; if you do not, the default is microphone (MIC).

☐   /M:*recording mode.* Use /M:STEREO for stereo recording, or /M:MONO for monaural recording. If you designate STEREO, your sampling rate will be automatically set for 22,050 Hz. The default, if this switch is not used, is MONO.

☐   /L:*n* designates the source volume for line-in and CD. This value varies from 0 to 15, where 15 is the maximum and 0 is the minimum. The default is 0, which effectively turns off the source. This has no effect on the microphone volume; Sound Blaster Pro has automatic gain control that adjusts the microphone level automatically for optimal recording.

Note   The VREC /L: switch setting is poorly named; it suggests line-in volume only. This switch actually controls either line-in or CD, whichever source is selected with the /A: switch.

☐   /F:*recording filter.* The filter setting can have two settings: LOW or HIGH. LOW suppresses audio components that exceed 4 kHz; the HIGH setting suppresses components above 8 kHz. The default, if this switch is not used, is LOW.

The following command example records from the line-in source, in stereo, at a reasonable volume:

VREC opera.voc /A:LINE /M:STEREO /F:HIGH /L:12

Note   You will hear the line-in source as soon as this command is issued, unless you first mute the output with the master volume control of SBP-MIX or SBP-SET, as described in Chapter 6.

Compression Influences on the Sample Rate

Sound Blaster and Sound Blaster Pro have similar hardware decompression capabilities, but do differ in their maximum sampling rate. Be aware that the sampling rate may need to be reduced if you do file compression. For more details, see the section on packing in Chapter 2. There you'll find a table with the maximum sampling rate for each Sound Blaster version.

PLAYCMF (All Cards)

PLAYCMF plays Creative Music File (.CMF) format songs, such as the sample files provided in the \SBPRO\PLAYCMF subdirectory with the .CMF file extension. (Creative Labs, early players in the music file business, pioneered their own version of MIDI files. These files are called Creative Music Files and have a .CMF filename extension. The .CMF files have a Creative Labs header attached that contains instrument assignments.)

 Note PLAYCMF can play audio files too large to fit into available memory. The Creative Voice Disk driver (CTVDSK.DRV) makes this possible. Look for this driver in your \SB\DRV or \SBPRO\DRV directory. If you don't have it, check the Creative Labs bulletin board (BBS) for an update, or call the Creative Labs support line.

Loading PLAYCMF

PLAYCMF is easy to use, but you must load the FM synthesizer driver first:

1. To load the Sound Blaster FM driver, switch to the Sound Blaster directory. Type **CD\SBPRO** or **CD\SB** and press ENTER. Then type **SBFMDRV** and press ENTER.

2. Switch to the PLAYCMF subdirectory by typing **CD\SBPRO\PLAY-CMF** or **CD\SB\PLAYCMF** and pressing ENTER.

Running PLAYCMF

To use PLAYCMF, simply type **PLAYCMF** followed by the filename you wish to call. For example, to play sample music file JUG.CMF, type **PLAYCMF JUG.CMF** and press ENTER.

To terminate a song before it is finished playing, press the ESC key.

When you are finished using PLAYCMF, you should unload the SBFMDRV driver from memory. To do so, switch to the Sound Blaster directory by typing **CD\SBPRO** or **CD\SB**, and then type **SBFMDRV /U** and press ENTER.

Note   To get help with PLAYCMF, type **PLAYCMF** and press ENTER.

Mastering PLAYCMF

PLAYCMF has two optional switches:

☐   /Q enables the Quiet mode, which suppresses on-screen display of PLAYCMF messages.

☐   /S= followed by a filename is used to start the music playing and then run another program once the music begins. To see how this works, type **PLAYCMF kentucky.cmf /S=DIR**. This will begin playing the KENTUCKY.CMF file and then do a directory listing while the music is playing.

Tip   Consider using the /S option to play a background song while displaying a software slide show.

Note   The Sound Blaster Pro toolkit, SBSIM, includes a program called MUSIC which plays both Creative Music File format .CMF files and MIDI files. MUSIC has many more features than PLAYCMF, such as repeat play, pause and continue play, change the tempo and transpose the music to a higher or lower key. See Chapter 7, which discusses Multimedia Presentation, for more information about MUSIC.

PLAYMIDI (Sound Blaster Pro and Sound Blaster 16)

PLAYMIDI plays MIDI song files with the .MID file extension. The MIDI song file format is used by musicians worldwide. It is part of a specification for a MIDI network of electronic instruments, keyboards, and computer-based sequencing programs that play and record MIDI songs.

Sound Blaster owners will have either \SB\MIDI or \SB\PLAY-MIDI on their drives. These subdirectories contain MIDI files for use with Windows Media Player. Sound Blaster owners are not provided with the program PLAYMIDI.EXE that plays these files from the DOS prompt.

 Note   PLAYMIDI will also play MIDI files recorded with a Sequencer, such as the Sequencer Plus Pro, which is bundled with the Sound Blaster Pro and available with the Creative Labs' MIDI kit.

Loading PLAYMIDI

Before running PLAYMIDI you must load the Sound Blaster MIDI driver. To do so, switch to the \SBPRO directory by typing **CD \SBPRO** and pressing ENTER. Then load the driver by typing **SBMIDI** and press ENTER.

Using PLAYMIDI

To use PLAYMIDI, switch to the PLAYMIDI subdirectory by typing **CD \SBPRO\PLAYMIDI**. To play a song, type **PLAYMIDI** followed by the song name. For example, to play the jazz sample file, type **PLAYMIDI JAZZ.MID** and press ENTER.

To terminate PLAYMIDI before the song is finished playing, press the ESC key.

When you are finished with PLAYMIDI, you should unload the SBMIDI driver from memory. First switch back to the \SBPRO directory, and then type **SBMIDI /U** and press ENTER.

 Note   To get help with PLAYMIDI, type **PLAYMIDI** and press ENTER.

Mastering PLAYMIDI

The PLAYMIDI command has two optional switches.

☐   /S=*filename* begins the MIDI music play and then runs another program while the music is playing. To use this switch, follow the /S= with the name of the program you want to run, as in the following example:

PLAYMIDI jazz.mid /S=DIR

This command will begin playing the MIDI file called JAZZ.MID and then do a directory listing while the music is playing.

Tip   A typical real-world use for the /S= option is to execute a program that runs, through your computer's serial port, a slide show.

☐/Q activates Quiet mode, suppressing PLAYMIDI's routine status messages from appearing on the screen. This keeps your screen from becoming cluttered with extraneous messages when you run PLAYMIDI from a batch file.

Note   The Sound Blaster Pro toolkit, SBSIM, includes a program called MUSIC that plays both Creative Music File (.CMF) files and MIDI files. MUSIC has many more features than PLAYMIDI, such as repeat play, tempo change, and transposing the music to a higher or lower key. See Chapter 7, which discusses multimedia presentations, for more information about MUSIC.

CDPLYR (Sound Blaster Pro Only)

The CD Player is an easy-to-use DOS utility program for controlling your CD-ROM drive.

Loading and Running CDPLYR

To load CDPLYR, first switch to the \SBPRO directory; then type **CDPLYR** and press ENTER.

The CD Player is easy to run. Use the LEFT ARROW and RIGHT ARROW keys, or TAB and SHIFT-TAB, to move to a button, and then press ENTER to select it. These buttons (Play/Stop/Pause/Next Track/Previous Track/Fast Forward/Rewind) work just like those on your personal CD player. Your Sound Blaster Pro manual has a full explanation of each button.

To quit the CDPLYR, press the ESC key.

Before you can use your CD-ROM player with CDPLYR, the CD-ROM installation must be complete. You must first install the software drivers provided on the disk that comes with your Creative Labs CD-ROM kit. If the drivers have not been installed yet, and you try to run CDPLYR, you will see a message stating that MSCDEX has not been loaded.

Microsoft Media Player (Windows)

The Microsoft Media Player plays MIDI music files (.MID) and wave digitized audio files (.WAV). In addition, it will control your CD-ROM. The Media Player is similar in capability to the DOS VPLAY and PLAYMIDI utilities, but has a far superior graphical user interface. The CD-ROM control is similar to that provided by CDPLYR in the DOS environment.

To load the Media Player, start Windows and double-click the Accessories group; then double-click the Media Player icon. To load a music file, pull down the File menu and select Open. Specify the correct file extension (either .WAV or .MID), and the drive and directory for your music files. To select a CD-ROM track, select Device and then CD Audio.

The Media Player operates like a tape or CD-ROM player: Simply click the Play, Pause, Stop, and Eject buttons with the mouse.

You can use your collection of .VOC digital audio files by converting them to Microsoft .WAV format. This conversion is performed by the VOC2WAV utility, described in Chapter 5.

Note Full instructions for using Media Player are in your Windows user's guide.

Multimedia Jukebox (All Cards Shipped after the Release of Windows 3.0)

The Multimedia Jukebox (Figure 4-1), which runs under Microsoft Windows, plays MIDI music files. Like a real jukebox, you can load a single song or a "stack" of songs.

To load the Jukebox, start Windows 3.1. Double-click on the Accessories group, and then double-click on the Jukebox icon. (This assumes you followed the Sound Blaster installation recommendation to

FIGURE 4-1

The Multimedia JukeBox with MIDI songs queued and playing

place Jukebox file MMJBOX, from the Sound Blaster drivers software, into the Accessories group.)

To select MIDI files to play, specify either the \SB\MIDI directory (Sound Blaster) or the \SBPRO\PLAYMIDI (Sound Blaster Pro) directory. Double-click on the Up Directory selection (the [..] in the drive list) to navigate to the correct subdirectory.

 Note Full instructions for using the Jukebox are in your Sound Blaster documentation. If your Jukebox doesn't work correctly, you may well have the Jukebox program written for Windows 3.0, which will not work well with Windows 3.1. If this is the case, contact Creative Labs for an update. See Appendix B for more information on this problem.

Microsoft Sound Recorder (Windows)

The Windows 3.1 Sound Recorder (Figure 4-2), provided by Microsoft as part of Windows 3.1, is an extremely easy-to-use tool for recording from the microphone, CD, or line-in. It has very exciting, albeit limited, editing and special effects capabilities.

 The Microsoft Sound Recorder

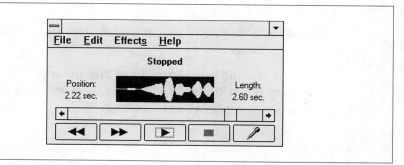

Loading the Sound Recorder

Before running the Sound Recorder, set up the mixer with the Sound Blaster Pro Mixer applet. Be sure to select the source you wish to record: microphone, line-in, or CD. The default mixer setting is for microphone input.

Start Windows 3.1. Double-click the Accessories group, and then double-click the Sound Recorder icon.

 Tip Arrange your Windows desktop to have both the mixer software and Sound Recorder visible in their own separate windows.

Running Sound Recorder

Follow these steps to make a recording:

1. Once the Sound Recorder is active, select File New.

2. Select the button with the microphone picture on it (the other buttons will be disabled). A waveform appears, to graphically demonstrate the audio input. You are now recording.

 Note If the recording level gauge still appears as an unwavering thick line, you need to check the mixer settings. Switch to the mixer's window, or bring up the mixer by clicking on its icon. Ensure that the correct source has been selected, and that the source volume level is at least halfway up.

3. Wait a few seconds, and click the button with the box to stop recording.

4. Use the mixer to turn down the microphone volume. If you don't turn down the source volume, you will pick up background noise when you play your recording.

Tip   The Sound Recorder doesn't talk to the mixer, so the recording sources are not shut off automatically when you play back a recording. Since the source volume is always louder than the playback volume, your recording may not be audible if your CD or line-in source is still playing.

5. Click on the Fast Rewind button (the double triangle pointing to the right). Then play your recording by clicking on the the Play button (the single triangle pointing to the right).

Mastering Sound Recorder

You will want to explore the Sound Recorder's special effects, such as sound reversal, speed change, and echo. This utility is handicapped by its rudimentary control over amplification and speed, but the capability to mix (overlay) sound files and insert one within another is very useful. Here are a few hints on using the effects provided by the Sound Recorder:

☐   *Volume.* Decrease Volume complements the Increase Volume menu choice. If you increase the volume by 25 percent and then select Decrease Volume, the original volume will be restored.

☐   *Speed.* Decrease Speed complements the Increase Speed menu choice. If you increase the speed by 100 percent and then select Decrease Speed, the original speed will be restored.

CHAPTER

Sample Editing and Manipulation

*T*his chapter discusses VOXKIT and VEDIT2, menu-driven programs that you use to record, edit, and play back digital audio files. Also in this chapter you will read about five command-line utilities used to manipulate digital audio files: WAVE2VOC, VOC2WAVE, JOINTVOC, VOC-HDR, and VSR.

☐ VOXKIT is an elementary digital audio file editor provided with Sound Blaster cards. VEDIT2 is a more powerful editor shipped with the Sound Blaster Pros. Both of these editors work with files recorded in the Creative Labs .VOC format. They cannot edit Microsoft wave (.WAV) files directly.

☐ WAVE2VOC and VOC2WAVE make it possible to convert digital audio files from the Creative Labs .VOC format to Microsoft's .WAV format and vice versa. These two utilities are provided with the Sound Blaster Pro cards only.

☐ JOINTVOC combines small voice files into larger ones. It can insert silence blocks, repeat a sound track, and even insert synchronization markers that trigger the next slide in a multimedia presentation. All cards come with this utility.

☐ VOC-HDR and VSR are special tools for creating and modifying, respectively, headers in .VOC files. VOC-HDR is provided with all cards. VSR is shipped with the Sound Blaster only.

VOXKIT (SB)

The VOXKIT is a very basic voice file editor. It will record and play Creative Labs voice (.VOC) digital audio files. VOXKIT can

☐ Record from either microphone or line-in (line-in on Sound Blaster version 2.0 only)

☐ Record to memory or to disk

☐ Play from memory or from disk

☐ Save from memory to disk

☐   Load from disk to memory

☐   Pack voice data in memory or on disk

Loading and Using VOXKIT

To start VOXKIT, switch to the \SB directory. Type **VOXKIT** at the DOS command line and then press ENTER. The VOXKIT main menu will appear.

You can advance to a menu item by either pressing the UP ARROW or DOWN ARROW keys, or by holding down ALT and pressing the letter key corresponding to the menu item. Then press ENTER to select the item. The arrow keys work on all menus.

When you first start VOXKIT, it displays "Memory" in the Status Box in the Work Space and stands ready to record to memory or to play voice data stored in memory. At this point, hook up a microphone or, if you have Sound Blaster 2.0, attach a stereo or other sound source to the line-in. Don't try to record from both at the same time.

Note   Voice files are limited to available memory (if recorded to memory) or to available disk space (if recorded to disk). Try to keep your recordings short. You can fill up available memory in about 40 seconds at the default sample rate of 8,000 Hz. At this rate, disk files will grow by 500K (one-half megabyte) for each minute of recording. See the discussion of sampling and sample rates in Chapter 2.

Recording to Memory

To record to memory, follow these steps:

1. *Caution:* Before recording to memory, be sure that the Status Box in the Work Space says Memory or MemMemory. Make sure either the microphone or line-in source is connected, but not both.

2. Select Record Voice.

3. Select Change Sample rate. Note the recording time available at the default sample rate of 8,000 Hz.

4. Press ESC to accept the current sample rate, or enter a new sample rate and press ENTER.

5. Select Record At. You are now recording. Press ESC as soon as you're done.

 Note   If you run out of memory, VOXKIT will stop recording automatically. The "Record to Memory" status indicator will disappear.

Playing from Memory

Caution: First make sure that the Status Box says Memory or MemMemory. Then select Play Voice. Press ESC to stop playback before the end.

Mastering VOXKIT

The sections below instruct you on how to accomplish the more advanced VOXKIT tasks, and give the step-by-step commands for each. In the previous section, you saw how to record and play back sound files to and from memory. This section shows how to save your recordings as sound files on disk. By recording to disk you can create larger audio files than by recording to memory. Once saved on disk, you have a permanent copy of the sound file.

Choosing Disk or Memory as the Work Space

Because of a screen display bug in the current version of VOXKIT (the one that ships with Sound Blaster at this writing), the Work Space Status Box in your version of VOXKIT may be somewhat confusing to you. The menu item immediately above the Exit option toggles (changes each time you select it) between the Use Memory option and the Use Disk option, changing the work space status message each time. The paragraphs that follow will help you become more comfortable using this menu item.

Select Disk   When you select Use Disk, you tell VOXKIT to operate on disk files. The Work Space box will show either Disk or Mem Disk (because of the display bug). This status indicates that the Record, Play, and Pack commands will operate upon .VOC files on disk.

Select Memory   When you select Use Memory, you tell VOXKIT to operate on voice files in memory only. The Work Space box will show either Memory or MemMemory (because of the display bug). This indicates that Record, Play and Pack commands will operate upon voice files in memory.

Switching Drives and Directories for Loading and Saving Files

When you first select the Save File or Load File command (explained in upcoming paragraphs), VOXKIT will go to the \SB\VOXKIT directory. You may, however, want to store your voice files in another drive and directory. Here's how to do this:

1. *Caution:* Ensure that the Status Box says Memory or Mem Memory. If it doesn't, toggle the Use Disk/Use Memory menu item.

2. Select Load File. You will see a box listing sample files.

3. *If you want to change the drive,* press F1. Enter the new drive letter and press ENTER.

4. *If you want to change the directory,* select the .. in the Load File list of files. You will now see a list of subdirectories. Move your cursor to the desired subdirectory and press ENTER to select it. (Once you are positioned in the correct directory, press ESC to return to the main menu. When you next select Save File or Load File, you will be positioned in this directory.)

Saving to Disk

After you have recorded your voice file to memory, you can save it to disk for later use. Here are the steps:

1. *Caution:* Ensure that the Status Box says Memory or Mem Memory. If it doesn't, toggle the Use Disk/Use Memory menu item.

2. Select Save File.

3. Enter the filename. You don't need to add .VOC at the end; VOXKIT will do this for you. The file will be saved to the current (VOXKIT) directory.

 Warning   Be careful when you choose a filename for recording or saving a file to disk. VOXKIT doesn't always warn you if you are about to overwrite an existing file. When you've made a recording that you are satisfied with, it's a good idea to copy the file to a "safe" location.

Loading from Disk

To load a file from disk, follow these steps:

1. **Caution:** Ensure that the Status Box says Mem or Mem Memory. If it doesn't, toggle the Use Disk/Use Memory menu item.

2. Select Load File.

3. Move the cursor to the desired file and press ENTER. Note that the filename is now displayed in the Work Space box.

Playing Files from Disk

When you play from disk, you are not limited to the space available in conventional memory. You can play files of any length.

To play a file from disk:

1. **Caution:** Make sure the Status Box says Disk or Mem Disk. If it doesn't, toggle the Use Disk/Use Memory menu item.

2. Select Play Voice.

3. Move the cursor to the file you wish to play, and press ENTER.

Recording to Disk

When you record to disk, you are not limited to the space available in memory. You can record voice files of any length, up to the maximum space available on your floppy or hard disk. Here are the steps to record to disk:

1. Connect either the microphone or line-in source. Don't try to record from both at the same time.

2. *Caution:* Make sure the Status Box says Disk or Mem Disk. If it doesn't, toggle the Use Disk/Use Memory menu item.

3. Select Record Voice.

4. Select Change Sample rate. Notice the recording time available at a default sample rate of 8,000 Hz. Either press ESC to accept the current sample rate, or enter a new sample rate and press ENTER.

5. Select Record At.

6. Enter the filename that will store your voice data. Press ENTER. You are now recording. Press ESC as soon as you are done.

Warning Be careful when you choose a filename for recording or saving a file to disk. VOXKIT doesn't always warn you if you are about to overwrite an existing file. When you've made a recording that you are satisfied with, it's a good idea to copy the file to a "safe" location.

Deleting Voice Files

There is no menu selection for deleting voice files. The steps to do this as follows:

1. Select Exit to quit VOXKIT, and confirm your command by pressing **Y**. You will be returned to the DOS prompt.

2. Switch to the \SB\VOXKIT subdirectory by typing **CD\SB\VOXKIT** and pressing ENTER. (If you've chosen another directory for storing your .VOC files, enter that directory name instead.)

3. Use the DOS Delete command to delete your files; they will have a .VOC filename extension.

Caution   Be careful to not accidentally delete the sample files provided with VOXKIT. These sample files will have a date prior to when you bought your sound card.

About File Size Limitations

Sound Blaster owners should bear in mind that, although VPLAY can play voice files larger than available memory, the VOXKIT voice editor cannot load and subsequently edit files this large. You have two choices for handling this dilemma: You can use Blaster Master, the voice file editor provided on the disk that accompanies this book (see Chapter 10). Or you can plan on creating smaller voice files—no more than about 500K (500,000 bytes) each, assuming you have a PC with 640K or more RAM installed.

Sound Blaster Pro owners don't need to be concerned about creating voice files that are too large. Creative Labs provides Sound Blaster Pro owners with VEDIT2, instead of VOXKIT. VEDIT2 can handle files that are too large to fit into memory.

Packing Files

When you select the Data Packing menu item, VOXKIT will compress your sound files, but there are trade-offs to this. Packing reduces the file size by up to 75 percent (4:1 compression), but you will suffer some degradation of audio quality. If you plan to do both data block and silence packing, do the silence packing first. For more information about packing in general, and silence packing in particular, see the section in Chapter 2 that explains packing and compression.

Warning   Be aware that a common accident is to pack a file on disk, accidentally overwriting the uncompressed sound file (the original recording). A similar accident is loading a file into memory, packing it, and then saving it again with the same file name. This type of mistake can be serious, because once a file is packed, it cannot be edited.

Packing Voice Files in Memory   If you want to pack voice files in memory,

1. ***Caution:*** Make sure the Status Box says Memory or MemMemory. If it doesn't, toggle the Use Disk/Use Memory menu item.

2. Select Data Packing.

3. Choose the Packing Method. You can do both silence and data packing. With silence packing, you can optionally revise the threshold value and window size.

Packing Voice in a Disk File   If you want to pack voice files on a disk:

1. ***Caution:*** Make sure the Status Box says Disk or Mem Disk. If it doesn't, toggle the Use Disk/Use Memory menu item.

2. Select Data Packing.

3. Move the cursor to the file you wish to pack and press ENTER.

4. Enter the target filename—that is, the name of the new, packed file that will be created—and press ENTER. VOXKIT will not let you overwrite the original, unpacked file.

5. Choose the Packing Method. You can do both silence and data packing. With silence packing, you can optionally revise the threshold value and window size. Unless you have very special needs, the default values should be fine.

VEDIT2 (SB Pro)

Voice Editor II (VEDIT2) is a feature-rich, full-screen program for recording, playing, editing, and enhancing your Creative Labs .VOC digital audio files. Just think of VEDIT2 as a complete recording studio for sound files. You can record from the microphone, line-in, or a CD-ROM . From the VEDIT2 editor you can see on your computer's screen the actual waveform that you hear when you play your digital audio file. You can mark a piece, listen to it, and then delete, move, or enhance that piece. You can, for example, remove words from a speech or change the order of sentences. You can also add special effects, such as fade-ins, stereo panning, and echoes.

Your Sound Blaster Pro manual has an extensive array of screen shots and detailed instructions to guide you through VEDIT2. This section is a supplement to your manual. Rather than step-by-step instructions and complete menu descriptions, here you will find information to fill in the "gaps" in your manual, pointing out interesting features of VEDIT2, and giving you tips on how to get the most out of this editor.

Starting and Quitting

To start VEDIT2, first switch to the SBPRO directory by typing **CD\SBPRO** from the DOS command line and pressing ENTER. Then type **VEDIT2** and press ENTER. You will see the opening screen, as shown in Figure 5-1. Press any key to progress to the next screen.

To exit from VEDIT2, select File from the main menu, and then select Exit. When prompted, confirm your command by typing **Y**.

Warning SPUTMON can interfere with VEDIT2. If you're using SPUTMON, disable it temporarily by typing **SPUTOFF** and press ENTER.

FIGURE 5-1   VEDIT2 opening screen

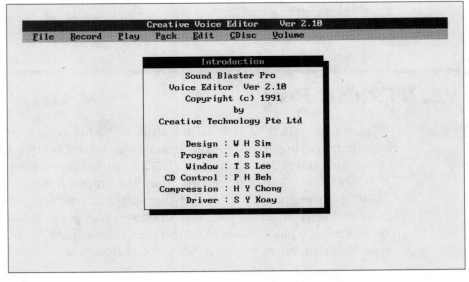

Keyboard Fundamentals

You work with VEDIT2 using keyboard commands similar to those of the FM Intelligent Organ. Commands are selected from a menu bar at the top of the screen, by holding down the ALT key and pressing a letter key. All other menu and dialog box selections are made by pressing just a single letter or number key.

Note   Because VEDIT2 is a graphically oriented program, you'll probably find that controlling the program with a mouse is more intuitive than with the keyboard. For the sake of brevity, and to ensure that everyone can follow the procedures described here, only keyboard instructions are provided.

Loading Files

To load a .VOC voice file, select Load from the File menu. This displays the File Directory screen that presents a list of .VOC files. Once you select a file, the Block Information screen appears, and all the blocks contained within that file are listed. You are now free to delete blocks, move them around, play specific blocks or the entire file, or switch to the Edit menu and modify a block.

Note   Chapter 2 touched upon data and sound blocks, the two most important components of a .VOC file. All of the block types are described in the section "Inserting Control Blocks" later in this chapter.

A typical Block Information screen, with a single voice data block that has been loaded into memory, is shown in Figure 5-2.

Working with Large Files

Some programs, such as VREC, record audio to disk as a single block that fills the file. More sophisticated programs, such as VEDIT2, record audio to disk as a sequence of smaller data blocks. In the case of VEDIT2, it fills an audio file with 32K data blocks. To edit a digital audio file, you must select from the Block Information screen a group of blocks that can

FIGURE
5-2

Block Information screen of VEDIT2

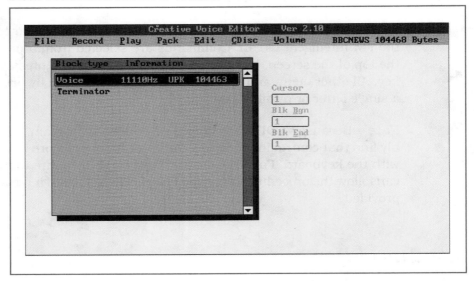

fit in memory. Unfortunately, there are two situations, both of which are very common, in which you cannot load all the blocks at once:

☐ *Audio File Consists of One Large Block.* In this case, VEDIT2 prompts you to split the block into smaller ones that can be loaded. You can split blocks repeatedly, as described in an upcoming section, until you have a block or group of blocks that will load into memory.

☐ *Audio File Consists of a Collection of Blocks Too Large to Load All Together.* In this situation, VEDIT2 prompts you to select which block or group of blocks you want to load. You can also split the blocks further, as described in an upcoming section, until you have a block or group of blocks that can be loaded.

Selecting Blocks

If a voice file is too large to fit into conventional memory, VEDIT2 displays the Message screen (Figure 5-3). Here the block selection window

FIGURE
5-3

Loading blocks from a large file

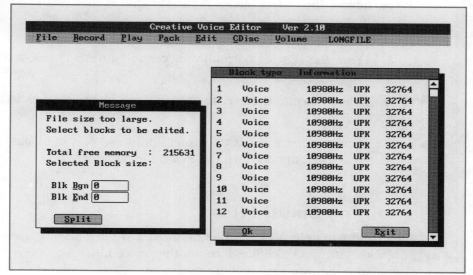

on the right provides a numbered list of all the blocks found in this file. The Message dialog box on the left prompts you to select the block or group of blocks you wish to load.

If your file consists of one large block too large to load, you can split that block by picking that block and then selecting the Split button.

If your audio file contains too many blocks to load, don't worry. Blocks that you load and then change will be automatically reinserted into the file when you save it to disk. For example, suppose you load the last data block only, and then add a fade-out to soften the music's abrupt ending. When you save your work by selecting File and then Save from the main menu, VEDIT2 will replace the last data block in the disk file with the edited version of this block from memory.

Splitting Large Files

If you find you're more comfortable working with smaller files, you can split a long audio file into several pieces, by selecting a group of blocks and then use the Write command to write them to disk. For example, if you have a file of ten blocks, you can split it into two five-block files. Follow these steps:

1. From the Block information screen (Figure 5-2) select a group of blocks.

2. Select File and then Write to save these blocks on disk in their own file.

3. Repeat steps 1 and 2 to extract additional sets of blocks, and then save them to disk with their own file name.

Joining Small Files

Unfortunately, VEDIT2 has no provision for inserting a voice file, or blocks within a voice file, into another voice file. If you need to do this, split the file into two or more pieces and then combine them with the JOINTVOC utility, described later in this chapter. You're likely to do this when creating multimedia presentations; otherwise, if you played many small files separately rather than as one combined file, you would hear a pause between sound bites.

Recording with VEDIT2

You can record from any one of the following sources: voice (microphone), CD, or line-in. You can record directly to memory or to a disk file. Before you begin recording, you must set up your recording environment by following these steps, all of which begin at the main menu:

1. Select the Volume menu, and then choose the source you wish to record from. Adjust the volume to a high setting, about 4/5 of the maximum volume level, to ensure a strong input signal.

2. Select the Record menu, and then choose Setting. The Setting window is discussed in the section just below.

3. Begin the recording by selecting either To Memory or To Disk from the Record menu. If you are recording from the microphone, begin speaking as soon as possible.

Choosing Recording Settings

Before you begin recording, you must choose Setting on the Record menu to enter the recording parameters on the Setting window (Figure 5-4). Note that once you pick a recording source, such as microphone or CD input, VEDIT2 makes an intelligent guess at what the other settings should be. For example, if you select Stereo and CD, VEDIT2 automatically establishes the 22.05 kHz sampling rate and the No Filter setting.

Unfortunately, VEDIT2 doesn't check that the volume control for the chosen source is set at a reasonable level. You are responsible for setting the volume to a suitably high level, probably 10 or more. Select Volume from the main menu to access the volume controls.

Two important issues—how to select a sample rate, and the considerations of recording to disk versus recording to memory—are discussed next.

FIGURE 5-4

The Record|Setting screen of VEDIT2

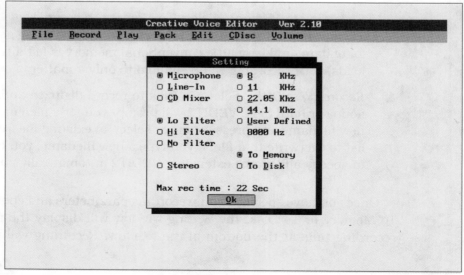

Note   Chapter 2 provides additional information to help you understand the recording settings (see the sections on sampling and filters).

Selecting the Sample Rate   When selecting the sample rate, keep three issues in mind:

☐   If you plan to work in the Windows environment, it's best to select 11, 22, or 44 kHz, since these rates are common to both .VOC and .WAV files.

☐   Use a higher sampling rate for music (44 kHz for monaural or 22 kHz for stereo) to accurately record the high-frequency components. Use a lower rate for voice (8 or 11 kHz).

☐   Beware of filling up your hard disk with voice files. At the 22 kHz maximum sampling rate for stereo, 44,100 (two channels each at 22.05 kHz) 8-bit (1-byte) samples are taken each second. This means you are consuming disk space at the rate of 44,100 bytes a second, or 2.65 million bytes a minute!

Selecting the Destination   In the Setting window you must select either the To Memory or the To Disk radio button. Your selection controls which menu item of the same name will be active. The item you do not select will appear dimmed on screen. As soon as you choose the destination, recording will begin.

☐   *Recording to Memory.* Select To Memory to record digitized audio in conventional memory. Since digital audio recording generates a lot of data, and very little conventional memory is left after VEDIT2 loads, your recording will be limited to only a matter of seconds.

☐   *Recording to Disk.* Select To Disk to record digitized audio to your floppy or hard disk. VEDIT2 will prompt you for a filename. Enter a new filename and press ENTER, or select an existing file from the file list to overwrite that file. If you type a new filename, you don't need to specify a filename extension; VEDIT2 automatically adds .VOC.

Once you have specified your recording parameters and chosen either To Memory or To Disk, the Setting window will display the maximum recording time at the bottom of the window. Recording will terminate automatically once memory is filled when you're recording To Memory, or when the disk is filled when you're recording To Disk.

Scanning Input

Select Scan Input from the Record menu to view the sound wave from your chosen source before you begin to record. The Scan Input screen is shown in Figure 5-5.

Scan Input is useful for ensuring that you've selected the correct source in the Setting window, and that the volume level is high enough. For the most dramatic demonstration of input scanning, set the source to be the microphone, choose Scan Input, and then speak into the microphone. If you see a flat line, VEDIT2 can't hear anything and you'll need to double-check your settings. Press the ESC key to return to the main menu.

Scanning input before recording

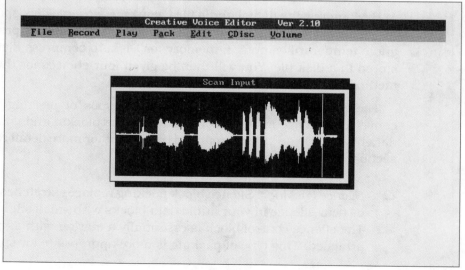

Recording from CD

The CDISK option from the main menu controls your CD player. This menu choice will be dimmed and unavailable if you don't have a CD-ROM player connected.

A very nice feature of VEDIT2 is that it automatically starts the CD player when you begin recording. This makes it easy to start your recording at the specific track you want. First, make certain you've selected CD as the recording source in the Setting window. Then pause at the location where you wish to begin recording. When you give VEDIT2 the command to start recording, by selecting either To Disk or To Memory, VEDIT2 will automatically start playing the CD from the specified starting point.

Conserving Disk Space

Recording sound files consumes disk space very rapidly. To conserve disk space you can either compress files or delete the ones you no longer need. These two alternatives are discussed below.

Compressing Files

By compressing digital audio files, you can conserve disk space. From the main menu, select Pack. Then choose Memory, to compress digital audio temporarily stored in memory, or Disk, to compress digital audio stored in a disk file. You will then be given four choices for the packing method.

There are two fundamentally different types of packing available: converting silence in the recording to silence blocks, and compressing data blocks. These are summarized below, but for more detail refer to the section on packing in Chapter 2.

☐   *Silence Packing.*   Silence block packing replaces stretches of silence or near silence in your audio data blocks with small silence blocks. The silence control block is essentially a marker with a time period attached. This type of packing is more appropriate for speech than for music, since long pauses are more common in speech. The savings in file size can be impressive; a speech file can often be reduced to half its original size.

☐   *Data Packing.*   You have three choices for performing data compression upon data blocks: 2:1, 3:1, and 4:1 compression. The greater the compression (4:1 is the highest), the more you lose in audio quality. The tightest overall file compression is provided by doing silence packing before data packing. Since silence packing can be quite effective in reducing file size without loss of sound quality, you may not need to do data packing at all.

Protect Your Unpacked Digital Audio   VEDIT2 can pack voice files already loaded in memory, or voice files on disk. When you pack digital audio recorded directly to memory, you will overwrite and lose the original raw (unpacked) sound recording. When you pack a file on disk, VEDIT2 will prompt you for both a source and target filename, and the packed audio will be placed in a newly created file. This is the preferable method for packing, since it minimizes the likelihood that you will lose a valuable recording by accidentally overwriting it. Always save your digital audio to disk, with the File Save command, before packing.

Packed Files Cannot Be Edited   There are some drawbacks and limitations to packing audio files. The major drawback is that you cannot further modify your files. This means you won't be able to move blocks around, cut blocks out, or add special effects like echo or panning. In addition, packed files cannot be used in the Microsoft Windows Multimedia environment.

Limitations on Packing   When you attempt to pack, you may get a message that "data cannot be packed." There can be several reasons for this. First, voice data with a high sample rate, such as stereo data, will not be packed by VEDIT2 because it knows that the decompression hardware of the Sound Blaster cards cannot keep up with the workload of simultaneously handling both a high sampling rate and doing decompression. Another reason you may encounter this message is insufficient memory. VEDIT2 needs a lot of memory to do packing, even when it packs a sound file on disk. If you encounter this limitation, you may have to split your file in two, pack the two pieces, and then join them together again, as explained earlier.

Deleting Files

You should frequently cleanse your \SBPRO directory of unneeded .VOC files. Unfortunately, there is no command to delete files on disk. You have to quit VEDIT2, return to the DOS prompt or your file manager, and then use the appropriate command to delete files with a .VOC extension.

Tip   If you are running out of disk space but don't want to quit VEDIT2 yet, you can free up space by compressing files you no longer need. Select 4:1 compression from the Pack menu to squeeze files as much as possible. You can also prepare for this contingency by creating a tiny (less than 1,000 bytes) digital audio file. Load this file into memory and then use the Save As command in the File menu to overwrite unneeded, much larger audio files.

Playing Sound Files

To hear your audio files, select Play from the main menu. You have three choices when playing files:

☐   From Memory lets you hear all of the audio file that you recently recorded to memory or loaded from disk.

☐   Selected Blocks lets you find the particular word, phrase, or melody you wish to manipulate.

☐   From Disk lets you listen to a voice file on disk.

Note   Before you play, you should turn off the source (for instance, shut off your microphone) or turn down the source volume by going to the Volume menu. The source is always louder than the digital audio playback, so you must turn down the source volume to hear your recording being played back.

Editing with VEDIT2

VEDIT2 is a powerful voice file editor. You can add control blocks, such as silence markers and ASCII comment blocks. You can also delete, move, and combine data blocks, as well as modify the actual waveform within a data block.

Once a file is loaded or recorded, the Block Information screen is displayed (look again at Figure 5-2). Voice data blocks, and control blocks if any exist, can be selected from this screen.

From the main menu select Edit to display the editing choices for selected blocks. The choices are organized into the following categories:

- Inserting control blocks

- Rearranging blocks (delete, move, copy, and combine)

- Modifying blocks

- Editing a data block waveform

Inserting Control Blocks

The Edit Insert commands insert various types of control blocks into your voice file. The inserted block is placed immediately above the current block (the block that is highlighted and whose block number appears as the Cursor number). To insert a block below the current block, select the Append button. The types of blocks you can insert and their purpose are explained below.

Silence   Select Silence to insert a silence block into the file. They are also created by silence packing, which compresses your file by replacing a period of silence or near silence with a small silence block. You specify the minimum duration of silence, in milliseconds, for which it's acceptable to replace silence digital audio with a silence block. One thousand milliseconds is equivalent to one second.

The silence block is very useful for conserving disk space, but there is a drawback. The Microsoft wave file format (.WAV) doesn't support this type of block. When you use VOC2WAV to convert from a .VOC to a .WAV file format, your silence blocks are converted back into "silent" data values, and your file size expands accordingly.

Marker   Select Marker to insert a marker block into the file. Markers are used by MMPLAY, the Multimedia Player, for synchronizing the display of animation flicks with your sound file. This has no effect upon sound output. For further explanation, see the description of MMPLAY in Chapter 7.

ASCII   Select ASCII to add a comment that helps document the sound file blocks that follow. This has no effect upon sound output, and expands the file size only minimally.

Repeat   Select Repeat to repeatedly play a single data block or a group of data blocks in your file. VEDIT2 will automatically insert both a repeat block and a matching end-repeat block. The repeat block feature is useful for conserving disk space, but there is a drawback. The Microsoft wave file format doesn't support this type of block, so repeated blocks are expanded when converted by VOC2WAV to wave format, and your file will grow significantly in size.

Rearranging Blocks

   You can easily and quickly make dramatic changes to the content of your sound file with the following commands. They are accessible by selecting Edit from the main menu:

   ☐   Delete

   ☐   Move

   ☐   Copy

   ☐   Combine

Note   The Delete command is always active. The Move, Copy, and Combine commands are available only if one or more blocks have been selected in the Block Information screen.

The Delete command has a very practical use. It is ideal for removing dead space, or a speech hesitation such as "umm..", or an accidentally repeated word. When deleting a repeat block, be careful to also delete the matching end-repeat block.

All of the first three commands offer considerable opportunity for mischief when manipulating speech. For example, you can change the order of words, and even completely change the meaning of a sentence by removing the word *not*.

 Tip   Silence packing can assist you in parsing recorded speech into small data blocks, each of which consists of a word, phrase, or sentence.

The Combine command has a different use. It combines two or more adjacent voice blocks into a single block. This is useful primarily for housekeeping purposes—for combining several small blocks into a larger, more easily managed block, for instance. Note that the sample rate must be exactly the same for all blocks you wish to join. You cannot combine silence blocks. Instead, delete one of the blocks and then modify the silence period of the remaining block.

Modifying Blocks

From the main menu, selecting Edit and then Modify displays a rich set of tools for revising your digital audio file. You can add or remove control blocks, perform special effects on voice data blocks, and even edit the waveform within a data block. Note that this set of tools operates only on a single block at a time. Most of the other commands you've used, such as Play from the main menu, let you select a group of blocks.

 Caution   Because the modifications described in this section are generally irreversible, make certain you have a copy of your voice data saved on disk before using Edit | Modify.

To modify a control block, highlight that block by using the block begin and block end numbers, and then select Edit | Modify. You'll then see a screen with options relevant to that type of control block. The screens that appear for silence, marker, ASCII, and repeat blocks are identical to those that appear when you create this block type from the Edit | Insert submenu.

To modify a voice data block, position the cursor on that block and select Modify. An entirely new screen, titled Editing Voice Data, appears. Figure 5-6 shows how the current block appears as waveform.

These menu choices are available in the Editing Voice Data screen:

☐   *Options.* Split the block or change the sample rate.

☐   *Edit.* Move a piece of the block by cut-and-paste, delete a piece, or create a waveform with the Insert and Fill commands.

☐   *Effect.* Add special effects like echo, fade in/out, and pan.

The Options submenu is self-explanatory. To take advantage of most of the edit and special-effect commands, you must first select a piece of the voice data block to modify. The paragraphs that follow tell you how

FIGURE 5-6   Editing a voice data waveform

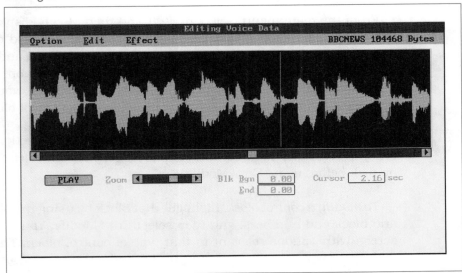

to expand and contract the waveform display by using the Zoom control, and then how to mark a piece of the data block. Then you'll read about editing the waveform and entering special effects.

Selecting a Piece of the Block Waveform

The user interface for VEDIT2's editing of the block's waveform (Figure 5-6) is somewhat mysterious, however, the following steps will help you master it quickly.

1. Type Z to select the Zoom control.

2. Hold down the LEFT ARROW key to stretch the waveform, so you can see it in more detail.

3. Press ENTER when you have finished zooming.

Stretching the waveform has no effect upon the sound you hear when you select the Play button. Also, notice that once you have stretched the waveform beyond the right edge of the screen, the meaning of the LEFT and RIGHT ARROW keys changes. The LEFT ARROW now moves you to the beginning of the waveform (the sound you hear at first), and the RIGHT ARROW moves you to the end. Notice how the Cursor box displays a number, which is the number of seconds of playing time from the beginning of the block to the cursor location.

The cursor, which is single vertical line that may be difficult to see, is used to mark a piece of the block to edit. To move the cursor to the right, press the TAB key. To move the cursor to the left, hold down the SHIFT key and press the TAB. The cursor moves in 8 or 9 jumps across the screen, so you can control the cursor position indirectly by using the Zoom control.

To select the beginning of a piece of the block, move the cursor to the start of the piece and press CTRL-B. Then move the cursor to the end of the piece and press CTRL-E. The selected piece is shown in inverse color. Note how Block Begin and Block End are automatically filled in with the location of this piece. When you work with the Block Information screen, you specify the beginning and ending block numbers. When you work in the Editing Voice Data screen, you specify the beginning and ending playing time within the current block.

Editing the Voice Data Block Waveform

You can make microscopic changes to the waveform of a digital audio data block. Once you've selected a piece of the block waveform as described just above, you can perform the following operations on this block:

☐ *Save.* Save this piece to disk.

☐ *Cut.* Remove the highlighted piece. Save it temporarily to the scrap heap (a temporary storage place in your computer). Use this command to copy or move a piece of the waveform.

☐ *Paste.* Insert, at the location of the vertical cursor, the contents of the scrap heap (not available until after you cut).

☐ *Fill.* Fill a piece with a single value.

☐ *Insert.* Insert a new piece that has the same length as the piece currently highlighted.

To move a piece of a block, first select Cut, then move the vertical cursor to where you wish to put the piece, and select Paste.

Custom waveforms, such as a square wave, can be made with the Fill and Insert commands. Unfortunately, you can only paste once, and you cannot insert a file from disk, so making custom waveforms is very tedious.

Using Special Effects

One of the most powerful features of the VEDIT2 editor is its capability to add special effects to your sound recording. Each of these effects are described in more detail below:

☐ *Amplify.* Select Amplify to amplify the relative amplitude (intensity) of this piece as compared to the rest of your block. The default value of 200% doubles the amplitude; 100% has no change on the amplitude; and 50% cuts the amplitude in half. If you amplify the voice data too much, it will be clipped and distortion will arise. Once clipping occurs, you have lost information and will have to reload the voice file from disk.

☐   *Echo.* Select Echo to add richness to the sound. This has the most impact if you first insert silence after the voice data you intend to echo. This way the echo can be heard distinctly as it rolls forward into the silent period.

☐   *Fade In and Fade Out.* Select Fade Out to gradually reduce the amplitude, or Fade In to gradually increase the amplitude. Use Fade Out at the end of a song or voice-over to provide a graceful fading of the sound. Use Fade In at the beginning of a song or voice-over to avoid shocking the listener.

☐   *Pan Left-Right and Right-Left.* Select Pan Left-Right when working with stereo voice data, to simultaneously fade out the left channel and fade in the right channel. By repeatedly panning from left to right and right to left, you will add a stereo effect to your presentation. If this is well done, it will add a dramatic impact to your presentation.

Caution   The special effect commands manipulate the waveform and cause irreversible change to your sound data. Be certain to have a copy of the voice file saved on disk before trying these special effects.

Listening to the Block

In Figure 5-6, you see the waveform for BBCNEWS.VOC. Press P to play the sound file. You can make changes to the waveform and immediately hear the results. If you enter a non-zero value for Block Begin and Block end, only that block will be played.

VEDIT2 Compatibility with the Windows Environment

VEDIT2 has one major limitation: It can only edit Creative Labs's own .VOC format digital audio files. When you work in the Windows multimedia environment, you will usually work with Microsoft wave (.WAV) digital audio files. Although VEDIT2 cannot edit wave files directly, you can use the WAV2VOC and VOC2WAV utility programs, described in the next two sections, to convert your files between the two formats. To work with .WAV files in VEDIT2, simply convert the files to .VOC files, edit them with VEDIT2, and then convert them back to .WAV format. Since both types of digital audio files store audio data in the same way, you can convert between the formats without loss of information.

WAV2VOC (SB Pro)

WAV2VOC is a utility that converts Microsoft .WAV files to Creative Labs .VOC files. This is useful if you have .WAV files you wish to include in a presentation built with MMPLAY, since MMPLAY can play .VOC but not .WAV files. Also, once they're converted to .VOC format, you can also modify these files with the VEDIT2 voice editor.

This utility is very simple, and handles issues such as sample rate conversion automatically. Here are the steps for using WAV2VOC:

1. Switch to the VEDIT2 subdirectory by typing **CD \SBPRO\VEDIT2** and then press ENTER.

2. To perform the conversion, enter the WAV2VOC command:

   WAV2VOC *wave_filename voc_filename*

   and then press ENTER.

VOC2WAV (SB Pro)

VOC2WAV converts Creative Labs .VOC files to Microsoft .WAV files. This is useful if you work in the Windows environment and have a collection of useful .VOC files. This utility is very simple, and handles issues such as sample rate conversion automatically. You can optionally override the defaults with command switches. Here are the steps for using VOC2WAV:

1. Switch to the VEDIT2 subdirectory by typing **CD \SBPRO\VEDIT2** and then press ENTER.

2. To convert a monaural file at the default sampling rate of 11 kHz, enter the VOC2WAV command in this format:

   VOC2WAV *wave_filename voc_filename*

   and then press ENTER.

VOC2WAV Switches

The /R Switch. Creative Labs .VOC files can have sample rates up to 44,100 kHz, and .WAV files can have only one of three rates: 11,025 kHz, 22,050 kHz, or 44,100 kHz (the default is 11,025 kHz). Use the /R switch to select the proper rate for the wave file you are creating. Ideally your .VOC and .WAV files will have the same sampling rate. If not, VOC2WAV will automatically convert the .VOC file (the sample rate is embedded in the file header) to the specified .WAV rate without noticeable degradation in audio quality.

The /S Switch. If your .VOC file contains silence blocks, the /S command switch controls whether they are ignored (Off) or converted to "silent" audio data values. The .VOC silence blocks provide a way to reduce the size of voice files containing long pauses. The silence block is very compact, typically much smaller than the silent audio it replaces. Unfortunately, the Microsoft wave file format does not support silence blocks, so the silence block is expanded into silence data, causing your file size to expand. Silence blocks are discussed more in the section on packing in Chapter 2.

The /L Switch. If your .VOC file contains repeated audio data blocks, the /L command switch controls whether only one copy of the audio data block is included (Off) or whether the audio data block is repeated (On) a specified number of times (this number is embedded in the .VOC file; you don't need to specify it). Unfortunately, Microsoft wave file format does not support this, and if the audio data block is replicated, the .WAV file will become significantly larger than the equivalent .VOC file.

The /C Switch. This selects stereo (/C:2) or monoaural recording (/C:1). The default is mono.

Note The loss of silence and repetition blocks in .VOC file conversion is not as problematic as it may seem. The MMPLAY utility has commands for introducing delays (.DELAY) and repeating digital audio and music files (.REPEAT and .END).

Example of VOC-to-WAV File Conversion

Here is an example for converting a voice file called BACH.VOC to a wave file called BACH.WAV. Since the voice file was recorded in stereo at 22 kHz, command switches are necessary to override the defaults of 11 kHz and mono.

To perform the conversion, you would type

VOC2WAV bach.voc bach.wav /C:2 /R:22

and then press ENTER.

Tip The VEDIT2 voice file editor that is provided with Sound Blaster Pro and described earlier in this chapter can be used to split up a digital audio file. This way you can extract each digital audio segment and save it to its own file before conversion to wave format.

JOINTVOC (SB and SB Pro)

JOINTVOC joins two or more digital audio files, in .VOC file format, into a single file. You can add silence blocks between the files, repeat one or more blocks, and add markers that synchronize application programs to the sound tracks (blocks).

First switch to the VEDIT2 directory by typing **CD \SBPRO\VEDIT2** and then press ENTER. To join two voice files together into a "target" that combines them, type the JOINTVOC command in this format:

JOINTVOC /T*targetfilename file1name file2name*

and then press ENTER.

To get on-screen help with this utility, type **JOINTVOC** alone at the DOS command line.

You can combine voice files with different sample rates, and you can join compressed and uncompressed files. (After combining files, use VPLAY to check your work.) For example, you may want to create a new voice file called MARKER.VOC that begins with one second of silence and then combines the CLP.VOC and MENTS.VOC voice files, inserting a synchronization marker with a value of 99 in between. Assuming all files are in the same directory, the following command line will do this:

JOINTVOC /Tmarker.voc /S10 voc clp.voc /M99 ments.voc

The command switches used in this command are as follows:

☐   /T. The target (result of the join) filename

☐   /S. The silence block time period, in units of 0.1 seconds

☐   /M. The synchronization marker number (value up to 999) used to synchronize audio and video in multimedia presentations

VOC-HDR (SB and SB Pro)

The VOC-HDR voice header program is primarily used to repair voice files that have been rendered unreadable because of damage to their header. It can also be used to attach a .VOC file header to a raw digital audio file. Adding a header makes it possible to load the file into VEDIT2 or VOXKIT and to listen to the file with VPLAY. The header provides information about the sound file, such as the sample rate and whether it is compressed or not.

Running VOC-HDR

To load VOC-HDR, follow these steps:

1. Switch to the VEDIT2 directory by typing **CD\SBPRO\VEDIT2** and then press ENTER.

2. At the DOS command line, type **VOC-HDR** followed by the filename of the raw audio file and the filename for the .VOC file you wish to create, in this format:

   VOC-HDR *raw_audio_filename VOC_filename*

   Then press ENTER. You should see the following response on the screen:

   ```
   Create <VOC file> with data in <raw audio filename>
   File without header
   ```

3. You will now be prompted with a series of questions. VOC-HDR will examine the raw digital audio file, before making any changes, and warn you if that file is already in .VOC file format. If so, you will see this message:

   ```
   Voice file already has new header. Change the header?
   ```

   To revise the header, type **Y**. (It is highly unlikely you'll need to add a header if one already exists, so don't enter N unless you think the utility program is confused.)

Note   Don't worry about whether you're guessing correctly on the answers to the questions in step 4. You can easily rerun VOC-HDR and change your responses.

4. You must now tell VOC-HDR the characteristics of this file: the sample rate and whether it is packed. Enter the number between 1 and 5 that corresponds to the type of audio data, either compressed (choose 4-bit, 2.5-bit, or 2-bit); or uncompressed monaural (8-bit); or uncompressed stereo (stereo). Type the number and then press ENTER. Then enter the sample rate for this file and press ENTER.

Note   You may want to refer to the discussions of sample rates and packing in this chapter and Chapter 2 for help with step 4. Also, see "Quick Summary of Packing Options" just below.

5. Once everything is correct, press **Y**. If you wish to change your responses, press **N**.

Getting Help

To get on-screen help with VOC-HDR, type **VOC-HDR** alone at the DOS command line and press ENTER.

Quick Summary of Packing Options

VOC-HDR prompts you for the raw audio data type (step 4, above). The choices are 8-bit (uncompressed), 4-bit (4x compression), 2.5-bit (3x compression), or 2-bit (4x compression). If you don't know which to choose, keep in mind that 8-bit is the most likely choice. For more information, see the section on packing in Chapter 2.

Note The medium compression choice (the 2.5-bit, 3x compression) is misnamed in this utility. All other utility programs that handle compression refer to 2.6-bit compression, which is the correct name for this choice.

How to Identify a .VOC File

A quick way to check whether a file already has the Creative Labs .VOC file header is to use the DOS Type command to display that file's contents on the screen. Enter **TYPE** followed by the filename, and press ENTER. If this is a .VOC file, you will see just "Creative Voice File" on the screen. If not, press CTRL-BREAK to terminate the type command.

Sound Blaster Pro Enhancements

The Sound Blaster Pro version of VOC-HDR has been upgraded to support stereo. Note that the sample rate for stereo is fixed at 22,050 kHz.

VSR (SB Only)

The VSR (Voice Sample Rate) utility revises the sampling rate, and hence the speed at which the file is played, of a .VOC format digital audio file. This program has limited usefulness. It can be used for improving the sound of a recording by making subtle changes to the pitch (by changing its playback speed) and for masking a person's voice. Speech played back 20 percent faster or slower can generally be understood, but you won't be able to recognize the speaker.

Sound Blaster Pro owners are not provided with VSR. They can revise the sample rate through the VEDIT2 voice edit utility.

To load VSR, switch to the VOXKIT directory by typing **CD \SB\VOXKIT** and then press ENTER. Then enter the VSR command and press ENTER. Here is the VSR command syntax:

VSR *<source filename> <target filename>* /R*nnn*

Note   The source file must have the .VOC file extension.

You specify the new sample rate by entering a percentage amount of change from the current rate. For example, for the *nnn* after the /R switch, enter **110** to set the new sample rate at 110 percent of the old rate, which is a 10 percent increase. The target file produced by VSR is identical to the source file, except that the header states a playback speed that is 10 percent higher. When you play the target file, perhaps with VPLAY, the speech or music will have a noticeably higher pitch, and will be about 10 percent shorter in duration.

You can add the /O command switch to play the target file when it is created. For example, the following command creates a new version of the TV4.VOC voice file that will play 2 percent slower:

VSR TV4.VOC TVNEW.VOC /R98 /O

The new sample rate of 98, just 2 percent slower than the original rate (or a sample rate of 102, just 2 percent faster than the original rate) is detectable to the ear.

To get on-screen help, type **VSR** alone at the DOS command line.

CHAPTER

Mixer Controls

Sound Blaster Pro owners quickly fall in love with the built-in *mixer*, a new feature of the Pro version cards. The major advantage of the mixer is that you can control the volume level of your individual sound sources. For example, your CD can provide subdued background music while you listen to louder voice annotations in a Windows document. In addition, you can control the overall volume level with a master volume control. The various mixer software programs also let you select which source to use for recording: either microphone, line-in, or CD.

 Note   Sound Blaster 1.x/2.0 versions, which don't have a mixer, will record whatever is detected from the microphone and line-in sources. With these Sound Blaster cards, you have to physically turn off or disconnect one of these two sources in order to record the other without interference.

The following mixer software is discussed in this chapter:

- SBP-MIX
- SBP-SET
- Sound Blaster Pro Mixer

SBP-MIX is a pop-up, memory-resident program that makes it easy to adjust the mixer on your Sound Blaster Pro card—even when other programs are running. You can control the source levels, master volume, and other features of the mixer. Whenever you want to change the settings, you press a hot-key combination and your mixer program will appear.

SBP-SET is the nonresident, DOS command-line equivalent of SBP-MIX. It is ideal for inclusion in your AUTOEXEC.BAT file, so you can set up your Sound Blaster Pro whenever you start your computer.

The Sound Blaster Pro Mixer is an applet (a little application program) that is installed in your Windows 3.1 Accessories group. It is the Windows mixer program that is functionally equivalent to the DOS mixer program, SBP-MIX, though it is not as feature rich.

SBP-MIX (SB Pro Only)

SBP-MIX is a pop-up, memory-resident program supplied with the Sound Blaster Pro cards. One of the key advantages of Sound Blaster Pro versions over Sound Blaster 1.x/2.0 versions is the mixer (see Figure 6-1) that is built into the sound card. The mixer lets you set the master volume level as well as the volume levels for all the audio inputs: microphone, line-in, CD, voice (digitized audio), and FM synthesizer. The Intelligent Organ, as well as the PLAYCMF and PLAYMIDI utilities, all play through the FM Synthesizer, so SBP-MIX gives you control over these programs, too. With the pop-up mixer, you can adjust the mixer while simultaneously running your favorite software programs.

Note SBP-MIX updates settings on the Sound Blaster Pro board, so your settings will stay in effect even if you must unload the pop-up mixer. As an alternative to SBP-MIX, you can run the SBP-SET utility at the DOS prompt. SBP-SET is described later in this chapter.

FIGURE 6-1   SBP-MIX main menu with Master Volume Control shown

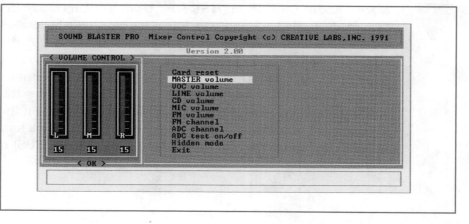

Loading SBP-MIX

When you run SBP-MIX it is loaded as a memory-resident program (also known as a terminate-and-stay-resident program, or TSR). It will then appear when you press the assigned hot-key combination. To load the mixer program:

1. Switch to the \SBPRO directory, type **SBP-MIX** and press ENTER. Notice the message on the screen that ALT-1 will activate SBP-MIX. ALT-1 is your hot key for the pop-up mixer.

2. Now hold down the ALT key and press the 1 key (the one located at the top of your keyboard), and you will see the pop-up mixer program appear.

The mixer program stays in memory, even after you select Exit from the mixer program's main menu and return to your computer's DOS prompt.

Note *To Windows Users:* When running Windows, you will use the Sound Blaster Pro Mixer for Windows, described later in this chapter. If you previously used your sound card in the DOS environment and used SBP-MIX, you must first unload SBP-MIX before running Windows applications that access your Sound Blaster sound card.

Note **About Conflicting TSR IDs:** If you get a message that SBP-MIX is already loaded though you know it's not, you have a conflict with another TSR (memory-resident) program that uses the same TSR ID as SBP-MIX, so the mixer program thinks it's already loaded. To solve this conflict, remove the other TSR (this may require rebooting). Or you can get an updated SBP-MIX program from Creative Labs that will load without any hitches; this updated version checks to see if the same TSR ID is already used before trying to load with that ID. Look for an updated mixer program on the Creative Labs bulletin board (BBS) or call their technical support line.

Selecting Another Hot Key for SBP-MIX

To select another hot key, run SBP-MIX /K and add one of the SHIFT keys: CTRI, ALT, SHIFT-L for left shift or SHIFT-R for right shift. Add a number between 1 and 9 after the SHIFT key names. For example, to change the hot key to ALT-5 you should type **SBP–MIX /KALT-5.**

Unloading SBP-MIX

You will usually want to keep SBP-MIX loaded, so you can pop it up while running other programs, but there are situations where you will need to unload it. (Bear in mind that by unloading it, you free up 75K for use by other programs.)

To unload the pop-up mixer, type **SBP–MIX /U** and then press ENTER.

Popping Up the Mixer Program

You can pop up the mixer program when working with other software programs, such as your favorite word processor, by pressing ALT-1, or whatever hot key you have selected. Some software programs, however, take over the keyboard and prevent the mixer program from seeing the hot-key combination. For example, the FM Intelligent Organ will let you pop up the mixer program from the Organ's main screen, the one which shows function keys F1 through F8, but not after you press F2 and go to the Play screen.

Popping Up the Mixer Program in Graphics Mode

Many software programs run in graphics mode. To avoid causing display problems in the graphics environment, SBP-MIX will appear only as a single command line at the bottom of your screen. You can see this by invoking SBP-MIX during a multimedia presentation, such as the MMDEMO multimedia demonstration. On the bottom of your screen you will see this:

```
SBP-MIX function: Exit
```

To work within this line and access the SBP-MIX functions available, press UP ARROW. Just imagine you are viewing the full-screen mixer program main menu, and moving the cursor from the bottom choice (Exit) to the top choice (Card reset). To adjust volume, for instance, once the desired volume function is displayed, use LEFT ARROW to reduce the volume and RIGHT ARROW to increase the volume. You can also use the LEFT ARROW and RIGHT ARROW keys to toggle on/off the choices offered by other functions, such as FM Channel.

In some circumstances, depending on the current graphics mode or the combination of foreground and background screen colors, you may be unable to see the value assigned to a mixer function. For example, you might be able to see the function name FM Volume but not the value indicating the current setting. Indeed, the function names themselves might not be clearly visible. You will then have to visualize what the mixer program control looks like while making adjustments. Try to avoid selecting Card Reset accidentally!

When you're done making adjustments, press DOWN ARROW until Exit reappears, and then press ENTER.

Using Hidden Mode

The recommended method for adjusting the mixer while in the midst of a multimedia presentation is to use the Hidden mode of SBP-MIX. You can turn on the Hidden mode by selecting the Hidden mode menu and then selecting On. Hidden mode lets you control all the mixer volume settings from the keyboard, without popping up the mixer program and interrupting your presentation.

Once Hidden mode is turned on, select the volume you want to control by pressing one of the following key-combinations:

Master volume   CTRL-ALT-M

Line-in   CTRL-ALT-L

FM   CTRL-ALT-F

CD   CTRL-ALT-C

VOC   CTRL-ALT-V

Microphone   CTRL-ALT-I

To control the volume, use the following key-combinations:

Increase volume   CTRL-ALT-U
Decrease volume   CTRL-ALT-D

You can also toggle sound output on and off with CTRL-ALT-Q.

Using the Features of SBP-MIX

Note   Many new features of the mixer program SBP-MIX, as discussed in this section, are not yet described in the Sound Blaster Pro User Reference Manual as this book goes to press. The SBP-SET program is better documented in the manual. The Windows Mixer program is also accurately portrayed in the most recent manual.

Card Reset

One of the most valuable features of SBP-MIX is the ability to reset your sound card from SBP-MIX. The SBP-MIX Card Reset menu selection restores the mixer settings, such as the source and master volume levels, to the default values. This is convenient because some software programs—games in particular—don't always return your sound card to its original state when they end, and may leave the controls at unnatural settings. By using the SBP-MIX Card Reset command, you can silence your audio card without having to press your computer's reset button or turn the power off. Note that CTRL-ALT-DEL will not reset your audio card.

Controlling the Master Volume and the Individual Source Volumes

SBP-MIX provides many useful controls, including those for setting the master volume and the volume for each source. For stereo sources and the master volume control, you can adjust both channels simultaneously, or the left and right channels independently.

You access all these controls from a menu that appears when you press the hot key. For example, when you first select the master volume control, a marker appears at the top of the middle slide, which shows the average sound level. Press the RIGHT ARROW key to move this marker to the slide on the right, and adjust the right channel volume up or down by using the UP ARROW or DOWN ARROW keys, respectively.

The ADC Test On/Off menu item, when it is selected, displays a horizontal sound-level meter (similar in concept to an analog "VU" meter) near the bottom of your screen. Before turning this meter on, select the input you wish to check from the ADC Channel menu item: microphone, CD, or line-in. The extent to which the bar spreads dynamically from the center shows the instantaneous sound level of the selected source. Note how the color of the bar changes with each measurement, helping your eye compare instantaneous changes in volume.

The ADC Channel menu item also lets you toggle between the low- and high-frequency settings for the input filter. This filter is useful for minimizing noise, especially aliasing (a high frequency ringing noise) that results from the analog-to-digital conversion process inherent to recording voice files.

Controlling FM Steering

SBP-MIX also lets you control FM steering, a feature not available with SBP-SET or with the Windows 3.1 Sound Blaster Pro Mixer. The FM channel settings are as follows:

☐ *No Steering.* The left channel FM synthesizer output is fed to the left speaker, and the right channel is fed to the right speaker. This is the usual, default setting.

- ☐ *Steer to Left.* Left and right FM synthesizer channel output is combined and fed to the left speaker; nothing goes to the right speaker.

- ☐ *Steer to Right.* Left and right FM channels are combined and fed to the right speaker; nothing goes to the left speaker.

- ☐ *Mute.* Neither FM channel is fed to the speakers.

 Tip Game software will sometimes direct both FM channels to one speaker and, when the game is ended, will leave your sound card in that state. If you hear sound coming out of one speaker only, try correcting the problem by selecting No Steering.

SBP-SET (SB Pros Only)

SBP-SET is similar to the pop-up SBP-MIX program—both programs control the mixer on your Sound Blaster Pro card. But SBP-SET does not load into and stay in memory, as does the pop-up mixer. You run SBP-SET, with a series of command switches, by typing a line at the DOS prompt.

SBP-SET is ideal for setting up your mixer before doing routine procedures, such as preparing for a recording session, because it can be executed from a batch file and doesn't take up valuable conventional memory. It is typically run from AUTOEXEC.BAT to set up the sound card every time the computer is turned on.

SBP-SET's Control of Mixer Features

The following mixer features can be controlled by SBP-SET, using the switches listed in the table when you enter the command to start the program. The default values for the settings are shown in square brackets.

Switch	Function	Values/[Default]
/R	Reset mixer	
/LINE	Input line volume control	0-15 [0]
/FM	Input FM synthesizer volume control	0-15 [9]
/CD	Input CD-ROM player volume control	0-15 [0]
/X	Input microphone volume control	0-7 [0]
/M	Master (output) volume control	0-15 [9]
/ADCS	Recording source selection	MIC/CD/LINE [MIC]
/ADCF	Input (recording) filter	LOW/HIGH [LOW]
/ANFI	Input filter switch	ON/OFF [ON]
/DNFI	Output filter switch	ON/OFF [ON]
/Q	Quiet mode (suppress message output)	

An important use of SBP-SET is to reset the sound output and mixer settings of your sound board to their defaults. Type **SBP-SET /R** at the DOS prompt and then press ENTER.

Note   SBP-SET has been improved recently, so what you read here may not match the description in your manual. To get a screen of help information indicating the capabilities of your mixer program, type **SBP-SET /H** at the DOS command-line prompt and then press ENTER.

Running SBP-SET

To run SBP-SET, first switch to the \SBPRO directory. Then type the start-up command followed by any optional command switches you want to use, and press ENTER. The command syntax is

SBP-SET /setting1 /setting2 /setting3 ...

The following command example shows how to set up the mixer for listening to your CD player:

SBP-SET /M:6,8 /X:0 /ANFI:OFF /DNFI:OFF /Q /CD:12

The switches in the above example establish the following controls:

☐   Master volume (/M) is set to a comfortable level with a little extra boost to the right speaker.

☐   Microphone input (/X) is turned off to avoid picking up ambient noise (or perhaps the on/off switch is broken).

☐   Input filter (/ANFI) and output filter (/DNFI) are disabled, so that you can hear CD sound at its richest.

☐   Unnecessary messages are suppressed (/Q is present).

☐   CD input level (/CD) is set to a suitable level

You can accomplish these same controls (except for control over the filters) from the pop-up mixer program SBP-MIX, but by placing these settings in a batch file you can easily restore your mixer settings.

Mastering SBP-SET

You don't have to specify all your mixer settings with one SBP-SET command. SBP-SET changes only the mixer settings you specify, so you may find it more convenient to first specify the master volume level, and then the individual sources' volume levels, and so forth.

Only the settings you specify are revised from their previous settings. For instance, the SBP-SET example provided just above, for listening to your CD player, does not include a command switch for setting the FM Synthesizer volume level. As a result, SBP-SET will not change the FM Synthesizer volume from its previous level.

 Note   Since SBP-SET doesn't restore settings to their defaults, you should always set the volume control to 0 for all sources you don't use.

The Input Filter

For the input filter (the /ADCF switch), the LOW setting is intended for voice recording through the microphone input, and the HIGH setting is recommended for high-quality speech and music. The default is on for /ANFI and off for /ADCF.

The Output Filter

The output filter (the /DNFI switch) is also a low-pass filter, similar in characteristics to the input filter in a HIGH setting. The purpose of the output filter is to suppress noise found in poor recordings. When playing your CD player, you will get the best fidelity by turning this filter off. When playing digital audio files, it is best to enable this filter. The default setting is ON.

Volume Settings

SBP-SET volume settings range from 0 to 15. The master volume control and all input sources except the microphone have 16 steps. The microphone has 8 steps only. This means, for example, that microphone settings of either 14 or 15 will result in the same volume, the highest volume level.

Sound Blaster Pro Mixer (SB Pro/Windows Only)

The Sound Blaster Pro Mixer (SB Pro Mixer) is a Windows mixer applet provided by Creative Labs. This easy-to-use mixer program, as shown in Figure 6-2, controls both the source and master volumes, and the input filter as well.

At this time, the two DOS mixer programs, SBP-MIX and SBP-SET have more features than the Windows SB Pro mixer. For example, controls available in SBP-MIX but not the Windows mixer program include FM channel steering and board reset.

FIGURE
6-2

The Sound Blaster Pro Mixer screen

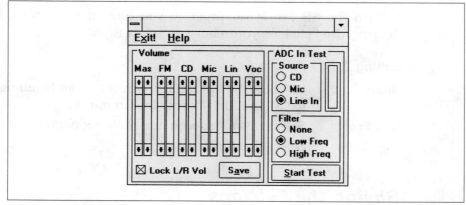

Loading and Running SB Pro Mixer

To load the SB Pro Mixer program, first start Windows 3.1. Double-click on the Accessories group, and then double-click on the Sound Blaster Pro Mixer icon. (This assumes you followed the installation recommendation to place the Sound Blaster Pro Mixer into the Accessories group; see Appendix A.)

Tip   Take advantage of Windows 3.1's ability to assign a shortcut to an icon. Assign a convenient hot key, such as CTRL-ALT-1, to your SB Pro Mixer program, so you can easily access it.

Volume Control

When the SB Pro Mixer program is first launched, both the left and right channels of the stereo volume controls are locked together. Remove the X from the Lock L/R Vol control to adjust the channels independently. Note that the leftmost volume control, titled Mas, is the master volume control.

Input Filter

With the SB Pro Mixer program you have three choices for input filtering. Just click on your choice to select it.

Setting	Function
None	Disables the input filter. Select this for listening to CD and high-fidelity line-in music.
Low Freq	Select this for speech and noise reduction.
High Freq	Select this for music.

Saving the Settings

To save your current settings, so that they will be automatically restored whenever you start Windows, click on the Save button.

The ADC Test

The SB Pro Mixer's ADC Test feature is like an analog "VU meter." The height of the bar indicates the intensity of the selected source. If the bar reaches the top, the source volume level is excessive and distortion is occurring. Click on the source you wish to monitor, and then click on the Start Test button. When done, click on the Stop Test button.

CHAPTER

Sound Blaster
Multimedia Software

This chapter presents a suite of programs for creating multimedia presentations. You are provided with a complete set of tools for combining video, music and voice-overs. The following programs are available with the Sound Blaster Pro and Sound Blaster 16 only:

- MMPLAY

- SBSIM

- VOICE

- MUSIC

- SOUNDFX

MMPLAY, the Multimedia Player, integrates other utilities such as VPLAY and VREC (see Chapter 4, "Play and Record Utilities,") into a tool for playing an eye-catching audio/visual presentation.

SBSIM is a toolbox that is the foundation for the Sound Blaster multimedia environment. It loads and unloads drivers for you automatically, reducing the complexity of selecting the correct drivers.

Once SBSIM is loaded, you can use SBSIM's sound utilities: VOICE, MUSIC, and SOUNDFX. VOICE is similar to VPLAY but is more powerful. MUSIC is similar to PLAYCMF and PLAYMIDI but has more power and flexibility. SOUNDFX does special effects such as panning and fading. VOICE, MUSIC, and SOUNDFX give you complete mastery over the audio component of your MMPLAY presentations.

Note This chapter is designed to supplement your Creative Labs manual sections about the above products. It clarifies areas of confusion, provides missing explanations, offers some hints, and reveals some secrets. This chapter is not intended to serve as a replacement for your manual, and so information that is readily accessible in your Creative Labs manual is not repeated here. Many of the utilities described, such as SOUNDFX, are extensively documented in the manual and need little additional comment.

Note Throughout this chapter you will encounter the abbreviation SB Pro (Sound Blaster Pro).

MMPLAY

The MMPLAY Multimedia Player is a powerful DOS tool for playing multimedia (audio/video) presentations. You can write a script, using a simple programming language, to combine Autodesk Animator screen animation (.FLI) files with Sound Blaster Pro audio, including digitized audio voice files (.VOC), Creative Music Files (.CMF), MIDI music files (.MID), and CD tracks.

 Note   To play Microsoft wave (.WAV) files, use the WAV2VOC utility to first convert them to .VOC files.

To get familiar with script writing for the Multimedia Player, you should start off by writing a simple script. Copy the MMDEMO.ACT sample script, eliminate all but the first few commands, and begin your experimentation with this script. Use a simple ASCII text file editor to create these scripts. (Chapter 2 tells you about ASCII file editing.)

The MMPLAY Commands

The information in this section supplements what you will read about MMPLAY commands in your SB Pro manual. Once you are comfortable using MMPLAY with utilities such as PLAYCMF, PLAYMIDI, and VPLAY, you will want to read the discussion of SBSIM in an upcoming section. The SBSIM utilities can add even more power to MMPLAY presentations.

 Note   When using MMPLAY, always start playing your audio sources *before* using the .APLAY or .APLAY1 commands to show animation.

About Synchronizing Animation with Sound

The .APLAY command "plays" an Autodesk Animator flick (.FLI) file containing a slide show of images. As MMPLAY is playing a flick file, it watches for *synchronization markers* that are embedded in audio voice (.VOC), MIDI (.MID) and Creative Music (.CMF) files. A synchronization marker is typically embedded at the end of the voice or sound track. When the marker is reached, the slide show is terminated, and the next command line in the script file is executed. Once .APLAY has been terminated by a synchronization marker, that marker is discarded. A new .SYNC command must be issued to establish the conditions for terminating the next .APLAY animation sequence.

.APLAY

The .APLAY command is best used in conjunction with the .SYNC command. When the synchronization marker specified by .SYNC is detected, .APLAY terminates and the next command in the script is executed.

Note It is recommended that you avoid using .APLAY without an accompanying .SYNC command, for the purpose of repeating an animation sequence until a key is pressed. This technique does not work reliably.

While testing new scripts, you may need to interrupt the .APLAY command. CTRL-END will stop the command but may cause MMPLAY to misbehave. If your screen display begins to look strange, press CTRL-C to interrupt MMPLAY.

If you find yourself in a screen display mode where the DOS prompt appears in large letters (or perhaps a blank screen), type **MODE CO80** to switch to normal color, 80-character mode, and press ENTER. MODE is a program that comes with DOS that should be in your DOS directory.

.REPEAT

MMPLAY will repeatedly execute all commands placed between the .REPEAT and .END commands. The .REPEAT command is followed by a number from 1 to 999 that specifies how many times to repeat the command sequence.

.PAUSE

The .PAUSE command causes MMPLAY to pause before executing the next command in the script. This is useful for pausing between .FLI animation sequences. Music continues to play while MMPLAY waits for you to press any key. This is similar to the slide presentation technique of pressing a button when you are ready for the next slide.

.WAIT

The .WAIT command is similar to the .PAUSE command; it causes MMPLAY to pause before executing the next command in the script. The .WAIT command is special, however, because it pauses execution until a synchronization marker, specified by an earlier .SYNC command, is encountered in the voice (.VOC), Creative Music (.CMF) or MIDI (.MID) file currently playing.

.SYNC

The .SYNC command posts a synchronization marker value which, when detected, terminates the .APLAY command or triggers the .WAIT command. The .SYNC markers are inserted into a .VOC file by Sound Blaster Pro's sound editor, VEDIT2. The markers can also be inserted into a voice file when using JOINTVOC, the utility program that combines small voice files.

.REM

The .REM statement lets you insert a remark into the script file. MMPLAY will ignore this line when it plays, automatically advancing to the next line.

Note You must follow an .REM with at least one space, or MMPLAY will become confused and report that the command is in error.

.VOUT

The .VOUT command plays a .VOC digital audio file. This usually consists of a short voice-over.

.EXECUTE

As its name suggests, .EXECUTE executes a DOS command line. It is most commonly used to run the sophisticated sound utilities provided in the SBSIM environment. It can also be used to trigger an external device, such as CD video player, by sending a command to the serial port.

The discussion of the SOUNDFX utility, part of the SBSIM Sound Blaster Standard Programming Tool, illustrates use of the .EXECUTE command.

Note   SBSIM and its related utilities are ideal companions for MMPLAY. Your MMPLAY script can run the SBSIM utilities through the .EXECUTE command. Once you have become familiar with MMPLAY, try writing MMPLAY scripts taking advantage of SBSIM.

Multimedia Script Example

To better explain the synchronization of animation graphics with sound, consider the following example that repeatedly plays a new product demonstration.

First, you need to create a voice file called MARKER.VOC containing a synchronization marker of value 99 embedded between two related voice tracks, as illustrated below in pseudo code:

```
"...and now introducing"
silence block
sync marker 99 block
"the new 586 PC"
```

The following extract from a script would begin to play the MARKER.VOC voice-over. Just before the words "the new 586 PC" are spoken, it will display an animation of a 586 PC appearing from behind a curtain:

```
.rem Previous flick's last screen still appears...
.rem "Introducing the 586 .."
.sync V99
.vout marker.voc
.rem Now show 586 PC floating down from space while
.rem announcer says "...what a beauty to behold"
.aplay 586.fli
```

You can add markers to voice files by using either JOINTVOC or VEDIT2. (See JOINTVOC in Chapter 5, "Sample Editing and Manipulation," of this book to learn how the file MARKER.VOC was created.) To add markers to MIDI files, use a sequencer program such as the Sequencer Plus Pro. At this writing there is no utility available to add a marker to a Creative .CMF music file.

Note   Windows 3.1 includes an application called the Media Player that is documented in their reference manual. Do not confuse the Windows Media Player with the Creative Labs MMPLAY utility. The Windows Media Player plays multimedia files and controls hardware devices, such as a videodisc player. Creative Labs's MMPLAY is a DOS utility program that integrates audio and visual files into a presentation. The Windows Media Player is similar in look to the Creative Labs CDPLYR DOS utility, and similar in function to Creative Labs JukeBox Windows utility; both these utilities are discussed in Chapter 4.

SBSIM

The Sound Blaster Pro is shipped with SBSIM (the Sound Blaster Standard Programming Tool environment), a powerful and easy-to-use environment for experimenting with sound sources and creating the right effects for audio/visual presentations. SBSIM has already proven its value—it was used by Creative Labs for presentations given to the investment community that led to Creative Labs, Inc.'s successful initial public offering.

SBSIM makes your life easier by loading and unloading necessary drivers. In addition, it reads a configuration file that remembers settings for buffer allocation, MIDI format, CD speaker switching, and so forth. SBSIM is the required foundation for using three powerful utility programs discussed in upcoming sections: VOICE, which plays digitized audio (.VOC); MUSIC, which plays Creative Music Files (.CMF) and MIDI music files (.MID); and SOUNDFX. VOICE and MUSIC are much more powerful than their simpler cousins, VPLAY, PLAYCMF, and PLAYMIDI. The SOUNDFX utility adds special effects, such as panning and fading.

SBSIM and its associated utilities are ideal partners for the MMPLAY Multimedia Player. The following batch files will make SBSIM even easier to use. They load both SBSIM and the optional drivers, and then unload them in the correct order.

Note   If the subdirectory location of your drivers does not match that shown below, you will need to revise these two batch files to specify the correct paths.

```
rem LOAD.BAT
rem Load SBSIM and optional drivers
\sbpro\sbfmdrv
\sbpro\playmidi\sbmidi
\sbpro\sbsim\sbsim

rem UNLOAD.BAT
rem Unload SBSIM and optional drivers
\sbpro\sbsim /U
\sbpro\playmidi\sbmidi /U
\sbpro\sbfmdrv /U
```

One drawback to SBSIM is that it may take more conventional memory than using just VPLAY or PLAYCMF alone. This is because the drivers are loaded regardless of whether they are really necessary. Your Sound Blaster Pro manual states that with SBSIM you can load voice files (.VOC) into extended memory, conserving scarce conventional memory. This feature is no longer important, however, because recent versions of VPLAY can play voice files that are larger than available conventional memory (see Chapter 4).

To run SBSIM utilities from MMPLAY, you will use the MMPLAY .EXECUTE command. For example, the following sequence will play the Creative Music File FAIRY.CMF in the \SBPRO\MMPLAY subdirectory, at half speed, and then launch animation flick Z2:

```
.execute \sbpro\sbsim\music /play:fairy /temp:50
.execute \sbpro\sbsim\soundfx start
.aplay1 z2
```

VOICE

The VOICE utility, which works in conjunction with SBSIM, is similar to VPLAY, a simpler utility for playing digitized audio (.VOC) files. VOICE has additional features, such as the ability to pause and resume playing.

Normally, VOICE returns control immediately to the DOS prompt or to a batch file. If you use the /WAIT command switch, VOICE waits until it has finished playing before returning control. If you use the /WAIT command with a synchronization marker specified, VOICE begins playing immediately but does not return control until after the marker is encountered.

Another feature of VOICE is that it can use extended memory, provided by SBSIM, to hold voice files. Although the Creative Labs manual suggests that this is important, it is not that significant given that VOICE can play voice files directly from disk.

MUSIC

The MUSIC utility, which works in conjunction with SBSIM, is similar to PLAYCMF and PLAYMIDI, simpler utilities for playing Creative Music (.CMF) and MIDI (.MID) files, respectively. MUSIC has many additional features, such as the ability to pause and resume, and to wait for a synchronization marker or until the end of the song. Other powerful features available for .CMF files are the ability to change tempo, transpose into another key, and do endless repetition.

SOUNDFX

SOUNDFX, as its name implies, is a sound-effects utility that works in conjunction with SBSIM to provide panning, fade-in, and fade-out effects to any single source or to the master volume.

SOUNDFX works as described in the manual, but the manual doesn't point out one very important fact: Nothing happens until you issue the start command! That command is

SOUNDFX start

Refer to your Sound Blaster Pro manual for the full list of SOUNDFX commands.

You will notice that the Sound Blaster Pro manual says that volume levels can range from 0 (no sound) to 255 (maximum sound), though the mixer on your sound card only supports 16 settings for the master volume control. SOUNDFX lets you specify values from 0 to 255, but all the values within a "step" have the same effect. For instance, any value entered from 0 to 15 has the same effect, that is, step 0, which turns off the sound.

CHAPTER

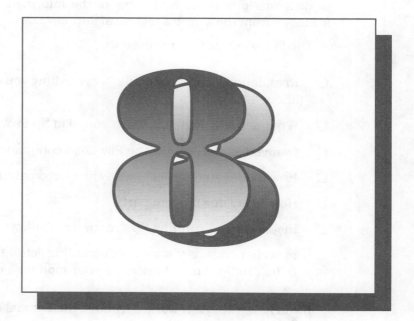

Sequencer Plus Pro

Voyetra's Sequencer Plus Pro (Sp Pro) is an introductory DOS-based MIDI sequencing and editing program that comes bundled with the Sound Blaster Pro and the Sound Blaster MIDI Kit. This MIDI kit can be purchased for the Sound Blaster, Sound Blaster Pro Basic, and the Sound Blaster MCV versions. Sp Pro is nearly identical to Voyetra's entry-level sequencing software, the Sequencer Plus Junior.

In this chapter you will find some tips and advice on using Sp Pro. The information included here was selected according to three criteria: Some facts are already presented in the Sp Pro manual, but not adequately emphasized. Some information wasn't available when the Sp Pro manual or disk was produced. And some of the information is new, based on feedback from the Voyetra technical support staff.

The following topics are covered:

- Installation issues, particularly everything you ever wanted to know about TAPI drivers.

- What actually happens when you load Sp Pro?

- Demystification of how the File Load command works.

- How to add stereo effects with the stereo panning feature.

- How to lay down drum parts.

- Installing and running Sp Pro under Windows 3.1.

- Miscellaneous hardware tips, including getting your MIDI keyboard to talk to Sp Pro and selecting your monitor's display mode.

If you haven't already worked through the Tutorial of the Sp Pro manual, this is a good time to do so. There you will find all the basic program commands; we are assuming you already have a familiarity with operating Sp Pro, such as how to start and stop song play (by pressing the SPACEBAR) and how to delete all the tracks (by the Delete All command).

Connecting MIDI Instruments to the Sound Blaster

This section provides extensive background on the TAPI drivers and Creative Labs sound board versions. The Sp Pro software will misbehave if the correct driver is not loaded, and the information presented here may save you time in diagnosing a problem. This information supplements the installation instructions provided in your Sp Pro manual.

 Note The illustrations and figures in this section display the 25-row screens of a CGA or monochrome/Hercules graphics monitor. If you have a high-resolution EGA or VGA monitor, your screens will look different from those illustrated here. Sp Pro takes advantage of your higher-resolution monitor to display more tracks or other information. We have used the 25-row screen shots because they are easier to see on the printed page.

All the Sound Blaster cards have a MIDI (Musical Instrument Digital Interface) port built in. The MIDI international standard defines how synthesizers, musical keyboards, and computers should communicate. By means of this standard, all electronic instruments can communicate regardless of their origin or of the make of computer.

MIDI data is in digital form and consists of a variety of messages. The most commonly used are Note On (when to play a note), Note Off (when to stop playing a note), Velocity (how loudly to play the note), and Instrument Number (what instrument should play the note).

Two pins on the Sound Blaster's joystick connector are used to receive MIDI data (MIDI In) and send MIDI data (MIDI Out). If you own a Sound Blaster Pro, the interface cable necessary for MIDI connections is included. If you own a Sound Blaster 1.x/2.0 or a Sound Blaster Pro Basic, you can purchase the MIDI Kit from Creative Labs, Inc.

The MIDI interface cable connects to the joystick port on the Sound Blaster card. On one end of the cable is a 15-pin male connector that plugs into the joystick port. On the other end is a female 15-pin connector and two 5-pin DIN-type connectors (the round ones). The female 15-pin connector is for your joystick, so that you don't lose the functionality of the joystick connector on the Sound Blaster card. The two 5-pin DINs are the MIDI In and MIDI Out connectors and are labeled as such.

When connecting a MIDI instrument such as a keyboard, the Out cable from the Sound Blaster MIDI interface connects to the In port on the back of the keyboard; and the In cable of the Sound Blaster MIDI interface connects to the Out port of the keyboard. This may sound backwards to you at first; to make it easier to understand, just remember that the data that comes *out* of the Sound Blaster goes *into* to the keyboard, and the data that comes *out* of the keyboard goes *into* the Sound Blaster.

Some keyboards and synthesizer modules also have a MIDI Thru connector. This connection simply duplicates any data that comes into the In port. By connecting a cable from the Thru port to another synthesizer's In port, the computer or keyboard can control two MIDI instruments. Then, if the second MIDI instrument also has a Thru port, it can be connected to the In port of another MIDI instrument.

 Caution   Hooking up more than a few synthesizers by means of MIDI Thru ports can affect the timing of music playback. The Thru port incurs a very short delay when copying the information from the In port. Thus, after several copies, a note can be noticeably delayed.

Once you have made the proper connections, anything you play on the keyboard can be recorded by the computer. Likewise, any data in the computer can be played back on the keyboard. Of course, you need software to accomplish the recording and playback; this software is called a *sequencer*. Voyetra's Sequencer Plus that comes with your Pro card (or MIDI Kit if you bought it separately) is just the software you need to record, edit, and play back your musical compositions.

Understanding the TAPI Driver

Sp Pro uses a special driver called the TAPI driver. (TAPI is an acronym for Tertiary Application Program Interface; "tertiary" because TAPI complements Voyetra's SAPI and VAPI drivers.) The TAPI driver allows the Sp Pro software to talk to the Creative Labs Sound Blaster sound cards.

Because Sp Pro uses this software driver, a single version of the program can work with all versions of Sound Blaster and Sound Blaster Pro.

The TAPI driver is a terminate-and-stay-resident program (TSR) that, once loaded, remains in memory. In order for Sp Pro to work, you must first load the correct TAPI driver. When you are done with Sp Pro, the TAPI driver is removed to free memory for other applications. The SP.BAT batch file that you use to start SP Pro, automatically loads the TAPI driver before it runs SPPro. After you quit SP Pro, the batch file automatically removes TAPI before it returns control to you at the DOS prompt.

There are two different TAPI drivers for the Sound Blaster: TAPISB and TAPISB3. TAPISB is used with the Sound Blaster 1.x/2.0 cards and the two-operator Sound Blaster Pro card. TAPISB3 is used with the newer four-operator Sound Blaster Pro 2 (CT-1600 is stenciled clearly on the Pro 2 circuit board; look for it close to the top edge). The installation program for Sp Pro examines the SET BLASTER= string in your AUTOEXEC.BAT file to determine the correct TAPI driver to install. The installation program also modifies the SP.BAT file to ensure that the correct driver is loaded for Sp Pro.

Checking for the Correct TAPI Driver

When you install your Sound Blaster software, the installation program detects the card model and modifies your AUTOEXEC.BAT file to identify the characteristics of the card. Your AUTOEXEC.BAT contains an environment variable called BLASTER that indicates the DMA, IRQ, I/O address, and card version number (the T number). Based on the value assigned to T, the Voyetra/Creative Labs Sp Pro installation program installs the correct driver.

Early versions of the Sound Blaster installation program didn't always set the BLASTER variable correctly. Accordingly, the Voyetra/Creative Labs installation program for Sp Pro is sometimes given incorrect information about which card is installed. As a result, it is possible that you have a TAPISB driver installed when you should have TAPISB3 installed. This should have little or no effect upon the performance of your Sound Blaster, but we recommend you contact Voyetra to receive instructions on how to install the correct driver.

There are two methods to find out which TAPI driver is loaded by Sp Pro:

□ Use the DOS Type command on the SP.BAT file in the \VOYETRA (or \SBPRO) directory, and look to see if it says TAPISB or TAPISB3.

□ While working with Sp Pro, you can display the Hardware Configuration screen by pressing F3 from the main screen and then typing H. If you see a name under Auxiliary Sound Drivers such as Voyetra OPL3 FM Driver for Sound Blaster Pro, or something similar that references OPL3, you have the TAPISB3 driver running.

Figure 8-1 below shows the configuration screen for a Sound Blaster Pro that has the wrong driver installed (TAPISB instead of TAPISB3). Note that this driver is the first version that supports General MIDI, indicated by the *GM*.

General MIDI TAPI Drivers

Newer versions of Sp Pro include TAPI drivers that provide Sound Blaster with a General MIDI implementation. Prior to establishment of the General MIDI standard, there was no single standard for the assignment of instrument sounds (*patches*) to channels. An even greater

Sp Pro Hardware Configuration screen

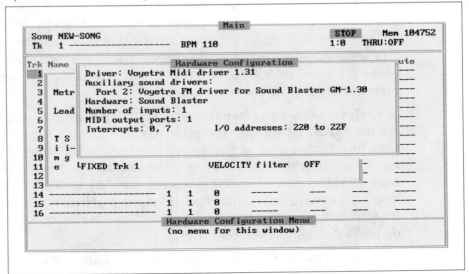

FIGURE 8-1

problem was that the *patch layout* (the assignment of numbers to patches) differed from synthesizer to synthesizer. As a result, a MIDI song might play different instruments on different synthesizers.

A General MIDI driver is one that conforms to the Standard MIDI File Specification, and uses the patch map and drum note map specified by the General MIDI standard. This means your MIDI song will automatically play the correct instrument on the FM synthesizer of your sound card. Without a General MIDI driver, you might have to use a MIDI mapper, such as the MIDI Mapper utility that comes with Windows 3.1, to make the correct assignments. In particular, the driver expects that channel 16 will be used for the drum parts of a base-level synthesizer. This assignment conflicts with the earlier Roland standard, but ensures compatibility with Microsoft Windows 3.1 multimedia extensions.

The new General MIDI-compliant TAPI drivers are identified by a version number of 1.30 or higher and a *GM* prefix in front of the version number. The version number is displayed when the driver loads. When you use the SP.BAT batch file to load the driver, you won't have time to see the driver version number. You can load the driver without loading Sp Pro by running the DRIVER.BAT batch file. Switch to the directory where your Sequencer is located by typing **CD\VOYETRA** (or **CD\SBPRO**) and then press ENTER. To load the driver alone, type **DRIVER** and press ENTER. Once you've checked the driver version, type **DRIVER /REM** to remove the driver from memory.

Almost all commercial MIDI files available today (including Voyetra's MusiClips library) are mapped for General MIDI. The main benefit of the new General MIDI TAPI drivers is that they allow you to play these files and use them with Sp Pro without having to remap them. The major changes to General MIDI TAPI drivers are as follows:

☐   The TAPI driver's default patch map and drum note map fully comply with General MIDI and are considerably different from the older TAPIs.

☐   Your Sound Blaster will now use channel 16 as its drum channel. Older versions of the TAPI drivers used channel 10.

Note   If you own an older TAPI driver that does not comply with General MIDI, you can obtain an update by contacting Creative Labs technical support at 408-428-6622. Or log onto the technical support bulletin board (BBS) at 408-428-6660. Voyetra Technologies also maintains a BBS at 914-738-7218. When you download the TAPI driver from the Creative Labs or Voyetra BBS, you can also download text files containing the new patch and drum maps, as well as instructions for remapping older MIDI files.

Starting Sp Pro and Loading Sound Files

Note   There are several versions of the installation program for the Sequencer Plus Pro. This chapter assumes your installation program has placed the Sp Pro software in a directory called VOYETRA. If your Sp Pro is in directory SPPRO instead, substitute SPPRO for VOYETRA in all the instructions throughout this chapter.

This section describes how to load and run Sp Pro on a DOS-based computer. From the DOS prompt, you will run the SP batch file (SP.BAT), which loads the TAPI driver, runs Sp Pro, and then automatically unloads the TAPI driver when you quit.

To start Sp Pro, type **SP** and press ENTER. You will see the Voyetra sign-on screen. Press any key to advance to the Main screen (Figure 8-2), or wait a few seconds for the Main screen to appear.

Note   If you type *SPPRO* instead of SP to start Sp Pro, you will receive an error message, "TAPI Driver Not Installed." Press any key to begin Sp Pro in demonstration mode. Then type *g* twice to return to the DOS prompt and start again.

Loading Sound Files to Play with Sp Pro

In this section you will find instructions for loading files to play in Sp Pro, including the two favorite types of sound files: Sequencer Plus song files (.SNG) and MIDI files (.MID). These procedures are a bit confusing in the Sp Pro manual.

FIGURE
8-2

Sp Pro Main screen

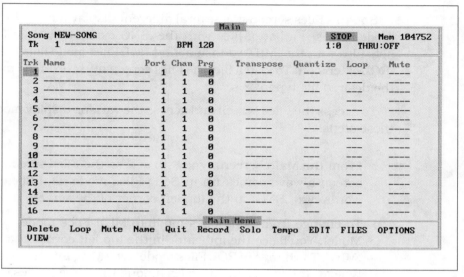

Tip If your Sound Blaster or Sound Blaster Pro works fine with other software packages that came with your sound card, but won't work with the Sp Pro, you probably have a DMA conflict. Refer to Appendix B for instructions on resolving this conflict.

You can load and play three different types of files with Sp Pro:

☐ Sequencer Plus song files (.SNG)

☐ Standard MIDI files (.MID)

☐ AdLib song files (.ROL)

Sp Pro comes bundled with a number of .SNG song files and standard MIDI files to get you started. Both the MIDI files and the .SNG files are located in the \VOYETRA\SONGS subdirectory. As with most programs, you must "navigate" to the drive and directory where the desired file is located in order to load it.

Switching Among the Files Display Modes

Sp Pro's Files screen has several different display modes. In Song Files mode, you see a list of files with the .SNG extension; MIDI Files mode lists files with the .MID extension; and ROL Files mode lists files with the .ROL extension. To load a file, the Files screen must be in the mode listing the desired file type.

To access the Files screen and access the various display modes, follow these steps:

1. From the Main screen, type **F** to access the Files screen. The Files screen always comes up in Song Files mode, as indicated by the words "Ext .SNG" in the top left corner of the screen.

2. To change from Song Files mode to MIDI Files mode, type **M**. (for Mode). You'll see the indicator in the top left corner change to "Ext .MID". To change to ROL Files mode, type **M** again. As you repeatedly type **M**, the Files screen cycles among the three modes.

3. After you're seen all the mode displays, press ESC to return to the Main screen.

Loading a Song (.SNG) File

Here are the steps to load a song (.SNG) file from the Files screen:

1. From the Main screen, type **F** to access the Files screen. The Files screen always comes up in Song Files mode, as indicated by "Ext .SNG" in the top left corner of the screen.

2. Using the arrow keys, highlight one of the listed files, type **L**, and then press ENTER to load the file.

Once the file loads, Sp Pro returns to the Main screen.

Loading a MIDI (.MID) File

When you load a MIDI file, its tracks are appended to other tracks.

1. If you're in the Main screen, which shows the track assignments, and want to clear out the existing tracks first before loading the file, type **D** and then **A** to delete all tracks.

2. From the Main screen, type **F** to access the Files screen. To switch to MIDI Files mode, type **M** until you see "Ext .MID" in the top left corner of the screen.

3. Using the arrow keys, navigate to the \VOYETRA\SONGS directory by highlighting SONGS (see Figure 8-3). Press ENTER to move into this directory.

4. Highlight one of the listed .MID files, type **L**, and press ENTER.

5. On the bottom left corner of your screen, you will see the word "Meters" highlighted. The message "Accept timesig" will appear below "Meters." Press ENTER again.

6. The file now loads. Sp Pro returns to the Main screen, and you will see track names, as well as port, channel, and program assignments.

FIGURE 8-3   Selecting SONGS directory containing MIDI files

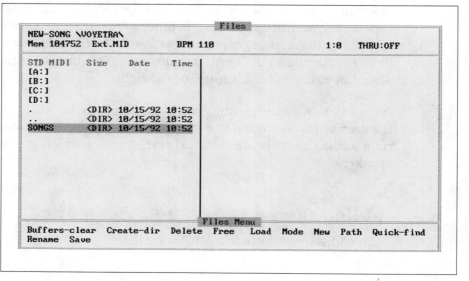

Some Special Techniques on Sp Pro

This section shows you how to take full advantage of the stereo capability of your Sound Blaster Pro by adding pan messages that give a stereo effect to your MIDI music. Another special technique described here is the procedure for quickly laying down a drum part using the QWERTY synthesizer. You'll also see how to do "one-finger" playing with the TAB key.

Stereo Panning

Sp Pro lets you control the left/right/center channel positioning of the Sound Blaster's on-board FM synthesizer, by using a type of MIDI message called a MIDI Pan message. *Panning* lets you assign individual tracks in Sp Pro to the left, right, or center channel of a stereo sound system. By using panning, you can often make a song sound fuller and more interesting. Also, changing the pan positioning as the song plays (that is, changing it dynamically) lets you add some unique and novel effects.

The various Sound Blaster models interpret MIDI Pan messages differently. Sound Blaster 1.x/2.0 and the older Sound Blaster Pro are capable of continuous panning. In other words, their notes can be placed left, center, right, or anywhere in between. The Sound Blaster Pro 2, on the other hand, can do "hard" panning only. This means its notes can be placed at either full left, center, or full right.

Note   Before experimenting with panning, make sure your Sound Blaster card is connected to a *stereo* sound system, and that the left and right audio channels are assigned correctly to your left and right stereo speakers.

Adding Stereo Effects to a Song File

To add stereo effects to a MIDI song file,

1. Load a song file and select a track to which you want to add panning effects.

2. Type **E** (for Edit) to bring up the Edit screen. Then type **M** to get the MIDI Edit screen. Examine Figure 8-4 to see what this screen looks like (on a VGA/EGA monitor it will look different).

3. The Class field is now highlighted. Press the + key on your numeric keypad to step through the MIDI event classes until you reach Controller.

4. Press DOWN ARROW to highlight the Type field. Enter the number **10** to select the pan positive controller, and press ENTER. The field now says "10 Pan Position."

Note The next step is to enter the pan value. This step requires that you know which version of Sound Blaster Pro you have. If you don't know this, refer to the previous section, "Checking for the Correct TAPI Driver."

5. Type **V** to input the pan position value

MIDI Edit screen for entering pan events

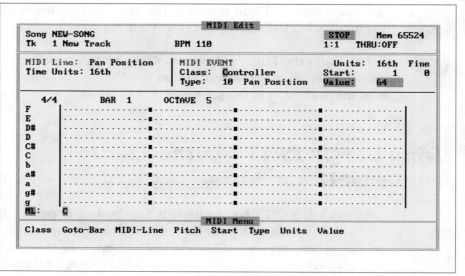

☐ *For Sound Blaster 1.x/2.0 and the two-operator Sound Blaster Pro,* enter a value between 0 and 127 (full left is 0, center is 64, and full right is 127). You can also enter values in between these; for example, 32 will position the notes halfway between left and center. This is called *continuous panning.*

☐ *For Sound Blaster Pro 2,* enter a value between 0 and 127 (full left is 0-31, center is 32-95, and full right is 96-127). Sound Blaster Pro 2 does *hard panning* only. Thus any value within these ranges will give the same result: a full left, center, or full right panning.

6. After entering a pan position value, press ENTER. This takes the highlight bar to the MIDI event line ("ML" at the bottom of the screen, above the menu selections).

7. To enter a pan event on the selected track, use the LEFT ARROW and RIGHT ARROW keys to move the cursor to the point (the note) on the MIDI Line where you want to insert the pan event. Then press the INS key, and you will see the letter *C* (for Controller) appear. You can enter additional pan events by repeating steps 5 through 7.

Tip   Once you've entered all the pan events you want, you can quickly move between them by pressing the TAB and SHIFT-TAB keys.

8. From the MIDI Edit screen or the Main screen, press the SPACEBAR to play back the song and hear your results.

Note   From the MIDI Edit screen, the play will resume from the first measure visible in the screen. From the Main screen, play will resume from the beginning of the song.

Using the QWERTY Synthesizer to Lay Down Drum Parts

Sp Pro's QWERTY (PC keyboard) Synthesizer is perfect for creating simple drum parts with your Sound Blaster card, especially if you don't feel like setting up your MIDI keyboard, or entering the notes manually from the Edit screen. So when you need to lay down a dance-type drum part that doesn't require much spontaneity, try using the QWERTY synthesizer.

Here are the steps to follow for laying down a drum part:

1. From the Main screen, choose an empty track and assign it to Port 2, Channel 16. Use the RIGHT ARROW key to move to these fields, type in the value, and press ENTER.

2. Set the tempo to about 110 beats per minute (BPM). Type **T** (for Tempo), enter **110**, and then press ENTER. Enable the Metronome by pressing F2.

Note Nothing on your screen will confirm that the Metronome is turned on after you press F2—trust that it works.

3. Type **R** to put Sp Pro into Record mode.

4. Press SHIFT-F1 to access the QWERTY Synthesizer. You will see a screen similar to Figure 8-5 (on a VGA/EGA monitor it will look different).

5. Use the + and – keys on the numeric keypad to set the Octave to 4.

QWERTY (PC keyboard) Synthesizer screen

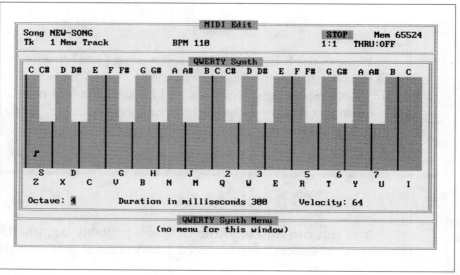

6. Try using the z key for bass drum and the x key for snare drum. You can even play the x and c keys with two fingers to do snare drum rolls.

7. Press the SPACEBAR to start recording your drum part. Press the SPACEBAR again when you're done.

Troubleshooting the QWERTY synthesizer

If, while following the steps above, you don't hear anything, or if you heard an instrument other than the drum from channel 16, you may have an older, non-General MIDI TAPI driver installed. If this is the case, first make certain you did select Octave 4 in step 5 above. The instrument mappings vary according to the octave, so selecting Octave 4 is essential.

If this doesn't solve your problem, check to see that the correct version of the TAPI driver is loaded. Display the Hardware Configuration screen by pressing F3 from the main screen, and then type H. At the top of the screen, in the Driver field, you should see something like "Voyetra Midi Driver 1.XX" where XX is a version number. If the version shown is earlier than 1.30, the TAPI driver supports the Roland MT-32 channel assignments. The Roland uses channel 10 for drums. If the version is 1.30 or later, the TAPI driver supports the general MIDI standard, with drums assigned to channel 16.

One-Finger Playing with the TAB Key

While in the Edit or Note Edit screens, you can advance from one note to the next using one finger, with the TAB key. This is sometimes useful for checking out a new melody, to find that one bad note in a track so you can edit it, or even just to have fun. Press SHIFT-TAB to go backwards one note at a time.

Using Sp Pro in Windows 3.1

You can run Sp Pro in the DOS compatibility box (the DOS prompt icon) within Microsoft Windows 3.1 environment, but special steps must be taken to do this. Although Windows 3.1 has drivers for the MIDI interface and FM synthesis, Sp Pro must use its own TAPI driver. In addition, Sp Pro and other DOS-based MIDI software cannot be loaded by Windows in 386 Enhanced mode (the default Windows mode on 386/486 computers). The TAPI driver must be loaded at the DOS prompt *before* you start Windows. Then Windows must be run in Standard mode; enter the command **WIN /S** at the DOS prompt.

Installing Sp Pro in the Windows 3.1 Environment

Before running a DOS application, such as Sp Pro, in Windows 3.1, you need to set up a Windows Program Item. You can put the Sp Pro icon in any Program Manager group you want.

How to Create an Sp Pro Icon

Follow the steps below to create an Sp Pro icon:

1. From the Windows Program Manager, double-click to activate the program group where you want to locate the Sp Pro icon. For example, you may want to put Sp Pro in the Accessories group.

2. From the File menu, choose New.

3. From the New Program Object dialog box, select Program Item then choose OK.

4. From the Program Item Properties dialog box, enter the word **Sp Pro** in the Description line.

5. For Command Line, type in the complete path and program file name of Sp Pro. In most cases, you will enter **C:\VOYETRA\SPPRO.EXE**.

6. From the Program Item Properties dialog box, click OK.

A new icon labeled "Sp Pro" will now be visible within the group that you selected.

If you have any trouble with the above instructions, or you wish to choose a different icon, refer to your Windows user's guide for further instructions on how to set up a Program Item for a DOS application.

Running Sp Pro in the Windows 3.1 Environment

Once you've designated the Sp Pro program icon, you can start it and run it exactly as if you loaded it from the DOS prompt. There is one major advantage of running Sp Pro from Windows, however: You don't need to load the SBP-MIX pop-up mixer program before running your Sp Pro program. While using Sp Pro in Windows, you can switch back to the desktop and use the Windows version of the Sound Blaster Pro Mixer program to control your sound card's mixer. See Chapter 6 for details on the mixer and mixer software.

Once you've created an icon for Sp Pro, it's very easy to run the program. (You might consider using a batch file to automatically load the TAPI driver and then start up Windows.) The steps for running Sp Pro under Windows 3.1 are as follows:

1. If you're still running Windows, exit to DOS.

2. Switch to the \VOYETRA directory by typing **CD \VOYETRA** at the DOS prompt and then press ENTER.

3. Load the TAPI driver by typing **TAPISB** or **TAPISB3**, and press ENTER.

Note If you're not certain which driver to load, review the previous section, "Checking for the Correct TAPI Driver."

4. Start Windows in Standard mode by typing **WIN /s**.

5. From the Program Manager, double-click on the Sp Pro icon.

If you have problems running Sp Pro from Windows 3.1—dropping MIDI notes, timing errors, or Windows error messages, for example—check to make sure you're running Windows in Standard mode, not 386

Enhanced mode. To find out what mode you're running in, choose About Program Manager... from the Program Manager's Help menu.

 Tip   If you have a modem, you can download an icon file for Sp Pro from the Voyetra Technologies Bulletin Board at 914-738-7218.

Some Tips About Sp Pro Hardware

The following hardware tips were provided by the technical support staff at Voyetra. These answer some of the most frequently asked questions.

MIDI Keyboard Problem: Beware of Cables Installed Backwards

Many first-time users of Sp Pro have trouble recording or playing with their external MIDI keyboard. Frequently this is because the MIDI cables connecting your Sound Blaster card and your keyboard are plugged in backwards. The ends of the Sound Blaster's MIDI cables are marked IN and OUT. The IN cable should be connected to your keyboard's OUT plug, because what your keyboard puts *out* is what the sound card takes *in*, and vice versa.

Controlling the Screen Display

 Note   If you have a Monochrome/Hercules or CGA monitor, this tip does not apply to your system. It concerns only computers with an EGA, VGA, or SuperVGA monitor.

If you have an EGA or VGA monitor, Sp Pro can take advantage of the monitor's high resolution to display up to 41 tracks (on a VGA monitor) and 3 octaves in the Edit screen. (If you have a monochrome or CGA monitor, Sp Pro will display only 16 tracks at most.) When you run Sp

Pro's installation program, it tries to correctly detect your computer's monitor type. In the earlier installation programs, the /ega switch was added to SP.BAT to force EGA/VGA monitors into 25-line mode (only 16 tracks). In later installation programs, the /ega switch was not added, so your program automatically appears with 41 tracks.

Here is a tip for controlling your screen display:

☐   If your Edit screen has 41 tracks, but you'd prefer 16 larger, easier-to-read tracks instead, type the following command to start SP.BAT (or edit the SP.BAT file to include this):

SP /ega

☐   If your Edit screen has 16 tracks, and you want more, edit your SP.BAT file to remove the /ega command option.

Note   To learn more about editing SP.BAT, refer to Chapter 2 for information on editing ASCII files.

Upgrading to Sp Classic or Sp Gold

All registered owners of Sp Pro are eligible for upgrades to Voyetra's intermediate and professional sequencing packages, Sp Classic and Sp Gold.

These programs offer a host of additional, advanced features. Most importantly, they offer Transforms functions. Transforms are preset editing commands that allow you a greater degree of flexibility in modifying and customizing your songs. Sp Gold even includes an editor for the original two-operator Sound Blaster driver, a full-featured MIDI data analyzer, and a Universal Librarian that supports more than 130 different MIDI instruments.

For upgrade information, contact Voyetra Technologies at 800-233-9377.

PART III

Using the Software
Included with This
Book

CHAPTER

Making Your System Come Alive with SPUTMON

By using the utility SPUTMON (short for Sputter Monitor), included on the disk that comes with this book, you can attach sound effects or music to hundreds of predetermined events in your system. You can also schedule sound effects or music to play at certain times or on certain days, launch other programs or events in response to another event, and much, much more.

SPUTMON is only part of the complete Sputter Sound System from VersaWare. The complete Sputter Sound System is capable of much more than can be covered in this book. The documentation for the Sputter Sound System includes that for the SPUTMON program. You can buy the complete system at a special discount by sending in the order form at the back of this book.

This chapter explains how the SPUTMON software has added various sounds to your system, and how you can customize your system with a host of other sounds and sound effects, using the SPUTMON software.

Note   The procedures in this chapter assume that you have already run SBSIM to load the drivers for MUSIC and VOICE.

Obtaining Sound Samples

Many of the samples that are included on the disk attached to *Sound Blaster: The Official Book* or referenced in this chapter came from the Creative Labs & Prosonus Sounds CD that's included with the Creative Labs Multimedia Upgrade Kit. This is hardly the only source of sound effects, however. In fact, with just the Sound Blaster card and a microphone you can create all the sounds and sound effects you'll probably ever need.

If that seems like too much work, there are other options, as well. At any computer show you'll find disks full of samples available for pennies (or less!). On-line services such as CompuServe have all sorts of samples for you to download. In addition, local BBSs (computer bulletin boards) often carry hundreds of recorded sound effects taken from many different sources. CompuServe even makes it easy to locate snippets of sound from movies and television shows, by dividing their samples into categories, such as science fiction and adventure.

Finally, there are companies whose sole business is selling quality samples. HSC Software (213-392-8441) sells libraries of ready-to-use sound effects and music on floppy disks. Then there's the granddaddy of sound effects, the Sound Effects Library from Sound Ideas (1-800-387-3030). This company sells literally hundreds of CDs packed with thousands of every conceivable kind of sample. If you need a recording of a car door slamming, for example, you'll find the Sound Ideas catalog has pages full of different car doors slamming—ranging from Ford Escorts to Porsches. Now, *that's* dedication.

What is SPUTMON?

SPUTMON is an event monitor program. Though written to run under DOS, it can also be loaded in a DOS window within the DESQview or Windows multitasking environments. SPUTMON is a memory-resident program that monitors the program activity on your PC, watching for any of the events to which you have attached sounds, music files, or programs. These events might be the deletion or transfer of a file, a beep, an error message, or other events of this type. Once you have defined the links to various events via the .DEF file, SPUTMON will monitor your system for these events and then perform when a particular event occurs. Once SPUTMON has performed, your system resumes normal operations.

As currently installed on your machine, SPUTMON will provide your computer with all kinds of new sounds. While you certainly don't need to change the default installation to enjoy SPUTMON's effects, you'll probably want to add your own sound touches to your system. The following sections explain exactly how SPUTMON works, and teach you how to customize SPUTMON's actions for your system.

SPUTMON and the Various Sound File Formats

When SPUTMON was first designed, sound board products were just emerging. Very few types of sound formats existed, so writing a utility to play them was fairly straightforward. However, as the development of sound boards progressed, all sorts of new sound formats arrived on the scene. AdLib introduced the first type of FM music format with its sound board, and called it an .ROL file. When Creative Labs arrived on the scene, they took the .ROL file format and enhanced it, creating the Creative Music File format, or .CMF file. Any file ending in .ROL and .CMF contains FM music.

The Sputter Sound System includes utilities to play most of the various file types. You'll find the utilities included on the disk that came with this book. They are SPUTROL (for playing .ROL files) and SPUTCMF (for playing .CMF files). In addition, SPUTMON can activate any sound-playing utility that comes along, so that SPUTMON is never out of date. You'll learn more about SPUTROL and SPUTCMF later in this chapter.

It's important to remember that SPUTMON only monitors the events; it doesn't actually play the related sound files, but rather only does what you instruct it to do. SPUTMON's default setup is to play back sounds using included utilities from the Sputter Sound System. These utilities are designed to play back all of the various types of sound files you're likely to encounter. Should you prefer, however, to use other sound-playing utilities, you can set up the SPUTMON.DEF file to use any player you desire.

About the Various File Formats

Many different sound file formats are currently in use in the PC software industry. The Sputter Sound System supports 24 of these diverse formats. If you don't know what format a sound file has, you can find out easily by typing the following at the DOS command line:

SPUT <pathname>/I

where pathname includes the drive directory and the filename. Sputter will display all of the information that it can discern about the sound file.

The file types you'll encounter most frequently are differentiated by their filename extension (for example, .VOC in SOUND.VOC). The most popular formats are described in the paragraphs that follow.

.VOC Files   The .VOC format was created by Creative Labs for use in defining and storing their digitized samples (sounds). Digitized samples are simply sounds (voices, music, sound effects) that have been recorded

and converted from their normal analog state to a digital state. Recording something to a cassette or video tape is an example of analog recording. Today, everything is moving to digital recording, which makes a copy that never degrades with use. A .VOC file is the same as a raw sample (see .SND), except that it contains information (called a header) that stores important information about the sample, such as the frequency at which the sample was recorded.

.WAV Files   Files with a .WAV extension are in the Microsoft Wave audio file format. They are almost exactly like .VOC files, in that they represent digital samples, but they're constructed differently. Because Windows 3.0 and 3.1 support .WAV files, they are becoming more popular.

.SND Files   Files that were originally recorded on a Macintosh and then transfered to a PC usually have an .SND extension. These files have header information followed by digitized samples similar to .VOC files. These files are commonly found on bulletin boards and can easily be converted to the more popular .VOC and .WAV formats.

.MOD Files   Files with a .MOD extension are Amiga sound files. They're much like .VOC files because they are digitized samples, but they're much more complex—like four .VOC files in one. Most .MOD files contain music that's been separated into four segments, usually by instrument. We discuss .MOD files and a utility to play them in Chapter 11, "Third-Party Software."

.ROL Files   Files with a .ROL extension are music files originally created using The Visual Composer, by Adlib Inc., for their Adlib boards. Today many utilities can create .ROL files, which can be played on any FM (Adlib)-compatible sound board containing an FM chip for music synthesis. These music files contain lists of notes, tempos, and instrument changes, similar to .CMF files, except that the events are grouped together by their type, and in order within each of the groups. To play .ROL files, a program must read the file, sort the events into their proper order, and then pass them to the Adlib driver SOUND.COM. This driver can only handle small amounts of data at a time, so the player program must pass events to the driver continuously to keep the song playing properly.

.CMF Files   Creative Music Files (.CMF) are the Creative Labs, Inc., equivalent of AdLib's .ROL files. .CMF files can be played on any FM-compatible sound board containing an FM chip for music synthesis. These music files contain a list of notes, tempos, and instrument changes, similar to .ROL files except that the events are already sorted and stored in the correct order to be played. This facilitates playing .CMF files in the background, because the player needs to call the Sound Blaster driver SBFMDRV.COM only once. This driver then processes the entire song without any additional prodding. A conversion program for converting .ROL files to .CMF files is available from Creative Labs, Inc.

.MID Files   Files with a .MID extension, are MIDI files. MIDI (Musical Instrument Digital Interface) is the standard used throughout the electronic music industry and is quickly becoming a standard in the computer industry. MIDI files are much like .CMF files in that they store music, not samples, but MIDI files are far more complex. Support for .MID files is also built into Microsoft Windows.

.SNG Files   Files with a .SNG extension are song files created with Sequencer Plus Pro by Voyetra, a MIDI recorder/arranger/editor program written for the Sound Blaster Pro sound cards and included in the Sound Blaster MIDI Kit.

The Heart and Mind of SPUTMON

SPUTMON's heart and mind is its definition file, called SPUTMON.DEF. This is a simple text (ASCII) file that defines and controls SPUTMON's activities. It can be found in the same directory as SPUTMON.

SPUTMON reads its definition file only once, when the program is first loaded into memory by your AUTOEXEC.BAT file, or when you type **SPUTMON** at the DOS command line. The program usually defaults to reading the SPUTMON.DEF file, but you can substitute any other customized file to be read at start-up. This file might be a special file for a particular day of the week, a particular month, a holiday, or even a user-specific file. For example, on one computer that's used by two or three people, each with their own preferences, each one might have a file—named, perhaps, JOE.DEF, SANDY.DEF, and TAYLOR.DEF. When Joe begins using the system, he types **SPUTMON JOE.DEF**, and SPUTMON will use that DEF file with Joe's preferences, overriding SPUTMON's use of any other DEF file.

Links to system events are created in SPUTMON by inserting command lines in the definition file. Each command line starts with a letter that represents the event that SPUTMON will watch for. The command lines will vary in length depending on which event type is being defined. All of the command lines end with the name of a sound file to be played or a program or batch file to be executed when the event occurs.

Some of the events that can be monitored are

☐   The system beep

☐   Arrival of scheduled dates and times

☐   Keystrokes

☐   Execution of certain programs

☐   File operations

☐   Disk accesses

And DOS functions, as well, can be monitored, such as

☐   Termination of certain programs

☐   Changes to other disk drives

☐   Changes to other directories

☐   Creation or deletion of directories

☐   Deletion or renaming of files

As you work through this chapter you'll read about all the different types of events that SPUTMON can handle, as well as the correct command lines to add to the definition file to accomplish the monitoring you want to do. More detailed information can be found in the documentation that comes with the complete Sputter Sound System package.

Note   All command lines referenced in this chapter should be entered into the SPUTMON.DEF file. Command lines may be entered in any order.

SPUTMON's Effects on Your System

Once you install the disk included with this book and restart your computer, you'll find that SPUTMON has made a number of subtle (and not so subtle) changes to your system. The changes that are made automatically when you install the disk and reboot your machine are listed below. Again, remember that these are just default settings and that you can change them to your liking.

- ☐ The system beep is replaced by a chirping bird.

- ☐ Whenever a file is deleted, you'll hear it scream into the afterlife.

- ☐ When you change from one disk drive to another, you'll hear the sound of a can opener.

- ☐ Changing directories is accompanied by the sound of a ratchet.

- ☐ Whenever you or a software program attempt to change your AUTOEXEC.BAT file, a voice will warn you,"Oops, watch out!"

- ☐ When a program ends, you'll hear the sound of a closing garbage can.

- ☐ If you use the DOS 5.0 editor (EDIT.COM), your editing session will begin with a very cute squishing sound.

- ☐ Running the CHKDSK utility will play a splash sound, followed by a ratchet sound because CHKDSK also changes directories.

- ☐ Pressing CTRL-1 gets you the sound of glass breaking, to demonstrate the effect of adding a sound to a keypress.

- ☐ You can run CHKDSK (and its associated sounds) by pressing CTRL-2.

- ☐ To show you how to pause SPUTMON during specific operations, a pause has been attached to the DOS utility LABEL.

- You'll never again need to guess when to start your lunch hour. Every day at at exactly 12 noon, you'll hear "It's time for some lunch."

- You'll know it's time to quit for the day at 5:00 P.M., when your machine begins playing Beethoven.

- You'll also know when you're officially burning the midnight oil when you hear a long sigh precisely at midnight each night.

Replacing the System Beep

The system beep is, without a doubt, the first thing people want to get rid of. Now that SPUTMON is active on your system, you'll find that your beep is gone. It's been replaced by the sound of birds chirping. We've accomplished this with the Beep command in the SPUTMON.DEF file.

If you look at the first command line of the SPUTMON.DEF file, found in the same directory as SPUTMON, you'll see the following:

```
B BIRD1-1
```

where the B stands for Beep, and BIRD1-1 is the actual sound file to play whenever the system beep is detected by SPUTMON. You can replace BIRD1-1 with any other sample of your choice. Maybe you'd like to record a gong or laser and play that instead. In fact, you can even have SPUTMON randomly choose between a whole group of samples (explained later in this chapter in the section called "Playing Randomly Selected Files").

Adding Speech to the System Beep

The Sound Blaster card family is capable of speech synthesis, and SPUTMON is ready to make your system speak.

Suppose you want your machine to say "An error has occurred" whenever your system beeps. To add this characteristic to your machine, change the beep command line to read as follows:

B /TL An error has occurred

where the B stands for Beep, and /TL tells SPUTMON to use Text-to-speech Language. Whatever you type after /TL will be spoken by your machine, using Sputter's text-to-speech synthesis.

Replacing the System Beep with Music

It's easy to add music to your system beep, though you will need to call a specific utility to play each of the various sound file formats. Directions for doing so follow.

Playing .ROL Files

To play a randomly selected .ROL file, using SPUTROL, type

B #R *.ROL

where the B stands for Beep, and the #R tells SPUTMON to use the utility SPUTROL to play a randomly selected group of .ROL files (*.ROL). For further information about SPUTROL, see the later section, "Adding Synthesized Music."

Playing .CMF Files

To play a random .CMF file in place of the system beep, using SPUTCMF, type

B #C *.CMF

The only difference between this command line and the previous one for playing .ROL files is the replacement of the #R with #C. The #C tells SPUTMON to use SPUTCMF to play a group of .CMF files. For further information about SPUTCMF, see the later section, "Playing Synthesized Music."

Playing MIDI Files

Playing .ROL and .CMF file formats seems simple enough, and it is. But what happens when a new file format comes along that SPUTMON isn't prepared for? The MIDI file format is an example of such a file format, and the solution to playing MIDI files is also a simple one. Creative Labs provides its own utility for playing these files on a Sound Blaster, called PLAYMIDI.

To play a MIDI file you will need to call the PLAYMIDI utility, by typing

B #D PLAYMIDI BEETHO10.MID

The #D in the above command line tells SPUTMON to use an outside DOS program to play this particular type of sound file format. In this case, we've told SPUTMON to replace the beep using the DOS utility PLAYMIDI. When SPUTMON executes this command it will play the same Beethoven music that its default DEF file currently uses to let you know when it's 5:00 P.M.

Other Sound-Playing Utilities

You can use all kinds of sound-playing utilities to play the different sound file types. As discussed in Chapters 4 and 7, your Sound Blaster comes with a number of these utilities. The following are a few brief examples of command lines used to incorporate these utilities into SPUTMON:

- ☐   B #D VPLAY <*filename*.VOC>

- ☐   B #D VOICE /OUT:<*filename*.VOC>

- ☐   B #D MUSIC /PLAY:<*filename*.CMF>

- ☐   B #D MUSIC /PLAY:<*filename*.MID>

- ☐   B #D MMPLAY <*script*>

- ☐   B #D VOICE/OUT:<*filename*.WAV>

Playing Randomly Selected Files

SPUTMON supports the DOS wildcard feature to select groups of files. (See your DOS manual for more information on DOS wildcards.) To play any randomly selected sample, just replace the default BEEP line (B BIRD1-1) with

```
B *.*
```

This command line causes a file to be randomly selected from SPUTMON's current directory whenever a beep is encountered.

You can also limit SPUTMON's random selection of files to groups of a certain type of file. For example, to have SPUTMON select randomly from only files in the Microsoft wave format (.WAV), enter this command:

```
B *.WAV
```

Teaching SPUTMON to Select Files from a Specific Directory

Unless you specify otherwise, SPUTMON assumes that it should select sound files from either the current directory or a directory specified by the SPUTDIR environment variable. However, you can tell SPUTMON to play files from anywhere on your computer using complete DOS paths and filenames. (See your DOS manual for more information on specifying paths and filenames.)

For example, let's say you've recorded your cat meowing and stored this sound effect in the file MEOW.VOC in the directory SOUNDS on drive C. To have this sound file play each time your system beeps, enter the following command:

```
B C:\SOUNDS\MEOW
```

Enlivening Your Computer's Clock/Calendar

Another hot feature of SPUTMON is based on the clock and calendar built into every computer system. Using this combination you can turn your computer into a talking and singing date-and-time reminder. As with all other SPUTMON features, you control the timer by manipulating the SPUTMON.DEF file.

Elements of the Timer

The timer portion of SPUTMON.DEF is divided into seven sections that look like this:

T 00-00-00 12:00 00-01-00 00:00 0 SOUND.VOC

Looking at the above command line, you'll note the following elements:

The Timer Command   The first command, the T, tells SPUTMON that you're describing a Timer event—just as a B in the BEEP commands described just above referred to a beep event.

The Start Date and Time Fields   The next two items, 00-00-00 and 12:00, represent the Start Date and Start Time fields. In the example above the Start Time is 12:00 (noon). By not specifying a specific Start Date (00-00-00) you tell SPUTMON that you want something to happen today at noon. To specify a date in this field, say July 4, 1995, you would enter 07-04-95 as the Start Date. Entering 07-00-00 as a Start Date would specify that something will happen at 12:00 noon every day in every month of July. Or 07-04-00 would tell SPUTMON to trigger an event every July 4 at noon. As you can see, the possible combinations are endless.

The Increment Date and Time Fields   The next two items in the T command line, 00-01-00 and 00:00, are the Increment Date and Increment Time fields. These fields are most useful for events that repeat multiple times during the current day or into following days. Notice in the foregoing example that the Increment Date field has the number 1 in the day portion; this means the file SOUND.VOC will play at 12:00 noon today and tomorrow only. One way to use Increment Time might be to turn your system into a lively clock. For instance, by setting Increment Time to 01:00 (or once an hour) and attaching a chime to this event, you'd get a chime every hour of the day.

The Repeat Field   The next item in the command line (0 in our example) is the Repeat field. The number here represents the number of times an event will be repeated, in relation to the previous settings. For instance, in the paragraph just above you read how to set a chime to go off every hour. If you want the chime to repeat every hour, but only for the next three hours after it begins, you would set the Repeat field to 3.

The Command Section   The last item in the command line is the Command section. Here is where you place, generally, the name of a file to play (such as SOUND.VOC in our example); however, you can enter any command supported by SPUTMON in this section. For example, you might use #D to have some other utility play a sound file, or even set SPUTMON to do a backup at a specific time and date. The following T command line example tells SPUTMON do a backup at 5:00 P.M. evey day:

T 00-00-00 17:00 00-01-00 00:00 0 #D BACKUP

The example above starts a timer event at 1700 hours (5:00 P.M.) every day, and runs a DOS file (#D) called BACKUP. To run a utility other than BACKUP, you would insert the startup command for that utility in place of BACKUP.

Attaching Sound Files To Keystrokes

Suppose you want to attach something fun to your F1 function key. For example, remember that old movie with Vincent Price called *The Fly?* In it there's a scene where a fly with a human head gets caught in a spider web. In a very eerie voice you hear him call out, "Help me. Hellllllp me..." You can easily attach that eerie plea to your F1 key, so that whenever you press F1 (which is usually the help key) you will hear the fly calling to you for help.

It's easy to pull off all kinds of tricks like this with SPUTMON, using its built-in Keystroke command. For example, your command in the SPUTMON.DEF file for attaching "Help Me" to the F1 key might look like this:

K 3B,00 HELPME.VOC

Here the K stands for Keystroke; the 3B,00 tells SPUTMON that we're referring to the F1 function key; and the HELPME.VOC assigns a sound file to the rest of the command.

You can do more with this Keystroke utility than just specify a sound file. You can use any supported command to do things such as linking the running of a program to a keystroke. As stated earlier, the SPUTMON.DEF file already contains a command to attach the DOS utility CHKDSK.COM to CTRL-2. This command line looks very similar to the one for attaching the sound file HELPME.VOC, as follows:

K 03,04 #D CHKDSK C:

Here again you see the K for Keystroke followed by the keycode for CTRL-2, which is 03,04 (keycodes are explained in the section that follows). Then you see the #D command followed by the program name CHKDSK. The C after CHKDSK tells CHKDSK to execute on drive C.

Keycodes

Long ago programmers developed a standard set of codes that specify all the keys (and key-combinations) available on the keyboard. They're called *keycodes*. The entire list of keycodes is quite lengthy, but most can be found in your MS-DOS manual. A few are special codes used only by SPUTMON, and these are in documentation for the complete Sputter Sound System. To get you started, we've included some of the more popular keycodes in Table 9-1.

TABLE
9-1

Function Key Keycodes

Keycode	Function Key	Keycode	Function Key
3B,00	F1	41,00	F7
3C,00	F2	42,00	F8
3D,00	F3	43,00	F9
3E,00	F4	44,00	F10
3F,00	F5	57,00	F11
40,00	F6	58,00	F12

The ,00 portion of the keycodes in Table 9-1 can be changed to specify combinations of function keys and other shift keys such as CTRL or ALT. The keycodes for those combinations are as follows:

00	No SHIFT key
01	Right SHIFT key
02	Left SHIFT key
04	CTRL key
08	ALT key
10	Either right or left SHIFT key

For example, 3B,04 represents CTRL-F1.

Remember that this is just a brief description of the complete capabilities of keystroke commands available to SPUTMON. The complete Sputter Sound System contains all the information you need to use SPUTMON to its fullest extent.

Adding Sounds to Program Execution

SPUTMON's Program command links sounds or other programs to the execution of any specified program. For example, the following command plays a sound whenever PKZIP.EXE is executed:

P PKZIP.EXE HIGLAS11.WAV

where P represents Program, PKZIP.EXE is the executable program file, and HIGLAS11.WAV is the sound file to be attached to PKZIP.EXE.

If you wish to use another player program, such as the VOICE utility program, you would enter

P PKZIP.EXE #D VOICE /OUT:D:\SOUNDFX\HIGLAS11.WAV

In this example, #D tells SPUTMON to go to a DOS program, rather than defaulting to the Sputter player. VOICE is the VOICE utility program, and D:\SOUNDFX\HIGLAS11.WAV directs VOICE to the directory containing the .WAV file you wish to attach to PKZIP.

Suspending SPUTMON's Operation

You may sometimes wish to temporarily suspend the SPUTMON event monitor while a certain program is running. For example, you might want to disable all sound effects while WordPerfect is running. To disable SPUTMON, add the command

PS WP.EXE

to the SPUTMON.DEF file. In this example, PS stands for Program Suspend. SPUTMON will resume normal operation when WordPerfect is terminated.

Turning Off SPUTMON Temporarily

To disable SPUTMON whenever a particular program, such as PCPLUS, is running, add

PD PCPLUS.EXE

to the SPUTMON.DEF file. In this example, PD stands for Program Disable. This command is useful when you're running a communications program and planning to do a download. In that case, you will not want sounds to occur while you are doing your download. The PD command keeps SPUTMON disabled even after Procomm Plus terminates. You must reenable SPUTMON when your specific program is executed, by typing

SPUTMON/E

at the DOS command line.

Automatically Reenabling SPUTMON

To automatically reenable SPUTMON after another program is run, add the following line to SPUTMON's DEF (definition file):

PE WORD.EXE

In this example, SPUTMON will be automatically reenabled once the Word program begins.

Linking Sounds to File Accesses

SPUTMON's File commands are used to link sounds to a number of types of file accesses. Any legal DOS wildcards may be used in the filename. The various File commands are discussed in the paragraphs that follow.

File-Open

The File-Open command is used to link a sound to the opening of a file, for read- or write-access. Here is an example:

FO AUTOEXEC.BAT CANSNAP1.WAV

where FO stands for the File-Open command. Once SPUTMON is loaded, this command line tells it to play CANSNAP1.WAV whenever your AUTOEXEC.BAT file is read.

File-Close

The File-Close command links sounds to the closing of a file. This command is particularly useful for creating slide shows. (See the later section, "Using SPUTMON to Create a Slide Show.") When using File-Close you will not hear the .VOC file until your data file has been closed. Here is an example:

FC MYFILE.TXT MYFILE.VOC

where FC stands for File-Close, MYFILE.TXT is a regular text file, and MYFILE.VOC is a .VOC file that has been recorded to be played whenever MYFILE.TXT is closed.

File-Read

The File-Read command is used to play sounds whenever a file is opened for read-only access. For example, to play a sound whenever any batch file is opened for read access, you type

FR *.BAT CANSNAP1

where FR stands for File-Read. This command line attaches the CAN-SNAP1 sound file to the opening of any batch file, represented by the * wildcard.

File-Write

The File-Write command links sounds to the opening of a file for write or read/write access. Here is an example:

FW * CANSNAP1

where FW stands for File-Write. This command line tells SPUTMON to link the CANSNAP1 file to the opening of any file for read/write access.

File-Name

The File-Name command is used to link sounds to the renaming of a file. Here is an example:

FN CONFIG.SYS CANSNAP1

where FN stands for File-Name. Once SPUTMON is loaded, this command line tells SPUTMON to play CANSNAP1 whenever CONFIG.SYS is renamed.

File-Delete

The File-Delete command is used to link sounds to the deletion of a file. In this example,

FD * GARBGEC1.WAV

FD stands for File-Delete. This command line tells SPUTMON to play the wave-format file GARBGEC1.WAV whenever any file on any disk in your system (represented by the * wildcard) is deleted.

Linking Sounds to Disk Accesses

The SPUTMON event monitor has the ability to link sounds or programs to almost any disk function. Some useful command examples are described in the paragraphs that follow. Refer to the documentation for the Sputter Sound System for a complete list of all disk function commands.

You will probably find that it is most helpful to link sound to disk access events in order to warn of unauthorized or unwanted disk write or format commands.

Linking Sound to Disk Format Track Commands

To warn that a Disk Format Track command is about to occur on any drive, type the following:

V 05,FF DEADM1-1.WAV

In this command line, V stands for Drive (since the D command has already been used to represent a DOS utility). The 05 represents a Disk Format command, and FF represents any drive. Should you wish to limit this command to drive A, you would replace FF with 00, where 00 represents drive A (the drive letters from A to Z are numbered from 00 to 25). Thus, to play a sound whenever the current drive changes to C, you would enter this command:

V 05,02 DEADM1-1.WAV

where 02 is the C drive.

Linking Sounds to a Write Disk Sector Event

To play a sound file when a Write Disk Sector is about to occur on drive A, type the following:

V 03,00 DEADM1-1

In this command line, V represents a Drive command; the 03 is the Write Disk Sector command; and 00 is drive A. The file DEADM1-1 will be played whenever a Write Disk Sector command is executed on drive A.

Linking Sounds to DOS Functions

The SPUTMON event monitor can link sounds or programs to almost any DOS function. The DOS functions that you will likely want to link sounds to are described in the paragraphs that follow, but all aspects of every command line are not necessarily explained. Refer to the documentation for the Sputter Sound System for a complete list of all functions.

Playing Sounds When a Program is Terminating

To play a sound file whenever a program is terminating, type the following:

D 4C,FF I-QUIT1

In this command line, D stands for DOS, 4C represents Program Terminate, and FF is any error code. The FF field is used for detecting various level settings (the documentation for the Sputter Sound System explains this field in more detail). In this case, I-QUIT1 will play whenever a program terminates.

Linking Sounds to a Change in Disk Drive

To play a sound whenever the current drive is changed, you would type the following:

D 0E,FF RATCHT1.WAV

where the second parameter, FF, specifies the drive. In this case, FF indicates any drive. Should you wish to specify a change to drive A, you would replace FF with 00, where 00 represents drive A. (The possible drive letters from A to Z are numbered from 00 to 25.) Thus, to play a sound whenever the current drive changes to C, you would type

D 0E,02 RATCHT1

where 02 is the C drive.

Linking Sounds to Directory Functions

To play a sound file whenever the current directory is changed, you would type the following:

D 3B,FF CANSNAP1

where D tells SPUTMON that this is a DOS function, and the 3B,FF combination indicates the Change Directory command. In this case, CANSNAP1 will play whenever there is a change in directory.

To play a sound file whenever a directory is created, you would type the following:

D 39,FF CANSNAP1.WAV

where D tells SPUTMON that this is a DOS function, and the 39,FF represents the Create Directory command.

To play a sound file whenever a directory is deleted, type the following:

D 3A,FF CANSNAP1

where 3A,FF represents the Delete Directory command.

 Note   SPUTMON can also watch for many other DOS functions that are not discussed in this chapter, such as memory allocation and string input and output. Refer to the Sputter Sound System documentation for more detailed information.

Adding Digitized Sounds to Batch Files

The simplest way to add sound to your system with SPUTMON is to add command lines to your existing batch files. The command lines will execute a player program when the batch file is executed. Various player programs are provided on the disk included with this book, and are used as described in the paragraphs that follow.

VPLAY

VPLAY comes with all versions of the Sound Blaster sound board and plays .VOC sound files. It can play sounds in the background when it is run from the DOS command line rather than from a batch file. See Chapter 4 for more information on using VPLAY.

To use VPLAY, insert a line in your batch file in this format:

VPLAY <*filename*.VOC>

where *filename* is the name of the sound file to be played.

SPUT

SPUT is part of the Sputter Sound System and recognizes sound files in many different formats, including .VOC, Macintosh .SND, and Atari sound files. To use SPUT, insert a line in your batch file in this format:

SPUT <*filename*>

To add some variety to your system operation, you can tell SPUT to randomly select a different sound file each time the batch file is executed. By placing the line SPUT *.* in your AUTOEXEC.BAT file, you will hear a different sound file each time your system is rebooted.

Adding Synthesized Music

Synthesized music files are played via the FM chip located on the Sound Blaster sound cards. This is the same chip that is on the AdLib board; any sound card containing this chip is "AdLib-compatible."

Three popular formats of files can be played via the FM chip: the .ROL file by AdLib, the .CMF file by Creative Labs, and the .MID (MIDI) file. Specific player programs and drivers are required to play each of the file formats. The simplest way to add synthesized music to your system is to add command lines to your existing batch files that will execute the appropriate player program. These command lines are described in the paragraphs that follow.

 Note In all the following examples, the *filename* variable represents the name of the song file to be played.

Playing .ROL Files

To play an .ROL file, insert a line in your batch file as follows:

SPUTROL <*filename.ROL*>

SPUTROL requires the AdLib FM driver SOUND.COM, but does not require that the driver be loaded prior to running SPUTROL. SOUND.COM is a memory-resident driver that requires a minimum of 32K. Since SOUND.COM is loaded by SPUTROL only for the duration of the .ROL file playback, you save 32K of memory. This is one of SPUTROL's great advantages over other .ROL players.

 Note Playing .ROL files with any player program other than SPUTROL requires loading a memory resident driver from AdLib called SOUND.COM. SPUTROL will temporarily load the driver automatically, and remove it from memory when it is finished.

To add some variety to your system, you can tell both SPUTROL and SPUTCMF (explained just below) to randomly select a different synthesized music file each time the batch file is executed. For example, if your AUTOEXEC.BAT file contains the line SPUTCMF *.*, you will hear a different song file each time your system is rebooted.

SPUTROL also has a feature that allows you to easily make instrument substitutions from the command line, adding variety to the same song each time it is played.

A conversion program called ROL2CMF, provided by Creative Labs, can be used to convert .ROL files to the .CMF file format.

Playing .CMF Files

To play a .CMF file, insert one of the following lines in your batch file:

SPUTCMF <*filename*.CMF>
or
PLAYCMF <*filename*.CMF>

SPUTCMF requires the Sound Blaster FM driver SBFMDRV.COM, but does not require that the driver be loaded prior to running SPUTCMF. SBFMDRV.COM is a memory-resident driver that requires a minimum of 6K. Since SBFMDRV.COM is loaded by SPUTCMF only for the duration of the .CMF file playback, you save 6K of memory. This is one of SPUTCMF's great advantages over other .CMF players.

 Note   Playing .CMF files with any player program other than SPUTCMF requires loading a memory resident driver from Creative Labs called SBFMDRV.COM. SPUTCMF will temporarily load the driver automatically, and remove it from memory when it is finished.

To add some variety to your system, you can tell both SPUTCMF and SPUTROL to randomly select a different synthesized music file each time the batch file is executed. For example, if your AUTOEXEC.BAT file contains the line SPUTCMF *.*, you will hear a different song file each time your system is rebooted.

Playing .MID Files

To play an .MID file, insert a line in your batch file as follows:

PLAYMIDI <*filename*.MID>

PLAYMIDI requires prior loading of the SBMIDI driver.

Using SPUTMON to Create a Slide Show

SPUTMON can be used to add sound capability to any presentation software package, such as Harvard Graphics, to provide you with a multimedia slide show. Both the File-Close and File-Open commands can be used to link sound files to graphic files. Both these commands and their application to slide shows are discussed in the paragraphs that follow.

When designing a slide show, consider writing separate definition (.DEF) files for each slide show. Then, when you are ready to play your slide show, you can simply type **SPUTMON** followed by the name of the .DEF file at the DOS prompt, for example, **SPUTMON COMDEX.DEF**. This will load SPUTMON with the settings in the .DEF file. You will then need to run your slide show, in this case the COMDEX slide show, using your presentation program. For subsequent slide shows, SPUTMON must first be unloaded from memory by typing the following command at the DOS prompt: SPUTMON /U. SPUTMON is then ready to be reloaded with the definition file containing the settings for the next slide show.

Using File-Close to Play a Sound File After a Graphic Is Drawn

The File-Close command is perfect for slide shows where you want to first draw the entire picture and then play the sound file.

Here is a sample command line for this purpose:

FC QUARTER.CHT #D VOICE /OUT:QUARTER.VOC

In this example, FC stands for File-Close. QUARTER.CHT is a chart in Harvard Graphics named Quarter. QUARTER.VOC is a .VOC file that has been recorded for playing whenever QUARTER.CHT is displayed in Harvard Graphics. VOICE will play the voice file, QUARTER.VOC, after QUARTER.CHT has been drawn in its entirety.

This command line is best used when the sound file exists as a short commentary on a slide. When using File-Close for a slide show, you must create one FC command line for each picture in your presentation.

Using FILE-OPEN to Play a Sound File While a Graphic Is Drawn

If you are using special effects with your slide show, such as fade-in or fade-out, and it will take some time to draw your slide on the screen, consider using the File-Open command. File-Open will play music or sound in the background while the graphic is being created.

Here is an example:

FO QUARTER.CHT #D MUSIC /PLAY:QUARTER.CMF

In this example, MUSIC will start playing the synthesized music file QUARTER.CMF in the background while the picture, QUARTER.CHT, is being drawn on the screen by Harvard Graphics. MUSIC is used in this case to play the .CMF file, instead of SPUTMON, because MUSIC will play QUARTER.CMF in the background. If #D MUSIC were omitted from the command, the sound file would be played first to completion, and then SPUTMON would let Harvard Graphics draw the chart.

CHAPTER

The Blaster Master
Sample Editor

*B*laster Master is a graphically based program designed for sample editing and processing—essentially a toolkit designed specifically for the Sound Blaster family of products—and it works with Sound Blaster .VOC, .WAV, and .SND files. It demonstrates features that are generally available only on Digital Audio Workstations, which normally cost many thousands of dollars.

One of the most significant features of the Sound Blaster and other PC audio cards is their ability to sample sound and play it back. Now you can tailor your own sound files using the Blaster Master program—a very fast EGA/VGA graphically based editor. Useless and noisy sample data at the beginning and end of .VOC files can be quickly removed, and sections from within the sample can be saved as a new sample file.

This chapter begins with background information on the Blaster Master user interface. The section "Using Blaster Master" describes the key steps for making a recording. The section "Transformations Using the Tools" provides a detailed description of the transformations available, such as adding an echo or changing the volume. Some transformations apply to the entire file, some work on only a section of a file, and some apply to both. The transformations that apply to the entire sound file are listed in "Modifying the Entire Sound File." Those that apply to only a section are listed in "Modifying a Section of the Sound File."

The present chapter concludes with additional topics, such as how to record from the CD-ROM, selecting and saving screen colors, and setting the Blaster Master default. If you have any problems running Blaster Master, see the "Troubleshooting Blaster Master" and "Performance Tips" sections at the end of this chapter.

Note The material in this chapter is an edited version of the Blaster Master documentation. It is printed here with permission. Full documentation for Blaster Master can be downloaded from the MIDI Forum in the CompuServe on-line service (do a keyword search for "Maddox"). In addition, Gary Maddox, author of Blaster Master, is a CompuServe sysop and can be contacted through that service.

The illustrations in this chapter are taken from Sound Blaster; Sound Blaster Pro owners will actually see a bit more information on their screens. For a view of what Blaster Master can do, look at Figure 10-1, which shows the Waveform Edit screen displaying a stereo sound file called BEA.VOC.

System Requirements for Using Blaster Master

Before you can run Blaster Master on your PC, your system must meet the following requirements:

☐   An 80286 PC or better, with an EGA or VGA graphics display, 640K of memory, a mouse, and a hard disk.

☐   Though an installed sound card is not required, without one the Blaster Master's Play, Record, and Scope functions will be disabled.

☐   Unregistered versions of Blaster Master will only process a 25-second sound file; the registered software will process any size sound file.

FIGURE 10-1   Waveform Edit screen showing stereo file

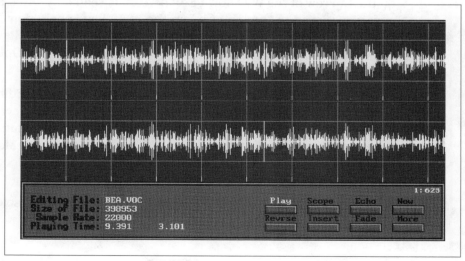

The Blaster Master User Interface

This section provides an overview of the Blaster Master user interface: how to issue commands, a summary of the major screens, and an explanation of the waveform screen where you edit your sound file.

The basic functions of working with a sound file—selecting it, importing it, recording it, and editing it—are covered in the following sections.

The Blaster Master Command Interface

This program is best controlled by a mouse, but you can use a keyboard for many operations. For example, you can select buttons by either clicking with a mouse, or in most cases, by pressing ALT plus the first letter of the button. For example, ALT-P will Play the currently selected sound file. For the few cases where ALT doesn't work, you can use the TAB and SHIFT-TAB keys to move forward and backward among buttons, and then press ENTER to select. The TAB and SHIFT-TAB keys are also useful for moving from place to place within the File Selection dialog box and the Recording dialog box.

The Vanishing Menu, which is a drop-down bar menu that appears on the top row of the Waveform Edit screen, is seen only when the mouse cursor is moved to the top or when the SHIFT key is held down. You can select a menu option with the mouse or hold down the SHIFT key and type the first letter of each option: SHIFT-F for File, SHIFT-O for Options, and SHIFT-H for Help.

The selection of buttons that appears in the Waveform Edit screen is context sensitive. You will only see buttons that are relevant to the current screen, and only for the most frequently used commands. Not all the buttons appear at one time. You may need to select the More button to see an additional set of buttons. Most of the tasks selectable by a button are also selectable from the Vanishing Menu.

You can leave most dialog boxes by pressing ESC or selecting the CANCEL button, when it is available.

The Three Major Screens

The Blaster Master is easily understood once you realize that there are only three main screens:

☐ The File Selection dialog box (titled Select Sound File) is where you specify the filename for the following tasks: Play, Record, Delete, Import (conversion from another file type), and Accept (load a Creative Labs .VOC file into the Waveform Editor). These tasks are executed by selecting a button.

☐ The Record dialog box (titled Record a Sound File) is where you set the recording parameters and perform the following tasks: Record, Scope (see what the current sound source looks like as a waveform), and Control the CD-ROM. You enter a filename, specify the recording parameters, and then select the Record button to begin recording.

☐ The Waveform Edit screen is where you can see and manipulate your sound file. This screen doesn't have a title, but when you move the mouse to the top you will see the Vanishing Menu. The Vanishing Menu consists of four choices: Block commands, File commands, Options (miscellaneous commands), and Tools. When you first examine a sound file, you will see the File pull-down menu option but not the Block. Once you mark a section of the waveform for editing purposes, the File pull-down menu option will be replaced by the Block menu option.

The Tools drop-down menu option is always accessible when you are working in the Waveform Edit screen. From here you can modify the entire sound file, such as changing the sampling rate or playback speed or adding a fade, pan, or echo. You can also mark a section of the sound file (you can see the actual waveform) and then take actions appropriate to a piece of the sound file, such as move it, change the volume, or change the pitch.

Waveform Edit Screen

In Blaster Master, much of your work is done in the Waveform Edit screen, where a graphic representation of the entire sample (sound file) appears on your monitor. The waveform overlays a grid that divides the sample into seconds to aid in selecting the *cut points*. When manipulating a section of the sample, you mark the two cut points. During playback, a pulsing index line is synchronized with the sound you hear, displaying the current position in the file being played. Figure 10-2 shows the Waveform Edit screen, with a monaural (single-channel) waveform displayed.

Note   A zero-crossing/phase approximation method allows you to select the displayed bytes (within the section), helping you choose the "cleanest" points for processing. Cross-fading is applied to splice points when needed.

FIGURE
10-2

Waveform Edit screen showing pulsing index line

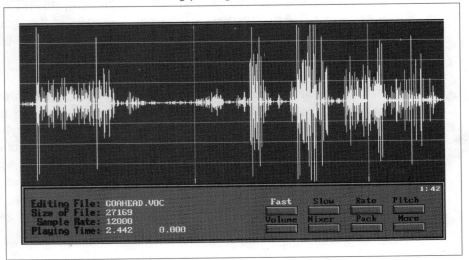

Selecting Colors for Your Screen

Blaster Master uses a full palette of colors to provide visual cues that help simplify use of this software product. You may need to change the color selection in this palette to make your screen more legible. Using your keyboard's function keys F1 through F10, you can control the colors displayed on the screen. Experiment with the available color combinations to find the one that best suits you. Once you've selected the right color combination, you can save it by selecting Options from the Vanishing Menu, and then the Save Screen Colors menu option.

Using Blaster Master

The usual sequence for working with Blaster Master is to begin with the File Selection dialog box. From here you either accept (load) an existing sound file, or select the Record button to display the Record screen. After either recording a new file or accepting an existing one on disk, you are automatically taken to the Waveform Edit screen. Most of the screen is filled with the actual waveform of your sound file, so you can see the effect of your changes and watch the sound bytes as the file is played. From the Waveform Edit screen you manipulate your sound file by issuing commands from either the Vanishing Menu at the top of the screen or the buttons at the bottom of the screen.

Starting Blaster Master

To run Blaster Master, switch to the Blaster Master directory by typing **CD\SBDISK\BMASTER** and then press ENTER. Now type **BMASTER** at the DOS command prompt and press ENTER. To start the program and load a sound file in one operation, type **BMASTER** followed by a space and the filename.

To quit the program, select the Quit button from the File Selection dialog box, or select File from the Vanishing Menu and then Quit. Press ESC to clear the advertisement.

Selecting a Sound File

If you don't specify a sound file when you start the Sound Blaster editor, a File Selection dialog box will appear. This dialog box has many components. Below the dialog box you will see scroll bars for the master volume control and the sources.

At the top of the dialog box you are prompted with the .VOC file extension wildcard; and in the large box below, all the files with a matching file extension are displayed. Once you select a file from this box by double-clicking (the easiest method for making selections), the filename will appear at the top of the dialog box.

To the right of this large box (which lists sound files), is a narrow list of the directories and drives that are available. Click on members of this list to change the drive or directory. Select the double dot (..) entry at the top of this list to move up one directory level.

After you have selected an existing sound file, or entered the name of a new one, issue a command by selecting a button. The buttons can be selected using the mouse or (in most cases) by pressing ALT plus the first letter of the option, as explained earlier. The buttons are listed below, and receive further explanation in the sections that follow:

☐   Play the sound file. While the file is playing you will see a dialog box describing the file.

☐   Record a new sound file.

☐   Delete an unwanted sound file.

☐   Import (load a sound file that is not a .VOC file).

☐   Accept (load an existing .VOC file).

☐   Quit the program and return to DOS.

After selection of Record, Import, or Accept, Blaster Master will display the Waveform Edit screen. Here you can see the data bytes that comprise your sound file, and you can access tools to manipulate the sound file.

Recording a Sound File

When you select the Record button from the File Selection dialog box, a new screen with a new dialog box appears, the Record dialog box. Figure 10-3 shows the Blaster Master about to record a file called NEW.VOC.

You need to do the following preparatory steps before starting to record:

☐ **Filename** Type the filename of the file you wish to create into the File Name box. If you specify a .VOC file that already exists, you will overwrite it.

☐ **Sample Rate** Select the desired sample rate from the scrollable Sample Rate list. Using a mouse, select the sample rate to use when recording: 13,000-4,000 Hz if using Sound Blaster 1.x/2.0, or 44,000-4,000 Hz if using Sound Blaster Pro. The higher the sample rate, the better the file will sound.

☐ **Sound Blaster Pro Settings** Select the mixer and/or filter parameters by selecting radio buttons (sets of buttons where only one

FIGURE 10-3

The Record dialog box

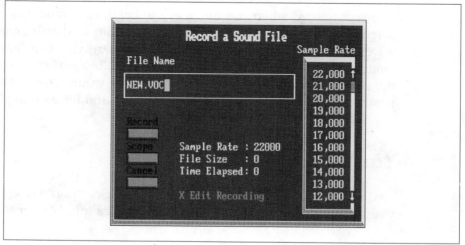

choice can be selected) from the Sound Blaster control box at the bottom of the screen.

☐   **CD-ROM Position**   Select the CD-ROM control buttons, in the slender horizontal box in the middle of the Record dialog box, if you have a CD-ROM installed and need to position it for recording.

Checking the Sound Source with Scope

The Scope option graphically displays real-time sample input, and is ideal for checking your source before starting the recording. To see this firsthand, select the Scope button from the Waveform Edit screen. Now speak into a microphone and see what your voice looks like, or play music directly into the Sound Blaster. (This works particularly well on faster machines and is an excellent way to check your system's quality.) When there is no sound input, you should see a straight, flat line that is exactly even with the white line on the sound file grid. Any spikes you see above or below this white line indicate that your system is registering noise of some kind. Pressing any key or either of the mouse buttons will cancel the Scope and return you to the Waveform Edit screen.

Starting the Recording

Select Record when you are ready to begin recording, and press ESC when you are ready to stop. Your sound file is then displayed as a waveform on the Waveform Edit screen where you can listen to and modify it. The sound file statistics are shown below the waveform. Note the number to the right of the Playing Time value. This is the current position of the bar that sweeps across the sound file as it is played.

Importing a Sound File

Choosing the Import option from the File Selection dialog box allows you to import .WAV, .NTI, .SND, and .8SV files into Blaster Master.

☐   .WAV files are in the Microsoft Multimedia format supported by the Sound Blaster Pro and Sound Blaster 16 and most sound card manufacturers.

☐   .SND files are raw wave data files (lacking header information).

☐   .NTI files are Amiga sample files as used by Tetra Compositor.

☐   .8SV is the extension normally used for Amiga IFF sound files. You can import Amiga IFF sound files, but you cannot save files in Amiga IFF format.

Note   You can also save .VOC files in the .WAV, .NTI, and .SND formats.

Accepting a Sound File

The Accept button serves to load the previously selected .VOC file into Blaster Master. (It really should be named Load.) If the sound file is multiblocked, Blaster Master will remove the blocks and convert it to a raw .VOC file. Voice file blocks are raw .VOC files, as discussed in Chapter 2.

Editing a Sound File

Once a file has been accepted (loaded), recorded, or inserted in another file by importing, you will see the Waveform Edit screen. This screen, which shows the sound file data as a waveform against a grid, is where you will have access to all the tools for performing digital (computer) transformation of the sound sample. You can cut and paste the waveform, add echoes and fades, pan stereo sounds, and do many other transformations.

In the Waveform Edit screen you issue commands by either selecting from the Vanishing Menu at the top of the screen, or selecting buttons at the bottom of the screen. Most of the button commands are duplicated in the Tools menu. They are offered as buttons for your convenience. Note that the More button will display additional buttons.

From the Waveform Edit screen you can either edit the entire file, or a section within the file. Once a section is marked by clicking with the left mouse button at two points along the horizontal grid, the Vanishing Menu changes. The File menu option is replaced by a Block menu option, and commands specific to working with blocks appear, such as Cut, Save, Move, and Copy. Both types of modifications are described in the sections that follow.

Transformations Using the Tools

This section of the chapter describes the *transformations* (modifications) applicable to an entire file. This is followed by a discussion of the transformations available to a section marked within a file.

Blaster Master supports several special digital processes, called *tools*, for modifying your sound files while they are displayed in the Waveform Edit screen. Among these are Scope, Echo, Reverse, Insert, Fast, Slow, Rate, Volume, Pitch, Pack, Fade, Vocals, Panning, and Mixer. Some of these transformations apply to either a section within a file, or to the whole file—and quite a few apply to either situation.

These transformations are available from the Waveform Edit screen. They can be accessed from either the Vanishing Menu's Tools menu option or from buttons on the Waveform Edit screen, or both. Not all the buttons can be displayed at the same time, so press the More button to see the next set of buttons. Figure 10-4 shows the Waveform Edit screen buttons, along with the Tools pull-down menu.

Setting a Marker

Blaster Master features a marker function which allows you to mark a point in a sound file. This function is especially useful for mixing (the Mix tool) and inserting sounds (the Insert tool) in sound files. To set a marker, position the mouse cursor at the appropriate spot on the blue bar just below the sound file grid. Then click the right mouse button on this position to place a white arrow on the blue bar, designating the marker.

FIGURE
10-4

Waveform Edit screen with Tools menu

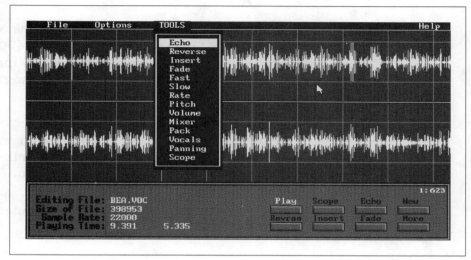

Note   This type of marker is not the same as the synchronization block marker used to coordinate music files with animation files.

Echo

The Echo option adds echo or delay to a .VOC file to give it a richer, fuller sound. This feature is also great for adding special effects. Figure 10-5 shows the Echo option dialog box.

FIGURE
10-5

Echo option dialog box

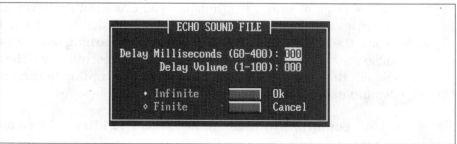

Two key parameters are used to determine the type of echo desired:

- **Delay Milliseconds** The "size" of the effect is determined by the number of milliseconds before the echo starts. Delays of 60-100 ms simulate the echo in a large room; larger delays (up to 200 ms) sound like the echo in a cavern or canyon. Type a number between 60 and 400 into this field.

- **Delay Volume** The mixture (how loudly the echo is mixed in) has an effect on the type of echo desired. A 30-60% mixture will sound more realistic than using a higher percentage volume for the delayed sounds. Type a number between 1 and 100 in this field.

To determine how the echo will repeat, click on either Infinite or Finite.

Reverse

You can reverse the playback of a .VOC file, which is effectively the same as playing a tape backwards. You Beatles fans can see for yourself if the song "Number 9" really does say "Turn me on, dead man" backwards. And did you know that the famous Tarzan yell sounds the same backwards as forwards? Try it!

Slow

This option extends the time domain without affecting the frequency domain. In plain English, that means the Slow transformation allows you to resample a .VOC file so that it will play back at approximately half speed, without affecting the pitch. This transformation doubles the size of the original sound file. Imagine you are a guitar player and want to learn the latest white-hot guitar licks from Joe Satriani or Eric Johnson—the Slow option makes listening and learning *much* easier. Slow is also very useful for preparing multimedia presentations. The amount by which the file is slowed will vary slightly according to the nature of the sound data.

 Tip Sound files with sample rates above 12 kHz produce a more natural sound.

Fast

We couldn't have a slow-down process without a speed-up process, could we? Unlike Slow, the Fast process includes a "slider" for selecting how much of a speed increase you desire. This function will decrease the size of the original sound file accordingly. To undo the effect of a Slow transformation, you need to approximately double the speed using the Fast transformation.

 Tip   Sound files with higher sample rates produce better results.

Rate

The Rate option allows a .VOC file created with a high sample rate to be down-sampled to a lower rate. Some PCs have difficulty playing .VOC files with the higher sample rates, so this Rate process gives you a way to change the sample rate to something more compatible with your PC. It is also a good way to make files smaller without the degradation associated with compression.

Once you select the Rate option, the Change Sample Rate dialog box appears, which displays the current rate and prompts you for the new rate. Type a value up to 44,100 for monaural sound or 22,050 for stereo sound and press ENTER.

A .VOC file recorded at 12,000 Hz or more that is down-sampled to 8,000 Hz will probably sound better than if it had been originally recorded at a rate below 12,000 Hz. Sound files sampled on a MacIntosh at 22,000 Hz can be down-sampled to 12,000 Hz or less with excellent results. The Rate process is also capable of up-sampling, although you will not gain any resolution.

Volume

This process either increases or decreases the amplitude of .VOC files. One way to get a very clean sample is to make your sample at a fairly low volume and then resample up to a higher volume. The Sound Blaster and Sound Blaster Pro have a tendency to introduce distortion as you increase the volume used for sampling.

The Volume process works very well for high-quality sampling that has been done directly from a CD or tape deck. You can increase or decrease the volume for the entire file by specifying a number that represents the desired percentage change in volume. Once you select the Volume menu option, the Adjust Volume dialog box appears. In the top data-entry field of the dialog box, enter either **I** to increase the volume or **D** to decrease the volume. In the bottom data-entry field enter the desired percent of change in volume.

Increasing the volume by values of 10 to 50 (10% and 50%) has a subtle effect on the resulting sound file. Values of 50 to 200 or more have a dramatic effect. Decreasing the volume by values of 1 to 99 causes the resulting file to have approximately the same volume as the percent of the number entered. Entering 50, for instance, will produce a sound file that is perceived as only 50% as loud as the original. Note that if a value greater than 100 is entered, the effect will be to *increase* the volume, even though you selected D for decrease.

Mixer

The Mixer process blends two .VOC files into a single sample. It is a good way to add special effects to your sound files. There is a volume mix parameter that lets you control how loud the mixed-in sample will be. The volume mix parameter can be a number between 1 and 100; 50 to 60 is often a very good mixing level. Before beginning the Mixer process (see the "Selecting a Marker" section above), select the point within your original file where you want to begin mixing. If you want to start at the beginning of your file, choose the farthest point to your left.

This process does not try to adjust the sample rates if the files are different.

Pack/Unpack

This command packs or unpacks a sound file, depending on its current state. Most of the transformations available in the Waveform Edit screen can be performed on unpacked files. Only a few transformations, such as Cut and Move, can be applied directly to packed files. Many sound files come packed, especially sound effects and speech files; once unpacked, all of the special Blaster Master features can be applied to these files. You then pack the file again, if you desire.

Pitch

The Pitch option alters the sample rate value contained within the .VOC file. If you want to raise or lower the pitch, select the slider. Altering the pitch will also affect the playback time, but not the size of the file.

Fade

The Fade menu option allows you to fade in or out the volume of a sound file at the file's beginning and ending. When choosing this transformation, you can specify the amount of time you want for the fade-in or fade-out; neither of these times can exceed one half the total time of the sound file. If, for instance, you wish to only fade out a sound file, use zero as the fade-in time.

When combining multiple files, a little fading can result in a smoother transition in the sound, making the switch between sounds less abrupt. This can be especially effective when a sound file has lots of background noise and the joining sound file does not.

Vocals (Stereo Files Only)

The Vocals transformation removes vocals from a stereo sound file. The effect varies significantly from song to song, depending on how it was originally mixed. For example, using the Vocals process on "I Feel Fine" by The Beatles will remove 99 percent of the vocal, whereas in "Eleanor Rigby" it has the effect of enhancing the vocals and reducing the cellos. This option actually inverts the left channel 180 degrees and mixes it back into the right channel. This has a tendency to cancel out all the center waves where vocals are often mixed in. The Vocals transformation is a lot of fun and works as well in removing vocals as hardware accessories costing as much as $350.

Panning (Stereo Files Only)

Panning adds left-channel to right-channel stereo panning, or right-channel to left-channel stereo panning. In other words, it allows a sound file to sweep gradually from one speaker to the next.

Insert

The Insert transformation allows another sound file to be inserted into the sound file you are currently editing. When you select Insert, the File Selection dialog box appears. From here, you can choose Select a .VOC file. You can also choose to record a new sound file or cancel the insert process, which will return you to the Edit screen. Once you have selected a .VOC file for insertion, the Blaster Master gives you the option of selecting the insertion point in the original file by using either the mouse pointer, the marker, a sample point in the file, or a point in time.

If the sample rate of the incoming sound file does not match the original file, the sample rate will be adjusted to blend in correctly.

Caution   Use care when inserting a sound file. If the incoming sound file is packed, contains silence blocks, or is a multiple-block .VOC file, the resulting sound file will not be optimal. If possible, identify and unpack packed files and convert silence blocks to silence data.

Modifying the Entire Sound File

The following button commands are available for working with the sound file as a whole. Many of the commands are explained above, in the section titled Transformations Using the Tools:

- ☐   **Play** Lets you listen to the entire file.

- ☐   **Scope** Displays the sound source as a waveform. This is described more in the section "Checking the Sound Source with Scope" near the beginning of the chapter.

- ☐   **Echo** Adds echo to the entire file.

- ☐   **New** Assumes you want to return to the File Section dialog box. It displays the Save dialog box for saving the current sound data to disk.

- ☐   **Reverse** Does just that. It reverses the order of sound bytes in the file so it plays backwards.

- ☐   **Insert** Puts into the current sound file the contents of another sound file on disk.

- ☐ **Fade** Gradually diminishes or increases the sound level.

- ☐ **Fast** Increases the playback speed.

- ☐ **Slow** Decreases the playback speed.

- ☐ **Rate** Changes the sampling rate, resampling the file.

- ☐ **Pitch** Increases or decreases the frequency of the sound sample.

- ☐ **Volume** Adjusts the volume level.

- ☐ **Mixer** Digitally combines two sound files.

- ☐ **Vocals** Removes much of the vocal component from a sound file, leaving the instrumental component.

Modifying a Section of the Sound File

To select a sound file section to edit, position the cursor over the graph at the first desired cut point, and press the left mouse button. Then position the cursor over the second cut point and press the left mouse button again. This marks the section with a blue box.

The following button commands are available for working with a section of the sound file. Many of the commands are explained above, in the section titled "Transformations Using the Tools":

- ☐ **Play** Lets you listen to that section only.

- ☐ **Cut** Removes that section from the file.

- ☐ **New** Has two different effects. If you've already selected a section of the waveform, picking the New button will undo that selection. If you haven't already selected a section, New assumes you want to exit, returning you to the File Selection dialog box.

- ☐ **Zoom** Expands the marked section repeatedly so you can see it with greater detail and edit the sound file with surgical precision. You can zoom the file until the resolution reaches 1:1. The current resolution is shown in the top-right corner of the control panel below the waveform display.

☐ **UnZoom** Reverses the effect of previous Zooms.

☐ **Save** Saves the section to disk as its own file. You will be prompted for the filename.

☐ **Move** Allows a selection to be moved to a new location in the same file.

Figure 10-6 shows the voice file BEA.VOC with a 1:2 zoom.

The following commands are displayed in a menu that appears when you select the Tools button or the Tools option from the Vanishing Menu. Many of the commands are explained above, in "Transformations Using the Tools":

☐ **Loop** Repeats a block up to 10 times, adding a Max Headroom-type stutter to the file.

☐ **Mute** Replaces the block with silence bytes, which is very useful for removing glitches and other undesirable noises without affecting the playback time.

FIGURE 10-6 Voice file with a zoom

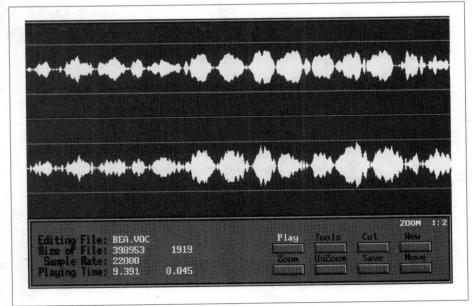

☐ **Reverse** Reverses the order of sound bytes in the block so it plays backwards.

☐ **Pitch** Changes the pitch of the block (lowering or raising it) and, as a side effect, changes the playback time.

☐ **Echo** Adds echo to the block.

☐ **Volume** Adjusts the playback volume level of the block.

The last four of these, Reverse, Pitch, Echo, and Volume, are also available for an entire file. These commands appear in the Tools menu, regardless of whether a section is marked, since they are equally valid transformations for an entire file.

File Menu

While in the Waveform Edit screen, you can select the following File menu items:

☐ **Save** Saves the current sound file. If the current sound file is untitled, you will be prompted for a filename.

☐ **Save As** Saves the current sound file under a new name or in a new file format.

☐ **Quit** Exits Blaster Master and takes you to DOS. If the current sound file is untitled, you will be prompted for a filename.

Figure 10-7 shows the Save dialog box. Click on the button for the desired file type before clicking on the Return to Edit button.

Options Menu

While in the Waveform Edit screen, you can select the following Options menu items:

☐ **Loop Play On/Off** Causes playback to be one line only (Off) or continuously looping (On). This applies to the entire file, or if a selection has been marked, to that section only.

☐ **Save Screen Colors** Saves the current screen colors. For more details, see the later section, "Working with Screen Colors." You won't see this if a section of the waveform is currently selected.

☐ **Play Block/Play All** This item doesn't appear until a section of the waveform is selected. It then toggles between Play Block and Play All, and controls whether just the block or the entire file is played when the Play button is selected.

Recording from CD-ROM (SB Pro and SB 16 only)

If you are using a CD-ROM from the Creative Labs Multimedia Upgrade Kit, you can use Blaster Master to sample recordings directly from your favorite CDs. The Blaster Master program creates excellent recordings with the Sound Blaster Pro using the CD-ROM. If you are equipped with a CD-ROM, a standard CD player control bar will appear in the Record dialog box. Blaster Master currently supports the following CD player controls—Play, Pause, Stop, Rewind, Fast Forward, Previous Track, and Next Track.

| FIGURE 10-7 | Save dialog box |

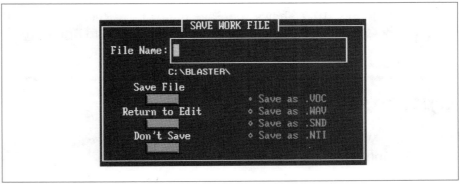

To sample from your favorite CDs, make sure you have selected CD as your input source when you display the Record dialog box. There are two ways to perform the recording. The obvious way is to start playing the CD-ROM and then select Blaster Master's Record button.

Alternatively, you can let Blaster Master synchronize the CD-ROM's play and Blaster Master's recording functions. Position on the desired CD-ROM track and place the CD-ROM on pause. When you are ready to begin recording, select the Record button. Blaster Master will automatically start the CD-ROM, perfectly synchronizing the start of digital audio recording and the start of CD audio playback. When you press ESC to stop recording, the CD playback will shut off automatically.

Working with Screen Colors

If you have a color VGA graphics display, you can choose from 256 colors. EGA users can choose from 64 colors. As you select colors, keep in mind that certain colors do not blend well with others. A poor choice of screen colors can result in unreadable dialog boxes and help screens. You can revise the colors while you run Blaster Master, as described in the section titled "Selecting Colors for Your Screen" at the beginning of this chapter.

The current color palette can be saved as your default colors. You can also start Blaster Master using one of the alternate screen palette files provided with your program. Both of these customizations are described below.

Saving Screen Colors

The color scheme of Blaster Master is specified in a configuration file named BMASTER.CFG that is automatically loaded when you start the program. To revise the default colors, select the Options menu item from the Vanishing Menu, and choose Save Screen Colors. You can restore the default screen colors by renaming or deleting this file.

Selecting an Alternate Color Palette

You can start Blaster Master with an alternate color scheme by loading a .PAL color palette file. To load a palette file, include the /P command switch followed by the filename. For example, to start the program with the OLDMOVE.PAL color palette, type **BMASTER /POLDMOVIE.PAL** as your start-up command.

To always start Blaster Master with the screen colors in your favorite .PAL file, copy the .PAL file to BMASTER.CFG. For instance, if you like the colors in OLDMOVE.PAL, type the following at the DOS prompt: **COPY OLDMOVIE.PAL BMASTER.CFG**, and then press the ENTER key.

The .PAL files are provided on disk in a compressed file called PALFILES.EXE. If you don't see the .PAL files, create them by typing PALFILES.EXE at the DOS prompt. This will create many small (32-byte) screen color files with the filename extension .PAL.

Setting Blaster Master Mixer Defaults (SB Pro and SB 16 Only)

When you select the Record menu option or the Record button, you will see the Recording dialog box and, at the bottom right of your screen, the recording default settings. (The settings are only visible for the Sound Blaster Pro.) The default setting is for microphone recording. You can customize your Blaster Master environment, specifying your choice for the recording parameter defaults, by using the SET BMDEFS= environment variable. A command line like the one below is inserted into your AUTOEXEC.BAT file:

```
              Input Source  Input Mode     Filter  Rate CDROM

SET BMDEFS= {CD/MIC/LINE} {STEREO/MONO} {LO/HI} {NN} {ROMx:}
```

The order of the parameters doesn't matter. Use the SET command alone at the DOS prompt to check your environment first. Then revise your AUTOEXEC.BAT file. Remember to save a copy of your original AUTOEXEC.BAT file before making any changes, and to reboot your machine to make these changes effective. See Chapter 2 for instructions on how to edit an ASCII file such as your AUTOEXEC.BAT.

For example, to set Blaster Master's default recording parameters to stereo line input with a low-pass filter and a sample rate of 22 KHz, use these parameters:

SET BMDEFS=LINE STEREO LO 22

 Note   Users of the Multimedia Upgrade CD-ROM may find a long pause on the File Selection dialog box when an Audio CD is in the drive. Use the {ROMx:} parameter to skip verifying that drive. To skip the CD-ROM drive F, for instance, use {ROMF:}.

Setting the Blaster Environment

Users of Sound Blaster 1.0 and compatible sound cards can override the address port/IRQ/DMA scanning by using the SET BLASTER= environment parameters supported by Sound Blaster 2.0 and Sound Blaster Pro versions.

If you have problems executing Blaster Master on your computer, try adding the following command line to your AUTOEXEC.BAT file:

SET BLASTER=A220 I7 D1

where A220 is the port I/O address, I7 is the interrupt, and D1 is the DMA channel. These settings are the default settings for the Sound Blaster; your installation may be different. For questions about your Sound Blaster installation, see Appendix A.

Troubleshooting Blaster Master

We promised to try and help you in this chapter with solutions to the most commonly occurring problems you might experience with Blaster Master, so here we go.

- ☐   **"Not enough 640K Memory Free"**   You will see this message when you try to run Blaster Master. See the section below about frequent crashes for an explanation of what to do.

- ☐   **Can't Hear Anything on Playback**   Verify in the File Selection dialog box that the master volume and source volume have been set to midrange or higher.

- ☐   **Frequent Crashes**   Blaster Master will crash frequently if your system doesn't have enough memory. You truly need as close to 640K as possible—580K or more free memory is ideal. Although your computer may have 640K or more memory installed, too much of the conventional memory (the first 640K) is already taken up by other programs, including drivers (such as for network connectivity), TSRs (such as SPUTMON), and memory managers (for placing drivers into high memory or creating a RAM disk or disk cache). The activity that uses the most memory is Echo with the maximum (400 milliseconds) delay. You should remove all unnecessary drivers before using this program. If necessary, you can further conserve memory by temporarily disabling your memory manager (such as the DOS 5 HIMEM, used for Microsoft Windows) and STACKS= command in the CONFIG.SYS by placing a REM before these statements. Remember to save a copy of your original CONFIG.SYS file before making any changes, and to reboot your machine to make these changes effective. See Chapter 2 for instructions on how to edit an ASCII file such as your CONFIG.SYS.

- ☐   **Unrecognized Graphical Interface**   It is possible that Blaster Master may not correctly identify your graphical interface. If Blaster Master tells you that you don't have EGA/VGA graphics but you know you do, try using the command switch /G. This switch forces graphics mode and bypasses the interface check.

- ☐   **Error 5**   This is a DOS error that means Illegal Function Call, which could signify just about anything. The most common occurrence of this is when you try to run Blaster Master on a PC with a graphics card that does not properly support 640 x 350 x 16 high-resolution EGA graphics mode. If you get this error immediately after typing the BMASTER command, then the problem is probably with your graphics card. The only fix in this case is to change your graphics card.

☐ **Mouse Cursor Erase Syndrome** A few users have reported instances of the moving mouse cursor seeming to erase the screen. This is a problem with the mouse driver. Blaster Master only makes calls to the Mouse API; it does not repaint the screen. In each case so far, switching mouse drivers has fixed this problem.

Performance Tips

Blaster Master works best on a very fast PC—one that has a fast processor, a fast graphics display, and a fast hard drive.

We recommend using floating-point operations for accuracy. A math coprocessor accelerates most of the functions by as much as 40 percent. For example, mixing two 50K files requires over one million calculations.

A slow graphics card can cause wait states on your processor. That bargain-priced VGA system may not be such a bargain if you save a mere $50 while slowing your PC down by 40 to 60 percent in graphics mode.

Blaster Master is designed to use virtual memory; that is, it uses your hard drive whenever possible. While this is slower, it is much more reliable and supports a wider system base. It also easily supports huge files. If you are lucky enough to have several megabytes of RAM, try running from a RAM disk, or at least use an extended/expanded memory disk cache. It makes a big difference in performance.

Disk fragmentation can lessen performance, regardless of what software you are running. Be sure to run optimization software regularly.

PART IV

Hardware and Software
Enhancements

CHAPTER

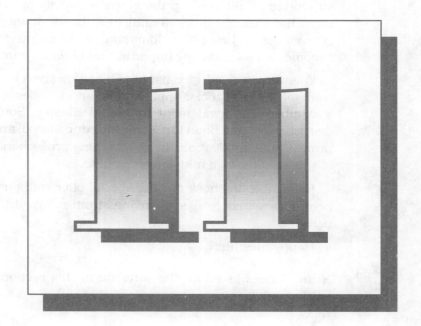

Third-Party Software

Sound, or rather the lack of it, has traditionally been one of the personal computer's few weaknesses. With the advent of the Sound Blaster sound cards, however, PC users no longer have to sit back and listen to (no pun intended) the raves of Apple Macintosh and Commodore Amiga owners about the great sound effects in their applications. As the de facto sound board standard, Sound Blaster is widely supported by software publishers. In fact, almost all contemporary PC game software supports Sound Blaster.

Microsoft and Windows also support Sound Blaster, and by virtue of this fact, most Windows applications will use Sound Blaster if sound is supported at all. The popularity and maturity of the Windows environment has brought about a shift in software development. As Windows gets closer to being the dominant desktop interface on PCs, sound becomes an increasingly important addition to your PC.

Following is a selected list (it is by no means a comprehensive one) of some of the best tools, applications, and utilities available to help you maximize your investment in Sound Blaster. Some of the programs described are just plain fun, some are educational, and others are serious professional applications (with matching professional price tags). Think of this chapter as a mini–buyer's guide.

Remember to check out the special offer coupons at the back of this book for exclusive, special savings from many of the publishers listed below.

Happy hunting.

 Note   Prices listed for the software in this section are current at this writing only.

Advanced Support Group

Advanced Support Group
11900 Grant Pl.
Des Peres, MO 63131
Orders Only: (800) 767-9611
Information & Registered Users Technical Support:

(314) 965-5630
CompuServe ID: 70304,3642

Whoop It Up! Fanfare
(Suggested Retail: $79.95)

Whoop It Up! attaches sound—both .WAV and MIDI files—to Windows events, such as Application Startup and Shutdown, Move, Minimize, Maximize, and many others. This program can also attach sounds to message boxes, such as those with the exclamation mark and question mark icon boxes. Each application can have its own custom set of sounds assigned to it. There is even a random feature that will select a random sound every time you use the application.

Over 2.5Mb of .WAV and MIDI files are included in Whoop It Up! Fanfare. Additionally, the following four utilities are all part of this collection:

☐ Yakkity Clock is a talking clock that features both preset and custom alarms, voice announcement of the time at various intervals, and both a male and female voice. It can be configured to display time maximized, or as icon text when minimized.

☐ Yakkity Monitor is a talking system monitor. It continuously monitors system resources and disk space and literally tells you when they fall below the preset levels. The program can be set to "stay on top" so that you can visually monitor Windows's current use of resources.

☐ Wave Editor is a 16-bit stereo .WAV file editor that boasts as wide a range of features as any professional sound editor. Besides basic functions such as recording and cut-and-paste, Wave Editor provides routines for fades, tranforms, filters, and echoes.

☐ Yakkity Savers is a collection of 14 screensavers that include sound and animation sequences. With Yakkity Savers loaded, you'll have fun with animated mice on pogo sticks and roller blades, skiing fruit, and various kaleidoscopic screensavers on your screen. These screensavers work with the standard Windows 3.1 screensaver.

Aristosoft

Aristosoft
7041 Koll Center Parkway, Suite 160
Pleasanton, CA 94566
1-800-338-2629 (outside CA)
1-800-426-8288 (inside CA)

Wired for Sound Pro (Suggested Retail $79.95)

The granddaddy of sound utilities, Wired for Sound Pro enhances
Windows by allowing you to attach sounds to Windows events. Wired for
Sound Pro's over 100 sound effects add audio excitement to even the
most mundane Windows events such as moving or resizing windows. A
talking system monitor, a talking clock, and a .WAV sound editor round
out this collection.

The Audio Solution

The Audio Solution
P.O. Box 11688
Clayton, MO 63105
(314) 567-0267

DigPak and MidPak
(License Fees: $69.95 to $5,000)

DigPak and MidPak are APIs (Application Programmers Interface) that
are widely used in the PC game industry. Other well-known game
publishers such as Strategic Simulations, Frontier, Software Toolworks,
Electronic Arts, and Spectrum Holobyte, among many others, have
embraced these APIs. DigPak and MidPak are the premier solution for
developers requiring music and sound effects in their applications—
whether the output medium is Sound Blaster or other sound cards on

the market. If you're a professional developer or programmer, or even just a budding amateur, and you want to take full advantage of Sound Blaster, these are the APIs you've been looking for.

DigPak is a set of TSRs that provide a simple API, through a user interrupt vector, to play 8-bit digitized sounds. C procedures for use with your program are included. Software compression and decompression of sound files are included, as well.

MidPak provides support for FM synthesis and MIDI music. The MidPak TSR works alone or in conjunction with the DigPak drivers to give a developer a complete sound solution. MidPak is a derivative of John Miles's Audio Interface Library, which is used in several computer games, including Interplay's Star Trek: The 25th Anniversary, Buzz Aldrin's Race Into Space, and Origin's Ultima Underworld and Strike Commander.

Bells and Whistles Software

Bells and Whistles Software
3829 Lawndale Ave.
Ft. Worth, TX 76133
CompuServe ID: 73527,2544

ToWave (Free; Available from CompuServe and Some BBSs)

ToWave (Figure 11-1) is a freeware Windows program that converts almost any sound file to a .WAV format sound file. ToWave works with any uncompressed sound file, including .VOC, .SOU, and .SND files. The file must be recorded at a sampling rate of 11, 22, or 44.1 kHz.

ToWave ignores the header of the different formats and simply adds a .WAV file header to whatever data is in the sound file. Because of this brute-force method of conversion, the resultant .WAV file may require editing to eliminate the few microseconds of gibberish or noise due to the old header. Windows's Sound Recorder program is more than adequate for this task.

FIGURE
11-1

ToWave

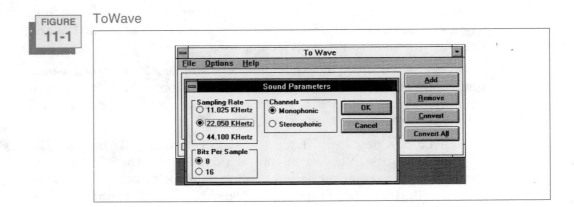

In order to use the program you will need the Microsoft Visual Basic Runtime DLL, VBRUN100.DLL, which should be available from the same BBS where you obtained ToWave.

Berkeley Systems

Berkeley Systems
2095 Rose Street
Berkeley, CA 94709
(510) 540-5535

After Dark (Suggested Retail $49.95)

After Dark is one of the widest-selling Windows utility programs. It was first made available for the Apple Macintosh, but has gathered quite a following in the Windows arena.

After Dark is a screensaver for Windows that includes the famous flying toaster and the ever-popular fish aquarium. The different modules sport different sounds, including "blub-blub" to accompany the air bubbles from the aquarium module. There are howling coyotes and screen-munching worms among the 40 or so modules. My favorite is the Swan Lake module, where beautiful swans and their cygnets float and swim gracefully across the screen.

Blaster Master (Shareware: $29.95)

Gary Maddox
1901 Spring Creek #315
Plano, TX 75023
CompuServe ID: 76711,547

Blaster Master (Figure 11-2) is a DOS-based program for working with Sound Blaster .VOC files, and .WAV, and .SND format files. It requires an EGA/VGA display, a mouse, a hard disk, and preferably a fast PC (386 or 486). Blaster Master is available as shareware. The unregistered version will only process a sound file of up to 25 seconds; while there is no such limit on the registered version. Features include the ability to convert between the different supported formats and sampling rates. You can add effects such as echoes and fades. The completely mouse-driven interface is easy to learn and use.

 Note   Blaster Master is included on the disk that comes with this book. Refer to Chapter 10 for more information.

Dr. T's Music Software, Inc.

Dr. T's Music Software, Inc.
124 Crescent Road, Suite 3
Needham, MA 02194
(800) 989-6434 or (617) 455-1454

FIGURE
11-2

Blaster Master

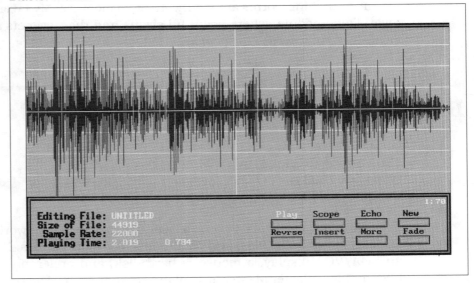

Boom Box (Suggested Retail: $59.95)

Are you ready to jam? Boom Box (Figure 11-3) is an exciting interactive title that allows you to get in the groove by triggering music samples using a keyboard, mouse, or joystick.

Boom Box draws heavily from popular rap and hip-hop styles. Dr. T's Music Software recruited musical engineers from New York City's acclaimed Unique Recording Studios to help create a number of the featured musical grooves. A lot of the grooves are actually created by some of the same people who do what you hear on the Billboard Top 100.

Boom Box's Remix screen lets you completely rearrange the songs, mix the different instruments and effects, trigger outrageous samples, and even record your virtuoso performances to disk. This is a party machine. You will love it, and your friends won't leave it alone. Paired with Sound Blaster, Boom Box transforms you from a computer nerd to the coolest guy on the block. Break it down; check it out!

FIGURE
11-3

Boom Box

QuickScore Plus (Suggested Retail: $149)

This DOS- and icon-based combination sequencer and notation program allows you to simply "draw in" notes with a mouse, or record a MIDI keyboard performance in real time. You can immediately see and play back your score, with up to 16 tracks simultaneously.

With Sound Blaster, a MIDI keyboard is not required for recording, editing, and/or playback in QuickScore Plus. The program allows you to enter any time or key signature, and add any tempo changes at any point in the score. You can also enter lyrics in a composition; but QuickScore Plus, or any other notation program for that matter, has yet to gain the ability to sing them.

Future Trends Software

Future Trends Software
1508 Osprey Drive, #103
DeSoto, TX 75115
(214) 224-3288

EZSound FX (Suggested Retail: $69.95)

EZSound FX is the Swiss Army knife of sound utilities for Windows. Six different modules or programs are included with EZSound FX, each one with specific capabilities.

- ☐ Digital FX (Figure 11-4), and Synth FX allow you to attach any sound or music to such mundane events as resizing a window or deleting a file. These are separate programs that can be run simultaneously. For instance, you can have Digital FX play a digitized gunshot when you close a window; Synth FX plays the beginning of Beethoven's Fifth whenever you resize a window.

- ☐ Music FX plays music files (.CMF and .ROL) in the background while you're working on other, more important matters. Over 100 such files, from classical to New Age, are included.

- ☐ CD FX is a CD player program included for those who have a CD-ROM drive connected to their Sound Blaster. Though a very basic program without any fancy displays or database features, it works well and is an adequate enhancement to the Windows Media Player when you want to listen to a CD.

- ☐ Master FX (Figure 11-5) is a versatile sound editor that fully supports stereo recording, editing, and playback on the Sound Blaster Pro series. It imports and converts sound files from various formats, even those from the Macintosh, Amiga, NeXT, and Sun environments. You should have fun experimenting with the over 100 included digital sound effects. The program supports sampling rates from 5,000 to 44,100 Hz, but cannot support 16-bit recording. That aside, it is very easy to use, and the variable view magnification and resizable window is a big improvement over the standard Windows Recorder.

FIGURE
11-4

Digital FX

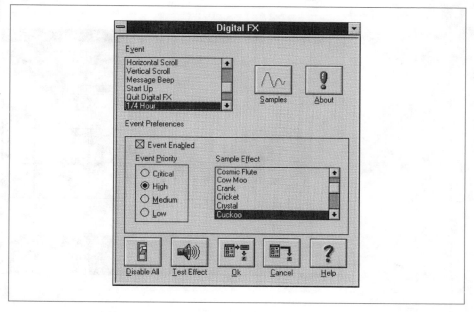

☐   Panel FX is a custom control panel for controlling the volume level of Sound Blaster. Additionally, you can use it to adjust and assign the Windows system error sound.

EZSound FX easily qualifies as the best bargain among Windows sound utilities for your Sound Blaster. The program interface is simple and intuitive. If your budget is tight this is the one to get.

Howling Dogs Systems

Howling Dogs Systems
Box 80405
Burnaby, BC
Canada V5H 3X6
(604) 436-0420
(800) 877-4266
CompuServe ID: 70044,2736

FIGURE
11-5

Master FX

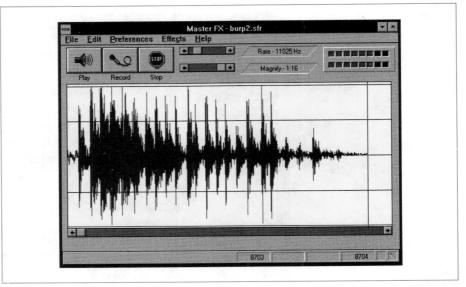

Power Chords (Suggested Retail: $84.95)

Power Chords (Figure 11-6), is an innovative sequencing program that distinguishes itself from other sequencers by using an on-screen guitar (or another stringed instrument) to build chords that are then used to build songs. Other music parts, such as drum and bass, can also be created and easily plugged into the song framework.

Power Chords actually lets you use the mouse to "play" the guitar. Guitarist and string players can even draw chords right on the screen. The program lets you pluck, strum, and do "string bends" and "hammer-ons," too. The on-screen instrument can have up to 12 strings and 24 frets, and can be tuned any way you want. You'll find it's simple to re-create the sounds of instruments such as guitars, banjos, and uku-leles, as well as create new, fantasy instruments.

Because of its unique interface, you do not need to know how to read scores or music notation. Writing music with Power Chords is easy. You

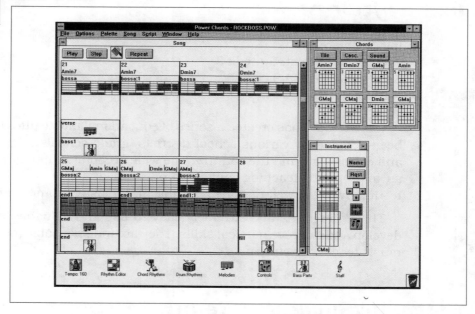

FIGURE 11-6

Power Chords

first create a chord progression and then build a plucking or strumming pattern. This chord progression repeats until another pattern is encountered. Drum and bass parts are created similarly and also repeat automatically. There is even a chord request feature: Request almost any chord, and Power Chords provides a number of different variations of it—no matter how many strings the instrument has or how it is tuned.

Power Chord's comprehensive scripting capability is best demonstrated by the interactive tutorial and demo, which was written entirely using this scripting feature. Lesson and presentation scripts can be created with relative ease. If you are a musician, the recording capability allows you to simply play and record your performance with a MIDI instrument. Any mistakes can be corrected using the built-in editor. Power Chords also imports and exports files in standard MIDI format.

Ibis Software

Ibis Software
140 Second Street, Suite 603
San Francisco, CA 94105
(415) 546-1917

Ibis Software has created a series of educational music titles that have been adopted by various school districts, grade schools, high schools, and colleges around the country. The wide acceptance of Ibis's software as appropriate teaching and learning tools at these varied levels is testimony to the well-designed, flexible, and mostly fun programs.

These programs are extremely easy to use and valuable in helping develop and improve musical skills. They are indispensable tools for any music teacher or student.

Noteplay (Suggested Retail: $49.95)

Designed primarily for people who want to learn to play music, or to improve their current playing abilities, NotePlay (Figure 11-7) can be used to teach the user how to read notes on a staff and play them from a keyboard. Using either the computer keyboard (which has been mapped to replicate an electronic keyboard) or an actual MIDI keyboard, you select and play back the notes displayed on a staff. In this game format, points are awarded for speed and accuracy. If you beat the timer, you get bonus points.

There are 36 drill levels, with new musical phrases introduced with every session. You can choose from three different play modes—slow, normal and automatic—tailoring the program to your level. Advanced drills include two-handed exercises dealing with counterpoint, intervals, and chords. You can choose to practice at a certain level as frequently as you like.

NotePlay for Windows is easy enough for beginners yet powerful enough for advanced musicians. The program's multilevel approach and various play modes make the program appropriate for users at all levels—beginner, hobbyist, student, or serious musician. The program

FIGURE
11-7
Noteplay

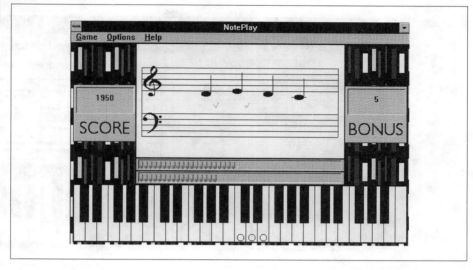

can also be used in an exploratory mode by disabling the game. Here you can randomly play notes and see them appear on the Grand Staff in their correct location and with their correct name. The attractive graphical interface and ease of use make the program as much fun as it is instructional.

NotePlay is available as either a DOS or Windows program.

Play It By Ear (Suggested Retail: $99.95)

Play It By Ear (Figure 11-8) provides a variety of self-paced ear-training exercises, featuring an on-screen piano keyboard and guitar fretboard. The program's strength is in its instant response to your actions, helping you to quickly identify and improve your weaknesses. You can use a mouse to play the on-screen instrument, or choose to apply the exercises directly to a MIDI-equipped keyboard or guitar.

Play It By Ear offers a variety of interactive melodic and harmonic exercises. Topics include note, chord, and interval recognition; chord and interval naming; pitches; scales; modes; and much more. In each

FIGURE
11-8

Play It By Ear

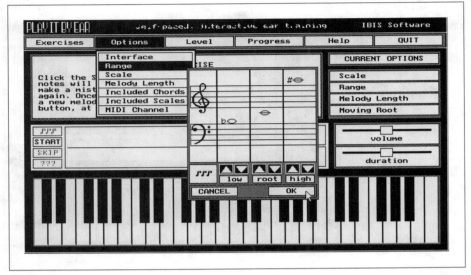

exercise, you are asked to play back or identify specific notes, melodies, intervals, or chords. The program tells you immediately if each answer is correct or incorrect. When you get stumped, ask Play It By Ear to highlight the correct location of the note, chord, or interval on the on-screen keyboard or fretboard. The program gives you another opportunity for the correct answer. A scorekeeper tracks your progress and displays it in a progress graph, a post-exercise summary, or an exercise report.

A suite of options gives you complete control over the content and difficulty of each exercise. For example, you can increase or reduce the range of the keyboard or fretboard covered by each exercise. Play It By Ear plays back melodies of from 2 to 16 notes, and also allows you to vary the playback speed. In all, the program offers six levels of challenge.

Play It By Ear will not cure the tone deaf, but will help the budding musician or singer to develop a keener sense of pitch and an improved ability to recognize notes, chords, and melodies.

RhythmAce (Suggested Retail: $99.95)

RhythmAce (Figure 11-9) is an interactive music education program featuring on-screen rhythmic notation. Offering a variety of different exercise modes, RhythmAce offers you flexibility in tailoring the presentation of drills to suit individual needs. Topics such as tempo, measures per drill, time signatures, notation values, and mixed meters provide for a complete rhythm-training regimen.

In a typical exercise, you hear a metronome ticking and are required to play back the rhythmic notation shown on the screen; you can use a mouse, the PC keyboard, or a MIDI keyboard. In another exercise, the program plays a rhythmic phrase, and you reproduce the notation by means of on-screen notation buttons. Drills are selected from a single user library, including a classical style that follows traditional notation rules closely, and a jazz style with a more relaxed notation. The program even includes the option of one- or two-handed rhythms.

RhythmAce provides comprehensive feedback about accuracy and improvement over time. In the notation area, a red X indicates a note or

FIGURE
11-9

RhythmAce

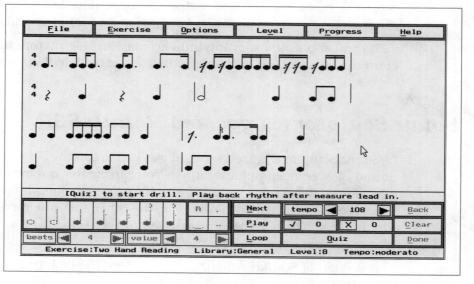

rest that was played incorrectly. Also, two timing diagrams display the expected response and the actual response, letting you know if notes and rests were held for the correct interval of time. Once the rhythm has been played correctly, the program calculates an accuracy figure based on expected and actual performance. At the end of a block of exercises, you can print a summary of the exercise just performed.

RhythmPlay (Suggested Retail: $49.95)

RhythmPlay (Figure 11-10) is a simpler version or subset of RhythmAce, and is presented in a game format. Special features include an audio and visual metronome; 24 types of drills; sustain and timing accuracy; timing diagram; high-score table; slow, normal, and automatic modes; and one- and two-handed exercises. This is an excellent program to help beginners get a feeling for rhythm. Experienced musicians can use it to hone their sense of timing. RhythmPlay isolates either sight reading or rhythm reading, to help you concentrate on just this skill.

The 24 types of drills are grouped into 6 levels, for a progressive introduction to reading and playing rhythms. You begin with simple rhythmic phrases using quarter- and half-notes in 4/4 time. As you progress, rests, eighth- and sixteenth-notes, dots and ties, changing meters, and two-handed phrases are introduced into the drills.

Typical applications for RhythmPlay may include rhythm training for church choir members, or training drummers to read rhythms from a score.

SoundSculptor (Suggested Retail: $39.95)

SoundSculptor (Figure 11-11), allows you to edit the FM sounds of the Sound Blaster in a graphical format. You can create your own sounds or edit some of the sounds included with the program. Sounds created with SoundSculptor can then be used in the other Ibis programs such as RhythmPlay. The sounds can be saved in the .BNK or .INS format, so that other programs can also use them.

A version of SoundSculptor is included on the disk that comes with this book.

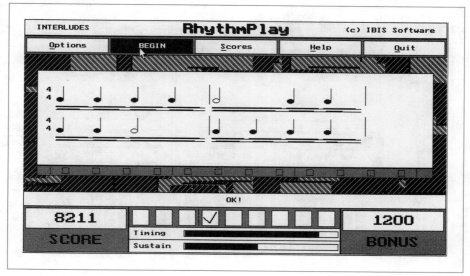

FIGURE 11-10   RhythmPlay

Icom Simulations

Icom Simulations
648 South Wheeling Road
Wheeling, DL 60090
(708) 520-4440

Intermission (Suggested Retail: $49.95)

Intermission is a Windows screensaver that includes many sound effects to accompany the colorful and action filled screens. It contains 55 zany modules. For example, you'll find a dancing disco pig complete with disco-era music and a disco ball; a fireworks module to light up the screen and blow up your speakers; a swarm of wasps buzzing around the screen; and battling mixers zapping each other with electricity.

Intermission will also use any After Dark module.

FIGURE
11-11

SoundSculptor

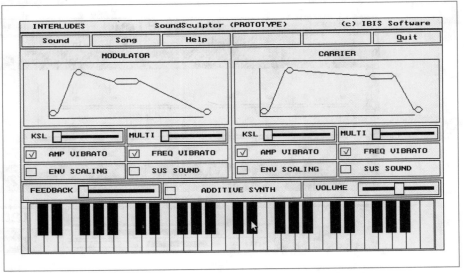

Midisoft Corporation

Midisoft Corporation
P.O. Box 1000
Bellevue, WA 98009
(800) 776-6434 or (206) 881-7176

Music Mentor for Windows (Suggested Retail: $149.95)

Music Mentor (Figure 11-12) offers an entertaining music tutorial and utilizes a notation-based MIDI sequencer. These features make music concepts spring to life—even for beginners. The product has lively text, graphics, animation, and MIDI-generated sounds.

For those just getting started in music, Music Mentor offers an introduction to basic music reading and explains the essential elements of all musical composition—rhythm, melody, harmony, timbre, texture,

FIGURE 11-12 MusicMentor for Windows

and form. The tutorial includes demonstrations of the ways in which famous composers have used musical elements during their own musical eras.

Because Music Mentor stores information in standard MIDI file (.MID) format, you can access and manipulate all musical examples in the program. After listening to various pieces and learning about their components, you can then alter sounds, tempos, and other aspects of the music however you please. Even beginners will find that concepts such as pitch and rhythm notation are easier to grasp with Music Mentor's multimedia approach.

Music Mentor includes a notation–based MIDI recording and editing utility, called Midisoft Recording Session for Windows (Figure 11-13). Music Mentor and the Recording Session utility interact in such a way that you can listen to an example in the tutorial session and, with a single command, open Recording Session to edit or play along with the piece. You can also create original music in Recording Session, or import MIDI files from other sources.

FIGURE
11-13
Midisoft Recording Session for Windows

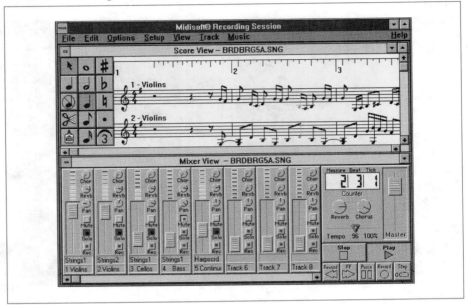

An important benefit of Recording Session is that it displays music in standard notation during both recording and playback—just like its upscale counterpart, Midisoft Studio for Windows. This capability sets it apart from common sequencer-style MIDI event lists and graphic editors, which tend to be less intuitive.

Multimedia Music Library (Suggested Retail: $79.95)

Multimedia Music Library is a compilation of over 100 .MID format files on floppy disks. The tracks in this collection comprise pop and orchestral music. The 14 main themes, 28 variations, and a wide assortment of snips and backgrounds are all original compositions and can be distributed royalty-free. Since the files are in standard MIDI format, they can be modified with any MIDI sequencer.

A simple interface, MIDIBase (Figure 11-14), facilitates access to these individual files. It stores information about the style and length of each piece. You can review descriptions and then listen to a selection while in MIDIBase. The music is organized into categories consisting of assorted related musical cues grouped around main themes.

Studio for Windows (Suggested Retail: $249.95)

This Windows-based program (Figure 11-15) is a MIDI music authoring and playback control program that allows music and multimedia enthusiasts to compose, record, edit, and print music with their Sound Blaster-equipped PC. It displays standard music notation in real time—a capability that, together with its Windows interface, provides an intuitive and spontaneous environment for creating music. Heading the list of powerful editing features contributing to the program's versatility are Punch, Loop, Splice Cut or Splice Paste, and Step Play.

FIGURE 11-14

MIDIBase

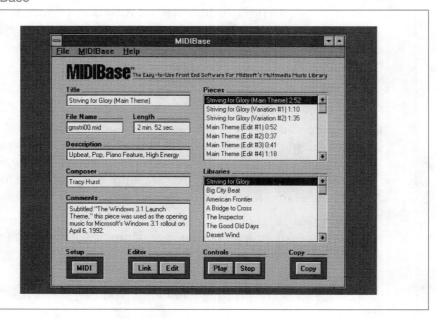

Midisoft Studio for Windows

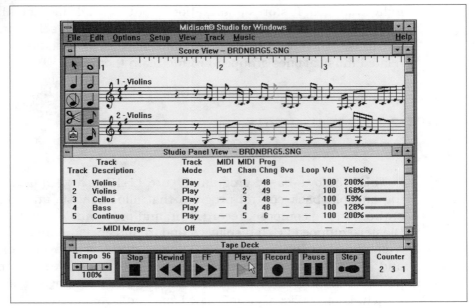

With *Punch*, you can record a new part and Studio automatically inserts it into a predetermined place within an existing track, quickly and accurately. This technique is often easier to do than editing the track manually.

Loop is a convenient feature to use when a phrase or section needs to be repeated. For example, you can record one or more measures, select them, and choose the number of repetitions.

Splice Cut removes a selected passage from a track and shifts all subsequent measures earlier in time to fill the empty space. *Splice Paste* takes a selection from the Clipboard and pastes it into a target area on a track. Subsequent measures are shifted later in time to make room for the pasted music.

Step Play is a mode for stepping through music one event at a time. This is useful for a dense passage of music when you want to isolate and hear each note or phrase.

Studio for Windows is the only notation-based MIDI sequencer that provides a score-printing capability. You can select the tracks you wish to print, including text for header and footer information, page numbers, track numbers, and measure numbers.

The program is tightly integrated with Windows 3.1. It supports the MIDI mapper feature, which lets you conveniently specify various mapping schemes with which to coordinate sound devices, using either General MIDI standards or Microsoft's authoring guidelines for MIDI files. With the Multi–MIDI Port feature, you have access to more than 16 MIDI channels and can easily assign different tracks to specific MIDI devices.

New Eden MultiMedia

New Eden MultiMedia
7652 Hampshire Ave.
Minneapolis, MN 55428
(612) 561-2557
CompuServe ID: 71020,2230

SoundWAV (Shareware: $45)

SoundWAV (Figure 11-16) lets you select and randomly change Windows 3.1 system sounds. SoundWAV operates very simply; using Windows system calls, it changes the sound file names assigned in your WIN.INI file. SoundWAV allows you to assign files to sounds, set the directory for .WAV files, and test-play the sounds, much as the Windows 3.1 Control Panel does. In addition, however, SoundWAV lets you name a directory for each individual system sound and determine whether sound files are to be selected randomly or sequentially (in ascending alphabetic order).

SoundWAV includes over 10Mb of sounds, free to registered users. You'll find everything from HAL's infamous "I'm sorry, Dave. I can't do that." to Fred Flintstone's "Yabba Dabba Doo."

FIGURE
11-16

SoundWAV

Passport Designs, Inc.

Passport Designs, Inc.
100 Stone Pine Rd.
Half Moon Bay, CA 94019
(800) 443-3210 or (415) 726-0280

Passport Designs is well-established in the Apple Macintosh market as one of the premier providers of MIDI and music software. With the Windows programs listed below, which echo their Mac siblings in capabilities, Passport gives you some of the best MIDI software around, at very resonable prices.

Encore (Suggested Retail: $595)

Encore is full-featured music notation software. Priced for the professional musician, it has all the features of MusicTime, plus a few other advanced features. Though MusicTime allows only six staves, Encore allows up to 64! This will come in handy if you're composing for an orchestra; so John Williams, please take note. Encore also does multiple part extraction for those complicated scores.

A header and footer capability helps you keep your pages organized. You can have more than one score open at any time. Using cut and paste, you can easily transfer or duplicate sections of one score to another.

Master Tracks Pro (Suggested Retail: $395)

Master Tracks Pro (Figure 11-17) is professional MIDI-sequencing software. It can record up to 64 tracks, do step-time input, and produce graphic and event list editing. The dizzying array of buttons and menu options on the screen may intimidate the uninitiated, but Master Track Pro delivers its powerful features with fast and intuitive operation.

Clearly aimed at the high end, Master Tracks Pro has some esoteric features: You can sync-lock your music to SMPTE (Society of Motion Picture and Television Engineers) via MIDI Time Code with MIDI/SMPTE interface (which allows you to sync your music to film, video, or tape); automatically chase MIDI controllers and program changes for automa-

Master Tracks Pro

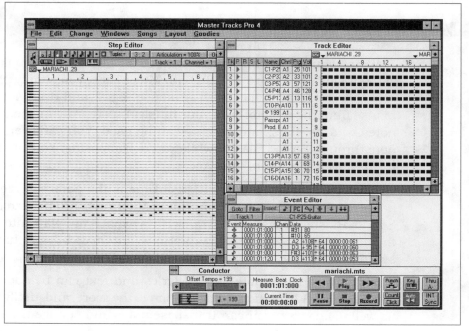

tion control; fit time to SMPTE time values; and control the music's feel by sliding regions forward or backward in time. The track sheet combines song and track information into one area. Adjustments to the volume fader can be recorded, which lets you do live mixing with immediate graphic feedback.

If you're a performing musician, you'll like the Song Play List feature. It allows you to cue up several files for automatic playback in any order. You can use a variety of ways to stop and start playback, including using a pedal hooked up to your MIDI keyboard. Also of interest to those who perform live, Master Tracks Pro has a Preset Palette feature that allows you to automatically select different sets of sounds for different keyboards. You can also edit this list and add banks of presets from synthesizers that are not included with factory-supplied sounds.

Master Tracks Pro sports other editing and recording features too numerous to list, and will prove more than adequate even for the most demanding professional musicians. The program has a consistent interface and is easy to learn. Like other sequencer programs, Master Tracks Pro really shines when you hook up a professional MIDI keyboard to the Sound Blaster.

MusicTime (Suggested Retail: $249)

Watch your music and songs come to life in standard music notation with MusicTime (Figure 11-18). With MusicTime, you simply place notes on electronic staff paper with a mouse. Click-and-drag notes with a mouse from the toolbox onto your musical score. Any musical symbol—notes, sharps, flats, and others—can be used. You can even play each note through Sound Blaster while you're composing. You can notate up to six staves with up to four voices.

One of the best features of MusicTime is the ability to record a live performance onto a score, if you have a MIDI keyboard hooked up to your Sound Blaster. MusicTime transcribes what you play into standard music notation. Score sheets can also be automatically produced from a standard MIDI file.

With MusicTime, note-aligned lyrics and text can be added to your composition. Add guitar chord notation to the score, and justify the music as well. Of course, you can transpose notes and change the key. When

FIGURE
11-18

MusicTime

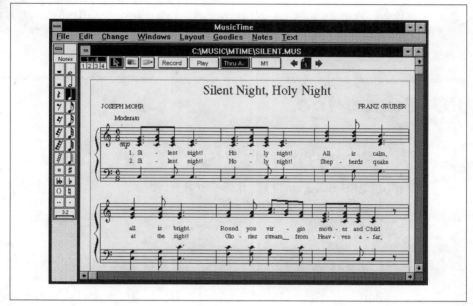

your masterpiece is printed on a laser printer, you will have professional-quality sheet music. This program is very useful for music teachers, band directors, and choir directors. You can easily enter a score by recording a performance; then, using the transpose function, switch to another key or transpose the score for another instrument. Finally, you can reprint the edited score for other performers or members of the group.

If you're a professional composer, the additional capabilities of Passport Designs's Encore (MusicTime's paradigm and elder brother) may be more suitable.

Trax (Suggested Retail: $99)

Trax is a MIDI sequencer that is based on Master Tracks Pro. Both siblings share a similiar interface. This scaled-down version does not have some of the esoteric functions and features (which may be a requirement for professional applications) found in Master Tracks Pro.

At the $99 bargain-basement price (for sequencing programs, any-way), Trax is a steal. Moreover, you can progress to Master Tracks Pro very easily when you outgrow Trax.

PG Music, Inc.

PG Music, Inc.
266 Elmwood Ave., Suite #111
Buffalo, NY 14222
(800) 268-6272 or (416) 528-2368
CompuServe ID: 75300,2750

Band-in-a-Box Pro (Suggested Retail: $88)

Band-in-a-Box Pro (Figure 11-19) is an amazing automatic music accompaniment program that is truly unique. One of the challenges for any musician or composer is to create the various accompaniments, or intrument parts, to any music. If you are to produce good music, this requires that you know how to play the main instrument as well as the accompanying instruments. Band-in-a-Box Pro allows you to just concentrate on your lead part, while it takes care of the drums, bass, piano, guitar, and string parts.

Creating a song with backup instruments is a cinch with Band-in-a-Box Pro. All that's needed is for you to first specify the chord progressions of any song, in simple chord notation (C, Fm7, and so forth). Second, select a musical style, from jazz swing to waltz to New Age; 75 styles are included with the program and an additional 25 are available separately for $29. Next, select a tempo, start the metronome, and off you go. The results can be very satisfying, and you'll often hear interesting, professional sounding material emanating from your Sound Blaster or MIDI instruments.

Not to worry if you have no idea where to start composing; Band-in-a-Box Pro includes some tunes in the package to get you started. Another 100 songs can be purchased for $29.

FIGURE
11-19

Band-in-a-Box

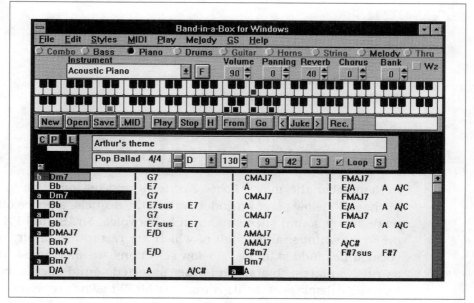

Elementary sequencer capabilities such as editing and saving to MIDI format files are built into Band-in-a-Box Pro. You can save a file with or without the melody (which can be a recording of your performance). These files can then be edited in other, more capable sequencers. You owe it to yourself to listen to what Band-in-a-Box Pro can do given a certain song and style. It is both educational and fun to just vary the style and listen to the different musical results from the program. Selecting various instruments (Fender Bass versus Upright Bass, for instance) can also dramatically alter a song.

The Band-in-a-Box Pro package includes both a DOS and Windows version and works with the Sound Blaster FM sythesizer or MIDI port. Files created by either program are completely compatible and interchangeable. A Band-in-a-Box Pro Standard Edition with 24 styles is available at a reduced cost of $59.

If you're lacking in one or more of the instrument skills necessary to becoming a one-person show, Band-in-a-Box Pro is the perfect solution—and certainly a most capable addition to your repertoire. It's the next best thing to having a live band at your disposal.

Prosonus

Prosonus
11126 Weddington St.
North Hollywood, CA 91601
(800) 999-6191 or (818) 766-5221

Mr. Sound FX (Suggested Retail: $24.95)

Remember the movie *Police Academy* and its long line of sequels? Michael Winslow played a cadet and, in the sequels, a police officer who made many sound effects using only his voice. Mr. Sound FX includes over 150 sounds, about half of which are recordings of Mr. Winslow's vocal antics. Added to the Winslow selections are short music cuts such as riffs, fanfares, "blats," and other assorted sound effects. With some incredible displays of vocal gymnastics, Mr. Winslow's repertoire includes some notable feats, from car crashes and squealing brakes to jet fly-by's, bird tweets, a UFO fly-by, a bouncing tennis ball, and breaking glass. You can integrate them all into your own multimedia presentations.

Mr. Sound FX is akin to a limited Whoop It Up! or Wired For Sound Pro (also described in this chapter)—you can assign sounds to events such as a program launching, moving, or minimizing and maximizing windows. The program also works with Norton's Desktop for Windows and many other Windows applications, including After Dark from Berkeley Systems, Screen Craze from Gold Disk, the Cathy calendar from Amaze Inc., and others.

MusicBytes (Suggested Retail: $99.95)

MusicBytes contains dozens of original tunes ranging from rock to classical and from industrial to novelty. The music and sound effects are designed to be used by developers of multimedia software and presentations.

In addition to their varying lengths, each tune is presented in various formats: 11 and 22 kHz .WAV files, 44.1 kHz standard Red Book audio, and MIDI sequences. (Red Book audio is CD audio and can be accessed using any standard CD player.) Each music clip is available pre-edited in 60-, 30-, 15-, and 5-second versions. The various file formats and lengths accommodate PC users from novice to power user. The .WAV format files permit you to edit music clips to any length, loop a section, or combine other music clips with a .WAV format editor such as the Windows Recorder.

Also included in MusicBytes is the Media Librarian (Figure 11-20), an easy-to-use software front-end, designed to audition, catalog, customize, and search for files on the CD-ROM. With the Librarian you can scroll through the files on your CD-ROM and select the desired music or sound effects file. Then the file can be auditioned without quitting the program. The Librarian also lets you rename, catalog, and make notes about the file. In addition, there's a Find File mechanism for easily searching for a specific file or category of files.

The MusicBytes CD-ROM features performances by several renowned artists: Scott Page (Pink Floyd, Supertramp); Jeff Porcaro (Toto, Paul McCartney); Steve Lukather (Toto, Michael Jackson); Neil Stubenhaus (Quincy Jones, Michael Bolton); Jeff "Skunk" Baxter (Doobie Brothers, Steely Dan); and Michael Lang (Barbra Streisand, Lee Ritenour, Neil Diamond).

Music and sound effects on MusicBytes can be used license-free. There are no extra copyright or licensing fees attached to MusicBytes for commercial applications. The tunes and effects on this CD are of consistently high quality and varied selection, and are highly recommended.

Turtle Beach Systems

Turtle Beach Systems
CyberCenter #33
1600 Pennsylvania Ave.
York, PA 17404
(717) 843-6916

Media Librarian

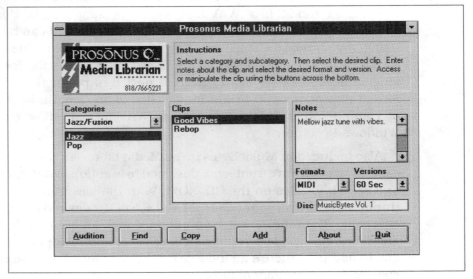

WAVE for Windows (Suggested Retail: $99)

WAVE for Windows, from Turtle Beach Systems, is a stunning graphical Windows software package designed to edit wave audio. WAVE provides recording, editing, and playback of digital sound. Once you've recorded your sounds, WAVE for Windows helps you shape your audio presentation.

WAVE's features let you rearrange a piece of recorded music, add fade-ins and fade-outs, boost the low end on sound effects with its parametric equalizer, remove unwanted pauses, and shorten material without changing pitch. The program's capabilities include the following:

☐   Cut/Copy/Paste for editing

☐   Gain Adjuster for changing the volume of all or part of a file

☐   Stereo Digital Equalizer for assigning center frequency, bandwith, and shelving capabilities

☐   Stereo Mixer for mixing up to three stereo sound files (including music, narration, and sound effects) to a fourth file

☐   Time Compression/Expansion for changing the length (time) of a file without affecting its pitch

Twelve Tone Systems

Twelve Tone Systems
P.O. Box 760
Watertown, MA 02272
(800) 234-1171 or (617) 926-2480

Cakewalk Professional for Windows (Suggested Retail: $349)

Cakewalk Pro (Figure 11-21) is a MIDI sequencer with an easy interface and a potent set of features. Having already taken a commanding share of the DOS sequencer market, Cakewalk's Windows version should set a few standards for other publishers to match.

Cakewalk Pro's greatest asset is its ability to have multiple views and editing windows on the screen at once. Changes made in one window are instantly reflected in all the other windows, and they all update during playback. These windows include a track/measure view, a piano-roll grid, and a staff view that can display up to ten staves at once. An event list can also be displayed alongside separate graphical controller and fader windows.

Other professional-level features found in Cakewalk Pro include fractional tempos (e.g. 120.34 beats per minute); pitch and velocity tranpositions; a built-in application language for creating, among other things, your very own chord generators and drum maps; and support for all four SMPTE (Society of Motion Picture and Television Engineers) and MTC (MIDI Time Code) synchronization formats. And though most sequencers record up to 64 tracks, Cakewalk Pro allows you to record and edit up to 256 tracks. A SysEx (System Exclusive) Librarian has 256 banks to store SysEx information from most synthesizers.

FIGURE
11-21
Cakewalk Pro

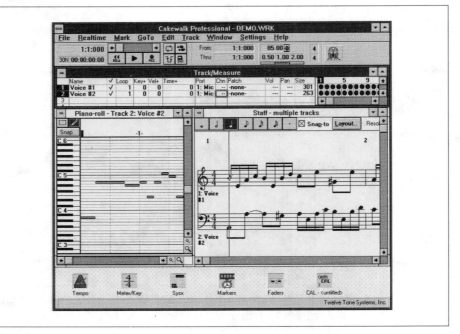

Cakewalk Pro also supports MCI (Media Control Interface) commands in tracks. This allows you to control and synchronize equipment such as CD players and VCRs to MIDI sequences. Digital audio data from a .WAV file can be embedded into a sequence, as well.

Cakewalk Pro has just about every feature a professional could ask for. The program lacks a printing capability, but it lets you store your sequence in standard MIDI format and use a notation program to print the score. Cakewalk Pro is arguably the best-executed MIDI sequencer on the market.

VOC Player (Freeware)

Doug Beachy
CompuServe ID: 73300,642

VOC Player is a menu-driven DOS shell program designed to play multiple .VOC files. The program requires either VPLAY.EXE (the latest driver) or VOUT.EXE (the older driver) from the disks included with your Sound Blaster. VOC Player will play up to 999 .VOC files in a row.

VoutBoot (Shareware: $5)

David Meltzer
7817 Old Orchard Ct.
Manlius, NY 13104
CompuServe ID: 72477,554

VoutBoot randomly selects a .VOC file and plays it through your Sound Blaster. Put it in your AUTOEXEC.BAT file to have a different greeting from your computer whenever you reboot. This shareware program can be found on CompuServe and other BBSs.

Voyetra Technologies

Voyetra Technologies
333 Fifth Avenue
Pelham, NY 10803
(800) 233-9377
(914) 738-4500
CompuServe ID: 71052,2416

Voyetra Technologies has a large number of products that support all of Creative Labs Sound Blaster cards, including the ones described below.

AudioView (Suggested Retail: $129.95)

AudioView (Figure 11-22) is a professional-quality graphical digital audio editor for Windows 3.1. It allows you to record, modify, edit, and play back .WAV and .VOC files with your Sound Blaster. You can also

FIGURE
11-22
AudioView

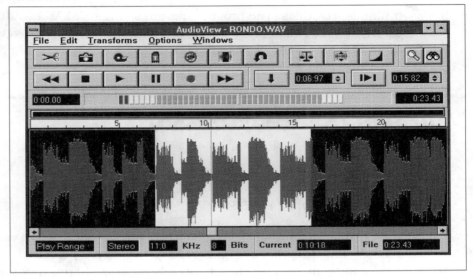

enhance these files with special effects such as compression, echo, reverb, sample rate conversion, and so forth. The program features an easy-to-use tape deck–style transport.

Multimedia Toolkit (Suggested Retail: $499.95)

Multimedia Toolkit features a special selection of DOS and Windows programs and utilities for your Sound Blaster, including the following:

☐ WinDAT is an entry-level digital audio editor for Windows.

☐ Windows Jukebox lets you arrange MIDI files, digital audio files, and CD tracks into custom playlists.

☐ SoundScript is a multimedia scripting language for DOS with which you can create multimedia presentations combining sound and animation.

☐   Command Line File Players allow you to play MIDI and digital audio from the DOS command line or from batch files.

Multimedia Toolkit includes 10 MIDI files and 10 digital audio files from Voyetra's extensive MusiClips library (described just below).

MusiClips (Suggested Retail: $69.95 and up)

MusiClips is Voyetra's huge library of MIDI files for multimedia productions. Eight different packages are available.

☐   Signatures Edition (three different groups) features styles characterizing different eras in pop music.

☐   Classics Edition (two different groups) includes symphonies, operas, piano concertos, Joplin rags, and much more.

☐   Collectors Edition (three different groups) contains popular favorites—ethnic, holiday, patriotic, original production music, and so on.

All MusiClips files are specially designed to work with your Sound Blaster, and they comply with Microsoft's Multimedia Authoring Standards for MIDI files.

PatchView FM

PatchView FM (Figure 11-23) is a Windows-based patch editor and bank arranger for your Sound Blaster's FM synthesizer. With PatchView FM you'll be able to graphically create new FM voices and sound effects, and arrange voices into custom banks. PatchView FM also includes Voyetra's enhanced Sound Blaster drivers for Windows. New patches can be utilized with the Sequencer Plus series (see below) and any Sound Blaster-compatible Windows application.

FIGURE
11-23
PatchView FM

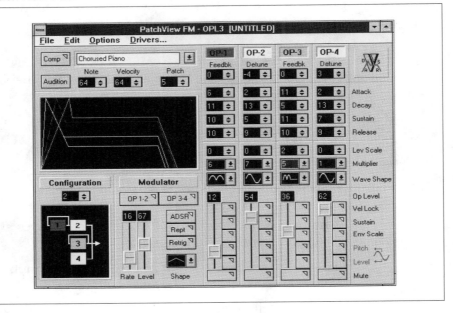

Sequencer Plus (Sp) Series (Suggested Retail: $69.95-$299.95)

The Sequencer Plus series is made up of the big brothers to Sp Pro, Voyetra's line of DOS-based MIDI sequencers/editors. The series includes Sp Jr, Sp Classic and Sp Gold. The Sp Jr series is illustrated in Figure 11-24. These sequencers are capable of addressing the Sound Blaster's internal FM sounds while simultaneously triggering external MIDI instruments.

Sound Factory (Suggested Retail: $199.95)

Sound Factory is a complete sound-development toolkit that gives DOS applications a level of sound functionality similar to that of Multimedia Windows. Sound Factory is built around the high-level Voyetra Multimedia Player (VMP) and a set of low-level APIs. This approach allows

FIGURE 11-24   Sequencer Plus JR

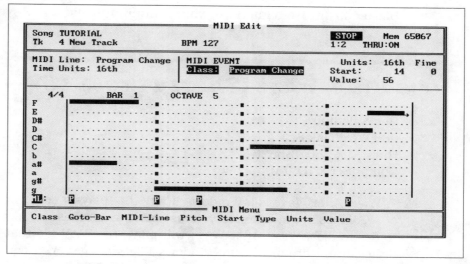

the programmer to create device-independent applications that support not only the Sound Blaster, but nearly every major sound card.

Sound Factory contains nearly 100 different functions for MIDI, synthesis, digital audio, CD audio, mixer control, SMPTE sync, timer services, and so forth. The program comes with extensive documentation, with complete function call specifications, programming support files, sample code, digital audio editor, a function call test utility, and sample MIDI and digital audio files.

V-Series MIDI Interfaces (Suggested Retail: $129.95-$389.95)

The V-series MIDI interfaces are a line of professional-quality MIDI interfaces. The line includes the V-22, a 2-in/2-out MIDI interface, and the V-24s, a top-of-the-line professional MIDI/SMPTE interface with 2-in/4-out and extensive SMPTE synchronization features. V-22 can be upgraded to V-24s with a simple daughter board.

Since Sequencer Plus and most Windows applications let you simultaneously use your Sound Blaster's FM synthesizer and a separate MIDI interface, the V-Series is the perfect solution for upgrading your Sound Blaster's 1-in/1-out interface, while continuing to use its FM synthesizer.

Wave After Wave (Shareware: $15)

Ben Saladino
660 West Oak St.
Hurst, TX 76053-5526
CompuServe ID: 71052,2416

Wave After Wave is a Windows utility that plays a series or sequence of .WAV files in a subdirectory. It also plays single files and has an option to delete files. Wave After Wave will play any .WAV file that has been dragged and dropped from Windows File Manager. You can associate .WAV files with Wave After Wave, and any .WAV file that you double-click in File Manager will play automatically. You can also call up your favorite wave file editor automatically from within Wave After Wave, with a simple click on the mouse button.

This shareware program can be obtained from CompuServe and other BBSs.

WinJammer Software Limited

WinJammer Software Limited
Dan McKee
69 Rancliffe Road
Oakville, Ontario
Canada L6H 1B1
CompuServe ID: 70742,2052

Software Excitement! (Attn: Registrations)
6475 Crater Lake Highway
Central Point, OR 97502
(800) 444-5457

WinJammer (Shareware: $50)

WinJammer (Figure 11-25) is a full-featured MIDI sequencer for Windows 3.1. It plays and records standard MIDI files. WinJammer may not be a match for other professional MIDI sequencers in the number of editing and performance features it offers, but sometimes less is more. In this case, the payoff is an uncluttered and simple interface. Even so, you won't find WinJammer too lacking in important features. You can create up to 64 tracks and use up to 256 MIDI channels. Editing is carried out in a traditional piano-roll notation window. WinJammer can send real-time system exclusive events (synthesizer specific data), as well.

WinJammer is the only sequencer we know of that reads .ROL files. This one feature clearly reveals the primary target audience for WinJammer: the beginner or amateur, and those who do not have a MIDI keyboard to accompany their Sound Blaster but would like to start creating music with its FM synthesizer.

FIGURE 11-25   WinJammer

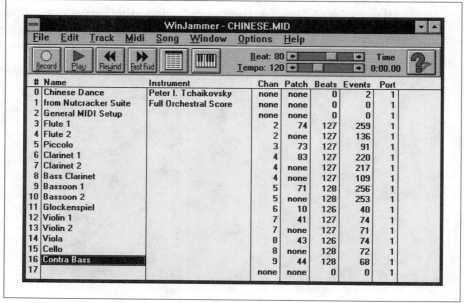

The WinJammer package includes a companion program called WinJammer Player, which is used to play MIDI song files in the background while you're working in Windows. The Repeat mode and Shuffle play options are two unique features found in this program.

For those who want a taste of MIDI without spending money up front, this shareware program might be just the ticket. It is available on most BBSs and can be found on CompuServe.

WOWII (Shareware: $20)

Jan Ole Suhr
Bockhorster Weg 28
2806 Oyten
Germany 04207-801033

MOD files are sounds and music created on the Commodore Amiga computers. Instead of using FM synthesis, MOD files consist of digitized samples of instruments played in sequence to create music. The results can sometimes be stunning. WOWII will play these files on the Sound Blaster. MOD files owe their popularity to their excellent sound, achieved by four independant digital channels. Depending on the speed of your machine, you can even have simultaneous colorful graphic displays while the music is playing.

CHAPTER

Getting the Most Out
of Your Speakers

We've taken almost an entire book to talk about sound cards and what you can accomplish with them. However, none of this would be of any use whatsoever without the ability to hear all the great sounds you create. So let's spend some time with one of the most important pieces of the hardware you use with your sound card: the speakers.

Thankfully, you don't need to spend very much money on speakers in order to enjoy your Sound Blaster. In fact, you don't even have to have a separate set of speakers in order to hear your sounds; a plain pair of headphones, like the type used with a Walkman, will do quite nicely. Most of you, though, will still opt for a pair of speakers—what good is a talking computer if you're the only one who can hear it? But the other side of the coin is equally compelling: Why spend a lot of money on good speakers when—and let's be honest here—the Sound Blaster family isn't exactly a high-fidelity product? In truth, the Sound Blaster isn't of the same class as a typical receiver or CD player.

Many people underestimate the potential uses of speakers. For example, now that you've added a Sound Blaster, how long will it be before you want a CD-ROM drive and better-quality sound? After all, CD-ROM drives are fully capable of playing CD audio music. Also, you might be thinking about connecting a small sound system or video system to your computer down the line, and these won't sound so impressive if they're coupled with cheap speakers. So consider all these possibilities when you start thinking about new speakers.

Deciding What to Buy

If you have not already bought a speaker, there are several issues that you should understand before your purchase. If you already have a speaker, the following sections will alert you to potential problems and could save you some aggravation.

The Basic Speaker Without An Amplifier

Before you begin to look for a set of speakers, decide what kind of sound you're hoping to get. If you want just enough to let you hear the music and speech coming out of the Sound Blaster, then an average set of speakers will probably be more than sufficient. Sound Blaster sound cards have an amplifier built right into them, and the volume produced may be more than enough for most people. If you fall into this category, then a trip to Radio Shack might be just the thing. Radio Shack carries a wide variety of speakers that will do the job and won't hurt your budget.

Powered Speakers for that Room-Shaking Effect

The Sound Blaster's 4-watt amplifier won't be enough to satisfy many people's needs. If you're looking for a bit more muscle in your sound output, powered speakers are the next step up. Powered speakers have their own built-in amplifiers whose power ranges from model to model. Some seem capable of imitating that old Maxell TV commercial, where the sound's power is cleverly represented by a strong wind blowing the proud Maxell owner's hair, tie, and very nearly his whole living room to parts unknown as he relaxes in his chair. In addition, powered speakers also offer a level of clear, crisp sound not found in ordinary speakers.

Problems with Powered Speakers

There are two issues you'll want to consider with powered speakers. The first is more of an irritation than a problem: As their name implies, powered speakers need power to provide their punch. This power is often supplied by batteries or AC adapters. Since many powered speakers do not include these power sources, and you have to buy them yourself, it's wise to ask about what kind of power source you'll have to budget for before you buy the speaker.

Another problem with powered speakers stems from their effect on batteries. Powered speakers have thus far been used most commonly with portable radios and such; computers were a secondary market for speaker manufacturers until recently. Since the amplifier in a powered speaker drains battery power quickly, many manufacturers added a battery-saving feature. This feature watches speaker output, looking for silence. After a predetermined interval occurs without any sound (generally one minute), the amplifier is switched off. When sound resumes, the amplifier is switched back on. Though this switching on and off extends battery life, it also causes a small piece of sound to be missed while the amplifier comes back on. This loss of sound may be acceptable on a portable radio, but it doesn't work so well with a computer.

Computer games often contain large sections of silence broken up by short sections of music or sound effects and speech. When you've got a battery saver at work that responds to silence, and you use your powered speakers with a computer game that has large sections of silence, you end up with a very disappointing game session. For example, suppose you start up your favorite game. If the game settles down, the amplifier shuts off. At this point you find a character who knows the secret password you've been searching for all over the place. But when the character turns to reveal the much-needed password, all you hear is a hissing noise. What has happened? When the character began to speak, the amplifier switched on, but not in time to catch the sound. The hiss you hear is that of your speaker's reactivated amplifier.

 Tip   Make sure you find out if this battery-saving feature is included in the powered speakers you consider. If it is, find out if it can be disabled. If it can't, look for another product.

About Speaker Cabling

One other thing to be aware of when considering speakers is the type of cabling they require. The Sound Blaster requires a 1/8-inch stereo miniplug. Some speakers come wired to handle this, but many come with the more common RCA-type connectors, which you will not be able to use as is. (RCA-type connectors are the type on most stereos.)

But don't despair if the speakers you want come with RCA plugs. Adapter cables for RCA plugs to 1/8-inch mini-stereo plugs are readily available.

Are Your Speakers Shielded?

Undoubtedly, the one item to be most concerned with when buying speakers is how they are *shielded*, or if they're shielded at all. The key component in a speaker is a magnet. Generally, the better the speaker, the bigger and more powerful the magnet. That's great for sound, but it's a nightmare for some unknowing computer owners.

Most people place their computer speakers on either side of their monitor, and therein lies the problem. Monitors are very sensitive devices on which magnets have a powerful effect. Over time, the speaker magnets will "pull" the monitor picture out of focus. Proper shielding in a speaker prevents this problem from occurring. It's important to ask your dealer about shielding in the speakers you're considering.

Demagnetizing With Degaussers

There is good news to report on the speaker magnet plus monitor mix: Many of today's higher-end, newer monitors come with a feature few people understand, and fewer can pronounce, but almost everyone can use. It's called a *degausser*, and it demagnetizes your monitor, thus removing the danger of damage caused by speaker magnets. This same remedy, applied by a repair center, would cost you more than $100. So don't forget to ask about shielding in the speakers you look at, and a degausser when you check-out a new monitor.

The Speaker Survey

In this section you'll find a mini-buyer's guide detailing many of the most popular and most suitable speakers available today for use with your Sound Blaster. Along with information about the manufacturer, a description of the product, and the current (at this writing) price, we've included two different technical specifications for each speaker: frequency response and watts per channel. Let's take a look at what these specifications tell you.

☐   *Frequency response* represents the range of sound that can be reproduced on the speaker system, for example, 50 Hz-20 kHz. The first number, 50 Hz, represents the speaker's ability to play bass. The lower the number, the deeper the bass response. The second number, 20 kHz, represents the high range or treble response. In this case, the higher the number, the higher the treble response. Common sense tells you that better speakers will have the widest range between these numbers, and generally this is so. Other factors, however, can make this perceived benefit an illusion. Quality construction and design cannot always be measured by frequency response alone.

☐   *Watts per channel* is the specification most of us know at least a little about. It generally represents the amount of power you can supply to a speaker. The numbers listed for the products in this survey are based on common usage, not the peak abilities of a speaker. Peak wattages are not listed here for the same reason that other technical specifications, such as signal-to-noise ratio, are omitted—that is, many of the manufacturers' technical specifications are not always realistic. In fact, many speaker specifications are controversial at best.

Remember that the bottom line is that speaker quality is a very subjective measure. What sounds good to one user may sound horrible to another. Specifications alone will not tell you whether you will like a particular pair of speakers. After reading the following discussions, your best bet is to get out and audition your choices before you lay down your money.

Now here are the speaker descriptions for your consideration. We've discussed some favorites first.

Note   Remember that the prices for pairs of speakers listed here are current only as this book goes to press.

Acoustic Research

Acoustic Research
330 Turnpike Street
Canton, MA 02021
(800) 969-AR4U (969-2748)

Acoustic Research, though virtually unknown in the computer market, is considered among the best in the audio world. The company is owned by Jensen, another very popular speaker manufacturer. Now that

Acoustic Research has added computer speakers to their line, it won't be long before they're known on the computer side of the world, as well.

Acoustic Research speakers offer quality sound and competive prices throughout their line. If you shop carefully, you should be able to find an excellent speaker to meet both your pricing and performance needs.

Powered Partner 22

Frequency Response: 100 Hz-20 kHz
Watts Per Channel: 3
Price: approximately $100

The Powered Partner 22s (an example is shown in Figure 12-1) are Acoustic Research's introductory entry into computer speakers. They are compact, but provide plenty of crisp, clear sound.

FIGURE 12-1 The Powered Partner 22 may be the entry-level product for Acoustic Research, but its sound is far from primitive

Powered Partner 42

Frequency Response: 80 Hz-20 kHz
Watts Per Channel: 8
Price: approximately $200

Tall, sleek, and with a punch to boot, the Powered Partner 42s (see Figure 12-2) are the middle of Acoustic Research's line both in price and performance. This speaker is ideal in many ways, and any would-be speaker buyer should check these out. They are well shielded and fit very nicely right next to your monitor, or anywhere else you might care to place them.

FIGURE
12-2

The AR Powered Partner 42 is well-suited for placement on both sides of your monitor

Powered Partner 622

Frequency Response: 50 Hz-20 kHz
Watts Per Channel: 8 (subwoofer: 30 watts)
Price: approximately $349

The 622, shown in Figure 12-3, is one of the best computer speaker systems on the market. The system has three components: a subwoofer, and two speakers called satellites. The subwoofer delivers incredibly deep base; the satellites fill in the midrange and the highs. All controls are housed on the subwoofer, including those for power, volume, bass, and treble.

If your goal is to put together a business presentation, either the 622 or the Powered Partner 570 (described next) will make sure that your point gets across.

FIGURE 12-3   The Powered Partner 622's subwoofer dominates the satellite speakers in size, and also dominates the competition in quality

Powered Partner 570

Frequency Response: 40 Hz-25 kHz
Watts Per Channel: 35
Price: approximately $475

Though not designed as computer speakers, the Powered Partner 570s (see Figure 12-4) are easily adaptable to the computer environment. They're a bit bigger than the mainstream computer speaker, and you'll need some cable converters to complete the task.

The 570s are the Rolls Royce of sound, and come in small triangular powerhouses that will simply blow away any competition. The strangest thing about them is their surprisingly heavy weight. Less than a foot tall, you'd expect them to weigh much less, but they are hefty despite their relatively small size because of all their potent magnets and heavy construction.

If you want the absolute best, look no further. If you start to balk at the price tag, remember the old adage, "You get what you pay for."

FIGURE 12-4   It just doesn't get any better than the Powered Partner 570

Monster Cable Products, Inc.

Monster Cable Products, Inc.
274 Wattis Way
South San Francisco, CA 94080
(415) 871-6000

Monster Cable currently is producing a line of speakers under the Persona label. Two excellent models are now available.

Persona Micro

Frequency Response: 150 Hz-15 kHz
Watts Per Channel: 6
Price: approximately $80

Persona Micro speakers, shown in Figure 12-5, offer surprisingly big sound for such a small set of speakers. Actually, they aren't as small as the "Micro" name implies—they're roughly 5-inches tall, which is easily bigger than many of the low-end speakers out there.

FIGURE 12-5   The Persona Micro offers a lot of bang for the buck

Persona PC

Frequency Response: 75 Hz-18 kHz
Watts Per Channel: 10
Price: approximately $229

The Persona PC, shown in Figure 12-6, is a tough speaker to beat. When we first heard a pair of these, the sound was so different from what I had been hearing that I disconnected them. A short time later I realized that what I had been listening to previously was simply poorer quality, and I had become accustomed to it. I reconnected the Persona PCs, and they've been on my desk ever since.

Persona PCs are designed to be placed right next to your monitor. They produce a sound image meant to be heard by someone sitting directly in front of the monitor. This design technology is commonly called *near-field imaging*, but Monster Cable calls it Sonic Imaging.

FIGURE 12-6

Persona PCs offer exceptional sound, based on their Sonic Imaging technology

Besides great sound, Persona PCs offer another nice touch: a headphone jack on the rear of the left speaker. This may not seem like a significant bonus, but no other speaker that we know of offers it, and it's nice to have a headphone jack so readily accessible. (Trust us on this one: Having amplified speakers on your system is great during the day but can mean trouble during late-night hours. It only takes one event of waking your spouse at 2:00 A.M. with an unexpected and highly amplified sound effect for you to realize the benefit of a built-in headphone jack!)

Persona PCs are not the most powerful speakers around, but their high quality and effective use of near-field technology make for a very enjoyable sound experience. Your ears will thank you again and again.

Altec Lansing Consumer Products

Altec Lansing Consumer Products
Milford, PA 18337-0277
(717) 296-4434
(800) 548-0620

ACS 200

Frequency Response: 100 Hz-20 kHz
Watts Per Channel: 18
Price: approximately $300

You'll probably notice the wiring of the ACS 200 (and especially of the ACS 300) before you notice anything else. The good news is that it all works fine once you figure out what to do with all that wire!

Altec Lansing has done a good job of providing all the creature comforts by giving you full control over all features. The ACS 200 comes complete with controls for volume, fading, treble, bass, balance, and DSP (Digital Signal Processing). The two ACS models come in a clamshell design that you can adjust in many different ways. You can open the speakers into an L-shape and sit them on a desk. You can also use them sideways in the L-shape, attached to the sides of your monitor. They can also be extended, fully opened, and attached to a wall.

The ACS speakers are powerful but pricey: upwards of $300. Be aware, too, that they also have more hiss than any of the other speakers covered in this survey.

ACS 300

Frequency Response: 35 Hz-20 kHz
Watts Per Channel: 18
Price: approximately $400

The ACS 300, shown in Figure 12-7, is like the ACS 200 except that the 300 includes a separate subwoofer featuring two 4-inch-long woofers. One warning about the subwoofer: It's not shielded, so don't place it anywhere near a monitor.

The ACS 300 adds a subwoofer unit to the original two-speaker system of the ACS 200

Labtec Speakers and Accessories

Labtec Enterprises, Inc.
11010 NE 37th Circle, Unit 110
Vancouver, WA 98682
(206) 896-2000

Labtec offers a wide variety of portable and computer speakers and accessories. They are also widely distributed, so you're likely to find Labtec speakers almost anywhere speakers are sold. Because there is such a wide variety of Labtec speakers available, we can't get too specific about specifications and model numbers. Your best bet is to call or write for a complete current catalog.

Within the industry, Labtec has been known as the "K-Mart" of speaker manufacturers, which is not necessarily a bad thing. The Labtec speakers can be quite adequate—their most popular models are low on features but also low in price.

Prices on Labtec speakers range from about $30 to $150; the speakers themselves span the whole spectrum, from entry-level to good-quality. Speakers at the low end of the line, such as the SS-50, aren't shielded, so you'll need to keep them away from your monitor; others, such as the CS-150, are fully shielded.

Labtec carries a nice assortment of headphones and even a dependable microphone (Figure 12-8), in addition to their speakers. All are well-suited for use with the Sound Blaster family.

Radio Shack Products

With over 6,600 stores, there's bound to be a Radio Shack somewhere near you. This company probably sells more speakers than anyone else in the business. There is a wide variety of Radio Shack speakers with model numbers and specifications that change frequently. Your best bet is to visit one of their stores to see the complete current selection.

FIGURE
12-8 Labtec's efficient microphone

The most important thing to remember when shopping for Radio Shack speakers is that most of them are not designed specifically for computer use, and therefore aren't shielded. Also, most of their powered speakers are intended for portable stereos or the like, and thus include the battery-saving feature discussed in "Problems with Powered Speakers" earlier in this chapter.

Bose Corporation

Bose Corporation
The Mountain
Framingham, MA 01701-9168
(508) 879-6541

Roommate Computer Monitor

Frequency Response: Not available
Watts Per Channel: approximately 15
Price: somewhat over $300

The Bose Computer Monitor speakers, shown in Figure 12-9, are well designed for computer use. Their cabling is right, and they can be positioned either vertically or horizontally. (In fact, you can even rotate the Bose logo, depending on what orientation you choose!)

Bose has a long-standing reputation for producing quality speakers. Though the Computer Roomates are not our personal favorites, they are well designed and should provide years of solid performance.

FIGURE 12-9 Computer Monitor speakers can be used either vertically or horizontally

Sony Corporation of America

Sony
Drive Park Ridge, NJ 07656
(201) 930-1000

Sony offers a wide range of speakers for computer use as well as more mainstream uses. It would be nearly impossible to discuss all of their models in detail in these limited pages, but we do recommend the following as their two best offerings for computer use.

SRS-58PC

Frequency Response: 100 Hz-20 kHz
Watts Per Channel: 3
Price: approximately $130

SRS-88PC

Frequency Response: 70 Hz-20 kHz
Watts Per Channel: 10
Price: approximately $200

Figure 12-10 shows an illustration of the SRS-88PC.

Summary

The collection of speakers outlined above is far from all-inclusive. Over the course of the last few years alone we've evaluated more speakers than most salespeople probably see in a lifetime. The speakers offered in this survey represent the best of what we've seen, along with the ones you're most likely to encounter in the market.

Remember—your choice of speakers is a very personal one. Some people can be quite happy using a set a speakers they found lying around gathering dust in their attic. Others won't be satisfied unless they can

FIGURE
12-10
Sony's SRS-88PC

get enough volume to shake the shingles off their roof. We happen to fall into the latter group. Our neighbor, on the other hand, is quite impressed with the Labtec speakers he picked up for mere pennies.

Once you decide which one of us you're more like, and make your purchase accordingly, your Sound Blaster will never sound better.

PART V

Appendixes

APPENDIX

Installing the
Sound Blaster Family

A correctly installed Sound Blaster card will provide you with count-less hours of fun and enjoyment. An incorrectly installed Sound Blaster will most likely give you countless hours of frustration and disappointment.

If you have any problems at all with your Sound Blaster, it is usually because of an improper installation. For many people, installation is a breeze. They just plug the board into an available expansion slot, attach a pair of speakers, and away they go. But for some of you, this may not be the case. After installing the board, you might find that the Sound Blaster will not function, or that some other part of your computer no longer works correctly.

This chapter will help you overcome many of the common (and not so common) difficulties associated with installation of the Sound Blaster family of sound boards. If you've already installed your board and are having problems, or are having trouble doing the installation, we suggest you at least give this chapter a good browse. And of course you'll want to read it thoroughly if you've just purchased your card and want to install it.

The chapter begins with some general information about the various Sound Blaster cards, and important tasks to perform before you begin an installation. The installation procedures themselves are divided into several sections, each one dedicated to a specific card in the Sound Blaster family. As you step through the instructions, you will be installing the DOS drivers and utilities that are included on the disks that came with your card. If you are running Windows, there is also a section on installing the Windows drivers. In addition to installation and testing instructions for each card, you will find lots of important information and many helpful tips. You will also want to check out Appendix B, which contains answers to the questions most often asked of the technical support folks at Creative Labs, which publishes the Sound Blaster products.

Note   If you get confused about some of the topics discussed in this chapter—such as hardware conflicts, joystick ports, or what to do with jumpers—don't despair. The troubleshooting topics you find in Appendix B will help you with that, too.

About the Sound Blaster Versions

This chapter discusses installation of the following versions of Sound Blaster:

☐   Sound Blaster 1.*x*/2.0

☐   Sound Blaster Pro, Pro 2, and Pro Basic

☐   Sound Blaster MCV and Pro MCV

If you don't know which version of Sound Blaster you have, refer to the sections throughout the chapter that tell you how to distinguish between the various cards, and pay special attention to the "Testing" sections.

Sound Blaster 1.x/2.0

The Sound Blaster 1.x/2.0 card can be used on an IBM PC/XT, AT, 386, 486, PS/2 (models 25/30); on a Tandy (except 1000 EX/HX); and on compatible computers.

Versions 1.0 and 1.5

Sound Blaster 1.0 and 1.5 are essentially the same card. The only difference is that the 1.5 card does not include the Creative Music System upgrade (CMS chips). The CMS upgrade was originally offered to provide backward compatibility with the older Game Blaster. (Support for the Game Blaster, and thus the CMS chips, has gradually fallen off and is almost nonexistent today, though you can still obtain the CMS chips and add them to your Sound Blaster. However, given the lack of support for the chips there is very little you can gain by adding them. Save your money for a good set of speakers.)

Another difference between 1.0 and 1.5 is in the Digital Sound Processor (DSP) versions. Some versions of the 1.5 card come with version 2.00 of the DSP, which is faster than the 1.05 DSP and is Windows 3.1-compatible. If you currently have a Sound Blaster 1.0 or 1.5 with the 1.05 DSP, you can upgrade it to a 2.00 DSP by calling Creative Labs, Inc.

Version 2.0

Sound Blaster 2.0 is quite different from the 1.x cards. Version 2.0 makes use of newer technology and, as a result, is smaller than its predecessors. The 2.0 card can play back digital files at sampling rates as high as 44.1 kHz, compared to the 1.x limit of 23 kHz; and can record at sampling rates as high as 15 kHz, compared to the 1.x limit of 12 kHz. (You'll learn more about sampling in Chapter 2.) It also has an additional connector, above the microphone input, for a line-level input signal. This connector can be used to attach a portable CD player or audio tape deck directly to the Sound Blaster for improved recording.

Sound Blaster Pro, Pro 2, and Pro Basic

The Sound Blaster Pro cards can be used on an IBM AT, 386, 486, and PS/2 (models 25/30); on a Tandy AT; and on compatible computers. With some limitations, Sound Blaster Pro can also be used on an IBM PC/XT, a Tandy (except 1000 EX/HX), and compatible computers with 8-bit slots.

The only significant difference between the Sound Blaster Pro and Pro 2 cards is in the FM synthesizer. You will learn more later in this chapter about how to recognize this difference.

Sound Blaster Pro Basic is a Sound Blaster Pro 2 in a new package. The only difference is that the Pro Basic does not include the MIDI adapter cable and MIDI sequencing software. As a result, it costs less than the complete Pro package. If you have Sound Blaster Pro Basic and later decide to add MIDI capability, contact Creative Labs, Inc., for a MIDI kit.

Sound Blaster MCV and Pro MCV

The Sound Blaster MCV (Microchannel Version) and Pro MCV cards can be used only on the IBM PS/2 model 50 and higher, and on computers that are 100%-compatible with the IBM PS/2 Microchannel bus architecture.

The Sound Blaster MCV is a Microchannel version of the Sound Blaster 1.5. The Sound Blaster Pro MCV is a Microchannel version of the Sound

Blaster Pro 2. The Microchannel architecture introduces no difference in sound quality. It is a proprietary type of connector for accessory cards, designed by IBM in an attempt to eliminate clones of its computers.

Sound Blaster Software

Various files (programs, drivers, and utilities) are bundled with the Sound Blaster cards. A driver is a special program that runs a hardware device—in this case, Sound Blaster—attached to your computer. A utility is a small program that accomplishes a specific task for the hardware device.

The installation instructions for each card include a procedure for copying the compressed Sound Blaster files onto your hard disk, and adding the Sound Blaster drivers and other software into the Windows environment.

Before Installing Sound Blaster

Before installing your Sound Blaster hardware and software, make backups of all the disks included with the Sound Blaster card. Put away the originals in a safe place, and use the copies for the installation process. Turn off the power to the computer and remove the cover. (See your computer's manual for details on removing the cover.)

 Caution   Read the following sections carefully before you begin your installation, to prevent potential problems with ports used for all versions of Sound Blaster, IRQ/interrupt conflicts, and other hardware conflicts.

Preventing Conflicts with Joystick (Game) Ports

The Sound Blaster comes equipped with a built-in joystick port (also called a game port). If your computer already has a joystick port, it will conflict with the joystick port on the Sound Blaster. To avoid this conflict you'll have to disable one of the ports. See the Sound Blaster manual for jumper locations.

☐   To disable the joystick port on the Sound Blaster 1.x card, remove jumper JP1; on Sound Blaster 2.0, remove jumper JP8.

☐   To disable the joystick port on Sound Plaster Pro, Pro 2, or Pro Basic, remove jumper JP4.

☐   To disable the joystick port on Sound Blaster MCV, remove jumper JP4; on Sound Blaster Pro MCV, remove jumper JP1.

If you don't yet know which version of the Sound Blaster you have, refer to the various sections later in this chapter that tell you how to tell the difference between the cards.

Resolving IRQ/Interrupt Conflicts

Before you install your Sound Blaster card, check your computer manual and the manuals of all peripheral cards in your system for possible conflicts with the default Sound Blaster card settings for I/O Address, IRQ, and DMA. Conflicts typically occur with handheld scanner cards (DMA 1), and on primary printer ports when used with laser printers (IRQ 7).

The default card settings and choices for changing them on each version of Sound Blaster are covered in the following sections that describe installation procedures for the various cards.

    Caution   If you have a hardware conflict with another device in your system, and you make changes to Sound Blaster's factory default settings, some software that uses Sound Blaster may not work. This is due to the fact that some programs are written to find the Sound Blaster only when it is set to the factory defaults. Fortunately, not many of these programs are still in use.

Sound Blaster 1.x/2.0

This section tells you how to install versions 1.0, 1.5, and 2.0 of Sound Blaster. Before you begin the installation, be sure you have read the prior section, "Before Installing Sound Blaster."

See Figure A-1 for an illustration of the Sound Blaster 1.x and Figure A-2 for an illustration of the Sound Blaster 2.0 cards.

Distinguishing Between Sound Blaster 1.x/2.0 Versions

The best way to determine which Sound Blaster version you have is by checking the DSP (Digital Sound Processor) version number. Thankfully, this is easily accomplished by running the test program TEST-SBC, described later in "Testing the Sound Blaster 1.x/2.0 Hardware."

After the test program finds the card's I/O Address, Interrupt, and DMA settings, it displays these, along with the DSP version, at the top of the screen. Use the DSP numbers to determine your version of the Sound Blaster. The DSP number for Sound Blaster 1.0 is 1.05. The DSP number for Sound Blaster 1.5 may be either 1.05 or 2.00. The DSP number for Sound Blaster 2.0 is 2.01 or 2.02.

Changing the Sound Blaster 1.x/2.0 Default Settings

Your Sound Blaster 1.x/2.0 card comes from the factory with the following default settings: I/O Port Address 220H, IRQ 7, and DMA channel 1.

☐ If another device in your system uses I/O Port Address 220H, you can change the Sound Blaster I/O Port Address by moving the I/O Address jumper to a value not used in your system. On the Sound Blaster 1.x, you can choose from 230H, 240H, 250H, and 260H. On the Sound Blaster 2.0, your only alternative is port 240H.

☐   If another device in your system uses Interrupt 7, you can change the Sound Blaster interrupt by moving the IRQ jumper to a value not used in your system. Choose IRQ 2, 3, 5, or 7, but bear in mind the following: IRQ 3 is used for the second serial port (COM2). IRQ 5 is sometimes used on bus mouse interface cards, as well as for hard disk controller cards on XT computers. The Tandy 1000 uses IRQ 7 internally and will not allow the Sound Blaster to use it.

☐   If another device on your system uses DMA channel 1, you will have to change the setting on that device, because Sound Blaster 1.x/2.0 can only use DMA channel 1. Consult the manual for the device in question to see how to select a different DMA channel. *Do not remove the DMA jumper on the Sound Blaster card.* The card will not work correctly without this jumper installed.

Installing the Sound Blaster 1.x/2.0 Hardware

Before you start the installation, be sure you know what version of Sound Blaster you have, and have handled possible port problems and card setting conflicts as explained in the earlier section, "Before Installing Sound Blaster." Then you can start your installation.

Follow these steps to install a Sound Blaster 1.0, 1.5, or 2.0 card:

1.   Plug the card into any free 8-bit or 16-bit slot.

Note   Other cards in your system may have an impact on the quality of recording and playback on a Sound Blaster. If possible, install the Sound Blaster away from other cards in your system. The most troublesome cards are usually disk controllers and video boards.

2.   Connect headphones, stereo speakers, or your home stereo system to the Sound Blaster speaker output connector. The connector requires a 1/8-inch stereo miniplug, like that used on portable audio tape player headphones. See Figure A-1 and A-2 for the location of the connectors.

3.   Adjust the volume knob on the Sound Blaster card; put it halfway between the maximum and minimum limits.

FIGURE A-1

The Sound Blaster 1.0/1.5

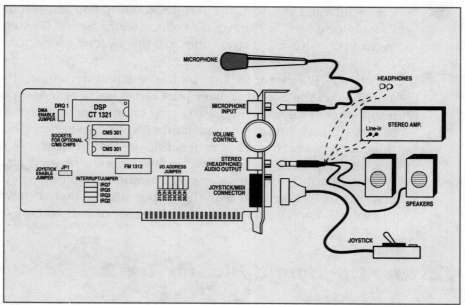

FIGURE A-2

The Sound Blaster 2.0

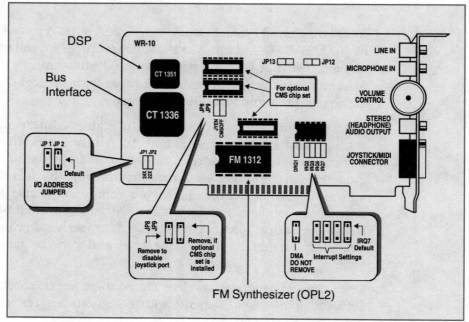

Tip   Although the microphone connector is considered to be the top of the card, when you turn the volume knob up you are actually turning the volume down. To turn up the volume on the Sound Blaster, you need to turn the volume knob down toward the joystick connector.

Warning   When turned up to the maximum volume, the built-in amplifier on the Sound Blaster puts out 4 watts of power per channel into 4-ohm speakers, and 2 watts per channel into 8-ohm speakers. Do NOT turn the volume up to maximum if your speakers are not rated for this much power. If you are connecting the Sound Blaster output to the line-level inputs of a stereo system, we recommend that you keep the volume about 3/4 of the way up. Turning the volume up higher can generate distortion or noise in the output signal. You may have to adjust the volume knob from this position for minimum distortion.

Testing the Sound Blaster 1.x/2.0 Hardware

Once you've installed the Sound Blaster card, you need to test it. Follow these steps to make sure that your installation has been successful:

1. Insert the Sound Blaster Disk 1 into drive A or B. Type **A:TEST-SBC** or **B:TEST-SBC**, and press ENTER. The test program will inform you of each test that is being performed and any conflicts that arise. Also, write down the DSP version number that is reported at the top of the test program, for future reference.

2. If the program reports a conflict in I/O Address, Interrupt, or DMA settings, turn off the computer and pull out the Sound Blaster card. Select a different I/O Address, Interrupt, or DMA setting, following guidelines in the earlier section about changing the default settings on the card. Also, double-check your computer's manual for guidance about conflicts in these settings. All conflicts must be resolved before the Sound Blaster card will work properly. After making the necessary changes, reinstall the card and run the test program again.

3. Once the test program has determined there are no conflicts in the settings, it displays a menu with selections for testing the FM

(music) and DAC (voice) output from your card. Highlight the FM test, and press ENTER.

4. As the music plays, turn up the volume knob on the Sound Blaster until you hear the music. (Remember—to turn the volume down, turn the volume knob up toward the microphone connector. To turn the volume up, turn the volume knob down toward the joystick connector.)

5. When the FM test stops, highlight the Voice test and press ENTER. You should hear a voice saying several times, "Hello there."

If you do not hear output from either of these tests, even after turning the volume knob to both extremes, you may have a bad card. Contact Creative Labs Technical Support or your nearest dealer to resolve the problem.

Installing Sound Blaster 1.x/2.0 Files

The Sound Blaster installation program runs under DOS only. The Sound Blaster drivers and software are stored in a compressed format and therefore should be installed on a hard disk; the decompressed files will not fit on a floppy. The easiest method for putting them on the hard disk is by running the hard disk installation program INST-HD.EXE. Here are the steps:

1. Insert the Sound Blaster Disk 1 into drive A or B.

2. Change to the drive that contains the disk, by typing **A:** or **B:** and pressing ENTER.

3. To install the software on drive C, at the DOS prompt type **INST-HD C:** and press ENTER. If you want to install the software on a different drive, type the letter of that drive in place of **C:**. For example, to install on drive D, type **INST-HD D:** and press ENTER.

When the installation program finishes, you will have a new directory named \SB, containing a number of subdirectories for the drivers, utilities, and other software.

Warning There is a subdirectory under \SB called DRV which contains all the drivers for the Sound Blaster card. Do NOT rename the DRV subdirectory. In order for programs to find the necessary drivers, this subdirectory must exist exactly as the installation program creates it. You can rename the \SB directory but not the DRV subdirectory.

The INST-HD Program's Effect on AUTOEXEC.BAT

The INST-HD installation program modifies your AUTOEXEC.BAT file to include two statements.

For versions 1.x/2.0, the statement SET SOUND=C:\SB (assuming you installed on drive C) is added. If you change the \SB directory name to something else, you must also change the SET SOUND= statement in the AUTOEXEC.BAT file so that programs will know where to find any necessary drivers.

The AUTOEXEC.BAT file will also contain the statement SET BLASTER=A220 I7 D1 T1. (The T1 parameter will be T3 if you have a Sound Blaster 2.0). Here are the parameters and their functions:

- **A**n Specifies the base I/O Address. The n value is either 220 or 240 (also 210, 230, 250, or 260 for Sound Blaster 1.x).

- **I**n Specifies the Interrupt setting. The n value is 2, 3, 5, or 7.

- **D**n Specifies the DMA channel. The n value is always 1.

- **T**n Specifies the card type. The n value is 1 for Sound Blaster 1.x, and 3 for Sound Blaster 2.0.

If this SET BLASTER= statement does not exist in your AUTOEXEC.BAT, use a text editor and add the line, based on the parameters described above. If you changed the hardware settings on your card from the factory defaults, you have to update the SET BLASTER= statement. You can change it manually by editing the AUTOEXEC.BAT file, or you can run the SET-ENV utility (it's in the \SB directory). If you have a Sound Blaster 1.x and you changed the hardware settings on your card from the factory defaults, you must run the INST-DRV utility (in the \SB directory) to update the drivers.

Note   If some of your programs cannot find the Sound Blaster card or drivers, move the SET SOUND= and SET BLASTER= statements to the beginning of your AUTOEXEC.BAT file. If you still have problems and you are running DOS 4.01 or an earlier version, look for an @ symbol at the beginning of the SET SOUND= and SET BLASTER= statements. If the @ exists, delete it.

Installing Sound Blaster 1.x/2.0 Software for Windows 3.1

Be aware that the following instructions for installing Sound Blaster 1.x/2.0 drivers and software for Windows have two conditions:

☐   The instructions are for Windows version 3.1 only.

☐   The drivers listed are for Sound Blaster 1.5 with DSP version 2.00, or Sound Blaster 2.0. They will not work with Sound Blaster 1.0 or Sound Blaster 1.5 with DSP version 1.05. If you have a Sound Blaster 1.x with version 1.05 of the DSP, you must use the Sound Blaster 1.0 drivers that come with Windows 3.1, or upgrade the DSP chip on the Sound Blaster. The DSP upgrade is available from Creative Labs, Inc.

Note   Before continuing, examine the README file that is included with the Windows 3.1 drivers. It may contain important updates to these installation instructions.

Here are the instructions for installing the Sound Blaster 1.x/2.0 drivers and software on a Windows 3.1 system:

1.   Start Windows, open the Control Panel, and select the Drivers icon.

2.   You should see the following driver names in the Drivers dialog box installed drivers list: MIDI Mapper, Timer, [MCI] MIDI Sequencer, and [MCI] Sound. If these drivers are not listed, add them before continuing. (See your Windows manual for instructions on adding drivers.) If you have other sound card drivers or Sound Blaster

drivers installed, remove them (click the Remove button). Then restart Windows.

 Note Whether you add or remove drivers, be sure you restart Windows after making changes to the installed drivers list. Until you restart your changes will not take effect.

3. Click the Add button.

4. Select Unlisted or Updated driver and click OK.

5. Insert the disk containing the drivers.

6. When Windows pops up a box requesting the location of the drivers, type in the letter of the drive containing the driver disk. (If you have an updated Windows 3.1 Drivers disk from Creative Labs, type **\SBW31** after the drive letter. For example, if you put the disk into drive A, type **A:\SBW31**.)

 Warning The actions in the following steps will overwrite your existing MIDIMAP.CFG file. If you want to keep your existing configuration, click Cancel, and make a copy of the existing MIDIMAP.CFG file before continuing the installation process.

7. Select Sound Blaster MIDI Synthesizer from the list of drivers and click OK.

8. Windows asks if you want to use the current MIDIMAP.CFG or install the new MIDIMAP.CFG. Select New and continue.

9. Windows prompts you for the Sound Blaster I/O Address. The default I/O Address is 220H. If you have changed the jumper on your card to a different I/O address, select that address.

10. Windows asks if you want to restart your system. Click Don't Restart, and then repeat steps 3 and 4. When Windows prompts for the location of the drivers, click OK.

11. Select Sound Blaster v1.5 or Sound Blaster v2.0 Wave and MIDI from the list of drivers, depending on which card you own. Click OK.

12. Windows prompts you for the Sound Blaster I/O Address, Interrupt, and DMA channel. Choose the settings that match your card and continue.

13. Windows asks if you want to restart your system. Click Restart.

14. An additional Windows application called Jukebox is provided on the drivers disk. It is a MIDI file player (like the Media Player that comes with Windows, except that Jukebox allows you to queue a series of MIDI files for playback). The filename is MMJBOX.EXE. Copy it into your Windows directory and add it to the Accessories Group. See your Windows manual for information on copying files and adding programs to program groups.

The Windows driver installation is now complete. This installation has no effect on your AUTOEXEC.BAT and CONFIG.SYS files.

Sound Blaster Pro, Pro 2, and Pro Basic

This section tells you how to install the Sound Blaster Pro, Pro 2, and Pro Basic cards. Before you begin the installation, be sure you have read the prior section, "Before Installing Sound Blaster."

Figures A-3 and A-4 shows pictures of the Sound Blaster Pro and Pro 2 cards.

Distinguishing Between the Pro Cards

Sound Blaster Pro and Sound Blaster Pro 2 are more difficult to tell apart than are the 1.0/1.5/2.0 versions. (As stated earlier, Sound Blaster Pro Basic is a Sound Blaster Pro 2 without the MIDI adapter cable and MIDI sequencing software.) All Pros have the same DSP version (3.01 or 3.02) and hence to the test program TEST-SBP.EXE, the cards appear the same. The name on the box is also the same—you won't find a store that carries the Sound Blaster Pro 2 actually labeled as such.

Fortunately, there are three things that do help you distinguish between the Sound Blaster Pros. At the store, look carefully at the front of the box. The box for the original Sound Blaster Pro states that the card is capable of 22 FM voices. The Sound Blaster Pro 2 box states that the card is capable of 20 FM voices. The difference is in the FM synthesizer.

FIGURE
A-3

The Sound Blaster Pro (CT 1330)

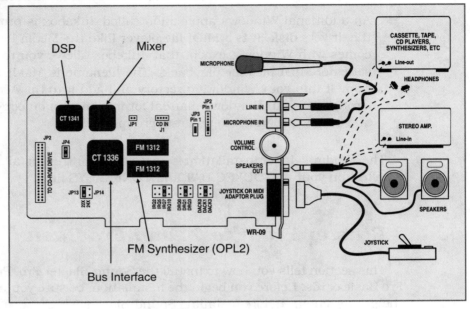

Sound Blaster Pro 2 (CT1600)

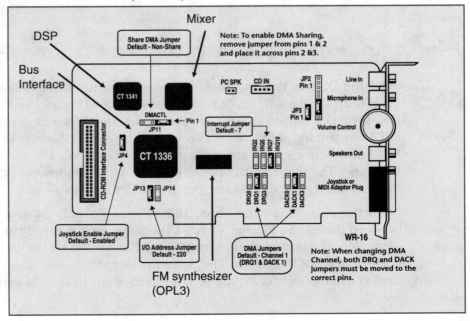

The Pro 2 uses a newer chip that provides stereo FM with only one chip, as opposed to the Pro's two.

On the cards themselves, the only significant difference between the cards is in the FM synthesizer. Sound Blaster Pro has two Sound Blaster FM chips (you will see these two chips labeled FM1312 on Figures A-3 and A-4). These are also known as OPL2 FM chips. Each one produces 11 FM voices, and since Sound Blaster Pro has two of them, the card is capable of producing 22 FM voices.

Sound Blaster Pro 2, on the other hand, does not have dual OPL2 chips. Instead, it has the newer stereo OPL3 FM chip (labeled YMF-262-M). This chip is backward-compatible with the older chips that use two-operator FM synthesis, but it also has a new four-operator mode that produces better sounding instruments. While in four-operator mode, Sound Blaster Pro 2 is limited to a maximum of six simultaneous instruments.

Programmer's Note The only way to distinguish between the Pro cards from your program is by reading the status register of the FM chip at I/O Address 388 hex. This address is independent of the I/O address jumper setting. If the card returns a value of 6, it is an original Sound Blaster Pro with dual OPL2 FM chips. If the card returns a value of zero, it is the newer Sound Blaster Pro 2 with the single stereo OPL3 FM chip.

Changing the Sound Blaster Pro Default Settings

The Sound Blaster Pro cards come from the factory with the following default settings: I/O Port Address 220H, IRQ 7, and DMA Channel 1.

☐ If another device uses I/O Port Address 220H, you can change the Sound Blaster Pro I/O Port Address by moving the I/O Address jumper to a value not used in your system. You have a choice of two I/O Addresses: 220H or 240H (jumpers JP14 and JP13, respectively).

☐ If another device uses Interrupt 7, you can change the Sound Blaster Pro Interrupt by moving the IRQ jumper to a value not used in your system. Choose from IRQ 2, 5, 7, and 10 (jumpers JP21, JP20, JP19, and JP18, respectively), but bear in mind the following: IRQ 3 is used for the second serial port (COM2). IRQ 5 is sometimes used on bus mouse interface cards, and for hard disk controller cards on XT computers. The Tandy 1000 uses IRQ 7 internally and will not allow the Sound Blaster Pro to use it.

☐ If another device uses DMA channel 1, you can change the setting on the Sound Blaster Pro by moving the DRQ and DACK jumpers. Choose from DMA 0, 1, and 3. The DRQ jumper value must match the DACK jumper value. In other words, for DMA 0, a jumper must be on JP5 and JP15 so that DRQ0 and DACK0 are selected. For DMA 1, a jumper must be on JP6 and JP16 so that DRQ1 and DACK1 are selected. For DMA 3, a jumper must be on JP7 and JP17 so that DRQ3 and DACK3 are selected.

Installing Sound Blaster Pro

Before you start the installation, be sure you know what version of Sound Blaster Pro you have, and have handled possible port problems and card setting conflicts as explained in the earlier section, "Before Installing Sound Blaster." Then you can start your installation. Follow these steps:

1. Plug the Sound Blaster Pro card into any free 16-bit slot in the computer. Sound Blaster Pro will also work in an 8-bit slot, but this will not allow access to IRQ 10 or DMA 0.

2. Connect headphones, stereo speakers, or your home stereo system to the Sound Blaster Pro speaker output connector. The connector requires a 1/8-inch stereo miniplug, like those used on portable audio tape player headphones.

3. The Sound Blaster Pro cards have a jumper labeled PC SPK. By connecting a cable from the speaker jumper on your computer's motherboard to PC SPK, the Pro will be able to amplify the computer's beeps. Most people do not use this feature because the amplified beeps are VERY loud. If you choose to hook your PC

speaker up to the Sound Blaster Pro, turn the volume down until you can judge the proper setting after you hear the system beep.

 Caution   If you connect the PC SPK jumper to your motherboard, be prepared for the resulting loud volume level of the computer's beeps. The PC SPK input is NOT connected to the Sound Blaster Pro MCV's mixer and can be very loud!

4. Adjust the volume knob on the Sound Blaster Pro card so it is between the maximum and minimum limits.

 Tip   Although the microphone connector is considered to be the top of the card, when you turn the volume knob up you are actually turning the volume down. To turn up the volume on the Sound Blaster Pro, you need to turn the volume knob down toward the joystick connector.

 Warning   When turned up to the maximum volume, the built-in amplifier on the Sound Blaster outputs 4 watts of power per channel into 4-ohm speakers, and 2 watts per channel into 8-ohm speakers. Do NOT turn the volume up to maximum if your speakers are not rated for this much power. If you are connecting the Sound Blaster output to the line-level inputs of a stereo system, we recommend that you keep the volume about 3/4 of the way up. Turning the volume up higher can generate distortion or noise in the output signal. You may have to adjust the volume knob from this position for minimum distortion.

Testing the Sound Blaster Pro Hardware

Once you've installed the Sound Blaster Pro card, you need to test it. Follow these steps to make sure that your installation is successful:

1. Insert the Sound Blaster Pro Disk 1 into drive A or B. Type **A:TEST-SBP** or **B:TEST-SBP**, and press ENTER. The test program will inform you of each test that is being performed and any conflicts that arise. Also, write down the DSP version number that is reported at the top of the test program for future reference.

2. If the program reports a conflict in I/O Address, Interrupt, or DMA settings, turn off the computer and pull out the Sound Blaster Pro card. Select a different I/O Address, Interrupt, or DMA setting. Also, double-check your computer's manual for guidance about conflicts in these settings. All conflicts must be resolved before the Sound Blaster card will work properly. After making the necessary changes, reinstall the card and run the test program again.

3. Once the test program has determined there are no conflicts in the settings, it displays a menu with selections for testing the FM (music) and DAC (voice) output from your card. Highlight the FM Music test, and press ENTER.

4. As the music plays, turn up the volume knob on the Sound Blaster until you hear the music. (Remember—to turn the volume down, turn the volume knob up toward the microphone connector. To turn the volume up, turn the volume knob down toward the joystick connector.)

5. After the FM test stops, highlight the Voice test and press ENTER. You should hear water sounds moving from the left speaker to the right speaker. (On fast computers, the water can sound like noise, so don't be alarmed.)

If you do not hear output from either of these tests even after turning the volume knob to both extremes, you may have to adjust the on-board mixer. (See the upcoming section, "Installing the Sound Blaster Pro Files," for instructions on installing the drivers and utilities, including the mixer program.) If you still have trouble even after turning up the mixer settings, contact Creative Labs Technical Support or your nearest dealer to resolve the problem.

Installing the Sound Blaster Pro Files

The Sound Blaster Pro installation program runs under DOS only. Sound Blaster Pro drivers and software are stored in a compressed format and therefore should be installed on a hard disk; the decompressed files will not fit on a floppy. The easiest method for putting them on the hard disk is to run the hard disk installation program INST-HD.EXE. Follow the steps given in the section on installing the Sound Blaster 1.x/2.0.

When the installation program finishes, you will have a new directory named \SBPRO, containing a number of subdirectories for the drivers, utilities, and other software.

 Warning There is a subdirectory under \SBPRO called DRV which contains all the drivers for the Sound Blaster Pro card. Do NOT rename the DRV subdirectory. In order for programs to find the necessary drivers, this subdirectory must exist exactly as the installation program creates it. You can rename the \SBPRO directory, but not the DRV subdirectory.

The INST-HD Program's Effect on AUTOEXEC.BAT

The INST-HD installation program modifies your AUTOEXEC.BAT file to include two statements.

For the Sound Blaster Pro cards, the statement SET SOUND=C:\SBPRO (assuming you installed on drive C) is added. If you change the \SBPRO directory name to something else, you must also change the SET SOUND= statement in the AUTOEXEC.BAT file so that programs will know where to find any necessary drivers.

The AUTOEXEC.BAT file will also contain the statement SET BLASTER=A220 I7 D1 T2. (The T2 parameter will be T4 if you have a Sound Blaster Pro 2 or Pro Basic). Here are the parameters and their functions:

- **A***n*   Specifies the base I/O Address. The *n* value is either 220 or 240 for Pro 2; 230, 250, or 260 for Pro.

- **I***n*   Specifies the Interrupt setting. The *n* value is 2, 5, 7, or 10.

- **D***n*   Specifies the DMA channel. The *n* value is 0, 1, or 3.

- **T***n*   Specifies the card type. The *n* value is 2 for Sound Blaster Pro, and 4 for Sound Blaster Pro 2 or Pro Basic.

If this SET BLASTER= statement does not exist in your AUTOEXEC.BAT, use a text editor and add the line, based on the parameters described above. If you changed the hardware settings on your card from the factory defaults, you have to update the SET BLASTER= statement. You can change it manually by editing the AUTOEXEC.BAT file, or you can run the SET-ENV utility (it's in the \SBPRO directory). There is no need to make any changes to the driver files themselves. Changes to the driver files were only required on earlier versions of the Sound Blaster 1.x.

Note   If some of your programs cannot find the Sound Blaster card or drivers, move the SET SOUND= and SET BLASTER= statements to the beginning of your AUTOEXEC.BAT file. If you still have problems and you are running DOS 4.01 or an earlier version, look for an @ symbol at the beginning of the SET SOUND= and SET BLASTER= statements. If the @ exists, delete it.

Installing the Sound Blaster Pro Software for Windows 3.1

Installation requirements for Sound Blaster Pro drivers and software in Windows are in a constant state of flux, due to the constantly changing hardware and software environment. Before continuing with this installation, be sure to examine the README file that is included with the Windows 3.1 drivers for important updates to the installation instructions that follow. Be aware that there may be significant changes.

Here are the instructions for installing the Sound Blaster Pro drivers and software on a Windows 3.1 system:

1. Start Windows 3.1, open the Control Panel, and select the Drivers icon.

2. You should see the following driver names in the Drivers dialog box installed drivers list: MIDI Mapper, Timer, [MCI] MIDI Sequencer, and [MCI] Sound. If you have the Creative CD-ROM driver installed, you will also see the [MCI] CD Audio driver. If these drivers are not listed, add them before continuing. (See your Windows manual for instructions on adding drivers.) If you have other sound card drivers or Sound Blaster drivers installed, remove them (click the Remove button). Then restart Windows.

Note   Whether you add or remove drivers, be sure you restart Windows after making changes to the installed drivers list. Until you restart, your changes will not take effect.

3. Click the Add button.

4. Select Unlisted or Updated driver and click OK.

5. Insert the disk containing the drivers.

6. When Windows pops up a box requesting the location of the drivers, type in the letter of the drive containing the driver disk. (If you have an updated Windows 3.1 Drivers disk from Creative Labs, type **\SBPW31** after the drive letter for Sound Blaster Pro, or **\SBP2W31** for Pro 2 or Pro Basic. For example, if you put the disk into drive A and you have Sound Blaster Pro, type **A:\SBPW31**.)

7. Select Sound Blaster Pro Auxiliary Audio from the list of drivers and click OK.

8. Windows prompts you for the Sound Blaster Pro I/O Address. The default I/O Address is 220H. If you have changed the jumper on your card to a different I/O address, select that address.

9. Windows asks if you want to restart your system. Click Don't Restart, then repeat steps 3 and 4. When Windows prompts for the location of the drivers, click OK.

 Warning   The actions in steps 10 and 11 will overwrite your existing MIDIMAP.CFG file. If you want to keep your existing configuration, click Cancel, and make a copy of the existing MIDIMAP.CFG file before continuing the installation process.

10. Select Sound Blaster Pro MIDI Synthesizer from the list of drivers and click OK.

11. Windows asks if you want to use the current MIDIMAP.CFG or install the new MIDIMAP.CFG. Select New and continue.

12. Windows prompts you for the Sound Blaster Pro I/O Address. Select the same I/O Address as in step 8.

13. Windows asks if you want to restart your system. Click Don't Restart and repeat steps 3 and 4. When Windows prompts for the location of the drivers, click OK.

14. Select Sound Blaster Pro Wave and MIDI from the list of drivers and click OK.

15. Windows prompts you for the Sound Blaster Pro I/O Address, Interrupt, and DMA channel. Choose the settings that are on your card and continue.

16. Windows asks if you want to restart your system. Click Restart.

17. Two additional Windows applications, Jukebox and SBPMixer, are provided on the drivers disk. Jukebox is a MIDI file player (like the Media Player that comes with Windows, except that Jukebox allows you to queue a series of MIDI files for playback). The filename is MMJBOX.EXE. SBPMixer is a utility for controlling the Sound Blaster Pro's on-board mixer. The filename is SBPMIXER.EXE. Copy these files into your Windows directory and add them to the Accessories Group. See your Windows manual for information on copying files and adding programs to program groups.

The Windows driver installation is now complete. This installation has no effect on your AUTOEXEC.BAT and CONFIG.SYS files.

Sound Blaster MCV

This section tells you how to install Sound Blaster MCV. Before you begin the installation, be sure you have read the section above, "Before Installing Sound Blaster."

Figure A-5 shows a picture of the Sound Blaster MCV card.

Installing the Sound Blaster MCV Hardware

Follow these steps to install a Sound Blaster MCV card:

1. If you have not yet done so, make a backup copy of your PS/2 Reference Disk. (And don't forget to make the usual backups of all the Sound Blaster disks.)

The Sound Blaster MCV

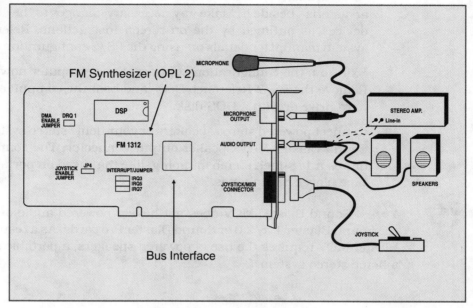

2. Copy the file @5084.ADF from the Sound Blaster MCV Disk 1 to the backup copy of the PS/2 Reference Disk.

3. Turn off the power to the computer and remove the cover.

4. Disable the joystick port, if necessary, as instructed in "Before Installing Sound Blaster" earlier in the chapter.

5. Plug the Sound Blaster MCV card into any free slot in the computer.

6. Insert the backup PS/2 Reference Disk into drive A and turn on the computer. The computer will report error 165, indicating that a change has been made to the adapter configuration. Select automatic setup and follow the on-screen instructions to configure your computer.

7. After the computer finishes its automatic configuration, it restarts. Leave the PS/2 Reference Disk in the drive. If you do not get an adapter configuration error at this point, skip to step 9.

8. Wait for the configuration software to come up. Select Set Configuration and then Change Configuration to view the adapter card

configuration screen. A conflicting adapter card will be listed with an asterisk beside it. Make any necessary changes to the conflicting devices as outlined by the on-screen instructions. Refer to your system manual for details on using the PS/2 configuration software.

9. Exit from the configuration software. Your computer now restarts. Remove the PS/2 Reference Disk, and boot the computer from the hard drive or with a DOS disk.

10. Connect powered stereo speakers or your home stereo system to the Sound Blaster MCV speaker output connector. The connector requires a 1/8-inch stereo miniplug, like that used on portable audio tape player headphones.

Note   Sound Blaster MCV does not have a powered audio output like the Sound Blaster 1.x/2.0 or Sound Blaster Pro cards. As a result, Sound Blaster MCV requires the use of powered speakers, a portable stereo, or a home stereo system.

Testing the Sound Blaster MCV Hardware

Once you've installed the Sound Blaster MCV card, you need to test it. Follow these steps to make sure that your installation has been successful:

1. Insert the Sound Blaster MCV Disk 1 into drive A or B. Type **A:TEST-SBC** or **B:TEST-SBC** and press ENTER. The test program will inform you of each test that is being performed and of any conflicts that arise.

2. If the program reports a conflict in I/O Address or DMA settings, repeat steps 6 through 9 of the hardware installation procedure (in the foregoing section) to select a different I/O Address or DMA setting. If there is an interrupt conflict, turn off the computer, pull out the card, and change the interrupt jumper setting. See the Sound Blaster MCV manual for jumper locations. You must resolve all system conflicts before the Sound Blaster card will work properly. After making the necessary changes, run the test program again.

3. Once the test program has determined there are no conflicts in the settings, it displays a menu with selections for testing the FM (music) and DAC (voice) output from your card. Highlight the FM Music test, and press ENTER.

4. When the FM test stops, highlight the Voice test and press ENTER. You should hear a voice saying several times, "Hello there."

If you do not hear output from either of these tests, even after turning the volume up on your speakers, you may have a bad card.

Installing Sound Blaster MCV Files

The Sound Blaster MCV installation program runs under DOS only. Sound Blaster MCV drivers and software are stored in a compressed format, and thus should be installed on a hard disk; the decompressed files will not fit on a floppy. The easiest method for putting them on the hard disk is by running the hard disk installation program INST-HD.EXE. Follow the steps as given in the section on installing the Sound Blaster 1.x/2.0.

When the installation program finishes, you will have a new directory named \SB, containing a number of subdirectories for the drivers, utilities, and other software.

Warning There is a subdirectory under \SB called DRV which contains all the drivers for the Sound Blaster MCV card. Do NOT rename the DRV subdirectory. In order for programs to find the necessary drivers, this subdirectory must exist exactly as the installation program creates it. You can rename the \SB directory, but not the DRV subdirectory.

The INST-HD Program's Effect on AUTOEXEC.BAT

The INST-HD installation program modifies your AUTOEXEC.BAT file to include two statements.

For the Sound Blaster MCV cards, the statement SET SOUND=C:\SB (assuming you installed on drive C) is added. If you change the \SB directory name to something else, you must also change the SET SOUND= statement in the AUTOEXEC.BAT file so that programs will know where to find any necessary drivers.

The AUTOEXEC.BAT file will also contain the statement SET BLASTER=A220 I7 D1 T1. Here are the parameters and their functions:

- ☐ **A***n*   Specifies the base I/O Address. The *n* value is 220 or 240.

- ☐ **I***n*   Specifies the Interrupt setting. The *n* value is 3, 5, or 7.

- ☐ **D***n*   Specifies the DMA channel. The *n* value is always 1.

- ☐ **T***n*   Specifies the card type. The *n* value is always 1.

If this SET BLASTER= statement does not exist in your AUTOEXEC.BAT, use a text editor and add the line, based on the parameters described above. If you changed the hardware settings on your card from the factory defaults, you have to update the BLASTER statement. You can change it manually by editing the AUTOEXEC.BAT file or by running the SET-ENV utility in the \SB directory.

If you changed the hardware settings on your card from the factory defaults, you must run the INST-DRV utility in the \SB directory to update the drivers. Simply execute the file from the DOS prompt and it will make the necesssary changes to the drivers.

Note   If some of your programs cannot find the Sound Blaster card or drivers, move the SET SOUND= and SET BLASTER= statements to the beginning of your AUTOEXEC.BAT file. If you still have problems and you are running DOS 4.01 or an earlier version, look for an @ symbol at the beginning of the SET SOUND= and SET BLASTER= statements. If the @ exists, delete it.

Installing Sound Blaster MCV Software for Windows 3.1

Installation requirements for Sound Blaster MCV drivers and software in Windows are in a constant state of flux, due to the constantly changing hardware and software environment. Before continuing with this installation, be sure to examine the README file that is included on the Windows 3.1 drivers disk for important updates to the installation instructions that follow. Be aware that there may be significant changes.

To install the Sound Blaster MCV drivers and software for Windows 3.1:

1. Start Windows 3.1, open the Control Panel, and select the Drivers icon.

2. You should see the following driver names in the Drivers dialog box installed drivers list: MIDI Mapper, Timer, [MCI] MIDI Sequencer, and [MCI] Sound. If these drivers are not listed, add them before continuing. (See your Windows manual for instructions on adding drivers.) If you have other sound card drivers or Sound Blaster drivers installed, remove them (click the Remove button). Then restart Windows.

Note   Whether you add or remove drivers, be sure you restart Windows after making changes to the installed drivers list. Otherwise your changes will not take effect.

3. Click the Add button.

4. Select Unlisted or Updated driver and click OK.

5. Insert the disk containing the drivers.

6. When Windows pops up a box requesting the location of the drivers, type in the letter of the drive containing the driver disk. (If you have an updated Windows 3.1 Drivers disk from Creative Labs, type **\SBW31M** after the drive letter. For example, if you put the disk into drive A, type **A:\SBW31M**.)

Warning   The actions in the following steps will overwrite your existing MIDIMAP.CFG file. If you want to keep your existing configuration, click Cancel, and make a copy of the existing MIDIMAP.CFG file before continuing the installation process.

7. Select Sound Blaster MCV MIDI Synthesizer from the list of drivers and click OK.

8. Windows asks if you want to use the current MIDIMAP.CFG or install the new MIDIMAP.CFG. Select New and continue.

9. Windows prompts you for the Sound Blaster I/O Address. The default I/O Address is 220H. If you have changed the jumper on your card to another address, select that address.

10. Windows asks if you want to restart your system. Click Don't Restart, and then repeat steps 3 and 4. When Windows prompts for the location of the drivers, click OK.

11. Select Sound Blaster MCV Wave and MIDI from the list of drivers. Click OK.

12. Windows prompts you for the Sound Blaster I/O Address, Interrupt, and DMA channel. Choose the settings that match your card and continue.

13. Windows asks if you want to restart your system. Click Restart.

14. An additional Windows application called Jukebox is provided on the drivers disk. It is a MIDI file player (like the Media Player that comes with Windows, except that Jukebox allows you to queue a series of MIDI files for playback). The filename is MMJBOX.EXE. Copy it into your Windows directory and add it to the Accessories Group. See your Windows manual for information on copying files and adding programs to program groups.

The Windows driver installation is now complete. This installation has no effect on your AUTOEXEC.BAT and CONFIG.SYS files.

The Sound Blaster Pro MCV

This section tells you how to install Sound Blaster Pro MCV. Before you begin the installation, be sure you have read the earlier section, "Before Installing Sound Blaster."

Figure A-6 shows a picture of the Sound Blaster Pro MCV card.

The Sound Blaster Pro MCV

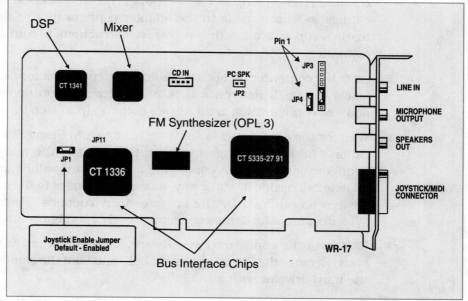

Installing the Sound Blaster Pro MCV Hardware

Follow these steps to install a Sound Blaster Pro MCV card:

1. If you have not yet done so, make a backup copy of your PS/2 Reference Disk. (And don't forget to make the usual backups of all the Sound Blaster Pro MCV disks.)

2. Copy the file @5103.ADF from the Sound Blaster Pro MCV Disk 1 to the backup copy of the PS/2 Reference Disk.

3. Turn off the power to the computer and remove the cover.

4. Disable the joystick port, as necessary, as instructed in "Before Installing Sound Blaster" earlier in the chapter.

5. Plug the Sound Blaster Pro MCV card into any free slot in the computer.

6. Insert the backup PS/2 Reference Disk into drive A and turn on the computer. The computer will report error 165, indicating that a change has been made to the adapter configuration. Select automatic setup and follow the on-screen instructions to configure your computer.

7. After the computer finishes the automatic configuration, it restarts. Leave the PS/2 Reference Disk in the drive. If you do not get an adapter configuration error at this point, skip to step 9.

8. Wait for the configuration software to come up. Select Set Configuration and then Change Configuration to view the adapter card configuration screen. A conflicting adapter card will be listed with an asterisk beside it. Make any necessary changes to the conflicting devices as outlined by the on-screen instructions. Refer to your system manual for details on using the PS/2 configuration software.

9. Exit from the configuration software. Your computer will now restart. Remove the PS/2 Reference Disk, and boot the computer from the hard drive or with a DOS disk.

10. Connect headphones, powered stereo speakers, or your home stereo system to the Sound Blaster Pro MCV speaker output connector. The connector requires a 1/8-inch stereo miniplug, like that used on portable audio tape player headphones.

Warning When turned up to the maximum volume, the built-in amplifier on the Sound Blaster Pro MCV outputs 1/2 watt of power per channel into 4-ohm speakers. Do NOT turn the volume up to maximum if your speakers are not rated for this much power. If you are connecting the Sound Blaster Pro MCV output to the line-level inputs of a stereo system, we recommend that you keep the volume about 3/4 of the way up. Turning the volume up higher can generate distortion or noise in the output signal. You may have to adjust the volume from this position for minimum distortion.

The Sound Blaster Pro MCV card has a jumper labeled PC SPK. By connecting a cable from the speaker jumper on your computer's motherboard to PC SPK, the Pro MCV will be able to amplify the computer's beeps. Most people do not use this feature because the amplified beeps are VERY loud.

Caution If you connect the PC SPK jumper to your motherboard, be prepared for the resulting loud volume level of the computer's beeps. The PC SPK input is NOT connected to the Sound Blaster Pro MCV's mixer and can be very loud!

Testing the Sound Blaster Pro MCV Hardware

Once you've installed the Sound Blaster Pro MCV card, you need to test it. Follow these steps to make sure that your installation has been successful:

1. Insert the Sound Blaster Pro MCV Disk 1 into drive A or B. Type **A:TESTPMCV** or **B:TESTPMCV** and press ENTER. The test program will inform you of each test that is being performed and any conflicts that arise.

2. If the program reports a conflict in I/O Address, Interrupts, or DMA settings, repeat steps 6 through 9 of the procedure for installing the Pro MCV card (in the section just above) to select a different I/O Address, Interrupt, or DMA setting. All conflicts must be resolved before the Sound Blaster Pro MCV card will work properly. After making the necessary changes, run the test program again.

3. Once the test program has determined there are no conflicts in the settings, it displays a menu with selections for testing the FM (music) and DAC (voice) output from your card. Highlight the two-operator FM test, and press ENTER. Then highlight the four-operator FM test and press ENTER.

4. When the FM test stops, highlight the Voice test and press ENTER. You should hear water sounds moving from the left speaker to the right speaker. (On fast computers, the water can sound like noise, so don't be alarmed.)

If you do not hear output from either of these tests, you may have to adjust the on-board mixer. (See "Installing Sound Blaster Pro MCV Files" for instructions on installing the drivers and utilities, including the mixer program.) If you still have trouble even after turning up the mixer settings, contact Creative Labs Technical Support or your nearest dealer to resolve the problem.

Installing Sound Blaster Pro MCV Files

The Sound Blaster Pro MCV installation program runs under DOS only. Sound Blaster Pro MCV drivers and software are stored in a compressed format, so running the hard disk installation program INST-HD is the easiest method for putting them on the hard disk in your DOS system. Follow the steps given in the section on installing the Sound Blaster 1.x/2.0.

When the installation program finishes, you will have a new directory named \SBPRO, containing a number of subdirectories for the drivers, utilities, and other software.

 Warning There is a subdirectory under \SBPRO called DRV which contains all the drivers for the Sound Blaster Pro MCV card. Do NOT rename the DRV subdirectory. In order for programs to find the necessary drivers, this subdirectory must exist exactly as the installation program creates it. You can rename the \SBPRO directory, but not the DRV subdirectory.

The INST-HD Program's Effect on AUTOEXEC.BAT

The INST-HD installation program modifies your AUTOEXEC.BAT file to include two statements.

For Sound Blaster Pro MCV cards, the statement SET SOUND=C:\SBPRO (assuming you installed on drive C) is added. If you change the \SBPRO directory name to something else, you must also change the SET SOUND= statement in the AUTOEXEC.BAT file so that programs will know where to find any necessary drivers.

The AUTOEXEC.BAT file will also contain the statement SET BLASTER=A220 I7 D1 T5. Here are the parameters and their functions:

☐ **A**n Specifies the base I/O Address. The n value is 220 or 240.

☐ **I**n Specifies the Interrupt setting. The n value is 3, 5, or 7.

☐ **D**n Specifies the DMA channel. The n value is 0, 1, or 3.

☐ **T**n Specifies the card type. The n value is always 5 for Pro MCV.

If this SET BLASTER= statement does not exist in your AUTOEXEC.BAT, use a text editor and add the line, based on the parameters described above. If you changed the hardware settings on your card from the factory defaults, you have to update the BLASTER statement. You can change it manually by editing the AUTOEXEC.BAT file or by running the SET-ENV utility in the \SBPRO directory.

 Note If some of your programs cannot find the Sound Blaster card or drivers, move the SET SOUND= and SET BLASTER= statements to the beginning of your AUTOEXEC.BAT file. If you still have problems and you are running DOS 4.01 or an earlier version, look for an @ symbol at the beginning of the SET SOUND= and SET BLASTER= statements. If the @ exists, delete it.

Installing Sound Blaster Pro MCV Software for Windows 3.1

As mentioned several times already, Windows 3.1 is a finicky creature. Installation of the Sound Blaster Pro MCV drivers is, therefore, not a cut-and-dried matter, so before continuing, examine the README file that is included with your Windows 3.1 drivers for important updates to these installation instructions.

Here are steps to install the Sound Blaster Pro MCV drivers and software for Windows 3.1:

1. Start Windows 3.1, open the Control Panel, and select the Drivers icon.

2. You should see the following driver names in the Drivers dialog box installed drivers list: MIDI Mapper, Timer, [MCI] MIDI Sequencer, and [MCI] Sound. If these drivers are not listed, add them before continuing. (See your Windows manual for instructions on adding drivers.) If you have other sound card drivers or Sound Blaster drivers installed, remove them (click the Remove button). Then restart Windows.

Note   Whether you add or remove drivers, be sure you restart Windows after making changes to the installed drivers list. Otherwise your changes will not take effect.

3. Click the Add button.

4. Select Unlisted or Updated driver and click OK.

5. Insert the disk containing the drivers.

6. When Windows pops up a box requesting the location of the drivers, type in the letter of the drive containing the driver disk. (If you have an updated Windows 3.1 Drivers disk from Creative Labs, type **\SBPW31M** after the drive letter. For example, if you put the disk into drive A, type **A:\SBPW31M**.)

7. Select Sound Blaster Pro MCV Auxiliary Audio from the list of drivers and click OK.

8. Windows prompts you for the Sound Blaster Pro MCV I/O Address. The default I/O Address is 220H. If you have changed the setting on your card to 240H, select 240H.

9. Windows asks if you want to restart your system. Click Don't Restart, and then repeat steps 3 and 4. When Windows prompts for the location of the drivers, click OK.

Warning   The actions in Steps 10 and 11 will overwrite your existing MIDIMAP.CFG file. If you want to keep your existing configuration, click

Cancel, and make a copy of the existing MIDIMAP.CFG file before continuing the installation process.

10. Select Sound Blaster Pro MCV MIDI Synthesizer from the list of drivers. Click OK.

11. Windows asks if you want to use the current MIDIMAP.CFG or install the new MIDIMAP.CFG. Select New and continue.

12. Windows prompts you for the Sound Blaster Pro MCV I/O Address. Select the same I/O Address as in step 8.

13. Windows asks if you want to restart your system. Click Don't Restart and repeat steps 3 and 4. When Windows prompts for the location of the drivers, click OK.

14. Select Sound Blaster Pro MCV Wave and MIDI from the list of drivers, and click OK.

15. Windows prompts you for the Sound Blaster Pro MCV I/O Address, Interrupt, and DMA channel. Choose the settings that are on your card and continue.

16. Windows asks if you want to restart your system. Click Restart.

17. Two additional Windows applications, Jukebox and SBPMixer, are provided on the drivers disk. Jukebox is a MIDI file player (like the Media Player that comes with Windows, except that it will allow you to queue a series of MIDI files for playback). The filename is MMJBOX.EXE. SBPMixer is a utility for controlling the Sound Blaster Pro MCV's on-board mixer. The filename is SBPMIXER.EXE. Copy these files into your Windows directory and add them to the Accessories Group. See your Windows manual for information on copying files and adding programs to program groups.

The Windows driver installation is now complete. This installation has no effect on your AUTOEXEC.BAT and CONFIG.SYS files.

Problems with PS/2s

At the time of this writing, some PS/2 machines have been known to experience a "Bus time-out error" when running Windows 3.1 in 386 Enhanced mode with the Sound Blaster Pro MCV. Microsoft has pinpointed the problem, and we hope it will have been addressed by the time you read this. If you encounter this problem, you can usually circumvent the error by running Windows in Standard mode first (type **WIN /S** and press ENTER). Then, immediately exit Windows and run it in 386 Enhanced mode (by typing **WIN**).

Some PS/2 machines also have a problem at power-up in resetting the Sound Blaster Pro MCV if it is on I/O Address 220H. Models 55sx and 57sx are known to experience this difficulty. As a result, Windows 3.1 will not start in 386 Enhanced mode. To remedy this problem, install SBPRESET into your AUTOEXEC.BAT file, as outlined in the file SBPRESET.TXT. You will find both of these files on the Windows drivers disk. On some machines, the problem can be solved by changing the I/O Address on the Pro MCV card to 240H. Contact Creative Labs for more information on this fix.

Installing a Creative Labs CD-ROM Drive

If you have purchased the Creative Labs CD-ROM drive, either separately or with the Multimedia Upgrade Kit, follow these steps to install it. The CD-ROM drive can only be connected to the Sound Blaster Pro/Pro 2/Pro Basic. It will not work directly with the Sound Blaster Pro MCV.

1. Turn off the power to the computer and remove the cover. See your computer's manual for details on removing the cover.

2. Locate an empty, half-height, 5 1/4-inch drive bay. Remove the blank plate that covers the bay.

3. If your computer case requires plastic runners on floppy drives and hard drives, use the four screws included with the kit to attach the runners to the CD-ROM drive.

4. Connect the flat ribbon cable to the drive, making sure that the edge with the colored stripe is closest to the audio connector. Also connect the small audio cable to the drive (it only goes in one way).

5. Carefully pull the audio and ribbon cables through the empty drive bay, and slide the CD-ROM drive into place.

6. Secure the drive with the mounting hardware that came with your computer. If you do not have the appropriate hardware to secure the drive, contact your computer system dealer.

 Warning   Do NOT tighten any of the mounting screws too tightly, or the drive may not work properly. If you have any problem after installation, try loosening the mounting screws.

7. Attach the flat ribbon cable to the large data cable connector on the Sound Blaster Pro card. Make sure that the colored stripe on the cable is toward the top of the Pro card. Also attach the audio cable to the CD IN connector on the Pro card (it will only go in one way).

8. Replace the cover on your computer and turn it on.

9. Insert the CD-ROM installation disk into drive A or B. Type **A:** or **B:**, depending on which drive contains the disk, and press ENTER.

10. To install the drivers on drive C, type **INST-HD C:** and press ENTER. If you want to install them on a different drive, enter the letter of that drive instead of the **C:**. It is recommended that you install on the same drive used to install the Sound Blaster Pro drivers.

 Note   The installation program copies the drivers SBPCD.SYS and MSCDEX.EXE into the \SBPRO\DRV directory on your hard disk. It also adds this line to your CONFIG.SYS file: DEVICE=C:\SBPRO\SBPCD.SYS /D:MSCD001 /P:220. If your Sound Blaster Pro is set to I/O Address 240H, change the /P:220 parameter to /P:240. If you have another CD-ROM drive in your system that uses the name MSCD001, change the /D:MSCD001 parameter to /D:MSCD002.

11. Restart the computer to enable the CD-ROM driver SBPCD.

12. At the DOS prompt, type **CDDRIVE** and press ENTER to enable the CD-ROM driver MSCDEX.

Note   The installation program does not load MSCDEX automatically because it takes up quite a bit of conventional DOS memory. If the amount of memory occupied by the driver causes you to run out of memory, you can load it as necessary by typing CDDRIVE at the DOS prompt. Creative Labs does not recommend loading this driver into high memory. If you prefer to have MSCDEX loaded automatically, add the contents of the file CDDRIVE.BAT (located in the \SBPRO directory) to the end of your AUTOEXEC.BAT file.

Troubleshooting Your Sound Blaster Installation

Though we have made every attempt in this appendix to anticipate all possible installation pitfalls, installing Sound Blaster can be a complicated matter. Follow the above instructions as closely as possible, paying attention to the various notes and tips, cautions, warnings, and so forth. If you do encounter problems, see the questions and answers in Appendix B, written by the tech support department at Creative Labs. Or you can call Creative Labs Technical Support directly at (408) 428-6622.

APPENDIX

Tech Support from Creative Labs

This appendix contains answers to many questions frequently asked about the Creative Labs sound cards. You'll find suggestions on how to solve a number of problems commonly encountered while installing or using the Sound Blaster and Sound Blaster Pro cards. Before calling Creative Labs's Technical Support line for assistance, read through these sections to see if your problem is answered there; chances are it can be solved quickly and easily. Since Creative Labs's Technical Support staff is a toll call away, the information here may save you time and money.

Note   If you are encountering a problem that's not mentioned here, the problem may be occurring because your Sound Blaster or Sound Blaster Pro has been incorrectly installed. You may well be able to eliminate the difficulty by reinstalling your sound card and software, using the detailed instructions provided in Appendix A of this book.

Note   In this appendix, the term Sound Blaster refers to all versions of the Sound Blaster card, unless otherwise noted.

Technical Support's Number-One Problem: Solving Device Conflicts

Here is the question most commonly asked of the staff at Creative Labs:

Problem: *I think I installed my Sound Blaster correctly, but when a game tries to play music or sound effects, the computer freezes or the sound doesn't play. What's wrong?*

Solution: Your problem is likely to be one of two things: Either the software program that's running incorrectly isn't configured properly for your Sound Blaster, or the card itself has a conflict with another peripheral in your computer. Before going any further, check to make sure that your software is configured properly to run with your version of the Sound Blaster. If it is, and setup does not appear to be the problem, read on.

Solving Conflicts with Other Peripheral Devices

When installing Sound Blaster in the typical PC or PC-compatible computer, there is a significant chance that you will encounter a problem called a *hardware conflict*. Conflicts will generally occur between two or more installed devices in your computer. These devices might include a network interface card, the parallel printer port, a modem, your mouse, a scanner, or even a hard disk or tape drive.

Conflicts come in three types: a conflict over an interrupt, over a port address, or over the DMA channel assignment. These conflicts are the result of having two devices in your computer that accidentally share the same setting for any of these three elements. If your computer tries to talk to a device, such as your sound card, and another device thinks it is being addressed, the computer's messages may be captured by that other device, causing your sound card to either sit idle or lose pieces of information.

Although a conflict is most likely to occur when you first install your Sound Blaster, it can just as easily occur when you install another device in your computer, if that new equipment is configured to use the same port, interrupt, or channel as your sound card. The more equipment you have installed in your computer, the more likely you are to encounter a conflict.

 Note   As mentioned earlier, a conflict with the sound card frequently occurs on a typical PC that has the Industry Standard Architecture (ISA) bus. If you are installing the Sound Blaster MCV, which is the Sound Blaster for the PS/2, you are much less likely to have a conflict, because the PS/2s use a more sophisticated bus, the microchannel bus, which was designed to avoid these conflicts.

Solving Installation Difficulties

The next paragraphs provide instructions for isolating and solving general installation problems. Although the process of isolating conflicts is not difficult, it is tedious and requires a methodical plan of attack.

If you are having a problem installing your Creative Labs sound card in the Windows environment, see the later section, "Troubleshooting Windows 3.1 Installations."

 Tip   Keep a list of the pieces of equipment installed in your computer and their settings. Using this list, you can avoid conflicts between devices when you next upgrade your machine. Your list should include each device's name and settings, such as port address (for example, COM1), memory address, interrupt request (IRQ), and DMA channel.

The following may be of help in isolating your particular type of installation problem:

☐   **Your Sound Card is New to Your Machine**   In this scenario, your computer was working fine until you installed your card. Now that you're installing a sound card, your computer doesn't work. Your solution is to change the settings on your sound card and try the installation again.

☐   **Your Sound Card Worked Fine Until You Added Another Device** In this scenario, Sound Blaster was working fine until you added another card (device) to your computer. Now either Sound Blaster or the new device, or both, won't work. Your solution in this case is to remove the new device and confirm that your Sound Blaster works without the other device installed. If it does, change the settings on the other device and try again.

Use Diagnostics to Isolate Your Problem

Once you've encountered a conflict, try to identify exactly what is conflicting, by running the diagnostic/testing program for your Sound Blaster or Sound Blaster Pro. This program is provided on your Sound Blaster program disk, and it diagnoses hardware conflicts. It is called TEST-SBC (for Sound Blaster cards) or TEST-SBP (for Sound Blaster Pro cards). The test program can probably identify whether the conflict occurs on an an IRQ, memory address, or DMA setting. Once a conflict is identified (possibly by the test program stopping), you can quickly zero in on fixing the problem.

For example, if you have an IRQ conflict, you can try each of the IRQ settings one at a time. If you have a DMA conflict, you will have to change the DMA setting on the other device, since your sound card is set to use one DMA channel only. Try to avoid changing DMA settings until you have ruled out IRQ and memory address as the likely conflict.

If All Else Fails

So you've tried everything, but you still can't seem to isolate the conflict?

Start by removing as many of the other cards from your computer as possible, and then reinstalling them one by one. This means you need to pull out all the cards—except the video display card and the hard disk/floppy disk controller card, if these functions aren't built into the motherboard. If you have an expanded memory card, you can leave it in, too, since it won't cause a conflict.

Now add the Sound Blaster card and confirm that it works. Next, add the other cards one by one (turn the computer off, insert a card, turn it on, and test), verifying that they all still work. For example, you should be able to listen to digital audio and do a directory listing on your hard drive at the same time, and use your mouse while playing the FM Intelligent Organ. As soon as you add a card and a problem occurs, you can zero in on changing the settings on that card to avoid the conflict.

The Last Resort for Solving Conflicts

The absolutely last-resort steps in problem resolution are as follows:

1. The Sound Blaster test program, like all diagnostic tests, can be fooled. If the test program doesn't help, or you don't trust its results, then you must follow a very methodical procedure. You must examine every card in your computer and, in conjunction with the manuals for that card, document what the settings are to ensure there are no conflicts.

2. If Sound Blaster still doesn't work properly, even though you've removed all other nonessential cards from your computer, contact Creative Labs. Your sound card may be defective.

3. The very last step you should take, after you know your Sound Blaster will work correctly only if other devices aren't installed in the PC, is to change the settings of these other devices. Be very careful to document their settings *before* making changes, in case you need to restore the original settings to get the devices to work again. The fundamental rule for car mechanics is also valid for reconfiguring devices in your computer: "If it ain't broke, don't fix it."

Miscellaneous Problems and Solutions

The following problems and solutions for the Sound Blaster and Sound Blaster Pro cards are supplied by the Creative Labs Technical Support Department. We have categorized the information to make it easier for you to find the answers you need.

Remember, unless otherwise noted, the terms Sound Blaster and sound card refer to all Sound Blaster cards.

Joystick Problems

Problem: *I've plugged a joystick into the game port on my sound card and loaded my game, but the joystick doesn't work at all.*

Solution: There is a jumper on the sound card that enables the joystick port on the sound card. When the jumper is removed, the joystick port is disabled. Check that this jumper is in place. (See Appendix A and Chapter 1 for more information on jumpers.) If the jumper is installed, then you probably already have another game (joystick) port active in your system. Only one can be active at a time, so your computer can't see the one on the sound card.

To determine if another game port exists, examine the back of your sound card to familiarize youself with what a game port looks like. (See

Chapter 1 or Appendix A for a labeled diagram of your version of Sound Blaster.) If you see another connector on the back of your PC with the same 15 pins as the game port on your Sound Blaster, you've probably found the offending game port.

Note   A game port is likely to be found on a combination I/O card that combines serial, parallel, and joystick ports on a single card. Usually, but not always, such a combination card will include a jumper for disabling the game port.

Problem: *I've purchased a Y-cable adapter so that I can connect two joysticks to my Sound Blaster joystick port. Everything works fine except for the two buttons on the second joystick, which don't do anything.*

Solution: The sound card MIDI/joystick port isn't 100% compatible with the standard game port, because it has been modified. Two pins, which provide power to the second joystick only, have been redefined to become the MIDI In and Out pins. As a result, many Y-cable adapters that expect a standard game-port pin assignment won't work correctly with your Sound Blaster.

There are several fixes to this problem. If you have the Creative Labs MIDI Kit, you have a game port extension cable whose connector is IBM standard. Simply plug the Y-adapter into this MIDI adapter cable, and plug the MIDI adapter cable into the sound card. If you don't have the MIDI Kit, you can order a special Y-cable adapter designed for dual joysticks from Creative Labs.

Problem: *I have a 386/25 MHz (or faster) machine, and I have my joystick plugged into the Sound Blaster joystick port. Some games work correctly with my joystick, but some don't. Most of the games won't let me center the joystick.*

Solution: Many games were designed for much slower computers than are now readily available. In the past, game software developers made assumptions about the computer's speed, which in turn influenced how the joystick position was measured. As computer speed has increased, the joystick position can no longer be measured accurately by these games.

If your computer has a "turbo" mode, you should first see if cranking down the computer's speed will make the joystick work correctly. Another solution is to forego the use of the Sound card game port and replace it with a "speed-aware" game port card (sometimes called 386-aware) that solves the game software problem with new game-port hardware. CH Products and Advanced Gravis sell the most popular speed-aware game ports. (If you install one of these special ports, be sure to disable your Creative Labs sound card port.)

If nothing else works, contact the game's manufacturer to see if they have an update that works correctly on the faster machines.

Sound Blaster Doesn't Work

Problem: *I've just added an IDE hard disk drive to my system for the first time (or added a Sound Blaster card to a system with an IDE disk drive), and now my Sound Blaster card doesn't work.*

Solution: An IDE controller card (the card your IDE hard drive plugs into) can conflict with Sound Blaster. Problems have been encountered with some of the cheaper controllers, which are incorrectly set to use DMA channel 1, and which cannot be altered. Since the Sound Blaster also uses DMA channel 1 for digitized audio, a conflict occurs between your sound card and your controller.

You can buy another controller for a nominal price, but be careful to select one that doesn't use DMA channel 1. If you encounter this problem with the Sound Blaster Pro, which has a choice of DMA channels, you can resolve things by changing the DMA setting on Sound Blaster Pro.

Volume Too Low on Sound Blaster Pro

Problem: *I've installed my Sound Blaster Pro correctly, but something must be wrong. The volume is always too low.*

Solution: This is the most common complaint about the Sound Blaster Pro, Pro 2, and Pro MCV. The problem usually results from the fact that the Sound Blaster Pro's mixer control is factory set to a medium level. The Sound Blaster 1.x/2.0 versions do not have a mixer.

Solve this problem by adding the utility SBP-SET to your AUTOEXEC.BAT file. SBP-SET, which is discussed in Chapter 6 of this book, sets the master and source volume levels. These levels range from 0 to 15. A setting of 12 or 13 will ensure that your sound card is audible.

Sound Blaster Line-In Source Doesn't Work

Problem: *I have a CD-ROM drive hooked up to the line-in input on my Sound Blaster, but I can't hear anything.*

Solution: You can't hear anything because the Sound Blaster doesn't have a built-in mixer that allows you to combine the regular Sound Blaster sounds, such as the internal FM synthesizer music or the microphone input, with the line-in sound from your CD-ROM. The line-in on the Sound Blaster is used for recording only; the sound is not passed on to the speaker and headphone output. The solution is to upgrade to a Sound Blaster Pro or Sound Blaster 16, both of which include a built-in mixer that allows you to simultaneously mix line-in, dedicated CD-ROM input, internal FM synthesizer sound, and microphone input.

Diagnostic Test Results Are Confusing

Problem: *When I run the test program (TEST-SBC for Sound Blaster and TEST-SBP for Sound Blaster Pro), I get digitized speech; but I hear nothing when I run the FM test.*

Solution: This problem usually occurs on 80486 machines with 50 MHz or higher speeds. The solution is to either slow the machine down (don't run it at turbo speed) or obtain an updated version of the test program from Creative Labs. This same problem will occur if you try to run the FM Intelligent Organ. You can get a software update that will fix both the TEST program and the FM Intelligent Organ problems by dialing into the Creative Labs BBS and downloading file 486-50MH.ZIP.

If you have Sound Blaster Pro 2 and you're still having problems with the FM, your motherboard may not be delivering a good timing signal. Contact Creative Labs for a software *patch* (a fix) to compensate for this motherboard problem.

Difficulty with Sierra On-Line Games

Problem: *I have a 486 computer, and when I run Sierra On-Line games I get the message "Unable to initialize sound hardware." What's wrong and what can I do about it?*

Solution: There are two solutions for this. The first is to contact Creative Labs for a software update (the 486SBDRV.EXE driver) that solves the problem. A more immediate fix is to turn off the turbo button on your machine (to slow your computer), if you have one, and wait until the music starts for the game. When the music starts, turn the turbo button back on. This problem stems from a bug in the sound driver embedded in Sierra's older games; in Sierra's newest games the bug has been fixed.

Parallel Printer Conflict

Problem: *I've just purchased a Sound Blaster and notice that the IRQ (interrupt request) is set to a default setting of 7. I've been told that my parallel printer port also uses that IRQ setting. Do I need to change the Sound Blaster's interrupt setting?*

Solution: Since the Sound Blaster family uses IRQs for digitized voices and MIDI IN, a conflict will occur only if you attempt to print while playing digitized voices or recording MIDI data through your sound card.

This conflict can become a factor, however, when multitasking with software such as Microsoft Windows or DESQview, in which printing occurs in the background. Also, some printer cards do not share their IRQ, especially if you're connected to a laser printer. If you have a problem, consider selecting another IRQ setting for your Sound Blaster. (Refer to Appendix A for more information about changing IRQ settings.)

Windows Jukebox Problems

Problem: *I have Windows 3.1, and when I run the Jukebox program everything seems fine until I quit Windows. When I go to exit, it locks up my system.*

Solution: The version of Jukebox you're using is most likely an earlier version meant for Windows 3.0 only. An update for Jukebox that supports Windows 3.1 is available from Creative Labs.

Problem: *I have the updated Jukebox from Creative Labs. When I attempt to play the MIDI files that are included with my Sound Blaster I get a dialog box that tells me this file will not play correctly with the default MIDI map setup. How can I fix this?*

Solution: In this case, the file does not contain a signature, which signifies that it conforms to Microsoft's specifications for MIDI channel, program numbers and such. While the file may play, it may not play correctly. To resolve this problem select the Basic FM map in the MIDI Mapper. If you still don't hear music, try EXT FM or ALL FM.

Choosing a Microphone

Problem: *I want to buy a microphone for my Sound Blaster. I don't know what kind to get.*

Solution: Any microphone will do, as long as it is rated at 600 Ω (ohm).

Troubleshooting Windows 3.1 Installations

This section discusses steps you should take to ensure that your Sound Blaster hardware and software run correctly under Microsoft Windows 3.1. The information presented here is very similar to what you'll find in the README file on the Creative Labs Windows Update disk. This disk, often referred to as the Windows driver disk, is available from Creative Labs at a nominal charge. The disk contains the latest drivers for all the Sound Blaster cards. As the Windows environment continues to evolve rapidly, it is to your advantage to have the most recent and finest drivers available.

Obtaining the Latest Drivers

You should get the latest drivers directly from Creative Labs. To order a disk with the latest drivers, call the Creative Labs sales line at (800) 998-LABS (998-5227). The cost for the disk (at this writing) is $7.50, plus shipping and handling and, if you're in California, sales tax.

 Note   The drivers found in the file CREAT.EXE on Microsoft's BBS and in the Microsoft Forum on CompuServe may be out of date and may not work correctly. Similarly, the drivers included with the Windows 3.1 Resource Kit may not be the most current and may not work properly.

The drivers and software patches are also available on the Creative Labs bulletin board for no charge. The BBS number is (408) 428-6660. The protocol is 8/N/1. There are eight lines, so you should be able to get through quickly. The BBS modems are V32bis and V42bis compatible, so you can download at up to 14,400 baud. If you have a problem getting through to the BBS, or don't see what you need, call Creative Labs Technical Support.

Once you have obtained a driver disk or downloaded the ZIP file from the bulletin board, be certain to examine the README file for the latest information on how to install the drivers and solve installation problems.

Correct Driver and System Initialization Settings

This section recommends a number of areas to investigate if you're having installation problems. In particular, you need to verify that you have the correct drivers loaded, and the correct settings in your SYS-TEM.INI file, for your particular Sound Blaster model.

The correct driver names and settings are named in the listings that follow. These lists are organized by Sound Blaster model type, and based on whether you have a typical PC ISA card or a PS/2 microchannel card. The Sound Blaster and Sound Blaster Pro cards are designed to fit in PCs that are equipped with an ISA (Industry Standard Architecture) bus. If you have the Sound Blaster MCV or Sound Blaster Pro MCV, your card is designed to fit into the microchannel bus of selected models of IBM PS/2 computers.

When comparing your Windows configuration information against the tables below, don't worry about capitalization or the order of drivers within a section, because Windows rarely cares.

 Warning Don't change the SYSTEM.INI or other Windows configuration files unless you follow the instructions below and understand what you are doing. Changing the Windows configuration information can dramatically alter your Windows environment.

Here are some issues to pay attention to:

☐   If you installed Windows 3.1 using the "Express Installation," Windows scanned your hard disk for programs to install. If you have Windows 3.0 versions of the Jukebox and Mixer, the Express Installation will have inadvertantly installed these along with the newer Jukebox and Mixer applications. You need to remove these icons. To do this, click on the icon once to select it, and then press the Delete key. Windows asks you to confirm this deletion. Repeat for each icon.

☐   If you've received a driver update disk, or downloaded a zip file with the latest drivers, compare the name, size, and date of all the driver files in the Windows SYSTEM directory against the listing in the README.TXT file included with the Windows driver update disk. Make sure that your hard disk has the latest drivers.

☐   Click the Drivers icon in the Windows Control Panel to confirm that you have the correct drivers installed. In the Installed Drivers list, you should have at least the driver names listed in the tables below.

Listings of Required Drivers for Windows

If any of the drivers listed below do not exist, you must install them using the Drivers applet in Control Panel (see your Windows user's guide for details).

The Sound Blaster Pro for the ISA bus should have the following drivers:

Creative Sound Blaster Pro Auxiliary Audio
Creative Sound Blaster Pro MIDI Synthesizer (early version Pro; model
    CT-1330 only)
Creative Sound Blaster Pro 2 MIDI Synthesizer (Pro 2; model
    CT-1600 only)
Creative Sound Blaster Pro Wave and MIDI

The Sound Blaster Pro MCV for microchannel bus (found on some PS/2 machines) should have the following drivers:

Creative Sound Blaster Pro MCV MIDI Synthesizer
Creative Sound Blaster Pro MCV Wave and MIDI
Creative Sound Blaster Pro MCV Auxilliary Audio

The Sound Blaster for the ISA bus should have the following drivers:

Creative Sound Blaster MIDI Synthesizer
Creative Sound Blaster 1.5 Wave and MIDI (1.5 only)
Creative Sound Blaster 2.0 Wave and MIDI (2.0 only)

The Sound Blaster MCV for the microchannel bus should have the following drivers:

Creative Sound Blaster MCV MIDI Synthesizer
Creative Sound Blaster MCV Wave and MIDI

All Sound Blaster and Sound Blaster Pro sound cards for both ISA and microchannel bus should have the following drivers:

MIDI Mapper
Timer
[MCI] MIDI Sequencer
[MCI] Sound

Sound Blaster and Sound Blaster Pro cards for the ISA bus should have the following driver (microchannel version lacks this):

[MCI] CD Audio

Drivers and Settings in SYSTEM.INI

Check your SYSTEM.INI file to verify that it has the drivers and settings listed below. You can view these files using the Windows system editor (SYSEDIT).

 Caution   As a precaution, you should use the File Manager to make a copy of SYSTEM.INI before browsing through this file with the editor. If you accidentally change SYSTEM.INI incorrectly, you can ruin your Windows setup.

From the Program Manager File menu, select Run. In the command-line box, type **SYSEDIT** and press ENTER. You will now see many overlapping windows, each containing part of your system configuration. Display the SYSTEM.INI window by clicking on the window title bar.

First, look near the bottom of the file, and find the [drivers] and [sndblst.drv] sections. Examine these sections, but avoid changing the file contents. Just look for the lines listed below; don't be concerned if there are other lines in the file. Also, it's not a problem if the entries are listed in a different order or have different capitalization from what is shown here.

```
[drivers]
Timer=timer.drv
Midimapper=midimap.drv
Aux=sbpaux.drv          (Sound Blaster Pro and Pro MCV only)

MIDI=sbfm.drv           (SB) OR
MIDI=sbpfm.drv          (early SB Pro) OR
MIDI=sbp2fm.drv         (SB Pro 2)

Wave=sb15snd.drv        (SB ver 1.5) OR
Wave=sb20snd.drv        (SB ver 2.0) OR
Wave=sbpsnd.drv         (SB Pro) OR
Wave=sbmcvsnd.drv       (SB for microchannel) OR
Wave=spmcvsnd.drv       (SB Pro for microchannel)
```

```
MIDI1=sb15snd.drv     (SB ver 1.5) OR
MIDI1=sb20snd.drv     (SB ver 2.0) OR
MIDI1=sbpsnd.drv      (SB Pro) OR
MIDI1=sbmcvsnd.drv    (SB for microchannel) OR
MIDI1=spmcvsnd.drv    (SB Pro for microchannel)

[sndblst.drv]
port=220
int=7
dmachannel=1
```

To close all the system configuration windows in one step, close the SYSEDIT window.

Checking the [mci] Section of SYSTEM.INI   If Windows refuses to install a device driver, or you get the error message "Device not found" when playing a Wave or MIDI file or a CD, you need to verify that you have the correct SYSTEM.INI drivers. Examine SYSTEM.INI as explained above, and look for the following settings in the [mci] section of SYSTEM.INI:

```
[mci]
WaveAudio=mciwave.drv
Sequencer=mciseq.drv
CDAudio=mcicda.drv (Sound Blaster Pro if CD-ROM is installed)
```

If any of these drivers do not exist, you must install it using the Drivers applet in the Control Panel (see the Windows user's guide for details). Do not type the missing entries into the SYSTEM.INI file, because the drivers have to be installed into your SYSTEM directory by Windows.

Lines to Delete from SYSTEM.INI   If you have upgraded from either Windows 3.0 or Windows 3.0 with Multimedia Extensions to Windows 3.1, and you've installed the new Windows 3.1 drivers from the Windows driver update disk, you may have a line that reads "device=vsbd.386" in the [386Enh] section of SYSTEM.INI. This is an old driver that has been replaced by VSBPD.386. The new driver will not work correctly until this line is removed. Make sure that a line reading "device=vsbpd.386" exists under the [386Enh] section in your SYSTEM.INI file. If you have a line that reads "device=vsbd.386", delete it.

Make sure the file VSBPD.386 is in your Windows SYSTEM directory. If it is not, get the drivers update disk and copy the file to your hard drive.

If you have a line reading "device=vadlibd.386" in the [386Enh] section of SYSTEM.INI, delete it. This is an early, AdLib driver. You also need to delete the line "MIDI=msadlib.drv" (or "MIDI1=..." or "MIDI2=...") from the [drivers] section of SYSTEM.INI, if the line exists. You don't have to remove these drivers from your hard disk. Deleting them from the SYSTEM.INI file is adequate.

Hints for Finishing the Upgrade from Windows 3.0 to 3.1

After installing Windows 3.1, verify that you have the lastest copy of the essential programs and drivers. If the disk contains more recent files, install these. In particular, check the creation dates of the following files:

☐ **Sound Blaster Pro (ISA)** MMJBOX.EXE, SBPFM.DRV, SBPAUX.DRV, SBPMIXER.EXE, SBPSND.DRV, and VSBPD.386

☐ **Sound Blaster (ISA)** MMJBOX.EXE, SBFM.DRV, SB15SND.DRV (SB 1.5) or SB20SND.DRV (SB 2.0), and VSBPD.386

☐ **Sound Blaster MCV** MMJBOX.EXE, SBFM.DRV, SBMCVSND.DRV, and VSBPD.386

☐ **Sound Blaster Pro MCV** MMJBOX.EXE, SBP2FM.DRV, SPMCVSND.DRV, SBPAUX.DRV, SBPMIXER.EXE, and VSBPD.386

For Sound Blaster Pro cards only, delete the file SBPMIXER.CPL in the Windows SYSTEM directory. The new mixer, SBPMIXER.EXE, is loaded automatically when you install the Sound Blaster Pro drivers.

Recent Improvments

The latest drivers make use of Device Virtualization. These drivers allow DOS applications running in Windows DOS prompt icon in Program

Manager to access your Sound Blaster when running Windows 3.1 in 386 Enhanced mode. Due to limitations in Windows 3.1, you shouldn't use timing-sensitive software—such as the Talking Parrot, SB Talker, and VOXKIT or VEDIT2 when they record or play back—in a DOS compatibility box. These four programs, and programs such as games that use digitized audio, do not run reliably in the DOS compatibility box. Even with the "exclusive" PIF setting, the flow of control to the DOS compatibility box is sufficiently uneven that digitized audio sound, which is very timing-sensitive, will not be handled correctly.

MIDI Mappings

A MIDI map has been created to make use of the FM synthesizer driver (SBPFM.DRV or SBFM.DRV). Feel free to use the MIDI Mapper icon in the Control Panel to customize the Map to your requirements. Under Windows 3.1, MIDI channel 10 is referenced as the drum channel. If your FM synth doesn't sound "right," try modifying the configuration with the MIDI Mapper. Table B-1 describes the existing MIDI Map configurations.

Note Channel 16 in the Basic FM mapping has been routed to channel 10 for proper access to the drum channel, based on Microsoft standards for MIDI authoring.

Solving a Microchannel PS/2 Lock-up Problem

PS/2 computers running Sound Blaster MCV and Sound Blaster MCV Pro may encounter a "Bus timeout error," or the system may lock up when running Windows 3.1 in 386 Enhanced mode. To get around this problem, run Windows in Standard mode after turning on your machine or rebooting it. Then exit Windows, and run it again, this time in 386 Enhanced mode.

TABLE B-1 FM and MIDI Maps

Map	Input Channel	Output Channel	Output Port	Map	Input Channel	Output Channel	Output Port
All FM	1	1	FM	All MIDI	1	1	MIDI
	2	2	FM		2	2	MIDI
	3	3	FM		3	3	MIDI
	4	4	FM		4	4	MIDI
	5	5	FM		5	5	MIDI
	6	6	FM		6	6	MIDI
	7	7	FM		7	7	MIDI
	8	8	FM		8	8	MIDI
	9	9	FM		9	9	MIDI
	10	10	FM		10	10	MIDI
	11	11	FM		11	11	MIDI
	12	12	FM		12	12	MIDI
	13	13	FM		13	13	MIDI
	14	14	FM		14	14	MIDI
	15	15	FM		15	15	MIDI
	16	16	FM		16	16	MIDI
Ext FM	1	1	FM	Ext MIDI	1	1	MIDI
	2	2	FM		2	2	MIDI
	3	3	FM		3	3	MIDI
	4	4	FM		4	4	MIDI
	5	5	FM		5	5	MIDI
	6	6	FM		6	6	MIDI
	7	7	FM		7	7	MIDI
	8	8	FM		8	8	MIDI
	9	9	FM		9	9	MIDI
	10	10	FM		10	10	MIDI
Bas FM	13	13	FM				
	14	14	FM				
	15	15	FM				
	16	10	FM				

Getting More Help

If, after reading this appendix and trying its suggestions, you still have an unresolved problem with your Sound Blaster card, call Creative Labs Technical Support (408) 428-6622, and consult your local Sound Blaster dealer.

APPENDIX

Programming the
Sound Blaster Family

The Sound Blaster contains a number of different devices to handle the various sound applications. One of these devices is called a Digital Sound Processor (DSP) chip. It handles the voice and MIDI sound operations. Another is the FM chip that produces synthesized music, and still another is the Mixer chip. The CD-ROM interface is not covered in detail in this book.

Low-level programming information is provided for each of these devices to give you an understanding of how they operate and interact with one another, so that you can program any simple sound applications. For more detailed information about the individual chips, refer to the Sound Blaster Developer's Kit from Creative Labs, Inc.

Throughout this appendix, an x included within an I/O port address indicates the jumper-selectable base I/O address. Thus, "2x6h" on a board jumpered for address 240h stands for "246h."

Sound Blaster I/O Port Addresses

The Sound Blaster 1.5 or earlier uses I/O port addresses from 2x0h to 2xFh, where x is the number of the selectable base address from 1to 6.

Base Address	I/O Addresses Used
210h	210h to 21Fh
220h	220h to 22Fh
230h	230h to 23Fh
240h	240h to 24Fh
250h	250h to 25Fh
260h	260h to 26Fh

The Sound Blaster 2.0 uses base I/O address 220h or 240h.

Base Address	I/O Addresses Used
220h	220h to 22Fh
240h	240h to 24Fh

The Sound Blaster Microchannel Version uses base I/O port addresses from 2x0h to 2xFh, where x is the number of the selectable base address from 1 to 6.

Base Address	I/O Addresses Used
210h	210h to 21Fh
220h	220h to 22Fh
230h	230h to 23Fh
240h	240h to 24Fh
250h	250h to 25Fh
260h	260h to 26Fh

The following address tables apply to SB, SB 2.0, and SB MCV:

2x0h	CMS Music Voice 1-6 Data port (write)
2x1h	CMS Music Voice 1-6 register port (write)
2x2h	CMS Music Voice 7-12 Data port (write)
2x3h	CMS Music Voice 7-12 register port (write)

Addresses 2x0h thru 2x3h apply only when the optional CMS chips have been installed.

2x8h	FM Music Data port (write)
2x8h	FM Music Status port (read)
2x9h	FM Music register port (write)

FM Music can also be accessed through I/O addresses 388h and 389h. These addresses are fixed and exist for backward-compatibility with the AdLib card's FM synthesizer.

2x6h	DSP Reset port (write)
2xAh	DSP Read Data port (read)
2xCh	DSP Write Data or Command port (write)
2xCh	DSP Write Buffer Status port bit 7 (read)
2xEh	DSP Data Available Status port bit 7 (read)

The analog Joystick port uses the standard joystick I/O addresses from 200h to 207h.

The Sound Blaster Pro uses 24 consecutive I/O addresses, selectable from 2 base I/O addresses (220h and 240h).

Base Address	I/O Addresses Used
220h	220h to 237h
240h	240h to 257h

The individual register definitions are as follows:

200h-207h	Analog Joystick port (read/write)
2x0h	Left FM Music Status port (read)
2x0h	Left FM Music register address port (write)
2x1h	Left FM Music Data port (write)
2x2h	Right FM Music Status port (read)
2x2h	Right FM Music register address port (write)
2x3h	Right FM Music Data port (write)
2x4h	Mixer Chip register address port (write)
2x5h	Mixer Chip Data port (read/write)
2x8h	FM Music Status port (read)
2x8h	FM Music register address port (write)
2x9h	FM Music Data port (write)
2x6h	DSP Reset port (write)
2xAh	DSP Read Data port (read)
2xCh	DSP Write Data or Command port (write)
2xCh	DSP Write Buffer Status port bit 7 (read)
2xEh	DSP Data Available Status port bit 7 (read)
2x0+10h	CD-ROM Data register (read)
2x0+10h	CD-ROM Command register (write)
2x0+11h	CD-ROM Status register (read)
2x0+12h	CD-ROM Reset register (write)
2x0+13h	CD-ROM Enable register (write)

FM music can also be accessed through I/O addresses 388h and 389h. These addresses are fixed and exist for backward-compatibility with the AdLib card's FM synthesizer. The internal registers of the FM chip(s) are outlined in Figure C-1. The internal registers of the Mixer chip are shown in Figure C-2.

Sound Blaster Interrupt Lines

The DSP also uses a hardware interrupt for some of its functions and is selectable between 2, 3, 5, or 7.

DSP Commands and Functions

Here are the DSP commands and functions:

10h	Direct mode 8-bit DAC (single-byte data transfer)
14h	DMA mode 8-bit DAC

FIGURE C-1   Yamaha 3812: Register address map

REG ADDR	D7	D6	D5	D4	D3	D2	D1	D0
01						TEST		
02	TIMER - 1							
03	TIMER - 2							
04	IRQ RST	MASK T1	T2				START/STOP T2	T1
08	CSM	SEL						
20 - 35	AM	VIB	EG	KSR	MULTIPLE			
40 - 55	KSL		TOTAL LEVEL					
60 - 75	ATTACK RATE				DECAY RATE			
80 - 95	SUSTAIN LEVEL				RELEASE RATE			
A0 - A8	F - NUMBER (L)							
B0 - B8			KEYON		BLOCK		F - NUMBER (H)	
BD	DEPTH AM	VIB	RHYTHM	BASS DRUM	SNARE DRUM	TOM TOM	TOP CYM	HI HAT
C0 - C8						FEEDBACK		CON

FIGURE
C-2

Register Map of MIXER Chip

REG ADDR	D7	D6	D5	D4	D3	D2	D1	D0
00H	DATA RESET							
02H	RESERVED							
* 04H	VOICE VOLUME LEFT				VOICE VOLUME RIGHT			
06H	RESERVED							
08H	RESERVED							
0AH	X	X	X	X	X	MIC MIXING		
0CH	X	X	IN FILTER			ADC		X
0EH	X	X	DNFI	X	X	X	VSTC	X
20H	RESERVED							
* 22H	MASTER VOLUME LEFT				MASTER VOLUME RIGHT			
24H	RESERVED							
* 26H	FM VOLUME LEFT				FM VOLUME RIGHT			
* 28H	CD VOLUME LEFT				CD VOLUME RIGHT			
2AH	RESERVED							
2CH	RESERVED							
* 2EH	LINE VOLUME LEFT				LINE VOLUME RIGHT			

16h	DMA mode 2-bit ADPCM DAC
17h	DMA mode 2-bit ADPCM DAC with Reference byte
20h	Direct mode 8-bit ADC (single-byte data transfer)
24h	DMA mode 8-bit ADC
30h	MIDI Read (polling mode)
31h	MIDI Read (interrupt mode)
34h	MIDI UART mode (polling mode)
35h	MIDI UART mode (interrupt mode)
38h	MIDI Write (polling mode)
40h	Set Time Constant
74h	DMA mode 4-bit ADPCM DAC
75h	DMA mode 4-bit ADPCM DAC with Reference Byte
76h	DMA mode 2.6-bit ADPCM DAC
77h	DMA mode 2.6-bit ADPCM DAC with Reference Byte
80h	Set Silence Mode Data length
91h	High-Speed DMA mode 8-bit DAC
99h	High-Speed DMA mode 8-bit ADC

D1h	Turn on Speaker
D3h	Turn off Speaker
D8h	Get Speaker Status
	00h = off
	ffh = on
D0h	Halt DMA in progress
D4h	Continue DMA
D1h	Get DSP Version
	low-byte = Major
	high-byte = Minor

Playing Sounds on a Sound Blaster

Programming each of the devices will be covered in generic step-by-step instructions without the use of any language-specific programming code. A working knowledge of programming techniques is both assumed and necessary to make use of the information provided in the remainder of this appendix.

Low-level programming information will be provided for each of the devices on the Sound Blaster, to enable you to program simple sound applications.

For more advanced sound applications, you should interface your program with the Creative Labs Sound drivers. Low-level programming information for each of these drivers has also been provided. For more detailed information about programming the individual chips, in-depth documentation on the sound drivers, or for language-specific routines, examples, and include files, refer to the Sound Blaster Developer Kit from Creative Labs, Inc.

Programming the DSP for Voice

The Digital Sound Processor (DSP) can be programmed in either Direct mode or Direct Memory Access (DMA) mode. Direct mode is simpler to program, but it requires that the application program perform all necessary timing operations. It also limits the application to playing only 8-bit Pulse Code Modulated (PCM) data, not compressed data.

DMA mode offers many advantages over Direct mode. Compressed or uncompressed data can be played, because the Sound Blaster is performing the data transfer from memory to the DSP, and performs any required data decompression automatically. All timing operations are also performed by the Sound Blaster, freeing the PC processor to perform other functions, such as video operations in the case of narrated animations.

Initializing the DSP for Voice

The DSP must be reset once before it can be programmed. This reset must be performed after each system reboot. The procedure is as follows:

1. Write a byte value of "01h" to the DSP Reset port (2x6h).

2. Wait at least 3 microseconds.

3. Write a byte value of "00h" to the DSP Reset port (2x6h).

4. Wait until the DSP Data Available Status port (2xEh) bit 7 is set (80h).

5. Read the DSP Read Data port (2xAh).

6. If the byte value read from the DSP Read Data port is equal to "0AAh," then you're done. Otherwise go back to step 4.

The DSP takes approximately 100 microseconds to initialize itself. As a result, if your program does not receive a value of 0AAh in step 6 the first time through, repeat steps 4 through 6 at least 40 to 100 times to be sure that the card has had enough time to reset itself. If you still do not receive a value of 0AAh after these attempts, the card has failed the reset.

DSP Read/Write Procedure

All Read and Write commands to the DSP ports require a special sequence of steps to ensure proper command handling by the DSP. These procedures are implied throughout the remainder of this appendix wherever a read or write to the DSP ports is indicated.

DSP Write Procedure

1. Read the DSP Write Buffer Status port (2xCh).
2. If bit 7 of the byte read from the DSP Write Buffer Status port is 1 (80h), then go back to step 1.
3. Write the data byte to the DSP Write Data port (2xCh).

DSP Read Procedure

1. Read DSP Data Available Status port (2xEh).
2. If bit 7 of the byte read from the DSP Data Available Status port is 1 (80h), then go to step 3. If not, go back to step 1.
3. Read the data byte from DSP Read Data port (2xAh).

The looping caused by checking the Status port in step 2 of both the DSP Write and DSP Read procedures ensures that the DSP is ready to receive and send the next data byte, respectively. Always remember to perform this check whenever you read or write to the DSP.

DSP Interrupt Handling

The DSP provides hardware interrupts for the following functions:

☐ DMA mode for Digital-to-Analog Conversion (DAC output)
☐ DMA mode for Analog-to-Digital Conversion (ADC input)

☐   Interrupt mode for MIDI input

An interrupt service routine must be set up before starting one of these functions in order to handle the interrupt when it occurs. For functions that provide data to be read, the data is read from the DSP Read Data port (2xAh) within the interrupt service routine. The interrupt must then be acknowledged by reading the DSP Data Available Status port (2xEh) once. Note that this is another detail that is easily overlooked and will cause your program to crash. There is no need to check for a value returned by this port. Reading from the port is all that is required to acknowledge the interrupt.

The interrupt service routine executes the End-Of-Interrupt (EOI) command (20h) to the interrupt controller, at the end of the routine.

Programming the DSP in Direct Mode

1. Write "10h" to DSP Command port (2xCh).

2. Write a single byte of data to DSP Write Data port (2xCh). This data must be in uncompressed 8-bit PCM format. No compressed data can be output in Direct mode.

 Caution   Don't forget to make sure that the card is ready before sending this byte! See the DSP Read/Write Procedure section above.

3. Wait for the correct timing, and then repeat steps 1 and 2 until end of data.

Programming the DSP in DMA Mode

1. Set up the interrupt service routine.

2. Program the sampling rate to the DSP in the following way:

    a. Turn on the speaker by writing "0D1h" to the DSP Command port (2xCh).

b.   Send the Set Time-Constant command by writing "40h" to the DSP Command port (2xCh).

c.   Send the Time-Constant value by writing the Time - Constant byte to the DSP Write Data Port (2xCh) where Time - Constant = 256 - (1,000,000 / sampling rate) Example for a 8,000 Hz sampling rate: to Time - Constant= 256.

3.   Program the DMA Controller for the first data block.

a.   Select DMA channel 1 by writing 05h to the DMA Mask register (0Ah).

b.   Reset the DMA transfer flip-flop to the lower byte. Write "00h" to the DMA Clear Byte Pointer register (0Ch).

c.   Select DMA mode for DAC output by writing "45h" to the DMA Mode register (0Bh), or for ADC input by writing "49h" to the DMA Mode register.

d.   Send the Data memory address to the DMA Controller by writing the low-byte of the address to the DMA ch1 Memory address register (02h). Then write the high-byte of the address to the DMA ch1 Memory address register (02h).

e.   Send the physical memory page number to the DMA controller by writing the page number to the DMA ch1 Page address register (83h).

f.   Send the DMA data-byte count (data length - 1) by writing the low-byte of the data-count to the DMA ch1 Transfer Count register (03h). Then write the high-byte of of the data count to the DMA ch1 Transfer Count register (03h).

g.   Enable DMA channel 1 by writing "01h" to the DMA Mask register (0Ah). The DMAC is now waiting for the DSP to read data.

4.   Program the DSP for the first data block.

a.   Send the DMA mode 8-bit DAC command by writing "14h" to the DSP Command port (2xCh).

b. Send the length of the data to be transferred by writing the low-byte of the length to the DSP Command port (2xCh). Then write the high-byte of the length to the DSP Command port (2xCh). The DSP now starts reading data from the DMAC.

5. Service the DSP interrupt.

a. Preserve the machine status.

b. Acknowledge the DSP interrupt by reading the DSP Data Available Status port (2xEh) once.

c. If there are no more blocks to transfer, go to step 5f.

d. Program the DMA Controller for the next data block (refer to step 3 above).

e. Program the DSP for the next data block (refer to step 4 above).

f. Output End-of-Interrupt to the Interrupt Controller by executing an EOI instruction (20h).

g. Restore the machine status.

h. Execute an IRET instruction.

6. Restore the original interrupt service routine.

Programming the Direct Memory Access Controller (DMAC)

The DMAC is an Intel 8237A chip that handles high-speed data transfers between memory and other PC devices and chips, such as the Sound Blaster's DSP chip.

The DMAC is programmed through the following ports:

0000h	DMA Channel 0, Memory address register (r/w)
0001h	DMA Channel 0, Transfer count register (r/w)
0002h	DMA Channel 1, Memory address register (r/w)
0003h	DMA Channel 1, Transfer count register (r/w)
0004h	DMA Channel 2, Memory address register (r/w)

0005h	DMA Channel 2, Transfer count register (r/w)
0006h	DMA Channel 3, Memory address register (r/w)
0007h	DMA Channel 3, Transfer count register (r/w)
0008h	DMA Status register (r)

bit 7 = 1 Channel 3 request
bit 6 = 1 Channel 2 request
bit 5 = 1 Channel 1 request
bit 4 = 1 Channel 0 request
bit 3 = 1 Terminal count on channel 3
bit 2 = 1 Terminal count on channel 2
bit 1 = 1 Terminal count on channel 1
bit 0 = 1 Terminal count on channel 0

000Ah	DMA Channel 0-3 Mask register (r/w)

bit 7-3 = 0 reserved
bit 2   = 0 Clear mask bit
        = 1 Set mask bit
bit 1-0 = 00 Select channel 0
        = 01 Select channel 1
        = 10 Select channel 2
        = 11 Select channel 3

000Bh	DMA channel 0-3 Mode register (r/w)

bit 7-6 = 00 Demand mode
        = 01 Single mode
        = 10 Block mode
        = 11 Cascade mode
bit 5   = 0 Address increment select
bit 4   = 0 Autoinitialized
        = 1 Non-autoinitialized
bit 3-2 = 00 Verify operation
        = 01 Write operation
        = 10 Read operation
        = 11 Reserved

	bit 1-0 = 00 Select channel 0
	= 01 Select channel 1
	= 10 Select channel 2
	= 11 Select channel 3

000Ch	DMA Clear Byte pointer (w)
000Dh	DMA Master clear (w)
000Eh	DMA Clear Mask register (w)
000Fh	DMA Channel 0-3 Write Mask register (w)

bit 7-4 = 0 Reserved
bit 3   = 0 Unmask channel 3 mask bit
         = 1 Set channel 3 mask bit
bit 2   = 0 Unmask channel 2 mask bit
         = 1 Set channel 2 mask bit
bit 1   = 0 Unmask channel 1 mask bit
         = 1 Set channel 1 mask bit
bit 0   = 0 Unmask channel 0 mask bit
         = 1 Set channel 0 mask bit

0019H	DMA Scratch register (r/w)
0081h	DMA channel 2, page table address register (r/w)
0082h	DMA channel 3, page table address register (r/w)
0083h	DMA channel 1, page table address register (r/w)
0087h	DMA channel 0, page table address register (r/w)

Note   See step 3 of "Programming the DSP in DMA mode" for programming details.

Special Notes on Programming the DMAC

The DMAC's data counter is always one byte less than the actual number of bytes to transfer.

The DMAC can transfer data only within a physical memory page. Any data block that crosses a physical memory page boundary must be divided into multiple requests for the DMA Controller. This limits the maximum data-transfer size to 64K (the size of a physical memory page).

Another limitation of the DMA controller is that it is only capable of accessing memory in the first megabyte of addressing space. When a program running within a multitasking system, such as DESQview or Windows, executes a DMA request into mapped memory, the Extended Memory Manager, such as QEMM or HIMEM, must reroute the actual DMA request into a temporary buffer in the first megabyte of memory, and then copy the data into the program's buffer in mapped memory. This process all happens without informing the application program, except when the original transfer size exceeds the size of the temporary buffer in the Memory Manager. This usually will cause a system crash, but the problem can be resolved by adding a parameter to the line in the CONFIG.SYS file that loads the Memory Manager to tell it to use a larger DMA buffer.

FM Music Synthesis

The FM music chip creates synthesized music using a technique called Frequency Modulation. Instruments and notes are defined by a set of parameters that control the modulation to produce the resulting waveform. These parameters are stored in a file, usually with a .CMF or .ROL extension, and passed to the FM chip, which will then produce the appropriate musical tones. Changing any single parameter while playing a music file, will result in changing the tone of a single instrument. It will not affect the other instruments.

Programming the Sound Blaster Drivers

- ☐ SBSIM.COM   Sound Blaster Standard Interface module
- ☐ CT-VOICE.DRV   Creative Memory Mode Voice driver
- ☐ CTVDSK.DRV   Creative Disk Double-Buffering Voice driver
- ☐ AUX.DRV   Creative Auxliary driver (Mixer)
- ☐ SBFMDRV.COM   Sound Blaster FM Music driver
- ☐ SBMIDI.EXE   The Creative MIDI Music driver

- ☐ SBPCD.SYS   CD-ROM Audio Interface Hardware driver
- ☐ MSCDEX.EXE   CD-ROM Audio Interface Software driver
- ☐ SBTALKER.EXE   Text-to-Speech Synthesis driver

Programming the Sound Blaster Standard Interface Module (SBSIM.COM)

SBSIM is a driver that combines and simplifies the interfaces to the Sound Blaster drivers. SBSIM loads the Sound Blaster drivers at start-up, thus relieving the application program of this task. SBSIM uses a Configuration file to specify which drivers will load and what memory will be reserved for buffers and files.

SBSIM supports .CMF music files by loading the SBFMDRV driver and .MID files by loading the SBMIDI driver. SBSIM also supports .VOC files played from memory, both conventional and extended, and also direct from disk. This is accomplished by loading the CT-VOICE and the CTVDSK drivers, respectively.

SBSIM gives you control of the source volumes when using the Sound Blaster Pro by loading the AUXDRV driver.

Startup/Configuration File

A Configuration file is used to define which drivers are to be loaded and what parameters are to be passed to the drivers. The Configuration file is read when SBSIM loads into memory. After SBSIM has been loaded, changes to the Configuration file will have no effect until SBSIM is reinstalled.

The format of SBSIM's Configuration file is based on the Windows .INI file format. A tag identifying the driver to be loaded is surrounded by brackets and followed by a set of parameters. This format is as follows:

```
[ <DriverTag> ]
<parm>=value                    ; parameters requiring values
```

```
              :
        <parm>=ON                    ;  switch parameters
        <parm>=OFF                   ;
              :
              :
```

Comments are also supported and are marked using a semicolon. Everything after the semicolon (;) on a line is ignored.

A Sample Configuration File for SBSIM

The following is an example of an SBSIM Configuration file:

```
; Load the FM driver
;
[FM]
BufferSize=32

; Load the VMEM driver
;      and use Extended memory
[MemVoice]
ExtendedMemory=on
SBSIMhandles=5
```

If a driver is not specified in the Configuration file, it will not be loaded into memory.

Supported Drivers and Their Parameters

The supported drivers and their associated parameters are as follows:

[FM]	Loads SBFMDRV.COM (.CMF files)
BufferSize:<nn>	Size of buffer in Kb (2..32)(32)
[DskVoice]	Loads CTVDSK.DRV (.VOC files from disk)
BufferSize:<nn>	Size of buffer in Kb (2..32)(32)
DMABufferSize:<nn>	Size of buffer in Kb (2..32)(8)
[MemVoice]	Loads CT-VOICE.DRV (.VOC files from memory)
ExtendedMemory:<OFF/ON>	Indicates if Extended memory is to be used. (OFF)

XMShandles:<*nn*>	Maximum No. of SBSIM handles, if XMS is specified. Refer to (4) below (10)
DMABufferSize:<*nn*>	Size of buffer in Kb (2..32)(8)
[Auxiliary]	Loads AUXDRV.DRV (Volume controls)
CDswitchSpeakers:<OFF/ON>	Switch specifying if CD-ROM output to the speakers should be swapped (OFF)
[MIDI]	Loads SBMIDI.EXE (.MID Files)
BufferSize:<*nn*>	Size of buffer in Kb(2..32)(32)
MidiMap:<*nn*>	MIDI mapper format to use 0 => GENERAL MIDI 1 => BASIC MIDI 2 => EXTENDED MIDI

General Application Programming Interface

The SBSIM functions are invoked by calling the interrupt that was defined when the driver was loaded. The driver is loaded into the first available interrupt between 80H and BFH. It may be identified by the signature string "SBSIM" at offset 103H of the segment to which the interrupt vector points.

Entry to the Driver

Upon entry to the driver, the following registers are used, as shown in the table below:

BH	=	Driver to Activate
		0 = Control
		1 = FM driver
		2 = DskVoice driver
		3 = MemVoice driver
		4 = AUX driver
BL	=	Desired function No.

AX	=	Input values (AL is used for byte values)
CX	=	Voice I/O handle to use, for SB16 voice drivers
DX:AX	=	Double-word input values

Exiting the Driver

Upon exiting the driver, values are returned to the registers listed below:

AX	=	Word results (AL is used for byte values)
DX:AX	=	Double-word results
AX	=	Error code (if carry flag is set)

All other registers remain unchanged.

 Note   There are exceptions to the format described above. Some functions may use other registers for their input. Refer to the detailed function descriptions below for the exact registers used.

Extended Memory Support in SBSIM

When using the CT-VOICE driver, SBSIM allows application programs to make use of Extended memory to store .VOC files. This option is available when the "ExtendedMemory" switch in the Configuration file is set to ON.

Normally, SBSIM will make use of Extended memory via a set of its own internal Extended memory (XMS) handles. These handles are referred to as SBSIM handles throughout this documentation. The number of handles is set to 10 by default but it may be modified by using the XMShandles parameter in the Configuration file. SBSIM-handle numbering begins with 1.

Alternatively, an application program may use its own XMS handles but it must relate them to an SBSIM handle. This can be done by using the function "Set XMS handle into SBSIM handle." All access to the .VOC file must be accomplished through this handle. Your program must free the SBSIM handle (the XMS handle is also freed) by making a call to the function "Free extended memory."

Error Codes Returned from SBSIM

Upon exit from SBSIM, the carry flag will indicate the success or failure of the requested operation. If the carry flag is clear, then the function has succeeded and the return value is in the AX register (or DX:AX in certain cases). If an error occurs in execution of the function, the AX register will contain the error code.

The complete list of error codes follows:

Error Code #	Name	Description
1	SIMerr_IsBusy	SBSIM currently in use
2	SIMerr_BadDriver	Bad driver specified
3	SIMerr_BadFunction	Bad function specified
4	SIMerr_VoiceActive	A voice process already active
5	SIMerr_VMEMnoStart	Could not start VMEM voice
6	SIMerr_VDSKnoStart	Could not start VDSK voice
7	SIMerr_BadSIMhandle	Invalid SBSIM handle
8	SIMerr_BadBuffer	Buffer not initialized yet
9	SIMerr_BadFile	Bad file name for load
10	SIMerr_Bad file handle	BadFileHandle
11	SIMerr_NotInited	Driver not START'ed yet
12	SIMerr_NoXMS	XMS driver not installed
13	SIMerr_NoSIMfree	No free SBSIM handles to use
14	SIMerr_BadFileType	Bad file type specified for load
15	SIMerr_BadFreeXMS	Couldn't free XMS block
16	SIMerr_AuxBadSource	Bad source for AUX functions
17	SIMerr_BadPanGet	Get pan position failed
18	SIMerr_BadPanSet	Set pan position failed
19	SIMerr_BadVolSet	Set volume failed
20	SIMerr_FPbadStart	Could not start fade/pan

21	SIMerr_FPbadStop	Could not stop fade/pan
22	SIMerr_FPbadPause	Could not pause fade/pan
23	SIMerr_FPbadType	Not fade/pan operation specified
24	SIMerr_FPbadMode	Bad mode for fade/pan
25	SIMerr_FPfailed	Could not start fade/pan
26	SIMerr_FPnotFadePan	Source not fading/panning
27	SIMerr_MusicActive	FM or MIDI already playing
28	SIMerr_BadMapper	Bad MIDI mapper format

Control Function (BH = 0)

The following programming section gives details on calling the drivers directly. This section discusses control functions for SBSIM. This will be followed by control functions for the individual drivers. Specifically, these drivers are FM, CTVOICE, CTVDSK, AUX, and MIDI.

The control functions are the calls made to the SBSIM interface. They perform functions such as requesting the entry address of the driver, the status of memory, and other address pointers.

Function 0: Query Version

This function returns a bitmask indicating which drivers are loaded. The definition of this bitmask is specified above in the section "General Application Programming Interface" (register BX).

Entry Upon entry to the driver the registers should be set as follows:

BH = 0
BL = 0

Exit Upon exit from the driver, the following values will be returned in the registers listed below:

AH   =   Major Version number

AL   =   Minor Version number

Possible Error Codes   This function returns no error code.

Function 1: Query drivers

This function returns the Version number of SBSIM.

Entry   Upon entry to the driver, the registers should be set as follows:

BH   =   0

BL   =   1

Exit   Upon exit from the driver, the following values will be returned in the registers listed below:

AX   =   bitmask indicating which drivers are loaded

          bit 0 = FM driver
          bit 1 = DskVoice driver
          bit 2 = MemVoice driver
          bit 3 = Auxiliary driver
          bit 4 = MIDI driver

Possible Error Codes   This function returns no error code.

Function 2: Query Driver Entry Address

This function returns a long pointer to the entry address of the specified driver. This allows application programs to call the drivers directly, thus bypassing SBSIM.

Entry   Upon entry to the driver, the registers should be set as follows:

BH   =   0

BL   =   2

AX   =   Which driver

           0 = FM

           1 = DskVoice

           2 = MemVoice

           3 = AuxDrv

           4 = Midi

Exit   Upon exit from the driver, the following value will be returned in the register listed below:

DX:AX   =   Driver entry address

Possible Error Codes   The following are possible error codes returned by this function:

SIMerr_BadDriver (2) - Bad driver specified, or driver not loaded.

Note   Because the FM driver is usually accessed through an interrupt, any calls made directly to this driver should simulate an interrupt call (push the flags on the stack, then make a far call to the driver entry address).

Function 3: Query Sound Status

This function returns a bit mask indicating which SBSIM sound sources are currently active.

Entry   Upon entry to the driver, the registers should be set as follows:

BH   =   0

BL   =   3

Exit   Upon exit from the driver, the following values will be returned in the registers listed below:

AX   =   Bitmask indicating which sound sources are playing

                bit 0 = FM

bit 1 = DskVoice

bit 2 = MemVoice

bit 4 = Midi

Possible Error Codes   This function returns no error code.

Function 4: Query XMS

This function either determines the availability of XMS memory, or determines if a specified SBSIM handle is free or not. If AX is zero upon entry, the function returns the number of free SBSIM handles. A return value of 0 indicates either that XMS is not available or that there are no more free SBSIM handles.

If AX is non-zero upon entry, the function checks to see if a particular SBSIM handle is free or not.

Entry   Upon entry to the driver, the registers should be set as follows:

BH = 0

BL = 4

AX = 0   =>   Returns number of free SBSIM handles

AX!= 0   =>   Tests if SBSIM handle free or not

Exit   Upon exit from the driver, the following values will be returned in the registers listed below.

If AX = 0 on entry:

AX = 0   =>   XMS not available

AX!= 0   =>   No. of free SBSIM handles

If AX!= 0 on entry:

AX = 0   =>   SBSIM handle is free

AX!= 0   =>   Actual XMS handle

Possible Error Codes   The possible error codes for this function are

SIMerr_BadSIMhandle (7) - An invalid handle number was specified for the handle test.

SIMerr_NoXMS (12) - XMS not installed, or not specified.

Function 5: Get Buffer Address

This function returns the address and size of the buffer that has been allocated by SBSIM for a driver (non-DMA buffers). Note that only the FM, DskVoice, and MIDI drivers require buffers.

Entry Upon entry to the driver, the registers should be set as follows:

BH	=	0
BL	=	5
AX	=	Which driver
		0 = FM
		1 = DskVoice
		4 = MIDI

Exit Upon exit from the driver, the following values will be returned in the registers listed below:

DX:AX	=	buffer address
CX	=	buffer size (in Kb)

Possible Error Codes The possible error codes for this function are the following:

SIMerr_BadDriver (2) - An invalid driver was specified for this function.

Function 6: Set Buffer Address

This function sets the address and size of a buffer for a driver. It must be called before starting the driver if the BufferSize in the Configuration file is set to 0.

Entry Upon entry to the driver, the registers should be set as follows:

BH	=	0
BL	=	6
AX	=	Which driver
		0 = FM
		1 = DskVoice
		4 = Midi
DS:DX	=	Pointer to user buffer
CX	=	Size of buffer (in Kb)

Exit Upon exit from the driver, the following value will be returned in the register listed below:

AX = 0 if there is no error

Possible Error Codes Possible error codes are as follows:

SIMerr_BadDriver (2) - An invalid driver was specified for this function.

Function 16: Load File into Extended Memory

This function loads a file into Extended memory. Currently, the only supported file type is the .VOC voice file. Only the data block of the file is loaded. The application must use a free SBSIM handle to hold the file. The SBSIM handle to use is specified in CX upon entry. If CX is zero, SBSIM will search for an empty handle to use.

Register AX returns the SBSIM handle used if the load was successful. This handle is to be used during further SBSIM accesses to the Extended memory block.

Entry Upon entry to the driver, the registers should be set as follows:

BH	=	0
BL	=	16
AX	=	File type (0 for VOC files)
DS:DX	=	Pointer to filename
CX	=	SBSIM handle No. (0 to use first available handle)

Exit Upon exit from the driver, the following value will be returned in the register listed below:

AX = SBSIM handle assigned

Possible Error Codes The possible error codes for this function are the following:

SIMerr_NoXMS (12) - XMS not installed, or not specified.

SIMerr_BadFileType (14) - An unsupported file type was specified.

SIMerr_NoSIMfree (13) - No more free SBSIM handles exist.

SIMerr_BadFile (9) - A bad file path was specified or the file was too large to load into Extended memory.

Function 17: Get XMS Handle

This function permits an application to set up its own XMS block and relates the obtained XMS handle to an SBSIM handle.

Entry Upon entry to the driver, the registers should be set as follows:

BH   =   0
BL   =   17
AX   =   SBSIM handle

Exit Upon exit from the driver, the following value will be returned in the register listed below:

AX = XMS handle (0 - SBSIM handle not in use)

Possible Error Codes The possible error codes for this function are the following:

SIMerr_NoXMS (12) - XMS not installed, or not specified.

SIMerr_BadSIMhandle (7) - An invalid handle number was specified for the handle test.

This function returns the actual XMS handle that is referenced by a particular SBSIM handle.

Function 18: Set XMS Handle into SBSIM Handle

This function allows an application program to set up its own XMS block, and to set the obtained XMS handle into an SBSIM handle.

Entry The registers should be set as follows for entry to the driver:

BH	=	0
BL	=	18
AX	=	SBSIM handle No. (0 - use first free handle)
DX	=	XMS handle

Exit Upon exit from the driver, the following value will be returned in the register listed below:

AX = SBSIM handle

Possible Error Codes The possible error codes for this function are the following:

SIMerr_NoXMS (12) - XMS not installed or not specified.

SIMerr_BadSIMhandle (7) - An invalid handle number was specified for the handle test.

SIMerr_NoSIMfree (13) - No more free SBSIM handles exist, or the specified handle was not free.

Function 19: Free Extended Memory

This function frees an SBSIM handle and the associated XMS block.

Entry The registers should be set as follows for entry to the driver:

BH	=	0
BL	=	19
AX	=	SBSIM handle No.

Exit   Upon exit from the driver, the following value will be returned in the register listed below:

AX = 0 if there is no error.

Possible Error Codes   The possible error codes for this function are the following:

SIMerr_NoXMS (12) - XMS not installed or not specified.

SIMerr_BadSIMhandle (7) - An invalid handle number was specified for the handle test.

SIMerr_BadFreeXMS (15) - Could not free the XMS block.

This function frees an SBSIM handle and the associated XMS block.

FM, DSKVOICE, MEMVOICE, MIDI DRIVERS (BH = 1, 2, 3, 5)

These functions pertain to the individual sound driver functions. They offer a simplified interface to the Voice, FM, MIDI, and Aux drivers.

Note that in the previous section we used the value of BH = 0 for the SBSIM control function. Values for specific driver calls are listed in the table below.

BH	=	1	=>	FM driver
BH	=	2	=>	DskVoice driver
BH	=	3	=>	MemVoice driver
BH	=	5	=>	MIDI driver

Function 0: Start Sound Source

This function sets up the specified driver for a subsequent sound output. For the FM driver, the specified .CMF file is loaded into the buffer, and the appropriate setup is performed. For the VDSK driver, the specified .VOC file is opened for input. For the VMEM driver, the driver is set up for output. For the MIDI driver, the specified .MID file is loaded into the buffer, and an appropriate setup is performed.

This function should be called whenever starting a sound process. However, sound will not start playing by calling this function. It will be played only when the PLAY function is invoked.

Entry   The registers should be set as follows for entry to the driver:

BL	=	0
BH	=	Driver
AX	=	Pointer to Filename (FM, MIDI, and DskVoice)
DX:AX	=	Pointer to data block (MemVoice, conventional memory)
AX	=	SBSIM handle (Extended memory)
DX	=	0 (Extended memory)

Exit   Upon exit from the driver, the following value will be returned in the register listed below:

AX = 0 if there is no error.

Possible Error Codes   The possible error codes for this function are the following:

SIMerr_BadBuffer (8) - Buffer not allocated yet.

SIMerr_BadFile (9) - A bad file was specified, or the file was too large to load into Extended memory.

SIMerr_VDSKnoStart (6) - The DskVoice driver could not be initialized.

SIMerr_VMEMnoStart (5) - The MemVoice driver could not be initialized.

SIMerr_BadSIMhandle (7) - A bad handle was specified.

This function initializes the specified driver for sound output as follows:

- ☐ For the FM driver, the specified .CMF file is loaded into the buffer and the appropriate setup procedures are performed.

- ☐ For the DskVoice driver, the specified .VOC file is opened for input and the appropriate setup procedures are performed.

- ☐ For the MemVoice driver, the driver is set up for output.

- ☐ For the MIDI driver, the specified .MID file is loaded into the buffer and the appropriate setup procedures are performed.

This function should be called to initialize the driver before starting a sound process. Sound will not start playing with this function.

Refer to the PLAY function to begin this process.

Function 1: Play Sound

This function starts the actual sound output.

Entry The registers should be set as follows for entry to the driver:

BH   =   driver (1, 2, 3, 5)
BL   =   1

Exit Upon exit from the driver, the following value will be returned in the register listed below:

AX = 0 if there is no error.

Possible Error Codes The possible error codes for this function are the following:

SIMerr_BadFileHandle (10) - A valid file has not been opened for voice output.

SIMerr_VDSKnoStart (6) - The DskVoice driver's Play function could not be started.

SIMerr_VMEMnoStart (5) - The MemVoice driver's Play function could not be started.

Function 2: Stop Sound

This function stops the current sound output.

Entry   The registers should be set as follows for entry to the driver:

BH   =   Driver (1, 2, 3, 5)
BL   =   2

Exit   No values are returned by the drivers upon exit.

Possible Error Codes   No error codes are returned by this function.

Function 3: Pause Sound

This function pauses the current sound output.

Entry   The registers should be set as follows for entry to the driver:

BH   =   Driver (1, 2, 3, 5)
BL   =   3

Exit   No values are returned by the drivers upon exit.

Possible Error Codes   No error codes are returned by this function.

Function 4: Resume Sound

This function resumes a previously paused sound output.

Entry   The registers should be set as follows for entry to the driver:

BH   =   Driver (1, 2, 3, 5)
BL   =   4

Exit   No values are returned by the drivers upon exit.

Possible Error Codes   No error codes are returned by this function.

Function 5: Read Sound Status

This function returns the value of the sound status word.

Entry   The registers should be set as follows for entry to the driver:

BH   =   Driver (1, 2, 3, 5)
BL   =   5

Exit   Upon exit from the driver, the following value will be returned in the register listed below:

AX = Sound status

Possible Error Codes   No error codes are returned by this function.

Function 6: Set Midi Mapper (for MIDI Driver Only)

This function sets a new MIDI channel mapper for the MIDI driver.

Entry   The registers should be set as follows for entry to the driver:

BH	=	5
BL	=	6
AX	=	New MIDI mapper

           0 - GENERAL mapper
           1 - BASIC mapper
           2 - EXTENDED mapper

Exit   No values are returned by the drivers upon exit.

Possible Error Codes   No error codes are returned by this function.

AUXDRV Driver

The following definitions apply to the Auxiliary driver functions:

Source

0	=	Master
1	=	Voice
2	=	FM
3	=	CD
4	=	Line-in
5	=	MIC
6	=	PC-SPK

Volume   For the Master, Voice, FM, CD, and Line-in sources:

Low byte = right speaker volume (0-255)
High byte = left speaker volume (0-255)

For the MIC source: Word value = volume (0-255).

FadePan Structure

The following is an assembly language structure for use with the FadePan functions:

```
FadePanStruc     STRUC

FadePanType      DW   ?     ; 1=Fade, 2=Pan
FadePanSource    DW   ?     ; source
FadePanMode      DW   ?     ; 0=unidir, 1=yo-yo
FadePanTime      DW   ?     ; time in millisec (0-65535)
FadePanCount     DW   ?     ; repeat count
PanInitPos       DW   ?     ; initial position (for pan only)
FadePanEndPos    DW   ?     ; ending position (for fade/pan)

FadePanStruc     ENDS
```

Function 0: Get Source Volume

This function returns the current volume of the specified source.

Entry   The registers should be set as follows for entry to the driver:

BH   =   4

BL   =   0

AX   =   Source

Exit   Upon exit from the driver, the following value will be returned in the register listed below:

AX = Volume (High byte = AH, Low byte = AL)

Possible Error Codes   The possible error codes for this function are as follows:

SIMerr_AuxBadSource (16) - A bad source was specified.

Note   The reading obtained may be an instantaneous value only if fading or panning has been invoked for the source.

Function 1: Set Source Volume

This function sets the volume level of a specified source. Note that when a source is currently undergoing a fading or panning process, its volume level cannot be set.

Entry   The registers should be set as follows for entry to the driver:

BH	=	4
BL	=	1
AX	=	Source
DX	=	Volume

Exit   Upon exit from the driver, the following value will be returned in the register listed below:

AX = 0 if there is no error.

Possible Error Codes   The possible error codes for this function are as follows:

SIMerr_AuxBadSource (16) - A bad source was specified.

SIMerr_BadVolSet (19) - Fading or panning is currently in effect for the source.

Function 16: Setup Fade and/or Pan

This function initializes a source for fading or panning. To start a fade or pan, use the START fade/pan function (function 17).

Entry   The registers should be set as follows for entry to the driver:

BH	=	4
BL	=	16
DX:AX	=	Pointer to FadePan structure

Exit   Upon exit from the driver, the following value will be returned in the register listed below:

AX = 0 if there is no error.

Possible Error Codes   The possible error codes for this function are as follows:

SIMerr_FPbadType (23) - A bad fading/panning type was specified. Currently the type should be 1 or 2 only.

SIMerr_AuxBadSource (16) - A bad source was specified for fading or panning.

SIMerr_FPbadMode (24) - A bad fading/panning mode was specified. Should be 0 or 1 only.

SIMerr_FPfailed (25) - Fading or panning initialization failed. Usually, this is due to a fading or panning already in progress on the source. Stop or clear the source before setting up again.

Setting Up Several Sources for Fading or Panning

Only one source is set up for fading/panning in this function. To set up several sources for fade/pan, call this function repeatedly for each source.

Only one setup is valid for each source. If a source is initialized a second time, then an error will occur.

The valid sources for fading and panning are as follows:

0)   Master
1)   Voice
2)   FM
3)   CD
4)   Line-in

Function 17: Start Fade/Pan

This function is called to start the actual fading or panning process after all the appropriate sources have been set up for fade/pan.

Entry   The registers should be set as follows for entry to the driver:

BH   =   4
BL   =   17

Exit   Upon exit from the driver, the following value will be returned in the register listed below:

AX = 0 if there is no error.

Possible Error Codes   The possible error codes for this function are as follows:

SIMerr_FPbadStart (20) - Fading or panning was not initialized properly. Usually, this is because set up has not been performed for any source, or because fading or panning is already in progress.

Function 18: Stop Fade/Pan

This function stops the fading or panning action of either a single source or of all the sources.

Entry   The registers should be set as follows for entry to the driver:

BH   =   4
BL   =   18
AX   =   Source (0FFFFh - stop all sources)

Exit   Upon exit from the driver, the following value will be returned in the register listed below:

AX = 0 if there is no error.

Possible Error Codes   The possible error codes for this function are as follows:

SIMerr_AuxBadSource (16) - A bad source was specified for the fading or panning.

SIMerr_FPbadStop (21) - Fade or pan could not be stopped. The usual reason for this is that the source has already stopped.

Function 19: Pause Fade/Pan

This function pauses the fading and panning action of all the sources.

Entry   The registers should be set as follows for entry to the driver:

BH	=	4
BL	=	19

Exit   Upon exit from the driver, the following value will be returned in the register listed below:

AX = 0 if there is no error.

Possible Error Codes   The possible error codes for this function are as follows:

SIMerr_FPbadPause (22) - Fading or panning could not be paused. Usually this is because there is no fading or panning action in process.

Function 20: Resume Fade/Pan

This function resumes previously paused fading/panning action.

Entry   The registers should be set as follows for entry to the driver:

BH	=	4
BL	=	20

Exit   Upon exit from the driver, the following value will be returned in the register listed below:

AX = 0 if there is no error.

Possible Error Codes   The following are possible error codes returned by this function:

SIMerr_FPbadStart (20) - Fading or panning could not be restarted. Usually, this is because no sources are actively fading or panning.

Function 21: Read Fade/Pan Status

This function returns the current fading/panning status of a source.

Entry   The registers should be set as follows for entry to the driver:

BH   =   4
BL   =   21
AX   =   Source

Exit   Upon exit from the driver, the following values will be returned in the registers listed below:

AX   =   FadePan status
                0 = Not fading or panning
                1 = Fading
                2 = Panning

Possible Error Codes   The following are possible error codes returned by this function:

SIMerr_AuxBadSource (16) - A bad source was specified.

Function 22: Get Pan Position

This function returns the current pan position of the specified source. If the source has not previously been initialized, then an error will be returned.

Entry   The registers should be set as follows for entry to the driver:

BH	=	4
BL	=	22
AX	=	Source

Exit   Upon exit from the driver, the following value will be returned in the register listed below:

AX = Pan position

Possible Error Codes   The following are possible error codes returned by this function:

SIMerr_AuxBadSource (16) - A bad source was specified.

SIMerr_BadPanGet (17) - The source is not initialized for panning.

Function 23: Set Pan Position

This function sets the pan position for a specified source. If the source is currently panning, then an error code is returned.

Entry   The registers should be set as follows for entry to the driver:

BH	=	4
BL	=	23
AX	=	Source
DX	=	Pan position

Exit   Upon exit from the driver, the following value will be returned in the register listed below:

AX = 0 if there is no error.

Possible Error Codes   The following are possible error codes returned by this function:

SIMerr_AuxBadSource (16) - A bad source was specified.

SIMerr_BadPanSet (18) - The source is currently undergoing panning.

Invoking the Respective Drivers Individually

An application program may obtain the entry address of any driver (except the Control driver (BH = 0)) and call it directly, thus bypassing SBSIM.

Warning   Intermixing direct calls to the drivers with calls to SBSIM may result in unpredictable results. Use this method carefully.

Programming the Creative Memory Mode Voice Driver (CT-VOICE.DRV)

The Creative Memory Mode Voice driver is a program-loadable file that contains all of the routines necessary to play sound clips from memory out to a Sound Blaster. All of the procedures discussed earlier for playing sounds using DMA output are implemented in the Voice driver. The Voice driver has a simple interface and can be called from a program written in almost any language.

If SBSIM was not previously loaded, the calling program must first allocate memory and load the driver at offset zero of a memory segment, before calling the driver.

Each of the functions performed by the Voice driver requires that certain registers be initialized before calling the driver. Except for registers AX and DX, all other registers are preserved, including the FLAGS register.

Function 0: Get Version Number

This function returns the Version number of the driver.

Entry   The register should be set as follows for entry to the driver:

BX   =   0

Exit   Upon exit from the driver, the following values will be returned in the registers listed below:

AH   =   Major Version number
AL   =   Minor Version number

Function 1: Set Base I/O Address

This function sets the base I/O address in the driver that is used by the Sound Blaster. The driver uses the default I/O address of 220h if this function is not called. If this function is used, it must be called before Function 3.

Entry   The registers should be set as follows for entry to the driver:

BX   =   1
AX   =   Base I/O address

The Sound Blaster Pro and Sound Blaster Version 2.0 have two possible addresses, either 220h or 240h.

The Sound Blaster Microchannel Version and the Sound Blaster have six possible base addresses. They are: 210h, 220h, 230h, 240h, 250h, and 260h.

Function 2: Set Interrupt Number for DMA

This function sets the interrupt number in the driver, which is used by the Sound Blaster to signal that a DMA transfer is complete. The driver uses the default interrupt 7 for DMA if this function is not called.

If this function is used, it must be called after Function 1 and before Function 3.

Entry   The registers should be set as follows for entry to the driver:

BX	=	2
AX	=	Interrupt number for DMA

The Sound Blaster Pro has four possible DMA interrupts: 2, 5, 7, and 10.

The Sound Blaster 2.0, Sound Blaster Microchannel Version, and the Sound Blaster have four possible DMA interrupts which are: 2, 3, 5, and 7.

Function 3: Initialize Driver

This function checks for the correct settings and functionality of the Sound Blaster. The speaker is turned on after the card has been initialized. This function must be called once, before Functions 4 through 13 can be used.

The DAC speaker is turned on after driver initialization.

Entry   The register should be set as follows for entry to the driver:

BX	=	3

Exit   Upon exit from the driver, the following values are returned in the register listed below:

AX	=	0 successful initialization
	=	1 voice card fails

	=	2 I/O read/write fails
	=	3 interrupt for DMA fails

Function 4: On/Off Speaker

This function turns the speaker connection on or off. The calling program must turn the speaker off before exiting.

The speaker must be turned off during voice input, or the recording will be output directly to the speaker.

Entry   The registers should be set as follows for entry to the driver:

BX	=	4
AL	=	0 turn speaker off
	=	1 turn speaker on

Function 5: Set Status Word Address

This function sets the address of the status word, located within the application program, that the driver will use to notify the application program of the voice input/output progress. The driver writes a zero to the status word at the end of a voice process or when the voice process is terminated. During voice output, the non-zero markers embedded in the Creative Labs voice files (.VOC) are copied into this location. Application programs can use the markers to synchronize the application's events with the sound file.

Entry   The registers should be set as follows for entry to the driver:

BX	=	5
ES:DI	=	Address of the status word

Function 6: Start Voice Output

This function uses the DMA Controller to output the sound. The buffer must contain voice data as defined by the Creative Labs voice file format (.VOC). ES:DI points to the start of the first voice data block. Control is returned to the calling program immediately with an 0FFFFh stored in the status word.

The calling program can perform any task that does not require DMA channel 1 while the sound is being played.

Entry   The registers should be set as follows for entry to the driver:

BX   =   6
ES:DI   =   Address of output buffer

Exit   Upon exit from the driver, the following values will be returned in the register listed below:

AX   =   0 successful
        =   1 failure

Function 7: Start Voice Input

This function uses the DMA Controller to input digitized sound. Control is returned to the calling program immediately with 0FFFFh in the status word.

Voice input ends when the buffer is filled, or input is terminated by Function 8.

Entry   The registers should be set as follows for entry to the driver:

BX   =   7
AX   =   Sampling rate
               SBPRO - 4000 to 44100 Hz mono
               SBPRO - 22050 or 44100 Hz stereo

The stereo sampling rate is the sampling rate of both channels.

SB 20 - 4000 to 1500 Hz mono
SB MCV - 4000 to 13000 Hz mono
SB - 4000 to 13000 Hz mono

DX:CX =   length of input buffer
ES:DI =   address of input buffer

Exit Upon exit from the driver, the following values will be returned in the register listed below:

AX   =   0 successful
        =   1 failure

Function 8: Stop Voice Process

This function terminates any voice input/output process and sets the status word to zero.

Entry The register should be set as follows for entry to the driver:

BX   =   8

Exit Upon exit from the driver, the following value will be returned in the register listed below:

Status =   0
word

Function 9: Terminate Driver

This function uninstalls the driver and resets the card, turning off the speaker's connection.

Entry The register should be set as follows for entry to the driver:

BX   =   9

Function 10: Pause Voice Output

This function pauses any sound that is currently being output. The status word remains non-zero while sound output is paused.

Entry   The register should be set as follows for entry to the driver:

BX   =   10

Exit   Upon exit from the driver, the following values will be returned in the register listed below:

AX   =   0 successful
     =   1 output not in progress

Function 11: Continue Voice Output

This function will continue any output that was paused.

Entry   The register should be set as follows for entry to the driver:

BX   =   11

Exit   Upon exit from the driver, the following values will be returned in the register listed below:

AX   =   0 successful
     =   1 nothing to continue

Function 12: Break Voice Output Loop

This function allows the application program to break out of a sound loop that is defined within the Voice file.

Entry   The registers should be set as follows for entry to the driver:

BX   =   12

AX   =   0 stop at end of current loop

       =   1 stop current loop immediately

Exit   Upon exit from the driver, the following values will be returned in the register listed below:

AX   =   0 successful

       =   1 no voice in loop

Function 13: Set User Function

This function sets the address of the optional user subroutine, which is called whenever the driver encounters the beginning of a voice data block.

Entry   The registers should be set as follows for entry to the driver:

BX   =   13

DX:AX   =   Address of user routine

DX:AX   =   0 to disable the user function

Upon entry to the user routine, ES:BX points to the first byte of the current data block, which is the block type. The user routine must observe the following conditions:

1. The function must perform a far return.

2. It must preserve the DS, DI, SI, and FLAG register except the carry flag.

3. It must clear the carry flag if the current data block should be processed by the driver. Setting the carry flag causes the driver to skip the current data block.

4. It must not set the carry flag if the current data block is the terminate block (block type 0).

Function 14: Start Voice Output from Extended Memory

This function outputs voice data from Extended memory.

Entry   The registers should be set as follows for entry to the driver:

BX	=	14
DX	=	Extended memory handle
DI:SI	=	Offset of extended memory block

Exit   Upon exit from the driver, the following values will be returned in the register listed below:

AX	=	0 successful
	=	1 failure

Function 15: Start Voice Input to Extended Memory

This function records voice data into Extended memory. The recorded data contains only the voice data block. The application should add a file header block to the front of this data block before saving to a file.

Entry   The registers should be set as follows for entry to the driver:

BX	=	15
DX	=	Extended memory handle
AX	=	Sampling rate in Hz
CX	=	Length of buffer in Kb
DI:SI	=	Offset of Extended memory block

Exit   Upon exit from the driver, the following values will be returned in the register listed below:

AX	=	0 successful

=   1 failure

Function 16: Set Recording Mode [SBPRO]

This function sets the driver either to mono or to stereo recording mode.

Entry   The registers should be set as follows for entry to the driver:

BX   =   16
AX   =   Recording mode
                    0 - mono (default)
                    1 - stereo

Exit   Upon exit from the driver, the following value will be returned in the register listed below:

AX   =   Previous recording mode

Function 17: Set Recording Source [SBPRO]

This function selects the recording source.

Entry   The registers should be set as follows for entry to the driver:

BX   =   17
AX   =   Recording source
                    0 - microphone (default)
                    1 - CD
                    2 - microphone
                    3 - line-in

Exit   Upon exit from the driver, the following value will be returned in the register listed below:

AX   =   Previous source used

Function 18: Set Recording Filter [SBPRO]

This function selects the recording filter.

Entry   The registers should be set as follows for entry to the driver:

BX   =   18
AX   =   Recording filter
       0 - low filter (default)
       1 - high filter

Exit   Upon exit from the driver, the following value will be returned in the register listed below:

AX   =   Previous filter status

Function 19: Set DMA Channel [SBPRO]

This function sets the DMA channel to be used by the driver.

Entry   The registers should be set as follows for entry to the driver:

BX   =   19
AX   =   DMA channel (0,1,3)

Function 20: Get Card Type

This function returns the card type supported by the Voice driver.

Entry   The register should be set as follows for entry to the driver:

BX   =   20

Exit Upon exit from the driver, the following values will be returned in the register listed below:

AX	=	1 SB and SB to MCV
	=	2 SBPRO
	=	3 SB 2.0

Function 22: Filter On/Off [SBPRO]

This function turns the filter on or off.

Entry The registers should be set as follows for entry to the driver:

BX	=	22
AX	=	I/O filter
		0 - recording filter
		1 - output filter
CX	=	option
		0 - on
		1 - off

Exit Upon exit from the driver, the following value will be returned in the register listed below:

AX	=	previous filter status

Function 26: Get Voice Sampling Rate

This function returns the maximum and minimum sampling rates for recording and output in different modes.

Entry The registers should be set as follows for entry to the driver:

BX	=	26
AX	=	Voice I/O process

		0 - recording
		1 - output
DX	=	Voice I/O mode
		0 - mono
		1 - stereo [SBPRO]

Exit   Upon exit from the driver, the following values will be returned in the register listed below:

DX:AX   =   Max:Min sampling rate

Function 27: Read Filter Status [SBPRO]

This function returns the current recording or output filter status.

Entry   The registers should be set as follows for entry to the driver:

BX	=	27
AX	=	I/O filter
		0 - recording filter
		1 - output filter

Exit   Upon exit from the driver, the following values will be returned in the register listed below:

AX	=	Current filter status
		0 - on
		1 - off

Programming the Creative Disk Double-Buffering Voice Driver (CTVDSK.DRV)

The Creative Disk Double-Buffering Voice Driver is a program-loadable file that contains all of the routines necessary to play sound files on a Sound Blaster using a double-disk buffering technique. The interface is similar to the Memory Mode Voice driver (CT-VOICE).

If SBSIM was not previously loaded, the calling program must first allocate memory and load the driver at offset zero of a memory segment, before the driver can be called.

Each of the functions performed by the Voice driver requires that certain registers be initialized before the driver can be called. Except for registers AX and DX, all other registers are preserved, including the FLAGS register.

Function 0: Get Version Number

This function is the same as Function 0 in the foregoing section, "Programming the Creative Memory Mode Voice Driver (CT-VOICE.DRV)."

Function 1: Set Base I/O Address

This function is the same as Function 1 in the CT-VOICE section above.

Function 2: Set Interrupt Number for DMA

This function is the same as Function 2 in the CT-VOICE section above.

Function 3: Initialize Driver

This function checks for the correct settings and functionality of the Sound Blaster. The speaker is turned on after the card has been initialized. This function must be called once, before Functions 4 through 13 can be used.

Entry   The registers should be set as follows for entry to the driver:

BX   =   3
AX   =   Buffer size in units of 2K per buffer
             (e.g., 16 = 32Kb buffers)

Exit   Upon exit from the driver, the following values will be returned in the register listed below:

AX   =   0 successful initialized
      =   1 failure

The DAC speaker is turned on after driver initialization.

Two buffers are allocated from the system using DOS calls. Buffer sizes range from 2K to 64K per buffer.

This function also intercepts the following interrupts for performing voice I/O in the background. However, your program is still free to access the disk using DOS functions.

- ☐   Timer Clock interrupt, INT 08h

- ☐   Video interrupt, INT 10h

- ☐   Disk interrupt, INT 13h

- ☐   DOS interrupt, INT 28h

These interrupts are released by the driver in Function 9 (Terminate Driver).

Function 4: On/Off Speaker

This function is the same as Function 4 in the CT-VOICE section above.

Function 5: Set Status Word Address

This function is the same as Function 5 in the CT-VOICE section above.

Function 6: Start Voice Output

This function outputs the voice file associated with the given handle. The calling program must open the voice file before calling this function. Control returns to the calling program immediately and voice output continues in the background.

Entry The registers should be set as follows for entry to the driver:

BX	=	6
AX	=	File handle

Exit Upon exit from the driver, the following values will be returned in the register listed below:

AX	=	0 successful
	=	1 failure

Function 7: Start Voice Input

This function starts the voice input process at the specified sampling rate.

Entry   The registers should be set as follows for entry to the driver:

BX   =   7
AX   =   File handle
DX   =   Sampling rate
                SBPRO mono - 4,000 to 44,100 Hz
                SBPRO stereo - 22,050 or 44,100 Hz
                (The stereo sampling rate is the sampling rate of the left and right channels combined.)

                SB 2.0 mono - 4,000 to 15,000 Hz
                SB to MCV mono - 4,000 to 13,000 Hz
                SB mono - 4,000 to 13,000 Hz

Exit   Upon exit from the driver, the following values will be returned in the register listed below:

AX   =   0 successful
       =   1 failure

The calling program must open a file for write access before calling this function.

Function 8: Stop Voice Process

This function is the same as Function 2 in the CT-VOICE section above.

Function 9: Terminate Driver

This function is the same as Function 9 in the CT-VOICE section above.

Function 10: Pause Voice Output

This function is the same as Function 10 in the CT-VOICE section above.

Function 11: Continue Voice Output

This function is the same as Function 11 in the CT-VOICE section above.

Function 12: Break Voice Output Loop

This function is the same as Function 12 in the CT-VOICE section above.

Function 14: Get Voice Process Error

This function will return the driver error code and the system error code after any driver function exits with an error.

Entry   The register should be set as follows for entry to the driver:

BX   =   14

Exit   Upon exit from the driver, the following values will be returned in the register listed below:

DX   =   System error code

AX   =   Driver error code

Function 15: Set Disk Double-Buffer Address

This function may be used if you prefer to allocate the buffer yourself.

Entry   The registers should be set as follows for entry to the driver:

BX   =   15
AX   =   Buffer offset
DX   =   Buffer segment
CX   =   Buffer size in 2K unit per buffer

This function must be called before Function 3 (Initialize Driver); otherwise, buffers will be allocated automatically from system memory.

Function 16: Set Recording Mode [SBPRO]

This function is the same as Function 16 in the CT-VOICE section above.

Function 17: Set Recording Source [SBPRO]

This function is the same as Function 17 in the CT-VOICE section above.

Function 18: Set Recording Filter [SBPRO]

This function is the same as Function 18 in the CT-VOICE section above.

Function 19: Set DMA Channel [SBPRO]

This function is the same as Function 19 in the CT-VOICE section above.

Function 20: Get Card Type

This function is the same as Function 20 in the CT-VOICE section above.

Function 21: Get Voice Sampling Rate

This function returns the maximum and minimum sampling rates supported in different I/O modes. For mono mode, multiply the returned value by 10 to find the actual maximum and minimum sampling rate. The actual sampling rate is returned for stereo mode.

Entry   The registers should be set as follows for entry to the driver:

BX	=	21
AX	=	Voice I/O process
		0 - recording
		1 - output
DX	=	Voice mode
		0 - mono
		1 - stereo [SBPRO]

Exit   Upon exit from the driver, the following values will be returned in the register listed below:

DX:AX	=	Max:Min sampling rate

Function 22: Filter On/Off [SBPRO]

This function is the same as Function 22 in the CT-VOICE section above.

Function 23: Read Filter Status [SBPRO]

This function returns the current recording or output filter status.

Entry   The registers should be set as follows for entry to the driver:

BX   =   27
AX   =   I/O filter
                    0 - recording filter
                    1 - output filter

Exit   Upon exit from the driver, the following values will be returned in the register listed below:

AX   =   Current filter status
                    0 - on
                    1 - off

Programming the Creative Labs FM Sound Driver (SBFMDRV.COM)

The Creative Labs FM driver is a resident program that contains all of the routines necessary to play .CMF music files on the FM chip of the Sound Blaster.

Each of the functions performed by the Voice driver requires that certain registers be initialized before calling the driver. Except for registers AX and DX, all other registers are preserved, including the FLAGS register.

Function 0: Get FM Driver Version

This function returns the Version number of the driver.

Entry   Upon entry to the driver, the register should be set as follows:

BX   =   0

Exit   Upon exit from the driver, the following values will be returned in the registers listed below:

AH   =   Major Version number
AL   =   Minor Version number

Function 1: Set Music Status Byte Address

This function sets the address of the status word, located within the application program, that the driver will use to notify the application program of the music output progress.

Entry   Upon entry to the driver, the registers should be set as follows:

BX   =   1
DX:AX =   Address of the music status byte

The status word is updated by the driver under the following conditions:

1. Reset to 0 during initialization.

2. Set to FFh when FM starts the music output.

3. Set to 0 when at the end of the music block as defined in the .CMF format.

4. Updated with the value of the Control data when the FM driver encounters a Control event (66h).

5. Does not change when music is paused and resumed.

6. Reset to FFh when the destructive Read status function is called.

Function 2: Set Instrument Table

This function sets the number of instruments and the location of the table of the instruments' definitions in memory.

Entry   Upon entry to the driver, the registers should be set as follows:

BX   =   2
CX   =   Number of instruments
DX:AX =   Address of instrument table

The driver uses this instrument table to program the FM chips whenever it encounters a Program Change event in the music block. The driver also associates the 16 channels in Melody mode or channels 1-11 in Rhythm mode with the first 16 or 11 instruments defined in this table. If the table contains less than 16 or 11 instruments, the driver reuses the instruments from the start of the table.

Function 3: Set System Clock Rate

This function informs the driver of the desired Timer 0 clock rate, to be used when the driver finishes the music output, and restores the Timer frequency.

Entry   Upon entry to the driver, the registers should be set as follows:

BX   =   3
AX   =   System clock rate divisor
divisor   =   1193180 / system clock frequency in Hz

If not called, or if AX=FFFFh, the Timer is reset to the default of 18.2 Hz.

Function 4: Set Driver Clock Rate

This function informs the driver of the desired Timer 0 clock rate to be used when it starts music output. The default is 96 Hz.

Entry   Upon entry to the driver, the registers should be set as follows:

BX   =   4

AX   =   Driver clock rate divisor

divisor   =   1193180 / driver clock frequency in Hz

The value to use in the above formula should be taken from offset 0C-0Dh of the .CMF header block.

Function 5: Transpose Music

This function tells the driver to transpose the music by the number of semitones in the AX register.

Entry   Upon entry to the driver, the registers should be set as follows:

BX   =   5
AX   =   Semitone offset

A positive value transposes to a higher key; a negative value to a lower key.

Function 6: Play Music

This function plays the music defined in the music block. The first byte of the music block must be a delta-time of an event, which is usually zero.

Entry   Upon entry to the driver, the registers should be set as follows:

BX   =   6

DX:AX =   Address of the music block

Exit Upon exit from the driver, the following values will be returned in the register listed below:

AX   =   0 successful
       =   1 failure

The music status byte is set to FFh. The driver reprograms the System Timer 0 using the clock rate set by Function 4, and intercepts the timer interrupt while playing the music block.

Function 7: Stop Music

This function stops the music from playing and sets the music status byte to zero.

Entry Upon entry to the driver, the register should be set as follows:

BX   =   7

Exit Upon exit from the driver, the following values will be returned in the register listed below:

AX   =   0 successful
       =   1 failure, no music was active

Timer 0 is reset to the clock rate as set by Function 3, and its original interrupt vector is restored.

Function 8: Reset FM Driver

This function turns off the FM chips and resets the instrument table to the default.

Entry Upon entry to the driver, the register should be set as follows:

BX   =   8

Exit   Upon exit from the driver, the following values will be returned in the register listed below:

AX   =   0 successful

         =   1 failure, music is active

If any music is active, first call Function 7 to stop music playing.

Function 8 must be called before the program can exit.

Function 9: Pause Music

This function pauses the active music. The music status byte is not altered.

Entry   Upon entry to the driver, the register should be set as follows:

BX   =   9

Exit   Upon exiting the driver, the values returned by the driver are listed below:

AX   =   0 successful

         =   1 failure, no music was active

Paused music can be resumed by calling Function 10 or stopped completely by calling Function 7.

Function 10: Resume Music

This function resumes the previously paused music.

Entry   Upon entry to the driver, the register should be set as follows:

BX   =   10

Exit Upon exiting the driver, the values returned by the driver are listed below:

AXAX   =   0 successful

        =   1 failure, no music was paused

Function 11: Set User-Defined Trap for System Exclusive Commands

This function notifies the driver that the calling program will handle system-exclusive events within the specified Trap routine.

Entry Upon entry to the driver, the registers should be set as follows:

BX   =   11

DX:AX   =   Address of trap routine

        =   0 to disable the routine

The driver performs an intersegment CALL to the Trap routine whenever it encounters a system-exclusive event in the music block.

Upon entry to the Trap routine, ES:DI points to the byte just after the System-Exclusive command. The Trap routine must preserve all registers and must return via an RETF instruction. The driver will then skip over the System-Exclusive command and proceed with the rest of the music block.

Sound File Formats

Most popular sound files are recorded as 8-bit Pulse Code Modulated (PCM) data. This produces one 8-bit byte of data for each sample of sound data. Stereo sound files contain two 8-bit bytes of data for each sample, one for each channel (left and right).

Some files, such as Turtle Beach .SMP files, use a 16-bit file format that uses two data bytes per sample, but gives a finer resolution and a higher quality sound at the cost of additional disk space to store the file.

The total number of bytes in the file depends on the recording frequency and the total length of the recording. The recording frequency, also called the sample rate, is the number of times a sound is sampled within one second. In 8-bit PCM format, each sample yields a single byte. Using higher frequencies, or sample rates, produces higher-quality recordings, but requires an appropriately faster machine to drive the Sound Blaster in Direct mode to be able to play back the recording at the proper speed. Again, the price of a higher-quality recording is still more disk space.

In order to make higher-quality recordings, without using so much disk space, many compressed file formats have been developed. These techniques often incorporate a method of encoding a long series of repeated bytes, such as silence, into a short sequence of 2 or 3 bytes. Many different compression algorithms are in use, which compress 8-bit PCM data down to 5, 3, 2 and even 1-bit Adaptive Differential Pulse Code Modulation (ADPCM). The trade-off here is that once a file has been compressed (to save disk space), it can no longer be edited or modified in any manner.

Creative Voice File Format (.VOC)

The .VOC file format consists of a header block and a data block. Within the data block, a number of different block types may exist. These different block types provide an elegant means of programming pauses, loops, and markers into the sound file, for synchronizing audio with video animations. Simpler applications probably will contain only a single block type (voice data).

When using the Creative Labs CT-VOICE driver, it is up to the application program to read the sound file, and pass only the data block to the driver. If you are writing your own driver, the driver must read the data block and handle the processing of the embedded block types appropriately.

Recording a .VOC file using the normal 8-bit PCM format will allow the file to be played on any internal or external sound device from another manufacturer, and even will permit the file to be transported to computers other than PCs.

If you decide to compress the .VOC file to save disk space, it is recommended that you first back up the original sound file on disk. This will ensure that you still have the option of editing the file at a future date, or transporting the file to another sound device or computer type. The following tables give you the byte-by-byte details for the header block, the data block, and the associated block types.

.VOC Header Block

The .VOC header block is divided into subblocks of data as follows:

Byte	Description
0-13	File type description
	"Creative Voice File", 1Ah
14-15	Offset of data block from start of voice file (usually 1Ah)
16-17	Voice file format Version number ("0A, 01" = 1.10)
18-19	Voice file identification code
	Complement of file format Version number + 1234h
	(for 1.10 = 1129h)

.VOC Data Block

The .VOC data block is divided into subblocks of data as follows:

Byte	Description
0	Block type
1-3	Block length following this byte
4-end	Block data

Block Type 0 - Terminator   Terminates the entire data block. It indicates that there is no other subblock after it.

Byte	Description
0	"00" End of block

Block Type 1 - Voice Data   Indicates that this subblock is a new set of voice data. It may use a different sampling rate or packing method.

Byte	Description
0	"01"
1-3	Block length
4	Time constant (256 - 1000000 / sampling rate)
5	Pack type
	0 = 8-bit unpacked
	1 = 4-bit packed
	2 = 2.6-bit packed
	3 = 2-bit packed
	4 = 1 channel multi
	5 = 2 channel multi
	6 = 3 channel multi
	7 = 4 channel multi
	8 = 5 channel multi
	9 = 6 channel multi
	10 = 7 channel multi
6-end	Voice data (length = block length = 2)

Block Type 2 - Voice Continuation   Defines a continuation of the voice data from the last voice data subblock.

Byte	Description
0	"02"
1-3	Block length
4-end	Voice data

Block Type 3 - Silence   Defines a silence period in the voice data.

Byte	Description
0	"03"

Byte	Description
1-3	Block length (always 3)
4-5	Period
6	Time constant

Block Type 4 - Marker This is a special subblock that specifies a marker in the voice data. Both the CT-VOICE and CTVDSK drivers update the status word with the contents of the marker value. Your program may check the status word for the desired marker value to perform synchronization with the voice output process.

The marker value can be inserted into the Voice file using the Sound Blaster Voice Editor, VEDIT 2.

Byte	Description
0	"04"
1-3	Block length
4-5	Marker value

Block Type 5 - ASCII Text This specifies a null-terminated ASCII string in the voice data file.

Byte	Description
0	"05"
1-3	Block length
4-end	ASCII data
end	"00" null byte

Block Type 6 - Repeat Loop Specifies the beginning of a repeat loop. The data subblocks between this block and the next end repeat loop subblock are repeated by the driver for Count +1 times.

Byte	Description
0	"06"
1-3	Block length (always 2)

4-5   Count (1 to FFFEh, FFFFh = endless loop)

Block Type 7 - End Repeat Loop   Specifies the end of a repeat loop.

Byte	Description
0	"07"
1-3	Block length (always 0)

Block Type 8 - Extended Block

Byte	Description
0	"08"
1-3	Block length (always 4)
4-5	Time constant
	Mono: 65536 - (256,000,000 / sampling rate)
	Stereo: 65536 - (256,000,000 / (2 * sampling rate))
6	Pack
7	Mode
	0 = mono
	1 = stereo

Block Type 8 must always precede Block Type 1. It carries voice attributes of the following voice data subblock, such as sampling rate, packing, and voice mode. It usually precedes stereo or high-speed voice data. When this block is present, the voice attributes in the next Block Type 1 are ignored.

Microsoft Waveform Audio File Format (.WAV)

This is an overview of the Waveform audio file format (.WAV). For more detailed information, refer to the Multimedia Specification available from Microsoft Corporation.

The Waveform audio file is organized in the RIFF (Resource Interchange File Format) structure. This structure was developed for multimedia resource files.

RIFF File Format

The basic building block of a RIFF file is called a chunk, which is formatted as follows:

<rID> <rLen> <rData(rLen)>

where

- [ ] *<rID>* 'RIFF' identifies the representation of the chunk data (4 bytes)
- [ ] *<rLen>* is the length of data in the chunk that follows (4 bytes)
- [ ] *<rData>* is the RIFF Data Chunk (rLen bytes long).

Within this block, many different RIFF forms are supported, but only the WAVE form will be discussed here.

WAVE Form Definition

The WAVE form of a RIFF Data Chunk is further divided into chunks. It must always contain a Format Chunk followed by a Data Chunk.

<rData> = <wID> <Format Chunk> <Data Chunk>

where *<wID>* 'WAVE' identifies the data as Waveform audio data (4 bytes).

WAVE Format Chunk

The Format Chunk contains data which specifies the format of the data contained in the Data Chunk. The syntax of the Format Chunk is as follows:

<Format Chunk>=   <ChunkId> <fLen> <wFormatTag> <nChannels>
<nSamplesPerSec> <nAvgBytesPerSec>
<nBlockAlign> <FormatSpecific>

where

- ☐ *<fId>* 'fmt ' identifies the block as a Format Chunk (4 bytes)

- ☐ *<fLen>* length of data in the Format Chunk that follows (4 bytes)

- ☐ *<wFormatTag>* indicates the Wave format category of the file (2 bytes). For example:

  1 = Pulse Code Modulation (PCM) format

- ☐ *<nChannels>* indicates the number of channels for output (2 bytes). For example:

  1 = mono, 2 = stereo

- ☐ *<nSamplesPerSec>* indicates sampling rate (in samples per second) at which each channel should be played back (2 bytes).

- ☐ *<nAvgBytesPerSec>* indicates the average number of bytes per second that the data should be transferred at (2 bytes).

  <nAvgBytesPerSec> = nChannels * nSamplesPerSec * (nBitsPerSample / 8)

- ☐ *<nBlockAlign>* indicates the block alignment (in bytes) of the data in the Data Chunk. Playback software needs to process a multiple of *<nBlockAlign>* bytes of data at a time, so that the value of *<bBlockAlign>* can be used for buffer alignment (2 bytes).

  <nBlockAlign> = nChannels * (nBitsPerSample / 8)

- ☐ *<FormatSpecific>* This field consists of zero or more bytes of parameters (2 bytes)

WAVE Data Chunk

The Data Chunk contains the actual .WAV audio data. The format of of the data depends on the *<wFormatTag>* value stored in the Format Chunk.

<Data Chunk> = *<dId> <dLen> <dData(dLen)>*

where

☐ *<dId>* 'data' identifies the block as a Data Chunk (4 bytes)

☐ *<dLen>* indicates the length of data in the Data Chunk that follows (4 bytes)

☐ *<dData>* is the actual waveform data (*dLen* bytes long).

Creative Music File Format (.CMF)

The .CMF file format consists of three different block structures including a header block, an instrument block, and a music block.

CMF Header Block

Offset	Description
00-03	File ID 'CTMF'
04-05	File format Version (current Version is 1.10)
	MSB = major Version
	LSB = minor Version
06-07	Offset of instrument block from start of file
08-09	Offset of music block from start of file
0A-0B	Ticks per quarter note (one beat) [default = 120]
0C-0D	Clock ticks per second [default = 96]
0E-0F	Offset of music title from start of file (0 = none)
10-11	Offset of composer name (0 = none)
12-13	Offset of remarks (0 = none)
14-23	Channel-in-use table (16 bytes long)
24-25	Number of instruments used
26-27	Basic tempo
28-	Title, composer and/or remarks are stored here

.CMF Instrument Block

The instrument block contains one 16-byte record for each of the instruments referred to in the music block. Each record is a 16-byte image of the register sets of the FM music chip. The format of the record is the same as those at offset 24-33h in the Sound Blaster Instrument (.SBI) file format, which is described in the section titled "Sound Blaster Instrument File Format (.SBI)." Refer to the .SBI file format for more detailed information.

Offset	Description
00	Modulator Sound Characteristic
01	Carrier Sound Characteristic
02	Modulator Scaling/Output Level
03	Carrier Scaling/Output Level
04	Modulator Attack/Decay
05	Carrier Attack/Decay
06	Modulator Sustain Level/Release Rate
07	Carrier Sustain Level/Release Rate
08	Modulator Wave Select
09	Carrier Wave Select
0A	Feedback/Connection
0B-0F	Reserved for future use

.CMF Music Block

The music block adheres to the Standard MIDI Format (.SMF). It is single-track, multichannel and polyphonic, with the maximum number of channels from 1 to 16.

The Standard MIDI File format specification defines three types of events: MIDI, System-exclusive, and Meta events. The .CMF file format uses only the MIDI events at the current time.

Delta-Time values are variable length fields, as defined by the Standard MIDI format.

The Music Block data appears in the following format:

<Music Block> = *<delta time>* *<MIDI event>* *<delta time>* *<MIDI event>* ...

where

☐   *<delta time>* is the amount of time before the following event stored as a variable-length quantity

☐   *<MIDI event>* is any MIDI channel message.

.CMF defines the following MIDI Control Change events:

Control Number	Control Data
66h	1 - 127
	Used as markers in the music
67h	0 - Melody mode
	1 - Rhythm mode
	Used to select the melody or rhythm mode of the FM chips

In Rhythm mode,, the last five channels are allocated as follows:

Channel	Rhythm
12	Bass Drum
13	Snare Drum
14	Tom-Tom
15	Top Cymbal
16	High-hat Cymbal

68h	0 - 127
	Changes the pitch of all following notes upward by the specified number of 1/128 semitones. Control data of 0 cancels the pitch change.
69h	0 - 127
	Changes the pitch of all following notes downward by the specified number of 1/128 semitones. Control data of 0 cancels the pitch change.

Sound Blaster Instrument File Format (.SBI)

Instrument files contain the data necessary to program the FM chip registers to synthesize a single instrument. The format of the .SBI file is as follows:

Offset	Description
00-03	File ID, ASCII string "SBI",1Ah
04-23	Instrument Name, Null-terminated ASCII string
24	Modulator Sound Characteristic
25	Carrier Sound Characteristic
	bit 7 Pitch Vibrato (AM)
	bit 6 Amplitude Vibrato (VIB)
	bit 5 Sustaining Sound (EGTYP)
	bit 4 Envelope Scaling (KSR)
	bit 3-0 Frequency Multiplier (MULTIPLE)
26	Modulator Scaling/Output Level
27	Carrier Scaling/Output Level
	bit 7-6 Level Scaling (KSL)
	bit 5-0 Output Level (TL)
28	Modulator Attack/Decay
29	Carrier Attack/Decay
	bit 7-4 Attack Rate (AR)
	bit 3-0 Decay Rate (DR)
2A	Modulator Sustain Level/Release Rate
2B	Carrier Sustain Level/Release Rate
	bit 7-4 Sustain Level (SL)
	bit 3-0 Release Rate (RR)
2C	Modulator Wave Select
2D	Carrier Wave Select
	bit 7-2 all bits clear
	bit 1-0 Wave Select (WS)
2E	Feedback/Connection
	bit 7-4 all bits clear

Offset	Description
	bit 3-1 Modulator Feedback (FB)
	bit 0 Connection
2F-33	Reserved for future use

Sound Blaster Instrument Bank File Format (.IBK)

A Bank file is a group of up to 128 instruments, combined into a single file in the following format:

Offset	Description
00-03	File ID, ASCII string "IBK",1Ah
04-803h	Instrument parameters, 128 instruments, 16 bytes each; Same as bytes 24-33h of the .SBI file
804-C83h	Instrument names, 128 instruments, 9 bytes each; Each Instrument name must be null-terminated

Musical Instrument Digital Interface File Format (.MID)

This is an overview of the MIDI file format. For more detailed information, refer to the Standard MIDI Files (.SMF) 1.0 specification available from the International MIDI Association.

MIDI files are made up of chunks. Each chunk has a 4-character type and a 32-bit length, which is the number of bytes in the chunk. Two types of chunks are currently defined, Header Chunks and Track Chunks.

A MIDI file always starts with a Header Chunk, and is followed by one or more Track Chunks.

'MThd' *<length of header data> <header data>*

'MTrk' *<length of track data> <track data>*

'MTrk' *<length of track data> <track data>*

MIDI Header Chunk

A Header Chunk provides a minimal amount of information pertaining to the entire MIDI file. The syntax of the Header Chunk is as follows:

<Header Chunk> = <chunk type> <length> <format> <ntrks> <division>

where:

☐   *<chunk type>* is the four ASCII characters "MThd"

☐   *<length>* is a 32-bit number of the bytes in the rest of the chunk

☐   *<format>* specifies the overall organization or contents of the file, where

    0 = single multichannel track

    1 = one or more simultaneous tracks of a sequence

    2 = one or more sequentially independent single-track patterns

☐   *<ntrks>* is the number of track chunks in the file

☐   *<division>* specifies the meaning of the delta-times. It has two formats: one for metrical time, and one for time-code-based time as shown here:

	0	Ticks per quarter-note	
bit:	15	14 ⟵—————————⟶ 0	

	1	Negative SMPTE format	Ticks per frame
bit:	15	14 ⟵————⟶ 8	7 ⟵—————————⟶ 0

MIDI Track Chunk

The Track Chunk is where the actual song data is stored. Each Track Chunk is simply a sequential stream of MIDI events, preceded by delta-time values. It may contain information for up to 16 MIDI channels. The concepts of multiple tracks, multiple MIDI outputs, patterns, sequences, and songs may all be implemented using several Track Chunks. The syntax of the track chunk is as follows:

<Track Chunk> = <chunk type> <length> <MTrk event> <MTrk event> ...

where

- ☐   *<chunk type>* is the four ASCII characters "MTrk"
- ☐   *<length>* is a 32-bit number of the bytes in the rest of the chunk

<MTrk event> = <delta time> <event>

where

- ☐   *<delta time>* is the amount of time before the following event stored as a variable-length quantity.

<event> = <MIDI event> | <sysex event> | <meta event>

where

- ☐   *<MIDI event>* is any MIDI channel message
- ☐   *<sysex event>* is a MIDI System-exclusive message as follows:

F0 <length> <data string>

or

F7 <length> <data string>

where

☐   *<length>* is stored as a variable-length quantity.

<meta event> specifies non-MIDI information for the sequencer as follows:

FF *<type>* *<length>* *<data string>*

where

☐   *<type>* is a single byte 0-127

☐   *<length>* is variable-length.

Meta events defined by the specification are as follows:

FF 00 02 ssss	Sequence Number
FF 01 *<len>* *<text>*	Text Event
FF 02 *<len>* *<text>*	Copyright Notice
FF 03 *<len>* *<text>*	Sequence/Track Name
FF 04 *<len>* *<text>*	Instrument Name
FF 05 *<len>* *<text>*	Lyric
FF 06 *<len>* *<text>*	Marker
FF 07 *<len>* *<text>*	Cue Point
FF 20 01 cc	MIDI channel Prefix
FF 2F 00	End of Track
FF 51 03 tttttt	Set Tempo
FF 54 05 hr mn se fr ff	SMPTE Offset
FF 58 04 nn dd cc bb	Time Signature
FF 59 02 sf mi	Key Signature
FF 7F *<len>* *<data>*	Sequencer-Specific Meta-Event

Some numbers in MIDI files are represented as variable-length fields. These numbers use from one to four bytes, where each byte uses the least significant seven bits to represent a value. All bytes except the last byte have the highest bit (bit 7) set. The last byte has bit 7 cleared.

Here are some examples of numbers represented as variable-length fields:

Number (hex)	Representation (hex)
00000000	00
00000040	40
0000007F	7F
00000080	81 00
00002000	C0 00
00003FFF	FF 7F
00004000	81 80 00
00100000	C0 80 00
001FFFFF	FF FF 7F
00200000	81 80 80 00
08000000	C0 80 80 00
0FFFFFFF	FF FF FF 7F

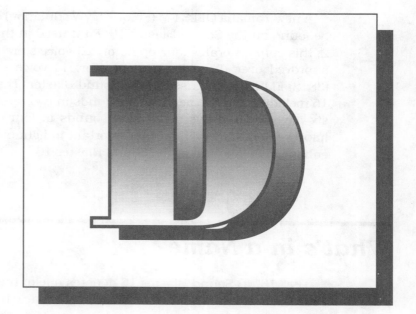

The Sound Blaster
16 ASP: A New
Wave in Sound

As with any evolutionary product, the Sound Blaster 16 is 100-percent compatible with the Sound Blaster and Sound Blaster Pro and shares much in common with each. The MIDI/joystick port and the CD ROM interface is unchanged. All software that supports the Sound Blaster MIDI port will work correctly with the Sound Blaster 16, and the Sound Blaster Pro's CD ROM drive and drivers will also work fine. The Sound Blaster's nonspeed compensating joystick port is carried over to the Sound Blaster 16, so you'll have to use another joystick port if you have a fast 386 or 486 PC. From the outside of the PC, the volume control wheel and input and output jacks on the back of the board look identical to the current crop of Sound Blasters.

A new Yamaha OPL3 FM (Frequency Modulation) synthesizer chip can be found on the Sound Blaster 16. First used in the Sound Blaster Pro 2, this chip generates four-operator, 20-voice stereo FM sounds. This is improved over the older two-operator, 11-voice mono Yamaha OPL2 (3812) FM chip, still used in the Sound Blaster. The OPL3 can generate 15 melodies and five percussion sounds in two-operator mode, but only six melodies and five percussion sounds in four-operator mode. This improvement, however, is less important in light of the more significant enhancements found in the Sound Blaster 16.

What's in a Name?

The "16" in Sound Blaster 16 denotes one of the new features of the board, namely the ability to record and play back 16-bit sound files. The 16-bit CODEC used in the Sound Blaster 16 is the same high-quality variety found in some professional DAT (Digital Audio Tape) machines. With the additional horsepower, the recording sample rate has also been fully extended to 44.1 kHz in stereo.

Chapter 2 of this book takes a look at the differences and advantages of 16-bit versus 8-bit sounds and higher sampling rates. When sampling an audio signal at 44.1 kHz, or 44,100 samples per second in 16-bit resolution, in stereo, a minute of recording requires the processing and storage of almost 10.6 megabytes. At this rate, you could gobble up 100 megabytes in under 10 minutes!

Many applications, including games, do not yet take advantage of the higher quality sound capability of the Sound Blaster 16. Sounds of this magnitude require enormous storage capacity, thus CD ROM will become more important as a distribution and storage medium for application software. Most of us just do not have the storage space on our hard disks for the next generation of full stereo 44.1 kHz 16-bit sound-enabled applications and games.

Be aware that the higher quality circuitry of the Sound Blaster 16 may make some bad 8-bit recordings sound even worse. A dusty dress on a mannequin may not seem as bad through a dirty window, but would look terrible through a clean one. The same principle applies with sound—the better the equipment, the more revealing it is of faults in the original material.

The Sound Blaster 16 will ruthlessly reveal the bad recording equipment and techniques of many applications, especially games. Sometimes, heavy filtering has to be used on the sound to make it presentable. The Sound Blaster 16 does not have this filtering circuitry as this circuitry was found to be detrimental to 16-bit sound. A quick 8-bit recording of a CD with the Sound Blaster 16 should demonstrate the quality and care that went into choosing its components and circuitry design.

The implications of the new 16-bit capability of the Sound Blaster 16 are exciting. Because this technology has such heavy storage requirements, data compression is almost a prerequisite to using it. That's where ASP comes in.

Advanced Signal Processing Technology

The DSP (Digital Sound Processor), similar to the one found in previous Sound Blasters, is primarily responsible for interpreting, processing, and dispatching sound commands to the Sound Blaster 16. The ASP in the Sound Blaster 16 moniker refers to the unique Advanced Signal Processor found only on the Sound Blaster 16.

The ASP is used primarily to handle all digital audio data. Since this processor is fully programmable, a variety of digital processing tasks can be handled at the same time, that is, multi-tasked.

This multi-tasking feature is important because even a fast 386 computer will be bogged down with the processing requirements of the massive amounts of data from converted stereo 44.1 kHz 16-bit sounds. The MPC (Multimedia PC) standards specify that audio playback at 44.1 kHz in 8-bit should not consume more than 15% CPU (Central Processing Unit) utilization. Even the fastest 386 CPU may have problems adhering to that specification if it is also required to decompress the sound file at the same time. If the CPU is preoccupied with processing the digital audio, other tasks requiring its attention will be slowed or held up indefinitely. For example, if you had a presentation with recorded music and accompanying animation, the frame rate may suffer considerably since the CPU has little time to spend on loading the next frame of animation.

As time and technology advance, the CPU will increase in speed until the simultaneous processing of high quality digital audio and video becomes a "non"-issue. But, for CPU-driven compression and decompression to be effective today, a more efficient plan is needed. The Sound Blaster 16's answer to this problem is mostly on the hardware level, with ASP. ASP behaves in your computer like a specialized digital audio CPU, much like what a math co-processor does for Computer Aided Design and spreadsheets.

How ASP Works

Let's examine how the ASP works with the recording process (see Figure D-1).

As shown in Figure D-1, before starting the recording, a program containing the data compression algorithm is downloaded onto the Sound Blaster 16's ASP. This is accomplished by using the ASP manager (described later in this appendix). The DSP, via any digital sound recording software such as the Windows Recorder, then informs the ADC (Analog to Digital Converter, explained in Chapter 2) to start converting analog data from an input device—a microphone in this instance—at a given sample rate and number of bits. The analog data is converted into digital data by the ADC and passed on to the ASP. The ASP compresses the digital data using the previously downloaded algorithm and sends it to the CPU. Finally, the CPU then moves this data to a storage device.

Recording compressed data with the ASP

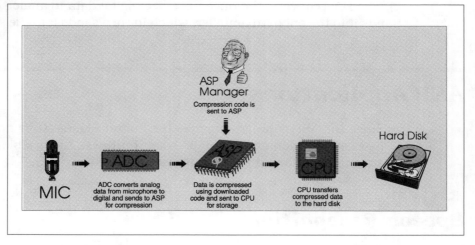

This process is reversed when playing back a previously saved recording (see Figure D-2).

Again, as shown in Figure D-2, a special decompression program is first downloaded via the ASP manager to the ASP. The data from the storage device is retrieved and sent to the ASP for processing. The ASP executes the program in its memory, decompresses the data, and sends

FIGURE
D-2

Playing back compressed data with the ASP

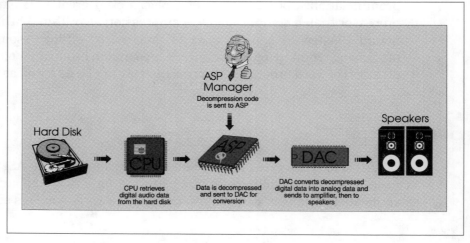

it onwards to the DAC (Digital to Analog Converter, discussed in Chapter 2). The DAC converts the uncompressed digital data to analog data and hands it to the onboard ampifier, which in turn sends it to the speakers.

ASP Applications

Since the ASP is programmable, the Sound Blaster 16 is not limited to just compression and decompression routines. The flexible ASP can be programmed for many other digital audio tasks.

Speech Recognition

One of the most exciting applications of ASP is in speech recognition. There probably isn't a soul who has seen *Star Trek: The Next Generation* who wouldn't want to be able to say, "Computer, what is the current location of Captain Picard?" and have the computer understand and process the request.

While Star Trek-like voice recognition remains far in the future, advanced voice recognition systems have made significant headway in recent years. There are PC programs today that will translate short verbal commands fairly accurately. However, these programs require a great amount of "training" before they will recognize particular voices or pronunciation. Speech recognition places even greater demands on a processor than a compression/decompression algorithm. With ASP, the Sound Blaster 16 can be used to process, or off-load, some of the processing required for future speech recognition products. Voice-to-text dictation of word processing documents may not be as far off as it seems.

Security

ASP also holds great promise for security applications: ASP allows a user to create a voice print and store it for later comparison and verification. The user can simply speak a password, which is sent to the

ASP for processing. Together with the CPU, the voice print and password can then be stored and used for future reference.

Time-Scale Modification

One esoteric use for the ASP is time-scale modification. Time-scale modification is a modification of the playback speed of a recorded signal that takes place without altering the pitch of the sound. Time-scale modification is particularly important in dictation, transciption, review, and other such applications. For instance, special algorithms can be used to speed up a speech, without making the speech sound like Mickey Mouse.

Special Effects

Special effects, such as echo and reverb, can also be performed real-time with the ASP. Since the ASP acts like a separate, optimized computer, adding these effects will not affect the performance of the main CPU all that much. Spatial and surround sound effects are also possible.

The ASP Manager

While all of the features of ASP may seem to require a lot of programming on the software developers part, in fact the opposite is true. The ASP manager actually takes care of tracking the code in the ASP. When applications require the ASP for any application, the ASP manager automatically loads the appropriate code into the ASP, if the code is not already loaded. The ASP manager will also unload any existing code to make room for new code on an as-needed basis.

This code-balancing act occurs transparently—neither user nor developer has to worry about it. For example, developers do not need to write the routines that compress or decompress a sound file; they simply have to call functions from an existing ASP routine. Even programs such as Microsoft Windows' Media Player, which knows nothing about sound decompression techniques, can work with fully compressed sounds. In most cases, such as the playback and recording of compressed data, the ASP manager will place the proper code into the ASP by simply specifying a compressed wave format.

Creative Labs has pledged to make new ASP programs readily available to both developers and end-users alike. While Sound Blaster 16's will always ship with all the latest ASP programs available at the time, updated ASP drivers and programs can be downloaded via modem, or on diskette by request. If a new 10:1 compression/decompression algorithm is discovered tomorrow, it can be translated into ASP code and made available rather quickly. These new ASP programs can then be copied to a hard disk and will be loaded transparently by the ASP manager when required.

During installation, the DOS ASP manager is automatically added to your CONFIG.SYS. This TSR (Terminate and Stay Resident) program is but a paltry 2.4K in size and is required by Windows and some DOS programs. You can conserve base memory by loading this driver high.

DOS and Windows versions of the ASP managers are already included with the Sound Blaster 16, while an OS/2 version is planned for the near future. The Sound Blaster 16 is more than adequately equipped to handle current MPC requirements. With the ASP's programmable nature, it should handle new sound technologies with aplomb.

Wave Blaster Upgrade Option

One of the most significant additions to the Sound Blaster 16 is the MIDI Extension Connector, made exclusively for attaching the Wave Blaster.

Wave Table Synthesis Technology

The Wave Blaster Upgrade is a daughter board that uses a patented wave table synthesis technology to generate 32-voice, multi-timbral stereo music. High quality 16-bit recordings of actual instruments are stored in four megabytes of ROM (Read Only Memory). These recordings are then manipulated digitally in real-time to produce the different notes on playback. A 7-point interpolation formula is used to perform the necessary calculations on sampled waveforms of musical instruments to achieve virtually perfect reproduction of these instrument sounds. The technology used in the Wave Blaster originates from E-Mu systems, a subsidiary of Creative Labs. E-Mu Systems has been providing this and other technologies to music keyboard synthesizer manufacturers for many years.

The difference between wave table synthesis sound and FM (frequency modulation) synthesized sound is like night and day. An FM synthesized acoustic guitar sounds pathetic when compared to a real acoustic guitar. Acoustic instruments produce the most difficult sound waves to reproduce with the simplistic FM algorithms. That's why the piano and guitar sounds are clearly the most improved sounds on the Wave Blaster versus the stock Sound Blaster. Instruments sound like the real ones played by professional musicians. And wait until you hear the drums—the difference is astonishing. Suddenly, the tinny sounds that used to emanate from the speakers are transformed into CD-quality music. Over 200 sounds are included.

A key advantage to having a quality synthesizer like the Wave Blaster is that you could use MIDI files (described in Chapter 2) for playing professional quality music in multi-media presentations. Quality recorded digital audio files in wave format, as we know, require a lot of processing and disk space. Since the quality of the sounds produced from the Wave Blaster can rival that of 16-bit CD sound, you can use the smaller and more efficient MIDI file format to store and play music. Instead of megabytes of storage for a short 20-second wave file, a MIDI file of a mere 20 kilobytes could play for several minutes.

Wave-table synthesis technology has been used in music keyboards and synthesizers for several years and accounts for some of the best and most realistically reproduced sounds you hear on the radio. This certainly is the next revolutionary step in sound boards. Creative Labs has provided some obsolescence protection by providing the Wave Blaster Upgrade for the Sound Blaster 16.

General MIDI Compatibility

The Wave Blaster is General MIDI compatible. This is good news for programmers and musicians alike. In operating a MIDI instrument, if you want a piano sound, you have to figure out which patch the instrument on that MIDI device is at and then send the MIDI messages to it via an appropriate channel. Different sounds in different synthesizers may be recalled using a different patch. For instance, violins may be patch 32 for synthesizer A and patch 18 for synthesizer B. This, of course, means lots of work for programmers and musicians to support every single synthesizer on the market.

The General MIDI specification was created to alleviate this confusion. In General MIDI, for example, patch 1 is always a piano sound, patch 41 always points to a violin sound, and patch 106 is a banjo sound. Different General MIDI-compatible synthesizers may have a different sounding violin, but it is always recalled as patch 41. This one feature of the Wave Blaster Upgrade will make the Wave Blaster Upgrade compatible with most of the MIDI, music, and gaming software on the market today—right out of the box.

Windows Software Included with Wave Blaster: WBPANEL and Cakewalk Apprentice

WBPanel, shown in Figure D-3, can be used to change the mappings and download different instrument banks to the Wave Blaster. Whenever you start WBPANEL, it automatically resets the Wave Blaster to its start up General MIDI-compatible bank list.

To get the full stereo effect, you may want to play with the pan sliders and turn them on. You can also change parameters like velocity curves or tune the Wave Blaster to another instrument.

Cakewalk Apprentice will get you started in the right direction for creating your musical masterpiece. It is a scaled down version of its bigger brother, Cakewalk Professional, which is described in Chapter 11. Remember to send in your registration card and also grab the excellent Romeo Music Cakewalk Series. It contains over 60 top-notch MIDI sequences—serving as great inspiration for budding musical prodigies.

MT-32 Compatible Instruments Map

The Roland MT-32 and CM-64 modules with the LAPC-1 board (replaced recently with the Sound Canvas General MIDI series) have

FIGURE
D-3

WBPanel for Windows

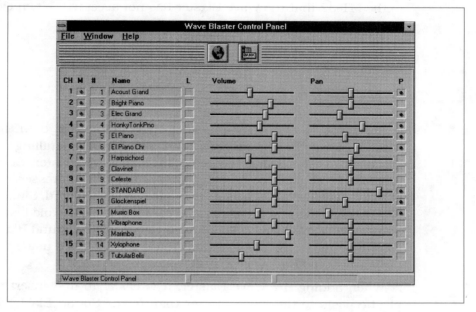

dominated PC MIDI add-ons. It is no wonder then that the Wave Blaster comes with a MT-32 bank-compatible setting. Keep in mind that the extended programming features and other advanced commands of the MT-32 are not supported. Many games will try to use these commands to set up the MT-32 and may hang up your computer if you specify that you have an MT-32 or compatible device. The MT-32 compatible bank mode of the Wave Blaster simply consists of alternate mappings of its intruments to match those of the MT-32.

There is no harm in trying to get better sound from applications that support the MT-32 but not General MIDI or the Wave Blaster directly. Use WBMODE to download the MT-32 compatible bank settings to the Wave Blaster by typing the following command:

WBMODE MT32

Now try reconfiguring your application to use an MT-32. If the program hangs, or will not continue when you try to start it, just reboot your machine and reset the sound selection back to the Sound Blaster mode. Even if it does work, you may get some funny sounding machine guns, for instance, since the program thinks it has downloaded a new sound to the MT-32 that the Wave Blaster has not accepted. When everything works and sounds correctly, you're in for a treat.

General Tips and Hints

For those of you lucky enough to have purchased both the Sound Blaster 16 and the Wave Blaster together, consider installing the Sound Blaster 16 by itself first before adding the Wave Blaster. Some of the jumpers to change interrupts, DMAs, and port addresses cannot be reached once the Wave Blaster is connected to the board. Since you may have to change the settings to avoid conflicts at first, avoid installing the Wave Blaster until you've successfully installed the Sound Blaster 16. If you must install them at the same time, at least avoid using the plastic posts untill you find a setup that works correctly.

When adding the Wave Blaster, it is easier to first insert the three plastic posts to the Wave Blaster than to the Sound Blaster 16. After putting on the posts, lay the Sound Blaster 16 on a flat hard surface like a desk or tile floor. Align the header pins and push down on the Wave Blaster at the four corners, starting with the side where the header pins are. You need to exert some force when trying to get the posts through the eyelets on the Sound Blaster 16.

You may have wondered how you can "play" the Wave Blaster, like you would a synthesizer keyboard. If you have a MIDI keyboard and the MIDI kit for the Sound Blaster, you can do this quite easily. Just attach your keyboard to the MIDI cable and use the special audition mode of WBPANEL by typing the following:

WBMODE A

If you got those bargain basement speakers when you purchased your Sound Blaster 16, consider new speakers when upgrading to the Wave Blaster. Better Speakers will reveal the true glory of the Wave Blaster's sound. The sound of its bass guitar and drums can really rattle any window with the right setup, and Wave Blaster can produce incredibly deep bass notes.

Certain software will only work with a MIDI device via a Roland MPU-401 MIDI port. This is not a problem since the Sound Blaster 16 and the Wave Blaster will operate in that mode. However, in Windows, some applications may change some settings in the SYSTEM.INI file to point to the MPU-401 driver, which is not loaded by default when installing Windows. If that is the case, you may get an error that says, "Failed to load MPU-401 driver" or, "Cannot initialize MIDI device" when you try to start Windows or load any software that uses the Wave Blaster. At this point, you can do one of two things. Keep in mind that the first method is the permanent fix, whereas the second fix may be "broken" again the next time you run the culprit program that changed your setup in the first place:

☐ Use the Windows Control Panel, select Drivers, click on Add, and double click on Roland MPU-401. Windows will ask for a certain numbered disk. Insert the required disk and click on OK. Windows will copy the required driver onto your hard disk. Follow the on-screen instructions and restart Windows. Your setup should work correctly from this point on.

☐ Use the Windows Control Panel, select Drivers, select the three Sound Blaster 16 drivers in sequence, and delete them. The drivers names are Creative Sound Blaster 16 Auxiliary Audio, Creative Sound Blaster 16 MIDI Synthesizer, and Creative Sound Blaster 16 Wave, and MIDI. Now reinstall the drivers by selecting Add, and click on Unlisted or Updated Driver, and type in the path to the latest Sound Blaster 16 driver location (typically C:\SB16\WINDRV), selecting each one of the above mentioned drivers. Restart Windows and everything should be back to normal.

Sound Blaster 16 Mixer Software and Controls

Enhanced sotware usually means new software, and the Sound Blaster 16 is no exception to the rule. The Sound Blaster 16 includes a number of enhanced programs, including new Windows programs that take advantage of the added capabilities of the hardware.

The SB 16 Mixers

A new mixer for both DOS and Windows is included with the Sound Blaster 16 (see Figure D-4). Both mixers include new tone controls and input and output level controls.

Treble and Bass Controls

The left and right channel treble and bass levels can be set independently in 15 levels from -14 dB (decibels) to +14 dB in 2-dB steps.

Volume Controls

Volume controls for the Master Volume, Digital Audio (DAC), CD Audio, FM Music, and Line In have been improved over the Sound Blaster Pro's stereo 8-level attenuation to stereo 32-level attenuation in 2-dB steps on the Sound Blaster 16. This finer level of volume control should permit smoother panning of sounds from left to right and vice versa.

Microphone Input

The Microphone input has also been increased from mono 4-level attenuation to mono 32-level attenuation in 2-dB steps. As for the PC speaker input, it is adjustable in 6-dB steps with 4-level attenuation in mono.

FIGURE
D-4

Sound Blaster 16 Windows mixer

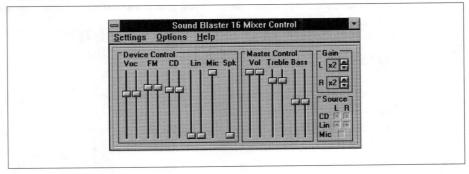

A microphone is actually included with the Sound Blaster 16. It is of adequate quality for voice recording, but you'll have to purchase a better one if you're after a quality 16-bit 44.1 kHz microphone recording.

Gain Control

Also new on the Sound Blaster 16 is the gain control, which allows the overall input and/or output levels to be increased by two, four, or eight times. The Automatic Gain Control, which can wreak havoc when recording from a microphone, can be disabled on the Sound Blaster 16 from either mixers.

Recording from More than One Source Simultaneously

A useful enhancement of the new Sound Blaster 16 is the ability to record from more than one source at a time. On the Sound Blaster Pro, you get to select only one source for recording. The Sound Blaster 16 mixer allows you to selectively choose discrete left and/or right channels of all inputs to record from. You can elect to record from the microphone while recording only the left channel from the line input, the right channel from the CD input, and both channels from the FM synthesizer (see Figure D-5). You can even record yourself singing to a tune with music accompaniment from a CD if you please!

The additional flexibility of the Sound Blaster 16 mixer also allows you to record the left channel of any input to the right channel or vice versa.

FIGURE D-5

Windows mixer recording input selector

Or you can record both channels from any input to the left or right channel only. The combinations are manifold, providing you with the most adaptable mixer yet for a Sound Blaster.

The DOS Mixer: SB16MIX

The DOS mixer, SB16MIX.EXE, is actually a large TSR (Terminate Stay Resident) program which eats up about 64K of memory. Once loaded in memory, it is activated by a hotkey (ALT-1 by default, but you can change that).

When the screen is in text mode, a window will pop up onto the screen (see Figure D-6) when the hotkey is pressed. When the mixer control panel is on the screen, it can be operated either with a mouse or with the keyboard. If you're running a graphics program like a VGA game for instance, the hotkey will use the line at the bottom of the screen, as shown in Figure D-7, and will only accept input from a keyboard.

Unlike the Sound Blaster Pro mixer (SBP-MIX.EXE), as long as the Sound Blaster 16 mixer (SB16MIX.EXE) is in memory, several key combinations can be used to control the volume of the various volume levels without necessarily bringing up the mixer panel. For example, you can press CTRL-ALT-M to enable the "master" volume control, followed by CTRL-ALT-U to "up" or increase the setting and CTRL-ALT-D to "down" or decrease the setting.

FIGURE D-6   Sound Blaster 16 DOS mixer in text mode

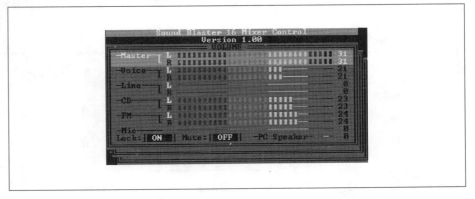

FIGURE
D-7

Sound Blaster 16 DOS mixer in graphics mode

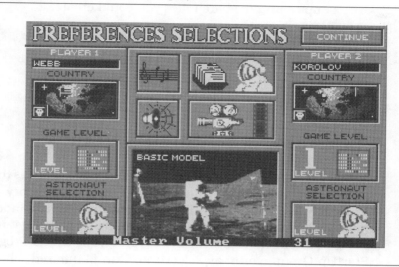

The Interactive and Command Line Mixer: SB16SET

Recognizing that SB16MIX.EXE may take memory away from programs that require the additional 64K to run, the traditional command line utility to set all the volumes and tone controls is also included. SB16SET.EXE works with the Sound Blaster 16 as SBP-SET.EXE does with the Sound Blaster Pro. Of course, the additional features found in the Sound Blaster 16 can be controlled using new command line switches for SB16SET.EXE.

SB16SET.EXE also includes a mouse-compatible interactive graphical interface for setting the various mixer levels. This is far more convenient than having to memorize the command line switches. It is a good idea to include the subdirectory in which SB16SET.EXE resides in your PATH= statement to gain access to this handy nonmemory resident mixer wherever you are in DOS. Alternatively, you could move SB16SET.EXE to a directory that is already in the DOS path.

For those of you who are not using an external amplifier, it is more convenient to use the mixer volume control than it is to reach behind the computer to adjust the volume control on the back of the Sound Blaster. Create some batch files with preset volume settings so that you can quickly change volumes by simply executing the batch command. Here are examples of some batch files you could create:

Batch File Name	Contents
SOFT.BAT	C:\SB16\SB16SET /M:130
MED.BAT	C:\SB16\SB16SET /M:180
LOUD.BAT	C:\SB16\SB16SET /M:240

The Windows Mixer: SB16WMIX

The Windows Mixer provides the same functionality as the DOS mixers described above. Since Windows alleviates most memory concerns, you can safely load SB16WMIX.EXE whenever you start Windows by adding it to the Program Manager StartUp Group or by adding it to the RUN= or LOAD= line in the WIN.INI file. If you add it to the Program Manager StartUp Group, you may select the "Run Minimized" check box in the Program Item Properties dialog box so that the mixer will show up as an icon at the bottom of your screen.

After adjusting the levels using the Windows Mixer, save the settings. The next time you start Windows and the mixer is loaded, your levels will revert to those that you had previously saved.

DOS Software for SOUND BLASTER 16

The traditional lineup of DOS programs, some enhanced versions of the Sound Blaster Pro counterparts, can be found in the Sound Blaster 16 box. The ones that remain unchanged and that are discussed elsewhere in this book are the following:

- ❑ SBTALKER, which works with Dr. Sbaitso
- ❑ FM Intelligent Organ
- ❑ SBSIM, the Sound Blaster Standard Interface Module
- ❑ MMPLAY multimedia player
- ❑ PLAYMIDI and PLAYCMF music utilities

The voice utilities like VPLAY.EXE and VREC.EXE have been updated to support the new stereo 16-bit 44.1 kHz recording capability of the Sound Blaster 16. This new Voice file format is version 1.20; utilities to convert to and from the previous version 1.10 to the new version are also included. Since the Wave file format already handles the new recording and playback capabilities of the Sound Blaster 16, only small changes to allow this capability were made to the other programs such as VOC2WAV.EXE, WAV2VOC.EXE, WPLAY.EXE, and WREC.EXE.

New Windows 3.1 Software

Besides the mixers and DOS programs, Creative Labs has included a whole slew of Windows applications for the Sound Blaster 16. First and of most importance are the Windows 3.1 drivers.

An automatic setup program makes the installation of these drivers a breeze. To install the drivers, you need only run WINSETUP.EXE while in Windows. When you run this program, the drivers are copied to the right directory, the Sound Blaster 16 program group is added to Program Manager, and all the changes take effect after Windows is restarted (see Figure D-8).

Windows provides an attractive and functional interface for the following programs that are bundled with the Sound Blaster 16. They are generally easier to learn and use than their cryptic DOS counterparts.

WaveStudio

WaveStudio is a recording, playback, and editing program for Wave format files. It has the ability to work with several of these files at one

FIGURE
D-8

Sound Blaster 16 Windows icons

time, allowing for cut and paste between them (see Figure D-9). Special effects such as echo, fade, amplification, reverse, and merge can be easily performed on any Wave file.

There is a button on WaveStudio's toolbar to run the mixer for adjusting input levels prior to the start of any recording. Working with the Sound Blaster 16, it will record from multiple sources at a time in 16-bit stereo, at a 44.1 kHz sampling rate. WaveStudio supports the drag and drop Windows interface, which allows you to simply drag a file from the Windows File Manager onto a window or icon and WaveStudio will load the Wave file for editing.

WaveStudio eliminates the frustration and complexity of working with the DOS voice utilities when recording on the Sound Blaster 16. This program is so superior that even if you need files in the Creative Labs Voice format, it's best to record using WaveStudio and then the DOS Wave-to-Voice translation utility (WAV2VOC.EXE) to convert the recording to the desired Voice format.

FIGURE D-9

WaveStudio with four open .WAV files

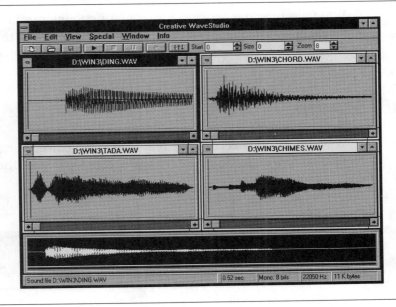

Talking Scheduler

Talking Scheduler is a scheduling program that will actually remind you of your appointments verbally. Using a text-to-speech engine and one of three animated characters, Simon, Perkins, or Igor, Talking Scheduler will actually call you by name and announce your upcoming appointment (see Figure D-10).

This multimedia program can even record your voice message and play it back as a reminder. OLE (Object Linking and Embedding), a Windows 3.1 feature, is fully supported by Talking Scheduler. By using OLE, you can easily attach a multimedia movie or spreadsheet, for instance, to an appointment—which can then be automatically retrieved when the reminder pops up on the screen. Imagine this: You can set a reminder for your wedding anniversary, have Igor tell you to go get a gift, have an animation clip showing Larry slapping Moe (from the Three Stooges) with the famous "woob woob" sound, and bring up your checkbook balance automatically. Is Talking Scheduler fun? You bet it is!

Talking Scheduler setup screen

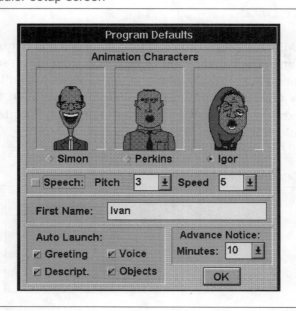

Soundo'LE

Soundo'LE is an OLE-compliant program that you can use to record and playback any Wave sound file in other Windows applications that support OLE (see Figure D-11). It is not significantly better than the Windows Recorder if you're only going to do basic voice annotation. However, Soundo'LE does support the full capabilities of the Sound Blaster 16. The Windows Recorder, on the other hand, makes selecting sample rates and other parameters difficult and does not support real time compression using the ASP manager.

Mosaic

Mosaic is a tile game with three difficulty levels and can be configured up to an 8-by-8 grid. Like Windows' own Solitaire game, it a very basic game, but is good for when you're on a coffee break. Creative Labs enhanced the game by adding sound and some colorful pictures (see Figure D-12).

MM Jukebox

MM Jukebox is a program that allows you to queue MIDI files and play them in the background while you're working on something else. The new version 2.2 actually allows you to insert a MIDI file as an OLE object into any OLE client program. It will also play MIDI files in full stereo. Use JukeBox with the Wave Blaster to provide CD-quality background music while you work in Windows.

FIGURE D-11   Soundo'LE screen

A Mosaic screen

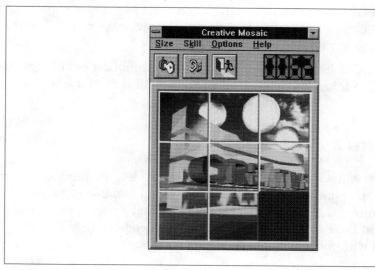

Fancy Commercial Software

Creative Labs aims to please with the Sound Blaster 16. Not only did they include the wealth of programs described previously, they made arrangements with other third-party companies to provide even more advanced applications. These programs would cost hundreds of dollars by themselves.

HSC InterActive SE

HSC InterActive SE from HSC Software is an interactive multimedia presentation authoring system. The description may be daunting, but what HSCIA allows you to do is to integrate sound, pictures, and animation in a variety of ways. HSCIA is a multimedia programming environment. Just like you would use Lotus 1-2-3 to create a spreadsheet, you would use HSCIA to create applications that would require multimedia elements like sound. These applications can then be used for presentations, tutorials, and the like. If you're adventurous, you could even use HSCIA to create a computer tour of your home.

Unlike traditional programming methods, HSCIA uses an icon-driven interface for authoring. Using a flowchart metaphor, you create an HSCIA application by simply building the flowchart with different icons that represent different actions.

HSCIA is a Windows program. An animation editor, graphics editor, and an image enhancement editor are all part of the HSCIA package.

PC Animate Plus

PC Animate Plus from Presidio Software is an animation studio. Much like the popular Autodesk Animator, you can use Animate Plus to create PC movies. A special effects generator and a paint program are included. If you have a compatible SuperVGA video board, you can create animation with pictures of up to 32,000 colors.

Monologue for Windows

Monologue for Windows may not sound as natural as Hal from the movie *2001: A Space Odyssey*, nor like the computer on *Star Trek: The Next Generation*, but it does a credible job of verbalizing text. This program permits other Windows programs to speak their mind! Using a patented text-to-speech utility, Monologue will read any text copied onto the Windows Clipboard. Using the DDE (Dynamic Data Exchange) or DLL (Dynamic Link Libraries) interface you can write to your own speech-enabled application if you're so inclined. In fact, the Talking Scheduler program uses this engine to create Igor's speech.

Speech synthesis is not quite perfect yet, and there are many reasons why this is so. Some of the reasons for this are discussed in Chapter 2. Monologue attacks some of the anomalies of spoken English with an "exception" dictionary. Here, you can use phonetics to force Monologue to pronounce a word more accurately. Also, you can vary the pitch and speed at which Monologue speaks.

At the very least, Monologue sounds better than Joshua, the talking computer from the movie *War Games*.

Miscellaneous Enhancements in Sound Blaster 16

The Roland MPU 401 MIDI card has been the standard for MIDI cards on the PC for several years. At the time the Sound Blaster was originally introduced, MPU 401-compatibility was important because it was the standard supported by all MIDI software.

The popularity of the Sound Blaster cards has brought about support for its proprietary MIDI port specification. In fact, since the coming of age of the Sound Blaster family, most MIDI software has been rewritten to support the Sound Blaster MIDI port.

Nevertheless, Sound Blaster 16 is still the first Sound Blaster to fully support the MPU 401 UART standard. The port is full duplex, buffered, and will automatically switch between Sound Blaster MIDI and MPU 401 modes.

To smooth the transfer of large amounts of digital data inherent in 16-bit recordings, the Sound Blaster 16 actually uses a 16-bit DMA channel in addition to an 8-bit DMA channel. Using a 16-bit DMA channel speeds up data transfer from the memory on the Sound Blaster 16 to the PC bus, and then to the PC memory by freeing the CPU from having to move the data. Some computers may have problems with these 16-bit DMA transfers, but thankfully the Sound Blaster 16 allows the use of an 8-bit DMA channel as a substitute (albeit at the cost of speed and processor cycles).

For users of powered speakers, the Sound Blaster 16 has a jumper to disable the internal 4W per channel amplifier. Bypassing the amplifier circuit should reduce hiss and interference. Since the bypass is post fader, all the input level and tone controls will still work fine. Try to locate the card as far away as possible from your video card, which is a major contributor of noise and interference.

The Sound Blaster 16 is undoubtedly a much improved card that is worthy of upgrade consideration—especially if you have one of the original Sound Blasters. If nothing else, the Wave Blaster Upgrade and additional software included with the Sound Blaster 16 at only a slight cost increase from the Sound Blaster Pro should help point you toward upgrading to the Sound Blaster 16.

The potential usefulness of the ASP cannot be accurately gauged at this moment. As new algorithms and programs are written for it, only then will we begin to see the capacity of the ASP. Regardless of this, the ASP promotes the stability and usability of multi-tasking operating systems such as Microsoft Windows and OS/2 today. By off-loading traditionally processor-intensive digital signal processing from the CPU, the ASP in the Sound Blaster 16 permits these operating systems more free time for running other programs concurrently—in other words, more breathing room.

Has the future of PC sound arrived? The answer from the Sound Blaster 16 with ASP and the Wave Blaster is a resounding yes.

APPENDIX

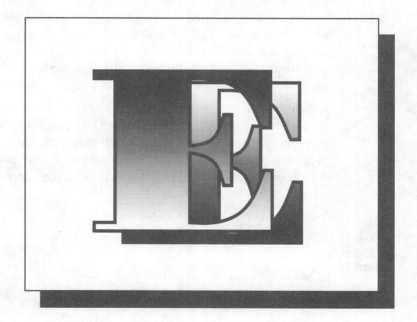

SoundSculptor

SoundSculptor by Ibis Software provides an easy-to-use graphical interface for programming the FM synthesizer with custom sounds on your Sound Blaster or Sound Blaster Pro. SoundSculptor lets you experiment with the FM synthesizer parameters that control the *timbre*, or the musical quality, of a note. By carefully sculpturing the timbre, you can simulate a wide range of nonpercussion instruments, from a guitar to a piano. This is the essence of music generation by your sound card.

Your Sound Blaster can be programmed to simultaneously play instrument sounds. To create these instrument sounds, the Sound Blaster FM synthesizer possesses 22 operators, and the Sound Blaster Pro has twice this number so it can produce stereo sound. Instrument sounds are simulated by combining two operators in series, using a technique known as "FM synthesis." Each operator is a source of sound with a constant, but different frequency. In essence, the carrier operator cell contributes the fundamental frequency, which is then modulated (modified) by the modulator.

The basics of FM synthesis are explained in Chapter 2, and much of this information is also contained in SoundSculptor's well-written help screens, accessed by pressing function key F1. The SoundSculptor screen is shown in Figure E-1, with the controls for the modulator operator cell visible on the left side, and the controls for the carrier operator cell visible on the right.

The SoundSculptor screen

When you load instrument files (.INS file extension) and instrument bank files (.BNK), the control sliders and buttons on the screen are automatically adjusted to show the FM synthesizer settings. The figure shows what the SoundSculptor controls when the program is first loaded. The timbre loaded by default, provided by Ibis Software, is named IBIS.

Starting SoundSculptor

Switch to the \SBDISK\SS subdirectory by typing **CD\SBDISK\SS** and then pressing ENTER. Then type **SS** and press ENTER to load this program. To quit SoundSculptor, select the File button at the top of the menu and then select Quit.

Using SoundSculptor

SoundSculptor requires a mouse to run. To adjust a slider, position the mouse cursor on the slider, hold the mouse button down, and then pull the control. Radio buttons, such as the Wave control, allow you to select only one button at a time. Toggle controls, such as Amp Vibrato and Freq Vibrato, can be toggled on and off repeatedly by the click of a mouse, The checkmark indicates they are toggled on. To play the piano keys you click on the piano key. Follow your instincts and experiment a little, and you will master the program in no time at all.

Important Function Keys

SoundSculptor has the following function keys, all of which (except F8) are accessible with the mouse:

F1	Help
F2	Save the current instrument to disk
F3	Load instrument sound
F8	Play built-in song with current instrument

F9   File menu for loading and saving your custom sounds

F10   View the numeric settings for the FM synthesizer controls

Screen Controls

All of the controls are documented in the SoundSculptor help screens, accessible by pressing F1. You can see the numerical equivalents for the control position by selecting the View (F10) button on the menu control bar at the top of your screen.

The list below describes those screen controls that have the most dramatic effect:

The Operator "Envelope"   The "envelope" of the carrier and modulator operators, visible in Figure E-1, controls the relative strength of the operator sound output over time. The graphs depict the relative strength of the note after a key is pressed. Each note reaches a peak, after which decay begins. The decay may stop temporarily at a plateau, known as the sustain level, or continue at a slower decline until the key is released. The final stretch of the sound output, after the key is released, is known as the release. With your mouse, you can stretch the envelope, assigning values for the attack/decay/sustain/release (A/D/S/R). See Chapter 2 for a discussion of FM Synthesis, which will help you visualize these concepts.

Output   Relative volume of each operator. Both operators need to be set relatively high to be audible.

Multi   This changes the frequency of an operator cell in multiples of a base frequency, causing a dramatic shift in instrument sound.

Freq Vibrato   Vibrato causes the operator cell frequency to waver in frequency by 6.4 Hz rather than stay at a steady frequency. This simulates the vibrato effect which is characteristic of most woodwind, string, and many brass instruments.

Amp Vibrato   This effect, also known as tremelo, causes a slight fluctuation at a frequency of 3.7 Hz (vibrations per second) to an operator's amplitude. This gives the operator the chracteristic of an electric guitar or a vibraphone.

Env Scaling Envelope scaling changes the A/D/S/R curve of the note as the frequency increases, simulating an effect familiar to piano players, where the higher notes diminish more quickly than the lower ones.

Sus Sound The sustain sound switch controls whether the sound slowly decays, such as the case for a piano sound, or quickly disappears.

KSL Key level scaling changes the volume of the sound according to the pitch. Higher tones of acoustic instruments sound softer (less loud) than lower notes.

 Note Detailed technical information on programming the Yamaha chip, which is used for your Sound Blaster's FM synthesizer, is available in the Creative Labs' Developer's Toolkit, which can be purchased by anyone, including the casual programmer, for a nominal cost. Appendix C of this book provides the Register Address Map for the FM synthesizer chip.

Index

BLASTER Master

The complimentary copy of **BLASTER Master** included in this book will only edit a file up to 25 seconds in length. To edit files up to 16 megabytes and support future releases, please register your copy by sending $29.95.

You will receive a code that unlocks your copy and all future releases of **BLASTER Master** , available from BBS's and Shareware Distributors worldwide.

Master the world of sound with your PC and **BLASTER Master**!

Complete Order Form and Return with Payment to:
Gary Maddox • 1901 Spring Creek #315 • Plano, Texas 75023

ORDER FORM

Name _____

Address _____

City _____ State _____ Zip _____

Telephone_____

Check or Money Orders Only
Please Make Checks Payable to Gary Maddox

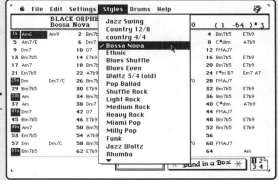

SPUTTER DISCOUNT COUPON

To order The Sputter Sound System from VersaWare for a single site, at the special book price, send this coupon along with your payment of only $35. *This is $10 off the regular registration price!*

Disk Size (Please check one):   ❑ 5 ¼"   ❑ 3 ½"

Make checks payable to Adrienne Cousins. Thank you.

Phone: 508-486-8507 - 24 hour Support BBS
        508-486-9351 - Technical Support (Mon.-Fri. 9am-4pm EST)

Name ....

Address ....

....

Phone: Home (...........) .... Work (.........) ....

Computer ....

Sound Equipment ....

Comments ....

....

....

Send to:

VersaWare/Adrienne Cousins
30 Jennifer Street
Littleton, MA 01460
U.S.A.

Sputter v1.16

The Police Quest Casebook
by Peter Scisco
Help Sonny Bonds win his ongoing fight against crime in the Police Quest series of adventure computer games from Sierra Online. Scisco provides all the information needed to win the games. You'll find maps, targeted solutions to specific problems, and much more.
$19.95, ISBN: 0-07-881823-0, 304 pages, 7 3/8 x 9 1/4

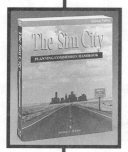

The SimCity Planning Commission Handbook
by Johnny L. Wilson
The SimCity planning simulator may be the most thought-provoking computer game of all, and *The SimCity Planning Commission Handbook* ensures that you'll enjoy all of the game's many dimensions. Author Johnny Wilson, the respected editor of Computer Gaming World, also presents prevailing theories of urban design, and challenges you to design a city that works for individuals and industry alike.
$19.95, ISBN: 0-07-881660-2, 193 pages 7 3/8 X 9 1/4

Buzz Aldrin's Race Into Space Companion
by Fritz Bonner
Get the right stuff with this hot new official book on Interplay's game for the IBM and compatible PCs. Race Into Space fans will get the inside scoop on all the hidden tricks and traps from the game's creator, Fritz Bonner.
$19.95, ISBN: 0-07-881938-5, 400 pages, 7 3/8 x 9 1/4

PCs Made Easy, Second Edition
by James Turley
If you've never used an IBM PC, PC compatible, Macintosh, or any other personal computer before, this book is for you. Turley's classic introduction has been updated to cover the latest computer models, software, and new technologies.
$19.95, ISBN: 0-07-881929-6, 464 pages, 7 3/8 x 9 1/4

▶ ─── Osborne **McGraw-Hill**   ■   **Available at local book and computer stores**

WordPerfect 5.1: The Complete Reference
by Karen L. Acerson
Every WordPerfect 5.1 user will want to have this fabulous reference, winner of PC Magazine's Editors' Choice Award. Commonly referred to as the "WordPerfect Bible," Acerson's book covers every WordPerfect 5.1 feature message, and menu item A to Z. Each topic includes keystrokes, tips, and hints and several applications where the features can be used.
$29.95, ISBN: 0-07-881634-3, 1327 pages, 7 3/8 x 9 1/4

Microsoft Word Made Easy, Fourth Edition
by Paul Hoffman
Whether you're new to Word or need information on the latest version, Paul Hoffman has thoroughly revised his bestselling book to cover all the powerful features of this popular wordprocessing software for the IBM PC and compatibles.
$19.95, ISBN: 0-07-881939-3, 412 pages, 7 3/8 x 9 1/4

Microsoft Word for Windows 2 Made Easy
by Paul Hoffman
Best-selling author Paul Hoffman will quickly teach you the newest version of Microsoft Word for Windows. Plenty of hands-on examples and helpful illustrations are included to build your skills fast. You'll also explore all of the powerful features including menus, linking documents, macros, and graphics.
$19.95, ISBN: 0-07-881770-6, 303 pp., 7 3/8 X 9 1/4

Microsoft Access Inside & Out
by Mary Campbell
Find out all about this revolutionary new database software in Mary Campbell's new book. Campbell quickly guides you from fundamentals to intermediate-level skills, then covers a range of advanced topics. You'll learn all the unique features that make this software a powerful new contender.
$27.95, ISBN: 0-07-881818-4, 784 pages, 7 3/8 x 9 1/4

▶ ────── Osborne **McGraw-Hill** ■ **Available at local book and computer stores**

Excel 4 for Windows Made Easy
by Martin S. Matthews
Excel expert Matthews offers you instruction, examples, and a handy reference for all your Excel questions. It's the very best way to get a quick start with the new release 4 of Microsoft's super-spreadsheet for Windows.
$19.95, ISBN: 0-07-881807-9, 512 pages, 7 3/8 x 9 1/4

FoxPro 2.5 for DOS Made Easy
by Edward Jones
FoxPro 2.5 DOS Made Easy is the best bet for busy people who want to upgrade their skills with the program. It's also a good introduction for first-timers who already know other major database programs. Jones selects FoxPro's most essential features and teaches them in the simple-to-use Made Easy format.
$24.95, ISBN: 0-07-881897-4, 720 pages, 7 3/8 x 9 1/4

Quicken 6 Made Easy
by David Campbell and Mary Campbell
Become productive fast with the latest version of this low-cost, user-friendly financial package through accounting experts David and Mary Campbell's easy, follow-along guide. The Campbells teach you all about using Quicken for home and business accounting, organizing your taxes, and tracking credit card purchases and much more.
$19.95, ISBN: 0-07-881890-7, 560 pp., 7 3/8 x 9 1/4

CorelDRAW! 3 Made Easy
by Emil Ihrig & Sybil Ihrig
and Martin S. Matthews & Carole Boggs Matthews
Osborne's best-selling book on this popular graphics program has been updated to cover the newest version 3.0. You'll find clear step-by-step instructions, easy-to-find reference m___ ial, along with numerous illustrations, all designed to guara_ _e a complete understanding of this top-selling program.
$29.95, ISBN: 0-07-881838-9, 850 pages, 7 3/8 x 9 1/4